Flash 8

THE MISSING MANUAL

*The book that
should have been
in the box*

OTHER RESOURCES FROM O'REILLY

Related titles

Dreamweaver 8: The Missing Manual

Creating Web Sites: The Missing Manual

Front Page 2003: The Missing Manual

Photoshop Elements 4: The Missing Manual

Flash 8: Projects for Learning Animation and Interactivity

---

oreilly.com

oreilly.com is more than a complete catalog of O'Reilly books. You'll also find links to news, events, articles, weblogs, sample chapters, and code examples.

oreillynet.com is the essential portal for developers interested in open and emerging technologies, including new platforms, programming languages, and operating systems.

Conferences

O'Reilly brings diverse innovators together to nurture the ideas that spark revolutionary industries. We specialize in documenting the latest tools and systems, translating the innovator's knowledge into useful skills for those in the trenches. Visit *conferences.oreilly.com* for our upcoming events.

Safari Bookshelf (*safari.oreilly.com*) is the premier online reference library for programmers and IT professionals. Conduct searches across more than 1,000 books. Subscribers can zero in on answers to time-critical questions in a matter of seconds. Read the books on your Bookshelf from cover to cover or simply flip to the page you need. Try it today for free.

Flash 8
THE MISSING MANUAL

E. A. Vander Veer

POGUE PRESS™

O'REILLY®

Beijing • Cambridge • Farnham • Köln • Paris • Sebastopol • Taipei • Tokyo

Flash 8: The Missing Manual

by E. A. Vander Veer

Published by O'Reilly Media, Inc., 1005 Gravenstein Highway North, Sebastopol, CA 95472.

O'Reilly books may be purchased for educational, business, or sales promotional use. Online editions are also available for most titles (*safari.oreilly.com*). For more information, contact our corporate/institutional sales department: (800) 998-9938 or *corporate@oreilly.com*.

Printing History:

March 2006:   First Edition.

 This book uses RepKover™, a durable and flexible lay-flat binding.

ISBN: 0-596-10137-6

[M]

Table of Contents

Part Two: Advanced Drawing and Animation

Part Three: Adding Interactivity

The Missing Credits

About the Author

 **E. A. Vander Veer** started out in the software trenches, lexing and yaccing and writing shell scripts with the best of them. She remained busy and happy for years writing C++ programs and wresting data from recalcitrant databases until reaching the proverbial fork in the road, when she chose the dark path—marketing. After a stint as an Object Technology Evangelist (yes, that's an actual job title), she found a way to unite all of her passions: writing about cool computer stuff in prose any human being can understand. Books followed—over a dozen so far—including *JavaScript For Dummies*, *XML Blueprints*, and the fine tome you're holding right now. Her articles appear in online and print publications including Byte, CNET, Salon.com, WEBTechniques, CNN.com (and a bunch you've never heard of). She lives in Minnesota with her husband and daughter. Email: *eav_mm@comcast.net*.

About the Creative Team

Nan Barber (editor) has worked with the Missing Manual series since its inception—long enough to remember booting up her computer from a floppy disk. Email: *nanbarber@oreilly.com*.

Michele Filshie (editor) is assistant editor for the Missing Manual series and editor of four of O'Reilly's Personal Trainer books. Email: *mfilshie@oreilly.com*.

Sohaila Abdulali (copy editor) is a freelance writer and editor. She has published a novel, several children's books, and numerous short stories and articles. She's currently finishing an ethnography of an aboriginal Indian woman. Sohaila lives in New York City with her husband Tom and their small but larger-than-life daughter, Samara. Web: *www.sohailaink.com*.

Greg Dickerson (tech reviewer) is a systems administrator at O'Reilly. During his time at O'Reilly, he has helped tech review several titles and was the QA lead for O'Reilly's Deluxe CD Bookshelf's product line.

Michael Hurwicz (technical reviewer) is a writer, animator, musician, and trainer who has written two books and a number of articles on Macromedia Flash and Studio. Web: *http://www.hurwicz.com*.

Michael D. Murie (technical reviewer) is a multimedia consultant and developer based in Boston.

Rose Cassano (cover illustration) has worked as an independent designer and illustrator for over 20 years, working for both corporate and nonprofit clientele. She lives in southern Oregon, grateful for the technology that makes working there a reality. Email: *cassano@highstream.net*. Web: *www.rosecassano.com*.

Acknowledgements

My name may be on the cover, but the fact is, this book wouldn't exist if it weren't for the tireless army of editors, technical editors, copy editors, production folks, and other O'Reilly professionals who shepherded it from manuscript to finished product. An especially heartfelt shout out to Sarah Milstein, who took a chance; Nan Barber, who made my life easier (while making this book ever so much better); and Michaels Hurwicz and Murie, whose eagle eyes straightened the bent, buffed the cloudy, and trimmed the fat. Quality is second nature to this team—and in this day and age, that's saying something.

—E. A. Vander Veer

The Missing Manual Series

Missing Manuals are witty, superbly written guides to computer products that don't come with printed manuals (which is just about all of them these days). Each book features a handcrafted index; cross-references to specific page numbers (not just "see Chapter 14"); and RepKover, a detached-spine binding that lets the book lie perfectly flat without the assistance of weights (or cinder blocks).

Access for Starters: The Missing Manual by Kate Chase and Scott Palmer

AppleScript: The Missing Manual by Adam Goldstein

AppleWorks 6: The Missing Manual by Jim Elferdink and David Reynolds

CSS: The Missing Manual by David Sawyer McFarland

Creating Web Sites: The Missing Manual by Matthew MacDonald

Dreamweaver 8: The Missing Manual by David Sawyer McFarland

eBay: The Missing Manual by Nancy Conner

eBay Business: The Missing Manual by Nancy Conner

Excel: The Missing Manual by Matthew MacDonald

Excel for Starters: The Missing Manual by Matthew MacDonald

FileMaker Pro 8: The Missing Manual by Geoff Coffey and Susan Prosser

FrontPage 2003: The Missing Manual by Jessica Mantaro

GarageBand 2: The Missing Manual by David Pogue

Google: The Missing Manual, Second Edition by Sarah Milstein, Matthew Mac-Donald, and J. D. Biersdorfer

Home Networking: The Missing Manual by Scott Lowe

iLife '05: The Missing Manual by David Pogue

iMovie HD 6 & iDVD 6: The Missing Manual by David Pogue

iPhoto 6: The Missing Manual by David Pogue

iPod & iTunes: The Missing Manual, Third Edition by Jude Biersdorfer

iWork '05: The Missing Manual by Jim Elferdink

Mac OS X Power Hound, Panther Edition by Rob Griffiths

Mac OS X: The Missing Manual, Tiger Edition by David Pogue

Office 2004 for Macintosh: The Missing Manual by Mark H. Walker and Franklin Tessler

PCs: The Missing Manual by Andy Rathbone

Photoshop Elements 4: The Missing Manual by Barbara Brundage

QuickBooks 2006: The Missing Manual by Bonnie Biafore

Quicken for Starters: The Missing Manual by Bonnie Biafore

Switching to the Mac: The Missing Manual, Tiger Edition by David Pogue and Adam Goldstein

Windows 2000 Pro: The Missing Manual by Sharon Crawford

Windows XP Power Hound by Preston Gralla

Windows XP for Starters: The Missing Manual by David Pogue

Windows XP Home Edition: The Missing Manual, Second Edition by David Pogue

Windows XP Pro: The Missing Manual, Second Edition by David Pogue, Craig Zacker, and Linda Zacker

Introduction

Flash has been the gold standard in multimedia creation software for almost 10 years. The program has come a long way since the mid-1990s, when professional animators—like those at Microsoft's MSN and Disney Online—used an early incarnation called FutureSplash. Over the years, Flash earned a following of programming geeks as an alternative to Java for creating vector-based Web graphics. In the 21st century, though, anyone with a desktop computer (or even a laptop) can be a Web animator. With Flash 8's easy-to-use panels and toolbars, you can create sophisticated, interactive animations that run on the Web, on standalone computers, on handhelds, on kiosks—virtually anywhere you find a screen (see Figure I-1).

Here are just some of the things you can create with Flash:

- **Drawings and animations.** Flash gives you the drawing tools to create original artwork and the animation tools to give it movement and life. You can then edit your Flash document in another program, add it to a Web page, or burn it to a CD or DVD. Flash recognizes multimedia files created using other programs, so you can enrich your animations with image, sound, and video files you already have (or that you find on the Web).

- **Multimedia Web sites.** You can create original drawings and animations with Flash, add in voice-overs, background music, and video clips, and then publish it all to a Web page with the click of a button. Using Flash's built-in scripting language, ActionScript, you can add interactive features like hotspots and navigation bars. You can even position elements on the screen precisely and then change the layout at runtime. With Flash, even regular folks can create real-time video blogs and eye-grabbing splash pages.

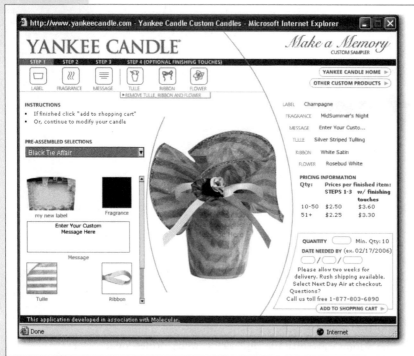

Figure I-1:
The Yankee Candle Company's Web site, www.yankeecandle.com, is just one example of the movement, interactivity, and polish Flash can add to a site. From the home page, clicking Custom Candle Favors → Custom Votives displays this Web-based Flash program.

- **Banner ads.** These blinking, flashing, animated strips of Madison Avenue marvelousness are easy to produce in Flash. Typically, banner ads consist of a skinny animation and a link to the sponsor site (see Figure I-2).

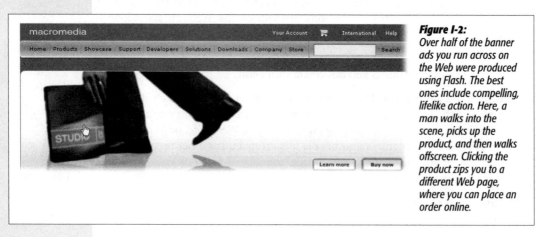

Figure I-2:
Over half of the banner ads you run across on the Web were produced using Flash. The best ones include compelling, lifelike action. Here, a man walks into the scene, picks up the product, and then walks offscreen. Clicking the product zips you to a different Web page, where you can place an order online.

- **Tutorials.** Web-based training courses, which often include a combination of text, drawings, animations, video clips, and voice-overs, are a natural fit for Flash. By hooking Flash up to a server on the back end, you can even present your audience with graded tests and up-to-the-minute product information.

You don't have to deliver your tutorials over the Web, though; you can publish them as standalone projector files (Chapter 14) and deliver them to your students via CDs or DVDs.

- **Full-length ads and product presentations.** Marketing types can use Flash to create slick, storyboarded, buy-our-stuff-now animations and program mock-ups.

- **Customer service kiosks.** Many of the kiosks you see in stores and building lobbies use Flash to help customers find what they need. For example, kiosks in photomats walk customers through the process of transferring images from their digital camera and ordering their own prints; kiosks in banks let customers withdraw funds, check interest rates, and make deposits.

- **Television and film effects.** The Hollywood set has been known to use Flash to create spectacular visual effects for TV shows and even smaller feature films. But where the TV and film industry is seriously adopting Flash is on promotional Web sites, where they wed Flash graphics to scenes taken from their movies and shows to present powerful trailers, interactive tours of movie and show sets, and teasers.

- **Games and other programs.** With support for runtime scripting, back end data transfers, and interactive controls such as buttons and text boxes, Flash has everything a programmer needs to create a cool-looking game (check out *www.addictinggames.com* for a few examples) or other *rich Internet applications* (Adobe/Macromedia's 20-dollar term for "Web-based program").

UP TO SPEED

Flash Is Everywhere

One of the reasons for Flash's success is that a version of Flash Player comes with most browsers (including AOL, Internet Explorer, Netscape, and Opera) and operating systems (including Windows and Mac). So, unlike Apple's QuickTime or RealNetworks' RealPlayer, Web surfers don't have to do anything special to play Flash animations embedded in Web pages. In fact, depending on whose figures you believe, somewhere between 70 and 98 percent of all the PCs and Macs connected to the Web can play Flash animations right out of the box.

This ubiquity is a huge boon for anyone interested in creating animations with Flash, because once you create your masterpiece, virtually everyone connected to the Internet will be able to see and enjoy it—with one caveat. If you use brand-new features introduced in Flash 8, folks running an earlier version of Flash Player (like Flash 6 or 7) may not be able to see your animation the way you meant for it to look until they download and install a copy of the Flash 8 Player.

Unfortunately, there's no such thing as a free lunch. If Flash is an incredibly powerful, useful program—and it is—it's also harder to use than a greased tightrope.

That's where this book comes in. You don't have to be a professional artist, animator, or software developer to create useful animations with Flash. All you need are this book and an idea of what you'd like to create. The examples, explanations, and step-by-step instructions you find in the next 14 chapters show you how to turn that idea into a working animation.

The Two Flavors of Flash 8

Flash 8 comes in two flavors: Flash Basic 8 and Flash Professional 8 (Figure I-3). Aimed at the corporate team developer, Flash Professional 8 offers everything Flash Basic 8 does, *plus*:

- **Additional graphic effects.** With Flash Professional 8, you get convenient extras like *filters* (predefined blurs, glows, and drop shadows), *blend modes* (transparency effects that make *compositing*, or combining images, easy), and *custom easing* (the ability to slow down or speed up animated tweens with the click of a button).

- **Support for mobile authoring.** Flash Professional 8 comes with mobile templates (to help you size your animations for handhelds), an emulator (to let you see how your animations will appear on every handheld that Flash supports), and built-in publishing options.

- **Support for high-end video manipulation.** You can embed video clips into your Flash animations using both Flash 8 and Flash 8 Professional (as you see in Chapter 8). But Flash Professional 8 gives you extra tools, including the Flash Video Exporter (a QuickTime plug-in that lets you create Flash video files using any Apple QuickTime–compatible video authoring tool) and the Flash Video Encoder (a standalone application that lets you convert regular video files to Flash video files). Using Flash Professional 8, you can link to external video files and even layer video clips on top of each other to create sophisticated composite effects.

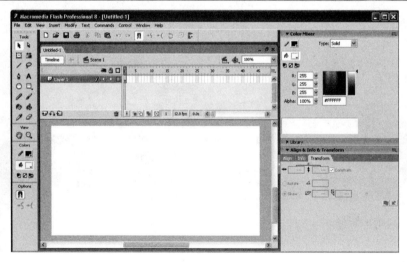

Figure I-3:
The Flash Basic 8 interface looks pretty similar to the Flash Professional 8 interface, shown here, except for the product description in the title bar. The big difference comes when you're using Flash Basic and trying to use a feature that exists only in Flash Professional 8, such as adding a filter effect (for example, a drop-down shadow) to a block of text. In this book, features that appear only in Flash Professional are so noted, so you won't waste time hunting for them if you're running Flash Basic.

What's New in Flash 8

Most of the improvements you see in Flash 8 compared to the previous version (Flash MX 2004) have to do with performance—always a good thing. But in addition, Macromedia also added a few usability tweaks, as well as a couple of new image-editing features.

Here's a short list of the differences in Flash 8 compared to Flash MX 2004:

- **Improved performance.** Improvements include better text *anti-aliasing* (smoother-looking text) and the ability to cache movie clips as bitmaps at runtime (and so cut down on playback time for super-complex vector graphics, which you learn about in Chapter 2). The big news: Macromedia added a new, faster, more efficient video *codec*, or video compression algorithm to Flash Player 8, which comes with both Flash Basic 8 and Flash Professional 8 as well as most Web browsers and operating systems (see the box on page 3). A more efficient codec means improved download and playback of any video clips you add to your animations.

- **Improved interface.** In Flash 8, you can drag a text block's resize handle and drag to expand it, which is simpler than having to resize the text block using the Property Inspector the way you had to in Flash MX 2004. A new drop-down list in the Flash 8 Library panel shows all other open libraries, making it easier to exchange imported media files and *symbols* between Flash documents. And scripting help is back in the form of the Scripting Assist mode. If you're running a Mac, you'll appreciate that the Mac version of Flash 8 lets you see all your open Flash documents in a single tabbed window, similar to the way you work with multiple documents in Flash when you're running Windows.

- **New image editing features.** Flash 8 introduces *object drawing mode* (Chapter 2), which lets you tell Flash whether you want it to treat shapes and their outlines as a unit (the way most people think of them) or separately. Flash 8 also lets you add sharp, mitered corners to rectangular objects. And Flash Professional 8 includes additional graphics effects (see the previous page).

- **Improved support for video editing (Flash Professional 8 only).** Both the Video Exporter and Video Encoder (see page 4) let you compress video clips using the new and improved codec—On2 Technologies' VP6—in addition to the Sorenson Spark codec supported in Flash MX 2004. New video *alpha channel* support lets you layer video clips using various alpha (transparency) settings.

Anatomy of an Animation

Animation is a complex subject, and Flash is a complex program. You'll have a much easier time plowing through the rest of the book if you start with a couple of basics under your belt: specifically, what an animation is and how you go about creating one in Flash. This section and the following one give you some background.

Animators typically develop animations in a frame-by-frame sequence, where every frame contains a different image. As the frames speed by on a projector, the hundreds (or hundreds of thousands) of static images create the illusion of moving characters.

Painstaking work? You bet. Before the age of computerized generation—which has really just come into its own in the last 15 years or so, with big names like Pixar—major animation houses employed whole armies of graphic artists, each charged with producing hundreds of drawings that represented a mere fraction of the finished work. What we yukked at for a scant few minutes took weeks and dozens of tired, cramped hands to produce. One mistake, one spilled drop of coffee, and these patient-as-Job types would have to grab fresh paper and start all over again. When everything was done, the animation would have to be put together—much like one of those flip books where you flip pages real fast to see a story play out—while it was being filmed by special cameras.

Well, Flash brings you the power of a design studio, expert tools, and the equivalent of a staff of highly trained detail people. You still have to come up with an idea for the animation, and you have to draw (or find and import) at least a couple of images. But beyond that, Flash can take over and generate most of the frames you need to flesh out your animation.

It's pretty incredible, when you think about it. A few hundred bucks and a few hours spent working with Flash, and you've got an animation that, just a few years ago, you'd have had to pay a swarm of professionals union scale to produce. Sweet!

Flash in a Nutshell

Say you work for a company that does custom auto refinishing. First assignment: Design an intro page for the company's new Web site. You have the following idea for an animation:

The first thing you want your audience to see is a beat-up jalopy limping along a city street toward the center of the screen, where it stops and morphs into a shiny,

An Animation by Any Other Name...

You may occasionally hear Flash animations referred to (by books, Web sites, and even Macromedia's own documentation) as *movies*. Perhaps that's accurate technically, but it sure can be confusing.

QuickTime .mov files are also called movies, and some people refer to video clips as movies; but to Flash, these two things are very different animals. In addition, Flash lets you create and work with *movie clips*, which are something else entirely. And "movie," with its connotations of quietly sitting in a theater balcony eating popcorn, doesn't convey one of the most important features Flash offers: interactivity.

Here's the most accurate way to describe what you create using Flash: a Web site or program with a really cool, animated interface. Unfortunately, that description's a bit long and unwieldy, so in this book, what you create using Flash is an *animation*.

like-new car as your company's jingle plays in the background. A voice-over informs your audience that your company's been in business for 20 years and offers the best prices in town.

Across the top of the screen you'd like to display the company logo, as well as a conventional navigation bar with buttons—labeled Location, Services, Prices, and Contact—that your audience can click to get more information about your company. But you also want each part of the car to be a clickable hotspot. That way, when someone clicks one of the car's tires, he's whisked off to a page describing your custom wheels and hubcaps; when he clicks on the car's body, he sees prices for dent repair and repainting; and so on.

Here's how you might go about creating this animation in Flash:

- Using Flash's drawing tools, you draw the artwork for every *keyframe* of the animation: that is, every unique image. For example, you'll need to create a keyframe showing the beat-up junker and a second keyframe showing the gleaming, expertly refurbished result. (Chapter 2 shows you how to draw artwork in Flash; Chapter 3 tells you everything you need to know about keyframes.)

- Within each keyframe, you might choose to separate your artwork into different *layers*. Like the see-through plastic *cels* that professional animators used in the old days, layers let you create images separately and then stack them on top of each other to make a single composite image. For example, you might choose to put the car on one layer, your company logo on a second layer, and your city-street background on a third layer. That way, you can edit and animate each layer independently, but when the animation plays, all three elements appear to be on one seamless layer. (Chapter 4 shows you how to work with layers.)

- Through a process called *tweening*, you tell Flash to fill in each and every frame in-*between* the keyframes to create the illusion of the junker turning slowly into a brand-new car. Flash carefully analyzes all the differences between the keyframes and does its best to build the interim frames, which you can then tweak or—if Flash gets it all wrong—redraw yourself. (Chapter 3 guides you through the tweening process.)

• As you go along, you might decide to save a few of the elements you create (for example, your company logo), so you can reuse them again later. There's no sense in reinventing the wheel, and in addition to saving you time, reusing elements actually helps keep your animation files as small and efficient as possible. (See Chapter 7 for details on creating and managing reusable elements.)

• Add the background music and voice-over audio clips, which you've created in other programs (Chapter 8).

• Create the navigation bar buttons and hotspots that let your audience interact with your animation (Chapter 7).

• Test your animation (Chapter 13) and tweak it to perfection.

• Finally, when your animation is just the way you want it, you're ready to *publish* it. Without leaving the comfort of Flash, you can convert the editable .fla file you've been working with into a noneditable .swf file and either embed it into an HTML file or create a standalone *projector* file your audience can run without having to use a browser. Chapter 14 tells you everything you need to know about publishing.

The scenario described above is pretty simple, but it covers the basic steps you need to take when creating any Flash animation.

The Very Basics

You'll find very little jargon or nerd terminology in this book. You will, however, encounter a few terms and concepts that you'll encounter frequently in your computing life:

• **Clicking.** This book gives you several kinds of instructions that require you to use your computer's mouse or trackpad. To *click* means to point the arrow cursor at something on the screen and then—without moving the cursor at all—to press and release the clicker button on the mouse (or laptop trackpad). To *double-click,* of course, means to click twice in rapid succession, again without moving the cursor at all. To *drag* means to move the cursor while pressing the button continuously. To *right-click* or *right-drag,* do the same as above, but press the mouse button on the right.

When you see an instruction like *Shift-click* or *Ctrl-click*, simply press the key as you click.

Note: Macintosh computers don't come with a right mouse button. With a one-button mouse, to do the same thing as a right-click or right-drag, press the Mac's Control key as you click or drag. (Or buy a two-button mouse.) See the next section for more Windows/Mac differences.

- **Keyboard shortcuts.** Every time you take your hand off the keyboard to move the mouse, you lose time and potentially disrupt your creative flow. That's why many experienced computer fans use keystroke combinations instead of menu commands wherever possible. Ctrl+B (⌘-B on the Mac), for example, is a keyboard shortcut for boldface type in Flash (and most other programs).

  When you see a shortcut like Ctrl+S (⌘-S on the Mac), which saves changes to the current document, it's telling you to hold down the Ctrl or ⌘ key, and, while it's down, type the letter S, and then release both keys.

- **Choice is good.** Flash frequently gives you several ways to trigger a particular command—a menu command, or by clicking a toolbar button, or by pressing a key combination, for example. Some people prefer the speed of keyboard shortcuts; others like the satisfaction of a visual command array available in menus or toolbars. This book lists all of the alternatives, but by no means are you expected to memorize all of them.

Macintosh and Windows

Flash 8 works much the same way in its Mac and Windows incarnations with the exception of a few interface differences and a slight variation in performance—Flash animations tend to run a bit slower on the Mac. This book's illustrations give Mac and Windows equal time, alternating by chapter, so you get to see how all of Flash's features look, no matter what kind of computer you're running.

There *is* one small difference between Mac and Windows software that you need to be aware of, and that's keystrokes. The Ctrl key in Windows is the equivalent of the Macintosh ⌘ key, and the key labeled Alt on a PC (and on non-U.S. Macs) is the equivalent of the Option key on American Mac keyboards.

Whenever this book refers to a key combination, therefore, you'll see the Windows keystroke listed first (with + symbols, as is customary in Windows documentation); the Macintosh keystroke follows in parentheses (with - symbols, in time-honored Mac tradition). In other words, you might read, "The keyboard shortcut for saving a file is Ctrl+S (⌘-S)." This book mentions any other significant differences between the Mac and Windows versions of Flash 8 as they come up.

About This Book

Flash has gotten more powerful and more sophisticated over the years, but one thing hasn't changed: woefully poor documentation. If Flash were simple to use, the lack of documentation wouldn't be such a big deal. But Flash is a complex program—especially if you don't have a background in programming or multimedia authoring software. Basically, because Flash's documentation alternates between high-level market-speak and low-level computer engineering jargon, you're pretty much out of luck if you're a normal, intelligent person who just wants to use Flash to create a cool animated Web site and then get on with your life.

Fortunately, there's an answer—and you're holding it in your hands.

This is the book that *should* have come in the Flash box: one that explains all the tools and shows you step-by-step not just how to create animations from scratch, but *why* you want to do each step—in English, not programmer-ese. You'll learn tips and shortcuts for making Flash easier to work with, as well as making your animations as audience-friendly as possible.

Flash 8: The Missing Manual is designed for readers of every skill level *except* super-advanced-programmer. If Flash is the first image creation or animation program you've ever used, you'll be able to dive right in using the explanations and examples in this book. If you come from an animation or multimedia background, you'll find this book a useful reference for mapping how you created an element in your previous program to how you do it in Flash. "Design Time" boxes explain the art of effective multimedia design (which is an art unto itself). And while the ActionScript programming language is far too broad a subject to cover in detail in this book, you do get working examples of the most common types of actions you'll want to create in ActionScript, along with suggestions for debugging your code and tips on where to go for a more in-depth look at scripting.

About the Outline

Flash 8: The Missing Manual is divided into five parts, each containing several chapters:

- **Part 1: Creating a Flash Animation** guides you through the creation of your very first Flash animation, from the first glimmer of an idea to drawing images, animating those images, and testing your work.

- **Part 2: Advanced Drawing and Animation** is the meatiest of the four parts. Here you'll see how to manipulate your drawings by rotating, skewing, stacking, and aligning them; how to add color, special effects, and multimedia files such as audio and video clips; how to slash file size by turning bits and pieces of your drawings into special elements called *symbols*; and how to create composite drawings using layers.

- **Part 3: Adding Interactivity** shows you how to add ActionScript actions to frames to create automatic effects and to buttons to create audience-controlled effects. You'll see how to loop and reverse a section of an animation, how to let your audience choose which section of an animation to play, and how to customize the prebuilt interactive components that come with Flash.

- **Part 4: Delivering Your Animation to Its Audience** focuses on testing, debugging, and optimizing your animation. You'll also find out how to publish your animation so that your audience can see and enjoy it and how to export an editable version of your animation so that you can rework it using another graphics, video editing, or Web development program.

- **Part 5: Appendix**

About → These → Arrows

Throughout this book, you'll find instructions like, "Open your Program Files → Macromedia → Macromedia Flash 8 folder." That's Missing Manual shorthand for much longer sentences like "Double-click your Program Files folder to open it. Inside, you'll find a folder called Macromedia; double-click to open it. Inside *that* folder is a folder called Macromedia Flash 8; open it, too." This arrow shorthand also simplifies the business of choosing menu commands, as you can see in Figure I-4.

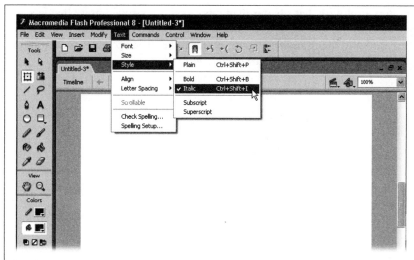

Figure I-4:
When you see instructions like "Choose Text → Style → Italic," think, "Click to pull down the Text menu and then move your mouse down to the Style command. When its submenu opens, choose the Italic option."

Flash Examples

As you read the book's chapters, you'll encounter a number of step-by-step tutorials. You can work through them using any Flash document of your own, or use the example files provided on this book's "Missing CD" page. You can download them using any Web browser at *www.missingmanuals.com/cds*. You'll find raw materials (like graphics and half-completed animations) and, in some cases, completed animations with which to compare your work.

About MissingManuals.com

At the *www.missingmanuals.com* Web site, you'll find articles, tips, and updates to this book. In fact, you're invited and encouraged to submit such corrections and updates yourself. In an effort to keep the book as up-to-date and accurate as possible, each time we print more copies of this book, we'll make any confirmed corrections you've suggested. We'll also note such changes on the Web site so that you can mark important corrections into your own copy of the book if you like. (Click the book's name and then click the Errata link to see the changes.)

In the meantime, we'd love to hear your own suggestions for new books in the Missing Manual line. There's a place for that on the Web site, too, as well as a place to sign up for free email notification of new titles in the series.

Safari® Enabled

 When you see a Safari® Enabled icon on the cover of your favorite technology book, that means the book is available online through the O'Reilly Network Safari Bookshelf.

Safari offers a solution that's better than e-books. It's a virtual library that lets you easily search thousands of top tech books, cut and paste code samples, download chapters, and find quick answers when you need the most accurate, current information. Try it for free at *http://safari.oreilly.com*.

Part One:
Creating a Flash Animation

1

Getting Around Flash

Computer programs these days strive to give you an intuitive work environment. A word processing document, for example, looks pretty much like a piece of paper and shows your words as you type them. Movie playing software has controls that look just like the ones on your home DVD player. Flash 8 provides the powerful and flexible tools that you need to create interactive animations, which is a more complex affair than producing text or playing media. Problem is, if this is your first time in an animation program, it may not be immediately obvious what to *do* with all these tools.

When you start with a blank Flash document, you find yourself staring at a blank white square and a dizzying array of icons, most of which appear to do nothing when you click them (Figure 1-1). You'd pretty much have to be a Flash developer to figure out what to do next. In this chapter, you get acquainted with all the different parts of the Flash window: the stage and main work area, the main menu, the toolbars and panels, the Timeline, and more. You'll also take Flash for a test drive and get some practice moving around the Flash screen. When you learn to create an animation of your own in Chapters 2 and 3, you'll feel right at home.

Note: For more help getting acquainted with Flash, you can check out the built-in tutorials by selecting Help → Flash Help → Flash Tutorials. You can read about them, along with the rest of Flash's Help system, in this book's Appendix.

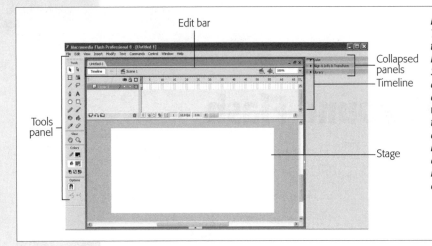

Edit bar

Collapsed panels

Timeline

Tools panel

Stage

Figure 1-1:
The white rectangle in the middle of the main Flash window—the Stage—is where you actually work on your animations. This entire window, together with the Timeline, toolbars, and panels identified here, is called the Flash desktop, the Flash interface, or the Flash authoring environment.

Starting Flash

Once you've installed Flash on your computer (page 435), you can launch it like any other program. Choose your method:

- Double-click the program's icon. You can find it on your hard drive in Program Files → Macromedia → Flash 8 (Windows) or Applications → Macromedia Flash 8 folder (Mac).

- Click Start → All Programs → Macromedia → Macromedia Flash 8 (Windows). If you're running Mac, you can drag the Flash 8 icon from the Macromedia Flash 8 folder to the Dock and from then on open it with a single click on the Dock icon.

Up pops the Flash start page, as shown in Figure 1-2. When you open the program, you're most likely to start a new document or return to a work in progress. This screen puts all your options in one handy place.

Tip: If Flash seems to take forever to open—or if the Flash desktop ignores your mouse clicks or responds sluggishly—you may not have enough memory installed on your computer. See page 435 for more advice.

When you choose one of the options on the start page, it disappears and your actual document takes its place. Here are your choices:

- **Open a Recent Item.** As you create new documents, Flash adds them to this list. Clicking one of the file names listed here tells Flash to open that file. Clicking the folder icon lets you browse your computer for (and then open) any other Flash file on your computer.

- **Create New.** Clicking one of the options listed here lets you create a brand-new Flash file. Most of the time, you'll want to create a Flash *document*, which is a

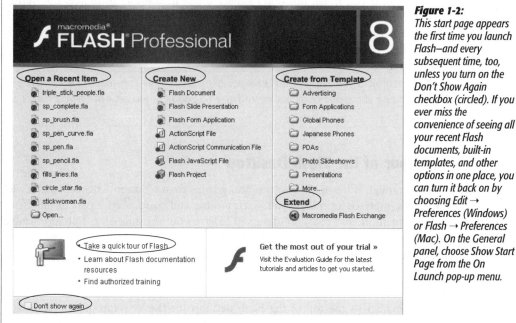

Figure 1-2:
This start page appears the first time you launch Flash—and every subsequent time, too, unless you turn on the Don't Show Again checkbox (circled). If you ever miss the convenience of seeing all your recent Flash documents, built-in templates, and other options in one place, you can turn it back on by choosing Edit → Preferences (Windows) or Flash → Preferences (Mac). On the General panel, choose Show Start Page from the On Launch pop-up menu.

plain garden-variety animation file. But you can also create a Flash *slide presentation* (a specialized kind of animation consisting of a bunch of still images); a Flash *form application* (an interactive animation that accepts data input and hooks into a server to process that input); an *ActionScript file* (a file containing nothing but ActionScript, for use with a Flash animation); an *ActionScript Communication file* (a file that uses ActionScript to transfer data between an animation and a server); a Flash *JavaScript file* (a file that transfers data between an animation and a Web browser using JavaScript); and a Flash *project* (useful if you're planning a complex, multifile, multideveloper Flash production and need version control).

• **Create From Template.** Clicking one of the little folder icons under this option lets you create a Flash document using a predesigned form called a *template*. Using a template helps you create a Flash animation quicker because a developer somewhere has already done part of the work for you. You'll find out more about templates in Chapter 7.

• **Extend.** Clicking the Macromedia Flash Exchange link under this option tells Flash to open your Web browser (if it's not already running) and load the Flash Exchange Web site. There, you can download Flash components, sound files, and other goodies (some free, some fee, and all of them created by Flash-ionados just like you) that you can add to your Flash animations.

• **Take a Quick Tour of Flash.** Why the Flash development team thought folks running Flash would want to sit through an ad is anybody's guess. Click this option if you must, but don't expect much in the way of usable, nitty-gritty information. Instead, a multimedia presentation shamelessly regales you with market-speak describing all the ways you can "enhance" the "engaging experiences" you create in Flash.

Tip: Except for the Macromedia Flash Exchange, which you find on the Help menu, all of the options on the start page also appear on the File menu (Figure 1-3 below), so you can start a new document any time.

A Tour of the Flash Desktop

Even though it has more controls and gizmos than a jumbo-jet cockpit, don't let Flash's interface intimidate you. Each toolbar and panel plays a part in the life of an animation, and most are designed to give you, the animator, full and flexible control over your creation. Once you know why and how to use each type of control, all becomes clear. That's what this section does.

Menu Bar

Running across the top of the Flash desktop (or the very top of your screen, if you're on a Mac), is the menu bar. The commands on these menus list every way you can interact with your Flash file, from creating a new file—as shown on page 46—to editing it, saving it, and controlling how it appears on your screen.

Some of the menu names—File, Edit, View, Window, and Help—are familiar to anyone who's used a PC or Mac. Using these menu choices, you can perform basic tasks such as opening, saving, and printing your Flash files; cutting and pasting sections of your drawing; viewing your drawing in different ways; choosing which toolbars to view; getting help; and more.

To view a menu, simply click the menu's title to open it and then click a menu option. On a Mac, you can also drag down to the option you want. Let go of the mouse button to activate the option. Figure 1-3 shows you what the File menu looks like.

Figure 1-3:
Several of the options on each menu include keystroke shortcuts that allow you to perform an action without having to mouse all the way up to the menu and click on it. For example, instead of selecting File → Save As, you can press Ctrl+Shift+S (circled) to tell Flash to save the file you have open. On the Mac, the keystroke is Shift-⌘-S.

Depending on what's on your screen, additional menus may appear, unique to Flash. You'll learn all about these options in upcoming chapters. For example:

- **Insert.** The options you find in this menu let you create complex drawings and turn static drawings into Flash animations by adding *symbols* (reusable bits of drawings and animations, as you'll learn in Chapter 7); *layers* (virtual transparencies that let you manipulate the elements of a composite drawing separately, as shown in Chapter 3); and *frames* (virtual "flip pages" that, when displayed rapidly one after the other, turn a series of drawings into an animation, as discussed in Chapter 3); and so on.

- **Modify.** Selections here let you make changes to your work. For example, this is the menu you want when you want to rotate or *scale* (shrink or enlarge) a piece of your drawing.

- **Text.** The options in this menu let you work with the text you add to your drawings. Here, you can set standard text characteristics such as font, alignment, and spacing; you can also run a spell check.

- **Commands.** Options here allow you to create and run *commands* (commonly called *macros* in other programs). Commands are series of tasks you perform in Flash. For example, if you know you'll be opening a bunch of Flash documents and making identical changes to each one of them, you can tell Flash to "watch" you make the changes once and save them as a *command*. The next time you need to make those changes to a different document, all you have to do is run the command.

- **Control.** This is the menu to use when you want to test your animation. You can run your animation, rewind it, or even slow it down so that you step through one frame at a time—great for troubleshooting.

The Stage

The *Stage*, located at the dead center of your Flash workspace, is your virtual canvas. Here's where you draw the pictures that you'll eventually string together to create your animation. The Stage is also your playback arena: when you run a completed animation—to test it out and see if it needs tweaking—the animation appears on the Stage. At the beginning of this chapter, you saw a Flash desktop with a blank Stage. Figure 1-4 shows one with an animation in progress.

Work area is the technical name for the gray area surrounding the stage, although many Flash-ionados call it the *backstage*. This work area serves as a prep zone where you can place graphic elements before you move them to the Stage and as a temporary holding pen for elements you want to move off the Stage briefly as you reposition things. For example, let's say you draw three different circles and one box containing text on your Stage. If you decide you need to rearrange these elements on the Stage, you can temporarily drag one of the circles off the Stage, as shown in Figure 1-4.

Work area
(backstage)

Work area
(backstage)

—Stage

Figure 1-4:
The Stage (white) is where you draw the pictures that will eventually become your animation. The work area (gray) gives you a handy place to put graphic elements while you figure out how you want to arrange them on the Stage. Here, a sketch of a flower is being dragged from the work area back to center Stage.

Note: The Stage always starts out with a white background, which becomes the background color for your animation. Changing it to any color imaginable is easy, as you'll learn in the next chapter.

You'll almost always change the starting size and shape of the Stage depending on where people will see your finished animation to appear—your *target platform*. If your target platform is a Web-enabled cell phone, for example, you're going to want an itty-bitty Stage. If, on the other hand, you're creating an animation you know people will be watching on a 50-inch computer monitor, you're going to want a giant Stage. You'll get to try your hand at modifying the size of the stage in the Flash Test Drive later in this chapter.

Toolbars

Flash lets you put all the menu options you use most frequently at your fingertips by displaying *toolbars* and *panels* like those shown in Figure 1-1. Toolbars and panels are very similar: they're both movable windows that display Flash options. The difference is that toolbars are small and show only icons; panels are larger and show whole rafts of settings you can change. (You can learn all about panels in the next section.)

Toolbars pack some of the most commonly used options together in a nice compact space that you can position anywhere you like. (See the box on page 22 for tips on repositioning toolbars.) Displaying a toolbar means your options are right there in front of you, so you don't have to do a hunt-and-peck through the main menu every time you want to do something useful.

Tip: When you reposition a floating toolbar, Flash remembers where you put it. If, later on, you hide the toolbar—or exit Flash and run it again—your toolbars appear exactly as you left them. If this isn't what you want, you can wipe away all your changes and return to the way Flash originally displayed everything by choosing Window → Workspace layout → Default.

Flash offers three toolbars, all of which you see in Figure 1-5:

- **Main.** The Main toolbar lets you one-click basic operations, such as opening an existing Flash file, creating a new file, and cutting and pasting sections of your drawing.

- **Controller.** If you've ever seen a video or sound recorder, you'll recognize the Stop, Rewind, and Play buttons on the Controller toolbar, which allow you to control how you want Flash to run your finished animation. (Not surprisingly, the Controller options appear *grayed out*—meaning you can't select them—if you haven't yet constructed an animation.)

- **Edit Bar.** Using the options here, you can set and adjust the Timeline (page 34) as well as edit *scenes* (named groups of *frames*) and *symbols* (reusable drawings).

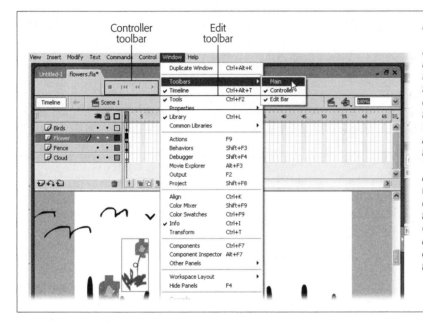

Figure 1-5:
To conserve space on Flash's jam-packed interface, only one toolbar—the Edit Bar toolbar—appears automatically. To display the other two, select Window → Toolbars → Main (to display the Main toolbar) and Window → Toolbars → Controller (to display the Controller window). The checkmarks on the menu show when a toolbar is turned on. Choose the toolbar's name again to remove the checkmark and hide the toolbar.

Panels

A Flash *panel* is like a toolbar on steroids: bigger and loaded down with more options, but built for the same reason—to let you keep the stuff you work with the most visible right there in front of you, where it's easy for you to find and use. Furthermore, unlike toolbars, panels offer options you can't find on *any* menu.

Flash offers you a ton of panels, each of which appears initially in one of two flavors: *docked* or *floating*. Docked panels appear outside your workspace, like the Color Mixer, Library, Property, and Actions panels shown in Figure 1-6.

Docked vs. Floating Toolbars

A *docked* toolbar or panel appears attached to some part of the workspace window, while a *floating* toolbar or panel is one that you can reposition by dragging.

Whether you want to display toolbars and panels as docked or floating is a matter of personal choice. If you constantly need to click something on a toolbar—which means it needs to be in full view at all times—docked works best. But if you usually just need a toolbar or a panel for a brief time and want to be able to move it around on the screen (so it doesn't cover up something else you need to work with, for example), floating's the ticket.

To turn a docked toolbar into a floating toolbar:

1. **Select the docked toolbar by clicking any blank spot on it.** An outline appears around the toolbar to let you know you've successfully selected it.

2. **Drag the toolbar away from the edge of the workspace window and release the mouse button.** Flash displays the toolbar where you dropped it. You can reposition it anywhere you like simply by dragging it again.

Here, the Controller toolbar has been dragged to make it float.

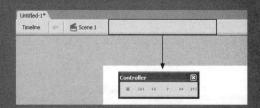

To dock a floating toolbar, simply reverse the procedure: drag the floating toolbar to the edge of the workspace window and let go of the mouse button. When you do, Flash docks the toolbar automatically.

You can have as few or as many panels showing at a time as you like. The Window menu lists all of Flash's panels, and you show and hide them by selecting to turn their checkmark on and off—exactly as with toolbars, as shown in Figure 1-5.

Besides keyboard shortcuts, there's only one way to display a panel—from the Window menu—but you have plenty of options for getting them out of your way. For example, you can click the X in the upper-right corner of a floating panel, as shown in Figure 1-6. For docked panels, you can *collapse* (shrink) them by clicking the down arrow in the upper-left corner.

Tip: To hide all the panels you've displayed in one fell swoop, select Window → Hide Panels or press the F4 key. You can also click the arrows just beneath (and to the right of) the workspace scroll bars. Whoosh! The panels below the Stage (or to the right of it) disappear, and you get to see a lot more of your workspace.

Tools Panel

All animations start with a single drawing. And to draw something in Flash, you need drawing tools: pens, pencils, brushes, colors, erasers, and so forth. The Tools panel, shown in Figure 1-7, is where you find Flash's drawing tools. Chapter 2 shows you how to use these tools to create a simple drawing; in this section, you get a quick overview of the four different sections of the Tools panel, each of which focuses on a slightly different kind of drawing tool.

Click to
collapse

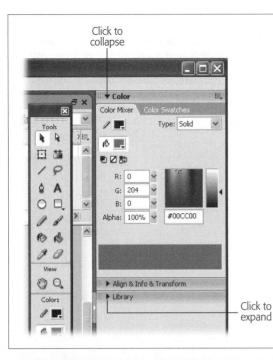

Figure 1-6:
Panels like the ones shown here group useful options together, so you can find what you want quickly and easily. To expand a collapsed panel and see what options it offers, click the miniscule right arrow you see next to the panel name. To collapse an expanded panel, click the miniscule down arrow.

Click to
expand

The Options Menu

In the upper-right corner of every expanded panel, you see a menu icon. When you click this icon, an options menu appears. The options menu is different for each panel. Here, for example, you see commands that let you edit how the Colors panel displays color choices. But a handful of options are common to all panels:

Group panel with. Displays a panel as a tab in *another* panel, which is a great way to save space on a crowded screen. Just like a tabbed Web browser, you can keep related panels neatly stacked together.

Close panel. Closes the panel (or tab) you're working with.

Rename panel group. Lets you rename the panel (not the tab) you're working with; for example, to a shorter name. (Flash doesn't let you open the panel by its new name in the Window menu, though.)

Maximize panel group. If the panel you're working with is docked, Flash redisplays the panel along the full length of your screen. Turning off the checkbox next to Maximize panel group minimizes the panel.

Close panel group. Closes the panel (not the tab) you're working with.

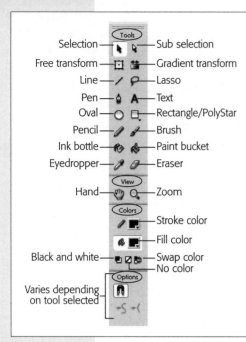

Figure 1-7:
The Tools panel shows up to four different sections, each relating to a different aspect of the drawing process: Tools, View, Colors, and Options. The icons that appear in the Options section change depending on which drawing tool you select. If you like, you can drag the docked Tools panel away from the edge of the workspace and turn it into a floating panel.

Labels on the Tools panel:
Selection — Sub selection
Free transform — Gradient transform
Line — Lasso
Pen — Text
Oval — Rectangle/PolyStar
Pencil — Brush
Ink bottle — Paint bucket
Eyedropper — Eraser
Hand — Zoom
— Stroke color
— Fill color
Black and white — Swap color
— No color
Varies depending on tool selected

Tools section

The Tools section displays the tools you need to create and modify a Flash drawing. For example, you might use the Pen tool to start a sketch, the Eyedropper to apply color, and the Eraser to clean up mistakes.

Tip: If you forget which tool does what and can't tell by looking at the icon (and frankly, it's pretty tough to tell what a black or white arrow is supposed to do), move your mouse over the icon and hold it there (don't click). After a second or two, the name of the tool pops up onscreen.

View section

At times, you'll find yourself drawing a picture so enormous you can't see it all on the Stage at one time. Or perhaps you'll find yourself drawing something you want to take a super-close look at so that you can modify it pixel by pixel. When either of these situations occurs, you can use the tools Flash displays in the View section of the Tools panel to zoom in, zoom out, and pan around the Stage. (You'll get to try your hand at using these tools later in this chapter; see page 37.)

Colors section

When you're creating in Flash, you're drawing one of two things, a *stroke*, which is a plain line or outline, or a *fill*, which is the area within an outline. Before you click one of the drawing icons to begin drawing (or afterwards, to change existing colors, as discussed in Chapter 2) you can use these tools to choose a color from the color palette, and Flash applies that color to the Stage as you draw.

Options section

Which icons appear in the Options section at any given time depends on which tool you've selected. For example, when you select the Zoom tool from the View section of the Tools panel, the Options section displays an Enlarge icon and a Reduce icon that you can use to change the way the Zoom tool works (Figure 1-8).

Figure 1-8:
On the Tools panel, when you click each tool, the Options section shows you buttons that let you modify that particular tool. In the Tools panel's View section, for example, when you click the Zoom tool, the Options section changes to show you only zooming options: Enlarge (with the plus sign) and Reduce (with the minus sign).

Accessibility Panel

Not everyone is blessed with perfect eyesight and hearing. To make sure vision- and hearing-impaired folks can enjoy the animations you create using Flash, you need to think about *accessibility:* the special techniques you can use to deliver your message via alternate means.

The Accessibility panel provides tools to help you in creating a design that provides at least some information to those whose vision or hearing is impaired. For example, using the Accessibility panel, you can give names and descriptions to certain sections of your drawings—descriptions that can be translated into speech by an assistive screen reader device, for example. Then, when a blind person surfing the Web views your animation of a car crunching into a thick brick wall, the assistive reader can speak the words, "the car crashes into a brick wall."

Note: Obviously, it's hard to translate any primarily visual medium like Flash into one that's spoken rather than seen. It's worth the effort it takes to try, though, because doing so gives impaired folks a chance to understand what you're trying to present.

To display the Accessibility panel, select Window → Other Panels → Accessibility (or press Alt+F2).

Actions Panel/ActionScript Debugger Panel

ActionScript is a serious developer-level scripting language that lets you add inter-activity to your animations by tying a graphic element (say, a button) to a specific action (say, opening up a specific Web page). In fact, that's how ActionScript got its name: it lets you tie an *action* to an object or element you designate. You use the

Why Accessibility Matters

The term *accessibility* refers to how easy it is for folks with physical or developmental challenges (such as low or no vision) to understand or interact with your animation.

As you can imagine, a Flash animation—which often includes audio in addition to video and still images—isn't going to be experienced the same way by someone who is blind or deaf as it is by someone who isn't impaired. But there is help. One of the features that conscientious Flash-ionados build into their animations is alternative information for those who can't see or hear. (Often, sight- and hearing-impaired folks use assistive devices to "report back" on what they otherwise can't access, so Flash animators build content into their animations that these assistive devices can access and translate.)

Thanks to U.S. legislation referred to as *Section 508*, local, state and federal Web sites absolutely have to be accessible and useable to the public. But if you're a private individual planning to incorporate your animation into a Web site, you can't ignore the issue of accessibility just because nobody's looking over your shoulder and forcing you to deal with it. If you ignore accessibility, you eliminate a whole audience who might otherwise benefit from your content.

For more information on accessibility, check out these Web sites:

- *www.alistapart.com/articles/wiwa/*
- *http://DiveintoAccessibility.org*
- *http://Section508.gov*
- *http://WebABLE.com*
- *http://WebAIM.org*
- *www.w3c.org/wai/*

Actions panel (see the next section) to build the ActionScript code that turns regular animations into interactive animations like clickable splash pages, navigation bars, and type-in forms.

The Actions panel lets you mix and match snippets of ActionScript code to build what's called an ActionScript *script*, which you can then attach to one of the objects in your drawing (or one of the *frames* in your animation) to make your animation "smart." *After* you create a script, the ActionScript debugger panel lets you to troubleshoot any scripting code that's giving you trouble. You'll learn how to write and debug ActionScripts of your own in Part 3.

Align Panel

Sometimes dragging stuff around the stage and eyeballing it works just fine; other times, you want to position your graphic elements with pinpoint precision. Using the Align panel, you can align graphic elements based on their edges (top, bottom, right, left) or by their centers. And you can base this alignment on the objects themselves (for example, you can line up the tops of all your objects) or on the Stage (useful if you want to position, say, the bottoms of all your objects at the bottom of the Stage, as shown in Figure 1-9). You can even distribute objects evenly with respect to each other.

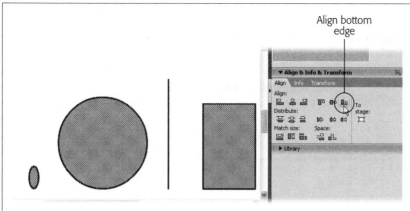

Align bottom
edge

Figure 1-9:
*The Align panel gives you
the opportunity to align a
single object (or whole
groups of selected
objects) along the left
side of the Stage, the
right side, the top, the
bottom, and more. Make
sure you select the
objects you want to align
first; then click the
alignment icon from the
Align panel.*

To display the Align panel, select Window → Align or press Ctrl+K (Windows) or
⌘-K (Mac).

Tip: More help for aligning stuff on the Stage comes from Flash's grids, guides, and rulers, which you
learn about in Chapter 2 (page 43).

Behaviors Panel

Flash comes with several common, pre-ActionScripted snippets of code called
behaviors that you can add to your animations. You'll find a behavior for most of
the really basic things you want to do with ActionScript, such as triggering a sound
file or jumping to a specific section of an animation.

All you have to do to use a behavior is display the Behaviors Panel (Window →
Behavior) shown in Figure 1-10 and then click the Add Behavior icon to display a
list of available behaviors. When you do, Flash pops up a helpful window (or two)
to step you through the process of customizing the behavior.

For example, if you want to trigger a sound file, you need to add the Play Sound
behavior, tie it to an event—such as a button clicking or a frame appearing—and
then customize your newly added behavior by telling Flash which sound file you
want it to play when the event occurs.

Color Mixer Panel/Color Swatches Panel

A good painter can create custom colors by mixing and matching a bunch of other
colors. In Flash, you can do that, too, through the Color Mixer panel. And, if you
like, you can save your custom color as a reusable color swatch in the Color
Swatches tab. That way, when you get the urge to draw another puce-colored
hedgehog, you'll be all set.

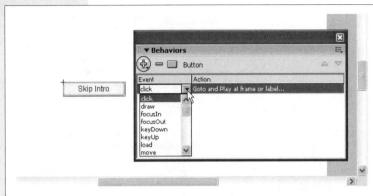

Figure 1-10:
*The easiest way to add a behavior is to select a frame or object (such as the Skip Intro button shown here) and then select Window →
Behavior. When you do, the Behaviors panel appears with a list of object-specific events (such as click) for you to choose from. Click Add Behavior to display a list of behaviors.*

Note: Color in Flash is a huge topic. To explore it further (including how you can specify hue, saturation, and luminescence for a custom color) check out Chapter 5.

Common Libraries

The three Common Libraries panels—Buttons, Classes, and Learning Interactions—display prebuilt clips (in other words, self-contained, preconstructed Flash documents) that you can add to your animations simply by dragging them to the Stage:

- **Buttons.** Here you'll find a wealth of cool-looking customizable push buttons, each as different from a dull gray HTML button as you can get.

- **Classes.** Useful only to heavy-duty ActionScript programmers, these compiled clips—DataBindingClasses, UtilsClasses, and WebServiceClasses—let you transfer information between your animation and server-side programs at runtime.

Note: To access the compiled classes that appear in the Common Libraries, you need to drag them from the Common Library to your document's Library; then you need to add specific ActionScript calls to your animation. Part 3 of this book introduces you to ActionScript and shows you how to add an action to your animation. You can find out more about the compiled classes Flash offers by choosing Help → Flash Help and searching All Books for the specific class you're interested in.

- **Learning Interactions.** In this panel, you find customizable components designed specifically for folks creating Flash tutorials, including fill-in-the-blank, multiple choice, and true/false.

Components Panel/Component Inspector Panel

A Flash *component* is a reusable, self-contained, customizable, interactive graphic that you can add to your animation. Technically, you (or anyone else, for that matter) can create your own components using a combination of Flash, ActionScript, and Macromedia's special component language. But right out of the box, the only

---

components that appear on the Components panel are standard user interface components (buttons, lists, text fields, and so on), animation controller components (MediaController, PlayButton, PauseButton, that kind of thing), and the handful of other assorted components that ship with Flash. To view and change the component's settings, all you have to do is click the component to select it and then display the Component Inspector panel by selecting Window → Component Inspector (or pressing Alt+F7).

UP TO SPEED

Deciphering Components

Components aren't unique to Flash. Most programming languages provide a way to create components, which are nothing more than reusable hunks of code known in the trade as *black boxes*. What that means is that you don't have to know how the component code works behind the scenes in order to use it. All you have to do is put stuff in (change a couple of settings) and take stuff out (watch the component do its thing).

In days gone by, software pundits predicted that components would be the next new thing. Since most people who

sit down to work with Flash or similar programs tend to want to create the same kinds of things—menus, buttons, clickable images, and so forth—the theory was that software developers would be falling all over themselves to create components, which other folks would shell out good money to buy.

Well, the world is still waiting. But if you look hard enough, you might be able to find useful third-party Flash components (some of them gratis) on the Web. Chapter 12 gives you some ideas for where to start looking.

History Panel

Flash keeps track of every little thing you do to a file, starting with the last time you opened (or created) it: every shape you draw, every file you import, every color you change. This behind-the-scenes tracking—which you can view using the History panel shown in Figure 1-11—comes in handy when you want to revert to an earlier version of an animation. For example, one in which the cartoon rabbits you drew actually look like rabbits instead of overfed mice. To display the History panel, click Window → Other Panels → History (or press Ctrl+F10).

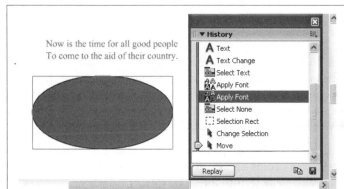

Figure 1-11:
When you move your mouse over one of the changes, Flash pops up a helpful detailed description of the change. To revert to an earlier version of your file, drag the slider until it's next to the last change you want to appear. To replay one or more changes, select the changes you want to replay and press Replay. If you do want to revert to an earlier version of your file, don't put it off: every time you close the file, Flash erases the file's history.

Note: Unless you tell it otherwise, Flash keeps track of the last 100 changes you made to a document starting with the last time you opened the document (or, if you've never saved the document, the last 100 changes since you created it). To increase this number, select Edit → Preferences. In the Preferences window that appears, select the General category. Then, in the Undo field, Specify Document-level Undo and type in the number of levels (changes) you want Flash to track. You can specify any number you like from 2 to 9,999.

Info Panel

The more complicated your Flash creations become, the more likely it is that at some point you'll want to know specific details about the objects on your Stage: details like the RGB values of one of the colors you used, the size of one of the objects in pixels, the XY coordinates of an object, and so on. This level of detail can be useful if you want to recreate a particular effect or if you want to rearrange objects on the Stage down to the last little pixel.

To display the Info panel, first head to the Stage and click an object to select it; then choose Window → Info or press Ctrl+I (Windows) or ⌘-I (Mac). As shown in Figure 1-12, the Info panel only displays information about the object you currently have selected.

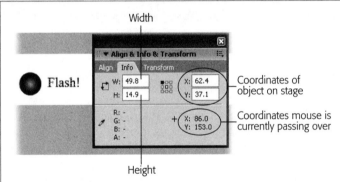

Width

Coordinates of object on stage

Coordinates mouse is currently passing over

Height

Figure 1-12:
Select an object on the Stage, and the Info panel shows you the object's width, height, XY coordinates, and color (expressed as RGB values and percentage of transparency). Move your mouse around the stage, and the bottom half of the Info panel shows you what color (and XY coordinates) your cursor is passing over.

Library Panel

The Library panel (Figure 1-13) is similar to the Common Libraries panel described on page 28: both display reusable components you can add to your Flash animations. The difference between the two is that while the Common Libraries panel displays components you can add to *any* Flash file, the Library panel displays objects you can add only to the file you currently have open. To show the Library panel, click Window → Library or press Ctrl+L (Windows) or ⌘-L (Mac).

Another difference between the Library panel and the Common Libraries panel is that the Library panel doesn't come preloaded with helpful buttons and such. You have to add your own reusable objects to the Library panel (which you see how to do in Chapter 7).

Let's say, for example, that you create a picture-perfect bubble, or sun, or snow-flake in one frame of your animation. (You learn more about frames on page 34.) Now, if you want that bubble, sun, or snowflake to appear in 15 additional frames, you *could* draw it again and again, but it really makes more sense to store a copy in the current project library and just drag it to where it's needed on those other 15 frames. Saves time and ensures consistency, too.

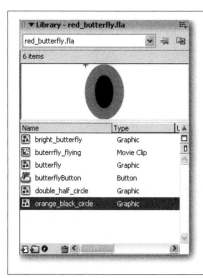

Figure 1-13:
Storing simple images as reusable symbols in the Library panel does more than just save you time: it saves you file size, too. (You'll learn a lot more about symbols and file size in Chapter 7.) Using the Library panel you see here, you can preview symbols, add them to the Stage, and easily add symbols you created in one Flash document to another.

Movie Explorer Panel

After you finish creating a Flash animation (which you see how to do in Chapter 3), you can find and edit specific animation details quickly and easily by using the Movie Explorer panel, shown in Figure 1-14. To display the Movie Explorer panel, select Window → Movie Explorer (or press Alt+F3).

Note: The Movie Explorer panel only shows you one scene at a time regardless of how many scenes your animation contains. If you want to work with multiple scenes, use the Scene panel described on page 34 in conjunction with the Movie Explorer panel.

If you're familiar with the Explorer tool in Windows, you may recognize the Movie Explorer Panel. Much as the Windows Explorer shows you a collapsible outline of all the folders and files on your computer, the Movie Explorer panel shows you all the components of your animation, organized by scene: the video clips, the sound files, the text, the images, and so on. (For more about scenes, check out the box on page 33.)

In addition to seeing an at-a-glance outline of your entire animation, you can use the Movie Explorer panel's Show icons to tell Flash which specific elements of your movie you want to view (just the buttons, say, or only the images, frames, and lay-ers). Or you can use the Find box to view specific elements (for example, you can hunt for an ActionScript script named *openNewBrowserWindow*).

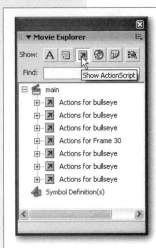

Figure 1-14:
The Movie Explorer panel lets you view the overall structure of your animation; it also gives you a way to find and edit specific elements quickly and easily. To find a specific element, use the Show icons or type the name of the element you're trying to find in the Find box. Right-clicking an element pops up a menu you can use to edit that element.

Output Panel

When Flash has something to tell you about your animation, it uses the Output panel. To view the Output panel, select Window → Output or press F2. For example, when you *export* your Flash animation (Chapter 14) or when you add buggy ActionScript code to your animation, Flash displays any problems it encounters in the Output panel.

Tip: To tell Flash to include a file size report in the Output panel every time you publish your animation, select File → Publish Settings. Then, in the Publish Settings window that appears, click the Flash tab; finally, turn on the checkbox next to Generate Size Report. The next time you export your animation, Flash adds a file size report to the comments its displays in the Output panel. (You want to keep on top of file size if you plan to include your Flash animation in a Web page, because the larger the file size, the more likely folks will have problems viewing it over the Web.)

Properties Panel/Filters Panel/Parameters Panel

The Properties panel (also known as the Property Inspector) appears automatically beneath the Stage when you open a new document. If you don't see the Properties panel, you can display it by selecting Window → Properties → Properties or by typing Ctrl+F3.

As you can see in Figure 1-15, the Property Inspector displays specific information about whatever object you currently have selected on the Stage. These details can be helpful if, for example, you're planning to incorporate your finished work into a Web page and need to know the dimensions of a particular drawing. In addition to just viewing the properties of a selected object, you can also edit those properties using the Property Inspector, as you'll learn in the "Test Drive" section of this chapter.

Anatomy of a Scene

A *scene* is a collection of one or more frames tied to its very own Timeline. Most of the time, you'll create animations consisting of just one scene; but if it makes sense to you organization-wise, you can choose to break your animation up into several scenes—for example, you might create an intro scene, a main scene, and a credits scene.

The benefit of breaking an animation up into a bunch of scenes is that it helps you reuse stuff. For example, say you use Flash to create 30-second Web advertisements for the company you work for. If every single ad you create needs to contain the same few seconds of animation at the beginning (a welcome message from your CEO) and the same few seconds at the end (a heartfelt "…and that's why you should buy from our company" appeal), it makes sense to designate these beginning and ending frames as separate, reusable scenes, perhaps naming them something descriptive like *Intro* and *Ending*. Then all you have to do to construct your next animation is create the meat of the new ad and sandwich it between the Intro and Ending scenes.

You'll notice two additional panel tabs in Figure 1-15: Filters and Parameters. The Filters panel tab lets you add special effect filters to text, movie clips, and buttons (Chapter 7); the Parameters panel tab lets you customize component parameters (Chapter 12).

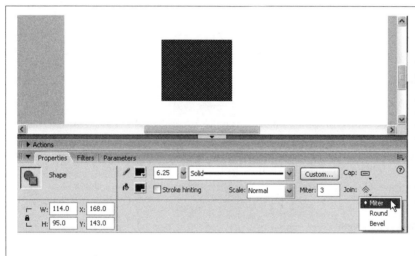

Figure 1-15:
The Properties panel (Property Inspector) shows only those properties associated with the object you've selected on the Stage. Here, because a square is selected, the Property Inspector gives you options you can use to change the thickness and color of the square's outline, to tell Flash what kind of corners you want your square to have (round, pointy, or blunted), and more square-related characteristics.

Note: Despite the important sounding name, the Property Inspector is a panel at heart. You can collapse it, expand it, right-click its options menu, and hide it, just as you can any other docked panel.

Scene Panel

You can create an animation in Flash that comprises just one scene, but you can choose to break your animations up into multiple scenes, too, if you like. (See the box on page 33 for the skinny on scenes and why you might want to organize your animation into multiple scenes.)

To add a scene to your animation (or to rename or delete an existing scene), you use the Scene panel, which you display by choosing Window → Other Panels → Scene. Figure 1-16 shows you what the Scene panel looks like.

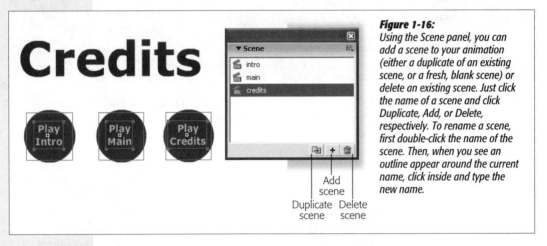

Figure 1-16:
Using the Scene panel, you can add a scene to your animation (either a duplicate of an existing scene, or a fresh, blank scene) or delete an existing scene. Just click the name of a scene and click Duplicate, Add, or Delete, respectively. To rename a scene, first double-click the name of the scene. Then, when you see an outline appear around the current name, click inside and type the new name.

Add scene
Duplicate scene Delete scene

Transform Panel

Transform is a $64 word meaning "to mess with." When you have an existing object that you want to mess with selected on your Stage—to scale horizontally or vertically, to rotate, to compress, to *distort* (pull out of shape like a wad of taffy), or to *skew* (slant horizontally or vertically)—you want, in animation terms, to *transform* that object. You can learn how to do all these transformations in Chapter 5 (page 133).

The Timeline

For a complex piece of software, Flash is based on a surprisingly simple principle—the old-fashioned slideshow. In case you're too young to remember, a slideshow consisted of a stack of slides loaded into a tray, a projector that displayed one slide at a time, and a human to run the show, determining the order in which the slides appear and how long each stays on screen. Well, a Flash animation is really nothing more than a souped-up slideshow. In Flash, the picture-containing slides are called *frames*, and instead of a person controlling the slide projector, you've got the *Timeline*.

The Timeline (see Figure 1-17) is what determines what order your frames appear in and how long each frame stays onstage. If you've decided to organize the images on your frames into separate *layers* (described in Chapter 3), the Timeline is also where you specify how you want your layers stacked: which layer you want on top, which one beneath that, and so on.

In addition to letting you put together a basic, plain-vanilla, frames-run-left-to-right, layers-run-bottom-to-top animation, the Timeline also lets you create spiffy effects, such as looping a section of your animation over and over again and creating tasteful fades.

Tip: The first time you run Flash, the Timeline appears automatically. But if you don't see it, you can display it by selecting Window → Timeline or pressing Ctrl+Alt+T.

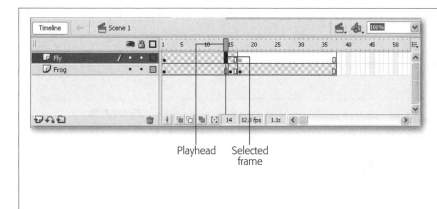

Playhead   Selected
frame

Figure 1-17:
The Timeline keeps track of all the frames that make up your animation, as well as what order you want them to appear in. Clicking a specific frame (or dragging the playhead to a specific frame) tells Flash to display the contents of that frame on the Stage for you to examine or edit.

In the rest of this chapter, you get to take Flash out for a test drive. You'll learn how to open, play, and save Flash animations; see the Timeline in action; and try your hand at two of the program's most important panels of all—the Tools panel and the Property Inspector.

Note: This book doesn't cover the less-used Filters, Parameters, Project, Screens, Strings, or WebServices panels.

The Flash 8 Test Drive

For the tutorials in this section, you need a Flash animation to practice on. There's one ready and waiting for you on the "Missing CD" page of the Missing Manuals Web site.

Tip: Much of the time, you'll be working with files that already exist—either because you've created them yourself or because you want to incorporate into your Flash animation picture, sound, or movie files you've found on the Web. To avoid the agony of downloading a file and not being able to find it later, create a folder called, say, Downloads in the My Documents (Windows) or Home → Documents (Mac) folder and keep them there. You can even set your Web browser's Preferences to stash all downloads in that folder automatically.

Opening a Flash File

Download the file rolling_ball.fla and save it on your computer. Then launch Flash (page 16), and choose File → Open (the Start page goes away automatically). When the Open dialog box appears, navigate to the file you just downloaded and then click Open. Flash shows you the animation on the Stage, surrounded by the usual Timeline, toolbars, panels, and (at the bottom) the Property Inspector. It should look like Figure 1-18.

Tip: To run the example animation, either press Enter or select Control → Play.

Figure 1-18:
Select an object on the Stage, and the Property Inspector automatically displays the properties (characteristics) of that object. You can change most of the properties in this panel; when you do, Flash redisplays the object on the Stage to reflect your changes. Here, looking at the details for a text box, you can change the text to centered or justified, or change the font or font color used.

Tip: If you don't see the Property Inspector, you can display it by selecting Window → Properties → Properties or by typing Ctrl+F3.

Exploring the Property Inspector

The Property Inspector appears automatically beneath the Stage when you open a new document. As shown in Figure 1-18, it displays specific information about whatever object you've selected on the Stage. Such details can be helpful when you want to recreate an object precisely in another program, or incorporate your finished animation into a Web page you've already created. For example, the Size button shows your animation's dimensions (550×200 pixels, say) which is information you need if you want to place your animation in a Web page by hand. (In Chapter 14, you'll learn how to tell Flash to create a simple Web page that includes your animation so you don't have to do this work by hand.)

To see how it works, click the letter "F" in the rolling_ball.fla example animation. On the Property Inspector, you'll see the following:

- **Height and width.** The pixel dimensions of this "F" are 10.4 wide $\times$ 13.0 high.

- **Color.** The color of this letter is black.

By typing in new values or changing a setting, you can edit the selected object. To see the Property Inspector in action, you'll use it to resize the Stage itself, described next.

Resizing the Stage

In addition to just inspecting the properties of a selected object, you can also edit those properties using the Property Inspector. In Flash, the size of your Stage is the actual finished size of your animation, so setting its exact dimensions is one of the first things you do when you create an animation, as you'll see in the next chapter. But you can resize the Stage at any time.

Here's how to change the size of your Stage:

1. **Click the Selection tool and then click on a blank area of the Stage (to make sure nothing on the Stage is selected).**

   Alternatively, you can click the Selection tool and then chose Edit → Deselect All.

2. **In the Property Inspector, click the Size button.**

   The Document Properties window appears. Around the middle of the window are boxes labeled Dimensions. That's where you're going to work your magic.

3. **Click in the width box (which currently reads 800 px) and type *720 px*. Click in the height box and change it from 600 px to *80 px*. Click OK when you're done.**

   Flash accepts the new dimensions and resizes your Stage, as shown in Figure 1-19.

Tip: If you resize the Stage so big that you can't see the entire thing, check out the scrollbars Flash puts at the bottom and the right side of your work area. You can use them to scroll around and see everything.

Zooming In and Out

Sometime in your Flash career, you'll draw a picture so enormous you can't see it all on the Stage at one time. The scroll bars let you move around a big Stage, but they can't help you get a full overview. Next, you'll learn how to use the Zoom tools to pull back your view and see the entire animation at once. You can find

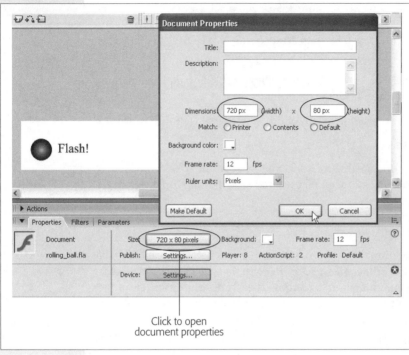

Figure 1-19:
Because your Stage is your canvas, you'll want to change its size and shape depending on how you want your finished animation to look. For an across-the-top-of-a-Web-page banner ad, for example, you'll want a long, skinny stage—somewhere around 720 ×80 as shown here, depending on the size of your target screen. Any modification you make to the size of the Stage immediately changes the dimensions of the Stage itself as it appears in your workspace.

Click to open
document properties

these tools in the View section of the Tools panel. They let you zoom in, zoom out, and pan around the stage. You can even get in so close, you can modify your drawing pixel by pixel.

Here's how the Zoom tools work:

1. **Click the Zoom tool (the little magnifying glass) in the View section of the Tools panel.**

   The tools panel usually sits at the left side of your screen (but you're free to move it, as described on page 22). As you can see in Figure 1-20, when you click the Zoom tool, the Options section at the bottom of the panel changes to show only zoom-related buttons.

2. **Move your cursor, which now looks like a magnifying glass with a plus sign on it, to the area on the Stage that you want to zoom in on and then click.**

   Flash enlarges the Stage and everything on it. The area where you clicked stays in full view.

3. **Click the Hand tool.**

   Your cursor turns into a little hand.

4. **Click anywhere on the Stage and drag your cursor around.**

   Flash moves the Stage beneath your cursor so you can get a better look at whatever section of your bigger-than-life drawing you're most interested in.

Zoom tool

Hand tool

Figure 1-20:
After you click the Zoom tool, each time you click your drawing, the Stage (which contains your drawing) appears larger. If it gets so big that you can't see the whole thing, click the Hand tool; then click the Stage again and drag to move the Stage around (as shown here).

Playing an Animation

Now that you've seen how to work on an animation while it's standing still, it's time for some action. After all, an animation by definition must move. Using the Controller toolbar, which you display by choosing Window → Toolbars → Controller (see the box on page 40), you can play, pause, and rewind, much like a videotape or DVD. When you click Play on the Controller, your animation plays once through from beginning to end.

For finer control, you can use the Timeline's playhead to click through your animation frame by frame, like the slideshow of yore. *Playhead* is nothing more than a fancy term for *currently selected frame*. Click a frame, and Flash displays the red playhead rectangle to show that you've successfully selected that frame (see Figure 1-21). If you select Control → Play to run your animation, your animation plays on the Stage, beginning with the selected frame.

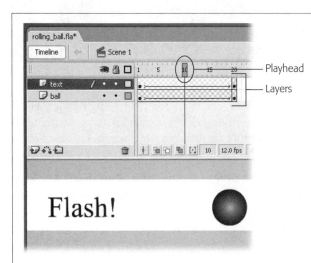

Playhead

Layers

Figure 1-21:
You select a frame (specify a playhead position) the same way you select everything else in Flash: by clicking. In this example, the currently selected frame (playhead position) is the tenth frame. You can watch the playhead move from frame to frame by selecting Control → Play. Dragging the playhead back and forth (called scrubbing) is an even quicker way to test portions of your animation—and a fun way, too: dragging the playhead from right to left displays your frames in reverse order.

UP TO SPEED

Controlling Playback with the Controller

If you've ever used a video deck or a tape player, the six icons on the Controller toolbar look comfortingly familiar. In Flash, here's what each one does, from left to right as they appear onscreen:

Stop. Clicking this square icon stops playback.

Go to first frame. Clicking this icon rewinds your animation. That is, it moves the playhead back to Frame 1.

Step back one frame. Clicking this double-left-arrow icon moves the playhead back one frame. If the playhead is already at Frame 1, this button has no effect.

Play. Clicking this right-arrow runs your animation on the Stage. Playback begins at the current position of the playhead. In other words, playback begins with the frame you selected in the Timeline and runs either until the end of your animation or until you press the Stop button.

Step forward one frame. Clicking this double-right-arrow icon moves the playhead forward one frame (unless the playhead is already at the last frame).

Go to last frame. Clicking this icon fast-forwards your animation to the very end. That is, it sets the playhead to the last frame in your animation.

You can also access these six functions by choosing them from the Control menu in the menu bar.

Keep in mind that certain elements Flash shows you when you're testing on the Stage—for example, *motion guide layers*, which you learn about in Chapter 3—don't appear in your finished animation. So while using the Controller panel is a great way to work the kinks out of your animation, it's no substitute for choosing Control → Test Movie, which exports (compiles) your Flash document and shows you *exactly* what your audience will see.

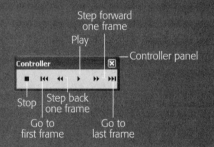

Saving a File

Saving your work frequently in Flash is a good idea. You might think you'll remember how to recreate a particularly great drawing or animated sequence if the unthinkable happens and your computer crashes, but why take the chance? You've got better things to do with your time.

The minute you finish a sizable chunk of work, save your Flash file by following these steps:

1. **Select File → Save As.**

   The Save As window appears (Figure 1-22). Choosing Save As (instead of Save) lets you create a new version of the file rather than overwriting the old one. Saving a new version of a file is always a good idea when you're experimenting, since some experiments invariably end up not working and you want to drop back to the previous working version of your file.

2. **From the Save In pop-up menu, choose the file folder where you want Flash to save your file.**

   If you like, you can skip this step. If you do—and you're running Windows—Flash assumes you want it to save your file in the My Documents folder. If you're running Mac, Flash assumes you want to save your file in the Home → Documents folder.

3. **In the File Name box, type a unique name for this file.**

   A short, descriptive name that helps you easily identify the file later like *rolling_ball_changes*) is your best choice. Make sure you either include the standard Flash file extension (.fla) or don't type any extension at all, as shown in Figure 1-22.

4. **Click Save.**

   Flash saves your file using the location and file name you specified.

Figure 1-22:
You have only to specify a name and location for your file the first time you save it. After that, all you have to do to save your file (including any changes you've made since the last time you saved it) is select File → Save.

Flash File Extensions

Flash gives each different type of file its own extension to help it (and you) tell files apart. For example, when you save a Flash document, Flash automatically appends the .fla file extension. Here's a quick rundown of the file extensions Flash uses when you tell it to save or export a file:

- **Flash document files and Flash form application files (.fla).** *Flash form applications* are HTML-like data entry forms you can create in Flash and hook up to a server on the back end to process the data that folks enter. This book doesn't cover Flash form applications.

- **ActionScript files (.as).** ActionScript files let script jockeys write ActionScript code by hand and attach it to their Flash documents at runtime, rather than stepping their way through Flash's build-a-script interface to include their ActionScript code directly into their Flash documents. (This book doesn't cover ActionScript files, but you will learn how to write Flash scripts of your own in Part 3.)

- **ActionScript Communication files (.asc).** Special ActionScript files that connect Flash animations to database back ends. This book doesn't cover ActionScript Communication files.

- **Flash JavaScript files (.jsfl).** Files that pass information from a Flash animation running in a Web browser to a JavaScript script. (JavaScript is a programming language built into Web browsers that Web developers can use in conjunction with HTML to create interactive Web pages.) This book doesn't cover Flash JavaScript files.

- **Flash project files (.flp).** If you need to create a large, complex Flash animation with a bunch of other people (for example, a corporate development team), you can use a Flash project file to keep track of all of the Flash documents, sound files, bitmaps, and other component files that make up that animation (including a copy of each version of the animation). This book doesn't cover Flash project files.

- **Flash runtime files (.swf, .exe, .hqx, and uncompressed Mac executable files with no file extension).** These *published* (compiled) files run in Flash Player (.swf), as an executable file that runs on Windows (.exe), as a standalone, self-extracting program on Mac (.hqx), and as a standalone, uncompressed program on the Mac (no file extension), respectively.

Creating Simple Drawings

The best way to get acquainted with Flash is just to dive in and create a simple animation. So this chapter starts with some tips for planning your work so you can get more done in less time (and be happier with the result). You see how to set up your Flash document and use the most popular Flash drawing tools—the Pen, the Pencil, the Shape tool, the Line tool, and the Brush—to draw a simple picture. Then you learn how to add color to your drawn shapes and move them around on the Stage.

In the next chapter, you add a few more drawings and string them together to create a simple animation.

Planning Pays Off

Drawing a single picture is relatively easy. But creating an effective animation—one that gets your message across, or entertains people, or persuades them to take an action—takes a bit more up-front work. And not just because you have to generate dozens or even hundreds of pictures: You also have to decide how to order them, how to make them flow together, when (or if) to add text and audio, and so on. In other words, you have to think like a movie director. With its myriad controls, windows, and panels, Flash gives you all the tools you need to create a complex, professional animation, but it can't do the thinking for you.

In this section, you see how the pros approach this crucial first step in the animation process: how to create a storyboard, come up with ideas, test your ideas, and benefit from others' successes.

Creating a Storyboard

Say you want to produce a short animation to promote your company's great new gourmet coffee called Lotta Caffeina. You decide your animation would be perfect as a banner ad. Now, maybe you're not exactly the best artist since Leonardo da Vinci, so you want to keep it simple. Still, you need to get your point across—BUY OUR COFFEE!

Before you even turn on your computer (much less fire up Flash), pull out a sketchpad and a pencil and think about what you want your animation to look like.

For your very first drawing, you might imagine a close up of a silly-looking male face on a pillow, belonging to a guy obviously deep in slumber, eyes scrunched tight, mouth slack. Next to him is a basic bedside table, which is empty except for what appears to be a jangling alarm clock.

OK, now you've got a start. After you pat yourself on the back—and perhaps refuel your creativity with a grande-sized cup of your own product—you plan and execute the frame-by-frame action. You do this by whipping out six quick pencil-and-paper sketches. When you finish, your sketchpad may look something like this:

- The first sketch shows your initial idea—Mr. Comatose and his jangling alarm clock.

- Sketch #2 is identical to the first, except for the conversation balloon on the left-side of the frame, where capped text indicates that someone is yelling to your unconscious hero (who remains dead to the world).

- In sketch #3, a disembodied hand appears at the left hand of the drawing, placing a cup bearing the Lotta Caffeina logo on the bedside table next to Mr. Comatose.

- Sketch #4 is almost identical to the second, except that the disembodied hand is gone now and Mr. Comatose's nose has come to attention as he gets a whiff of the potent brew.

- Sketch #5 shows a single eye open. Mr. Comatose's mouth has lost its slackness.

- Sketch #6 shows a closeup of the man sipping from the cup, his eyes wide and sparkling, a smile on his lips, while a "thought bubble" tells viewers, "Now, *that's* worth getting up for!"

In the animation world, your series of quick sketches is called a *storyboard*.

Figure 2-1 shows a basic storyboard.

Five Questions for a Better Result

Creating your Flash animation will go more smoothly if you can answer these five basic questions before you even turn on your computer (much less start working in Flash):

Figure 2-1:
Spending time up-front sketching a storyboard lets you set up your basic idea from start to finish. Don't worry about how sophisticated (or unsophisticated) it looks; nobody but you will see this rough working model.

- **What do you want to accomplish with this Flash creation?** Besides knowing whether you want your creation to be fun or serious, cutesy or slick, you should have a concrete, stated goal, like "show my company's new line of scooters" or "generate 1,000 hits per month for my personal Web page."

- **Who's your audience?** Different types of people require different approaches. For example, kids love all the snazzy effects you can throw at them; adults aren't nearly as impressed by animation for animation's sake. The more of a sense you have of the people most likely to view your Flash creation, the better you can try to target your message and visual effects specifically to them.

- **What third-party content (if any) do you want to include?** *Content* refers to the stuff that makes up your Flash animation: the images, the text, the video and audio clips. Perhaps all you want your animation to contain are your own drawings, such as the ones you see how to create in this chapter. But if you want to add images or audio or video clips from another source, you need to figure out where you're going to get them and how to get permission to use them. (Virtually anything you didn't create—a music clip, for example, or a short scene from a TV show or movie—is protected by copyright. Someone somewhere owns it, so you need to track down that someone, ask permission, and—depending on the content—pay a fee to use it. Chapter 8 lists several royalty-free, dirt-cheap sources of third-party content.)

- **How many frames is it going to take to put your idea together, and how do you want them to be ordered?** For a simple banner ad, you're looking at anywhere from a handful of frames to around 50. A tutorial or product demonstration, on the other hand, can easily require 100, 200, or more frames. Whether you use storyboarding or just jot down a few notes to yourself, getting a feel for how many frames you'll need helps you estimate the time it's going to take to put your animation together.

Tip: Try to get your message across as succinctly as possible. Fewer frames (and, therefore, images) typically means a smaller file size, which is important if you plan to put your Flash animation up on the Web. (Folks surfing with dial-up or on a cellphone often have trouble viewing large files.)

- **How will you distribute it? (In other words, what's your target platform?)** If you plan to put your animation up on a Web site, you need to keep file size to a minimum so people with slow connections can see it; if you plan to make it available to hearing-impaired folks, you need to include an alternative way to communicate the audio portion; if you're creating an animation you know will be played on a 100" monitor, you need to draw large, bold graphics. Your *target platform*—the computer and audience most likely to view your animation—always affects the way you develop your animation.

Preparing to Draw

Even if you're familiar with animation software (but especially if you aren't), you need to know a few quick things before you roll up your sleeves and dive into Flash—sort of like the quick where's-the-turn-signal once-over you do when you jump into a rental car for the first time.

In this section, you see how to get around the Stage and how to customize your Flash document's properties. You'll also learn a couple of basic Flash terms you need to understand before you use the drawing tools (which you see how to do on page 58).

But first you need to open a new Flash document page so that you can follow along at home. To do so, launch Flash and choose Create New Flash Document on the start screen. You can also create a new file using the Flash main menu. Here's how:

1. **From the main menu, choose File → New.**

   The New Document window opens. If the window doesn't show the General tab shown in Figure 2-2, click that tab to make it active.

2. **In the Type list, select the type of new file you want to create and then click OK.**

   The New Document window disappears and Flash displays a brand-new blank document. You can tell it's a new document by the name Flash gives it: for example, *Untitled-1*.

Customizing Your Stage

The Stage, as you may recall from Chapter 1, is your electronic canvas: it's where you'll be drawing your lines and shapes and adding your text. Figure 1-1 shows you the way the Stage appears the first time you create a new document in Flash. There's certainly nothing wrong with it, but you may want to make yours larger (or smaller) or add helpful positioning guides, such as rulers and gridlines. This section shows you how.

Tips from the Trenches

Starting out on a learning curve as steep as Flash's can be daunting. Sometimes, it's helpful to hear what the pros think—to get advice from folks from who've been there, done that, and want you to know that you can, too.

Here are the top ten recommendations from the experts:

1. **Analyze other people's animations.** As you begin to explore Flash content on other Web sites, think about it critically. Don't just focus on whether the result is dazzling or colorful, but also consider whether it's effective. What do you think it was designed to do? Get you to buy something? Get you interested in a product? Did it work? If not, why not? What detracts from the overall effect? Keep a notebook so you can apply what you learn to your own efforts.

2. **Don't sell yourself short.** Don't think you can't create great animations just because you're not a professional artist with a background in design. You'll find that Flash helps you through lots of tough spots (like correcting your shaky lines and generating frames out of whole cloth), and frankly, you're probably not shooting for a Picasso- or Tarantino-level result anyway. You get better at everything with practice; Flash is no exception.

3. **Always start with a storyboard.** Whenever you're working with anything but the simplest design (anything more than a couple of frames), create a storyboard (page 44). It can be as rough or as detailed as you want; some folks just jot notes to themselves. But do it you must. Every minute you spend planning will save you hours of hair-pulling later.

4. **Practice, practice, practice.** There are a lot of software programs out there that you can probably sit down and nail in 20 minutes flat. Flash isn't one of them. And while reading is a great way to begin learning Flash, no amount of book learning is going to substitute for rolling up your sleeves and actually producing an animation or two. (That's why this book

contains hands-on examples for you to work through.)

5. **Join an online Flash community.** Real-time help from knowledgeable Flash-ionados is a beautiful thing. Use the online resources outlined in Appendix A to join a Flash community where you can ask questions, get help, and share ideas.

6. **Don't throw anything away.** You might be tempted to discard your mistakes. But if the "mistake" is interesting or useful, save it: you may be able to use it later for a different project. (While you're at it, write down a few quick notes about how you achieved the result so you can recreate it if you want to.)

7. **Spread yourself thin.** Many Flash pros like to have several different projects going at once, all of various types, so they can switch around when they get stuck on one. Keeping a lot of balls in the air can be an excellent way to help you think about things from different angles, which will help develop your skills.

8. **Always test your work in a live environment.** Don't rely on Flash's testing environment. If you're creating a Flash animation to display on a cell phone, test it on a cell phone before you go live. If you're targeting a Web site, upload your animation to a Web server and test it in a browser.

9. **Solicit (and incorporate) viewer feedback.** After you finish an animation, ask for feedback. Choose people you know will take the time to look at your work carefully and give you an honest evaluation.

10. **Never, ever sacrifice content for the sake of coolness.** The purpose of tools like Flash is to help you get your message across, not to see how many special effects you can cram into a 5-second spot. Pay more attention to whether you're creating an effective animation than whether you're adding enough colors, shapes, or audio clips.

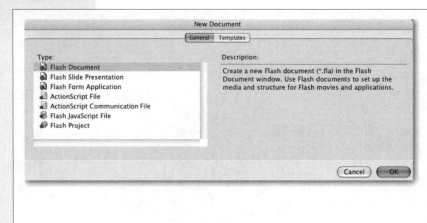

Figure 2-2:
In every case but one (Flash Project), selecting a document type and then clicking OK tells Flash to create a crisp, new document for you. (Flash projects are really nothing more than lists of other files with version control added so that multiple designers can work on the same Flash project without overwriting each others' changes.)

Change the size of the Stage

The size of your Stage is also the size of your finished animation. The standard 550 × 400 pixel Flash Stage is a good compromise between large-enough-to-see-with-out-glasses and small-enough-not-to-hog-the-whole-screen. Flash automatically shows you this size Stage because 550 × 400 is the minimum decent screen size for someone running a computer with a typical resolution of 800 × 600.

But you may not want to keep that size. In some cases, you'll actually need the Stage to hog the whole screen: for example, if you're designing an animation targeted for a very large size display monitor. In the case of the Lotta Caffeina banner ad, you want a wide, short Stage (typically somewhere around 640 × 40). If you're designing for those itty-bitty mobile devices, you'll want to shrink the Stage accordingly.

The best way to ensure that your finished animation is the right size is to start with the right sized Stage out of the gate. You set the size of the Stage in the Document Properties dialog box (Figure 2-3), which you can open by using one of these methods:

- Right-click the Stage. From the shortcut menu that appears, choose Document Properties.

- Click the Size button in the Property Inspector (page 32).

- Choose Modify → Document.

Then, in the Document Properties window, type the new height and width in the Dimensions boxes. Figure 2-3 shows dimensions of 200 × 200 pixels, which is about the right size for a small pop-up ad. Click OK to close the window and return to the now-resized Stage.

Taking Advantage of Templates

How can some template designers I've never even met possibly know what kind of drawings I want to put in my animation, or how long I want my animation to be, or what kinds of sounds I want to add? They can't–so how on earth can Flash templates save me time?

The predesigned templates that come with Flash save you time on the grunt work associated with several commonplace kinds of animations. For example, the Interactive Advertising Bureau (*www.iab.net*) recommends certain dimensions for certain types of Web ads, including pop-up windows and banner ads. When you open up a template for a pop-up ad, for example, the Stage is already preset to the dimensions for a standard sized pop-up in a standard sized browser window. You don't have to research the issue, and you don't have to customize the Stage yourself.

Or say you want to create a slideshow in Flash, complete with buttons that let folks click forward and backward through your pictures. Putting an interactive animation like this together from scratch would require a fair bit of work, but if you use a slideshow template, all you have to do is add your images and captions. The template takes care of the rest.

On the downside, documentation for how each Flash template behaves and what you need to do to customize it is a bit skimpy. (When you select Help → Flash Help and, in the Help window that appears, search for "Using Templates," you get some vague overall hints on what the templates to do and how to modify them, but no specific instructions.)

To see the templates Flash offers, select File → New to display the New Document window; then click the Templates tab. Here are the main categories:

- **Advertising:** Pop-up, skyscraper (skinny vertical), banner (skinny horizontal), and full-page ads.

- **Form applications:** Data input forms that you need to hook up to a server on the back end.

- **Global phones:** For Flash animations targeted for certain (Symbian) phones.

- **Japanese phones:** For Flash animations targeted for Japanese phones.

- **PDAs:** For Flash animations targeted for Nokia, Motorola, Sony, and other personal digital assistants (handhelds).

- **Photo Slideshows:** For Flash animations showing JPG images overlaid with Forward and Back controls.

- **Presentations:** Automatic (noninteractive) slideshows.

- **Quiz:** Simplified data input forms that allow the audience to page through multiple screens and answer yes/no questions.

- **Slide Presentations:** Similar to Photo Slideshows, but tailored for multiple images per frame.

You can learn more about templates, including how to create your own, in Chapter 7.

Tip: If you know you're going to be printing your work, you don't have to futz around with pixel dimensions; you can just turn on the Match: Printer radio button, which automatically resizes your Stage so that it prints out nicely on 8.5 × 11 paper.

Setting the background color

Because the Stage is your canvas, the color of the Stage will become the background color of your drawing. If white's okay with you, you're in luck: A fresh new

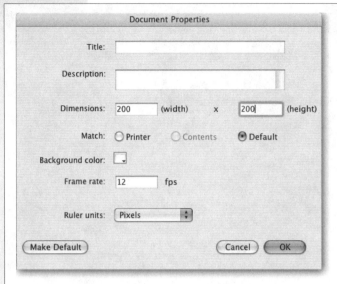

Figure 2-3:
You use the Document Properties window to set the size and color of your Stage (which will also be the size and background color of your finished animation). When you type the dimensions, you can type out the units of measurement (px, or even pixels, for example). But it's not necessary: The value in the Ruler Units field tells Flash which unit of measurement you're using.

Stage always appears white. But if you want to create a drawing with a different-colored background, here's how you go about it:

1. **Select Modify → Document (or press Ctrl+J in Windows; ⌘-J on a Mac).**

   The Document Properties window shown in Figure 2-4 appears.

2. **On the Background Color box, click the down-arrow and choose the color you want to use for the Stage (and for the background of your drawing). Then click OK.**

   Flash turns the Stage lime green (or whatever color you chose in step 2).

Tip: Because background color changes the way foreground objects appear, you might want to experiment with the color of the Stage, beginning with one color and changing it as you add objects to the Stage until you get the effect you want. (You can change the color of the Stage at any time, even after you've completed your drawing.)

Add helpful measurement guides

Even professional artists can't always draw a straight line or estimate three inches correctly. Fortunately, with Flash, they (and you) don't have to. Flash offers several tools that help you spot precisely where your objects are on the Stage and how much space they take up: rulers, a grid, and guides. You can see an example of these tools as they appear on the Stage in Figure 2-5.

Here's what each tool does, and how to display each of them:

- **Rulers.** This tool displays a ruled edge along the left and top of the Stage to help you determine the location and position of your objects. To turn on Rulers,

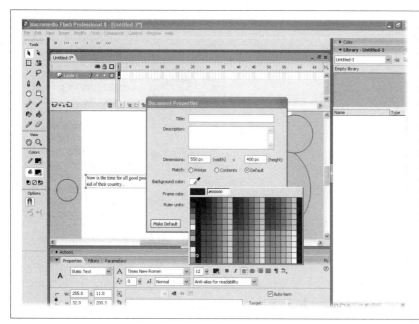

Figure 2-4:
Changing the color of the Stage is an easy way to change the way your drawing looks. It can also make constructing your drawing easier. For example, if you're working with light-colored shapes, a nice dark background will help you see what you're doing better—even if you end up changing the Stage back to a lighter color when you're finished.

right-click (Windows) or Control-click (Mac) the Stage. Then, from the short-cut menu, choose Rulers → Show Rulers.

- **Grid.** This tool divides the Stage into evenly sized squares, which is great for helping you get the location of objects exact. To turn on the Grid, right-click (or Control-click) the Stage. Then, from the shortcut menu choose Grid → Show Grid.

- **Guides.** If you want a tool that helps with straightedge alignment—like the grid—but you want more control over where the straight edges appear on the Stage, you want guides. To turn on guides, you first have to turn on rulers (see above). Then, right-click (or Control-click) the Stage and, from the shortcut menu, choose Guides → Show Guides. A checkmark appears next to Show Guides to indicate they're turned on, but you don't actually see any guide lines until you drag them onto the Stage. You can drag as many guide lines as you want down from the top ruler or over from the left ruler. To add a guide, click on a ruler (don't let go of the mouse) and drag your cursor to the Stage. Release the button when you get to the spot where you want your guide.

Tip: Grids and guides would be helpful enough if all they did was help you eyeball stuff, but Flash takes them one step further. If you turn on *snapping* and then drag, say, a circle around the Stage, Flash won't let you drop it just anywhere. Instead, Flash only lets you drop (position) the circle when it's lined up pre-cisely with either a grid or guide mark. To turn on snapping, simply right-click (Control-click) the Stage and choose Snapping → Snap to Guides (or Snapping → Snap to Grid).

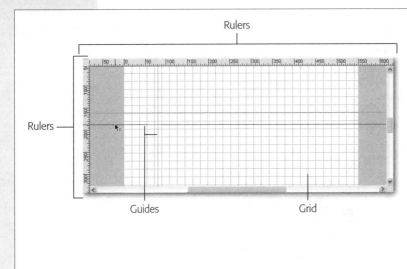

Rulers

Rulers

Guides

Grid

Figure 2-5:
Grids, guides, and rulers are Flash's answers to graph paper and T-square. To change the unit of measurement for the ruler, right-click the Stage and choose Document Properties from the shortcut menu. From the Ruler Units drop-down menu, select whatever measurement unit you want. You can also change the unit of measurement for the guides and the grid. To do so, right-click (Control-click) the Stage and choose Guides → Edit Guides and Grid → Edit Grid, respectively.

Choosing a Drawing Mode

Flash's selection tools, as you'll see in the next section, behave differently depending on which of Flash's two *drawing modes* you choose: the *merge* drawing mode (which was the only way you could draw in Flash up till now) or the new *object* drawing mode (which is more like the familiar drawing modes in Adobe Illustrator, AppleWorks, or Microsoft Word). The way you work with your drawings on the Stage depends on the drawing mode you choose, too, so it pays to understand the differences between the two:

- **The merge drawing mode.** Flash assumes you want to use the merge drawing mode unless you tell it otherwise. In this mode, if you overlap one shape with another shape, Flash erases the overlapped portion of the first shape—a fact you discover only when you move the overlapping shape, as shown in Figure 2-6 (bottom).

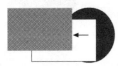

Figure 2-6:
Top: Say you're in merge mode and you drag a rectangle to overlap a circle, as shown here. Your only clue that you're in Flash's merge drawing mode is that the objects (or portions of objects) that you select appear to be covered by a dotted pattern.

Bottom: Drag the selected rectangle away, and you see that Flash has erased the overlapped portion of the circle. Notice, too, that Flash repositioned the rectangle's fill, but left the outline in place. That's typical in merge drawing mode, where Flash treats shapes not as complete objects, but as a collection of disparate elements.

- **The object drawing mode.** New in Flash 8, the object drawing mode tells Flash to think of shapes the way most humans naturally think of them: as individual, coherent objects. Overlapping shapes in object mode doesn't erase anything, and when you select a shape, you select the *entire* shape—not just the fill, or line, or portion of the shape you selected. Figure 2-7 shows you an example.

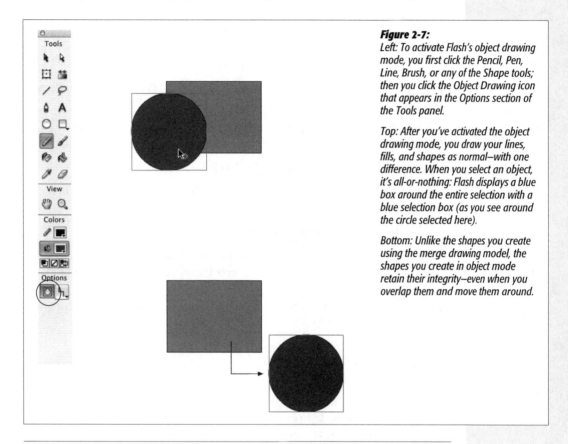

Figure 2-7:
Left: To activate Flash's object drawing mode, you first click the Pencil, Pen, Line, Brush, or any of the Shape tools; then you click the Object Drawing icon that appears in the Options section of the Tools panel.

Top: After you've activated the object drawing mode, you draw your lines, fills, and shapes as normal—with one difference. When you select an object, it's all-or-nothing: Flash displays a blue box around the entire selection with a blue selection box (as you see around the circle selected here).

Bottom: Unlike the shapes you create using the merge drawing model, the shapes you create in object mode retain their integrity—even when you overlap them and move them around.

Note: The drawing mode you select isn't document-specific; it affects all of the documents you create in Flash. If you choose the object drawing model, for example, each time you create or switch to another open document, Flash assumes you want to use the object drawing model.

When to use merge drawing mode

As shown in Figure 2-6 (bottom), when you overlap objects in merge drawing mode, Flash erases the overlapped portions of the objects. You'll probably want to stay with the merge drawing model if you fall into one of the following three categories:

- You're familiar (and comfortable) with an older version of Flash. (Merge was the *only* drawing mode before Flash 8.)

- You plan to create no more than one shape or object per layer anyway, so overlapping isn't an issue.

• You want to be able to select portions of objects, or create a deliberate "cut out" effect by overlapping objects and letting Flash do the cutting for you.

Since Flash assumes you want to work in merge drawing mode, you don't have to do anything special to activate it the first time you use Flash. But if you (or someone you share your copy of Flash with) has activated object drawing mode (page 52), here's how to tell Flash to return to merge mode:

1. **Click to select one of the drawing tools (Line, Pencil, Pen, Brush, Oval, Rectangle, or Polygon).**

   In the Options section of the Tools panel, Flash displays the Object Drawing icon (Figure 2-7, left). The icon appears white, showing that it's selected.

2. **Click the Object Drawing icon to deselect it.**

   The icon appears gray after you've deselected it, indicating that you're in merge drawing mode.

3. **Using the drawing tool you selected, draw an object on the Stage.**

   Flash lets you work with your drawing (select it, overlap it, and so on) using merge drawing mode. Page 56 explains how the selection tools work in this mode.

Tip: If you've already created an object in object drawing mode, you can break it apart by selecting it and then choosing Modify → Break Apart.

When to use object drawing mode

In the days before Flash 8, you had to create your objects on separate layers if you wanted to overlap them with impunity. In Flash 8, simply activate object drawing mode and bingo—Flash lets you stack and overlap your objects on a single layer as easily as a deck of playing cards. Choose object mode if you want to work with entire objects (as opposed to portions of them).

Here's how to activate object drawing mode:

1. **Click to select one of the drawing tools (Line, Pencil, Pen, Brush, Oval, Rectangle, or Polygon).**

   In the Options section of the Tools panel, Flash displays the Object Drawing icon (Figure 2-7, left).

2. **Click the Object Drawing icon to select it.**

   The icon appears white after you've selected it, meaning you're in object drawing mode.

3. **Using the drawing tool you selected, draw an object on the Stage.**

   Flash lets you interact with your drawn item (select it, stack it, and so on) using object drawing mode. On page 56, you see how the selection tools work in this mode.

Tip: If you've already created an object in merge drawing mode, you can integrate it (in other words, tell Flash to treat it as a single, complete object just as though you'd created it in object drawing mode) by selecting the object and then choosing Modify → Combine Objects → Union.

Selecting Objects on the Stage

Once you draw a line or shape on your Stage (which you see how to do on page 58), you need to select it if you want to do anything else to it: for example, if you want to change its color, make it bigger, move it, or delete it.

Note: This section gives you a quick introduction to Flash's selection tools. Chapter 5 (page 133) shows you the finer points of selecting objects.

As you can see in Figure 2-8, the Tools panel offers three selection tools you can use to select an object on the Stage. How these tools behave depends on whether you've created your drawings in merge or object drawing mode (see the previous section).

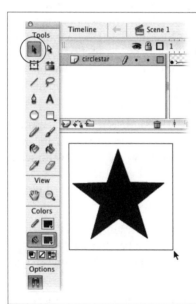

Figure 2-8:
Selecting an object on the Stage to work with should be easy—and most of the time, it is; all you have to do is click the Selection tool (circled) and then either click your object or click near it and drag a selection box around it. But if your Stage is crowded and you're trying to pick out just one little tiny angle of a line or portion of a drawing to manipulate, you'll need to use either the Subselection tool or the Lasso tool.

• **Selection tool.** This tool lets you select entire shapes, strokes, and fills, as well as symbols and bitmaps. (If you've created objects in merge mode, the Selection tool also lets you select rectangular portions of those objects.) After you've made your selection, you can then work with it—move the object around the Stage by dragging, for example.

— **Using the Selection tool in merge mode.** To select a rectangular portion of a shape you've drawn in merge mode, click near the shape and drag your cursor to create a selection box around just the portion you want to select. To select an entire shape, create a selection box around the whole shape.

To select a symbol, a bitmap, or one element of a shape (just the fill portion of a rectangle, for example, or just the outline of a star) simply click the symbol, bitmap, or element. Flash surrounds selected symbols and bitmaps with a rectangular outline; all other selections appear covered with a dotted white pattern.

— **Using the Selection tool in object mode.** To select an object created in object mode, click anywhere on it. A rectangular outline appears around the selected object.

• **Subselection tool.** The Subselection tool lets you reposition the individual points that make up your strokes and shape outlines.

— **Using the Subselection tool in merge mode.** To select a stroke or an outline created in merge mode, click the Subselection tool and then click the line you want to move or change. Flash automatically redisplays that line as a bunch of individual points and lines. (Technically, these doohickeys are called *anchor points* and *segments*; see page 61 for more details.) As you move your cursor over the selection, Flash displays either a black (move) box or white (edit) box. Drag a black *move box* to move the entire stroke or outline; click and drag a white *edit box* to edit it (to change the individual points and segments).

— **Using the Subselection tool in object mode.** The Subselection tool works the same way on objects drawn in object mode as it does in on objects drawn in merge mode except that on objects drawn in object mode, you can also select an entire object by clicking the Subselection tool and then clicking a fill. When you do, Flash displays a rectangle outline around the selected object, just as if you'd selected it using another selection tool.

• **Lasso tool.** The Lasso tool is the one to use when you want to select a weirdly shaped portion of an object—say, you want to create a hand-shaped hotspot in the middle of a square bitmap—or when you need to select a weirdly shaped object that's super-close to another object.

— **Using the Lasso tool in merge mode.** To select a nonrectangular portion of an object drawn in merge mode, first click the Lasso tool; then click near (or on) the object and drag your cursor (as if you were drawing with a pencil) to create a nonrectangular shape.

— **Using the Lasso tool in object mode.** To select an entire object drawn in object mode, select the Lasso tool, click near the object, and then drag your cursor around the object (as if you were drawing with a pencil) until the object is completely encircled.

Note: If you need to deselect an object after you've selected it (say, you changed your mind and don't want to change the object's color after all), you have three choices. You can press Esc, you can click somewhere else on the Stage, or you can select Edit → Deselect.

Essential Drawing Terms

In Flash, a cigar isn't just a cigar. A circle isn't even just a circle. Every single shape you create using Flash's drawing and painting tools is composed of one of the following elements, as shown in Figure 2-9:

- **Strokes.** A *stroke* in Flash looks just like the stroke you make when you write your name on a piece of paper. It can either be a plain line or the outline of a shape. You draw strokes in Flash using the Pen, Pencil, and Line tools. When you use one of the Shape tools (for example, to create a square or polygon), Flash includes a stroke outline free of charge.

- **Fills.** Flash recognizes two different kinds of *fills:* the marks you make with the Brush tool, and the interior of a shape (in other words, everything inside the strokes that form the outline of a shape).

In a lot of cases, your shapes comprise both strokes and fills, like the shapes you see in Figure 2-9. You can create fill- and stroke-containing shapes in one fell swoop using Flash's shape tools—Oval, Rectangle, and PolyStar—or you can draw them by hand using the Pen, Pencil, and Line tools.

Why bother to learn the technical terms "stroke" and "fill" when all you want to do is draw a smiley face? For one very important reason: Flash treats strokes and fills differently. You use different tools to create them and different tools to modify them. If you don't know the difference between a stroke and a fill, you won't be able to do a whole lot with the drawing and painting tools described in this chapter.

Creating Original Artwork

Before you can create an animation, you have to have some drawings to animate. You start with one drawing and then create a bunch more (often by altering the first drawing slightly). For example, if you want to create an animation showing a raccoon marching in place, you need to draw a picture of a raccoon standing still; another picture of the same raccoon lifting its left foot; and still more pictures showing the raccoon putting its left foot down, lifting its right foot, and so on. Put them all together using Flash's Timeline (as you learn in Chapter 3) and you've got yourself an animation.

Note: You're not limited to using your own drawings. Flash lets you *import,* or pull in, existing drawings and photos—and even sound clips and video clips. Page 243 shows you how to import files.

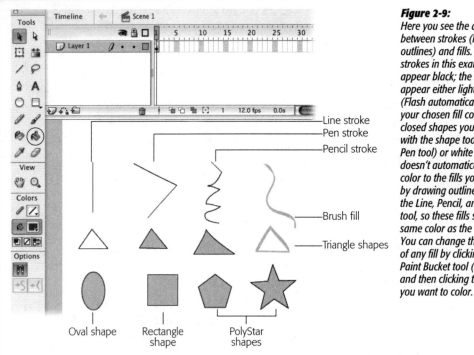

Figure 2-9:
Here you see the difference between strokes (lines and outlines) and fills. The strokes in this example appear black; the fills appear either light gray (Flash automatically adds your chosen fill color for closed shapes you create with the shape tools or the Pen tool) or white (Flash doesn't automatically add color to the fills you create by drawing outlines with the Line, Pencil, and Brush tool, so these fills stay the same color as the Stage). You can change the color of any fill by clicking the Paint Bucket tool (circled) and then clicking the fill you want to color.

This section shows you how to use basic Flash tools to create a simple drawing (*really* simple; it's a stick person!). You see the Line, Pencil, Pen, Brush, and shape tools (Oval, Rectangle, and PolyStar) in action, and learn the differences among them (some are better for creating certain effects than others). You also find out how to add color to a Flash drawing and erase your mistakes.

Drawing and Painting with Tools

One of the true beauties of creating digital artwork—besides not having to clean up a mess of paint spatters and pencil shavings—is that you don't have to track down your art supplies: the one pen that feels good in your hand, the right kind of paper, the sable brush that still smells like paint thinner. Instead, all you need to do is display Flash's Tools panel.

In this section, you see Flash's drawing and painting tools in action: the Line, Pen, Pencil, Brush, and shape tools. You also see the tools Flash provides (Lasso, Selection, and Subselection) that allow you to select the your drawings so you can modify them. And finally, you get a quickie introduction to color—specifically, you see how to change the colors of the strokes and fills you create.

Line tool

You use the Line tool in Flash to draw nice, straight lines—perfect all by themselves or for creating fancy shapes like exploding suns and spiky fur.

To Thine Own Self Be True

When asked about her artistic process, a celebrated 20th century painter said that in order to create, she had to toss aside everything she knew about matching colors, standard techniques, and even the way she held her pencil and her paintbrush. As a right-handed person with a strongly analytical mind, she discovered her ability to create only after she started drawing with her *left* hand. She learned to ignore what everyone else told her about how she *should* be working.

There's a moral to this story: Just because one person finds the Pencil or Brush the easiest tool to use so that she sticks to it almost exclusively doesn't mean you should do the same. Experiment and find what works best for *you!*

To help get your juices flowing, the stick figure you see in this chapter demonstrates several ways you can use Flash's painting and drawing tools. Each of these tools has its pros and cons, so try them all out for yourself. After all, the Flash police aren't going to arrest you if you sketch a beard and moustache on your stick figure using the Brush tool instead of the Pencil.

Here's how to start drawing your stick figure using the Line tool:

1. **In the Tools panel, click the Line tool, as shown in Figure 2-10.**

   Flash surrounds the Line tool with a white background to let you know you've successfully selected it; when you move your cursor over the Stage, you see it has turned into crosshairs.

2. **Click anywhere on the Stage and drag to create a short horizontal line. To end your line, let go of the mouse.**

   Your line (technically called a *stroke*) appears on the Stage.

3. **Click above the horizontal line and drag down to create a vertical line.**

   The result is a cross. Next, you'll add legs by drawing diagonal lines.

4. **Click the bottom of the vertical line and drag down and to the left; then click the bottom of the vertical line again and drag down and to the right.**

   You see the result in Figure 2-10. It doesn't look like much yet, but it's actually the basis for a stick figure you'll create as you experiment with Flash's drawing and painting tools in the following sections.

Pencil tool

The Pencil tool lets you draw freeform strokes on the Stage, similar to the way you draw using a regular pencil on a regular sheet of paper. Unlike the Line tool, the Pencil tool doesn't make you stick to the straight and narrow, so it lends itself to curving lines and fine details, like hands and face. To use the Pencil tool:

1. **In the Tools panel, click the Pencil tool.**

   Flash surrounds the Pencil tool with a white background to let you know you've successfully selected it, and Pencil-related options appear in the Options section

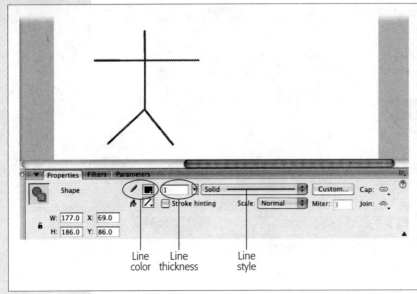

Line color   Line thickness   Line style

Figure 2-10:
The Line tool is the easiest, quickest way to create straight lines in Flash (like the four straight lines you see here). If you'd like to customize the way your lines look, head down to the Property Inspector. There you find options that let you make the line thicker, change it to a different color—even turn it into a dashed or dotted line, instead of a plain solid line. (If you don't see the Property Inspector, choose Window → Properties to display it.)

of the Tools panel. When you move your cursor over the Stage, you see it has turned into a miniature pencil.

2. **In the Options section of the Tools panel, click the down arrow.**

   A pop-up menu appears.

3. **In the pop-up menu, turn on the checkbox next to Smooth.**

   The *Smooth* option gently corrects any jiggles you make as you draw with the pencil—essential when you're trying to draw small lines, such as the face and hands you draw in this example.

4. **Click the Stage and drag to draw a little face, hands, and feet similar to the ones you see in Figure 2-11.**

   While you're on the Options section, there are other ways you can modify how the Pencil tool works: The *Straighten* option emphasizes the corners you draw with the Pencil (for example, turning squarish circles into squares or roundish squares into circles—definitely *not* what you want when you're trying to draw the feet you see in Figure 2-11), and the *Ink* option leaves your Pencil strokes just as they are, jiggles and all.

Tip: You can also straighten or smooth a line you've already drawn. To do so, select the line you want to modify using the Lasso tool (page 56), then select Modify → Shape → Straighten or Modify → Shape → Smooth.

Figure 2-11:
*Don't be surprised if your results look a bit shakier than you might
expect. If you've got an extra hundred bucks lying around, you can
buy a graphics tablet (see the box below) to make drawing in Flash a
bit easier, but most people start out using a computer mouse to
draw—and it's a lot harder to do than it looks. Fortunately, Flash offers
Pencil options you can use to help you control your drawing results.*

Mouse vs. Graphics Tablet

If you expect to do a lot of Flash work, do yourself a favor: ditch your mouse and get yourself a *graphics tablet* (sometimes referred to as a *digitizing tablet, graphics pad,* or *drawing tablet*). A graphics tablet is basically an electronic sketch board with a stylus that doubles as a pen, pencil, and brush. Today's graphics tablets connect through the Universal Serial Bus (USB) typically located at the front or back of your computer, so they're a snap to connect and remove.

With a graphics tablet, drawing and painting feels a whole lot more natural. Your results will look a lot better, too.

When you use a graphics tablet, Flash recognizes and records subtle changes, such as when you change the pressure or slant of the stylus—something you don't get with a plain old mouse. (In fact, if you install your graphics tablet correctly, Flash displays extra icons on the Tools panel that relate only to graphics tablets.)

Expect to spend anywhere from $100 to $500 on a good graphics tablet.

Pen tool

If you want to create a complex shape consisting of a lot of perfect arcs and a lot of perfectly straight lines, the Pen tool is your best choice.

To create straight lines with the Pen tool, click on the Stage to create *anchor points*, which Flash automatically connects using perfectly straight *segments*. The more times you click, the more segments Flash creates—and the more precisely you can modify the shape you draw, since you can change each point and segment individually (see Chapter 5).

If you click and drag the Pen tool (instead of just clicking), the Pen lets you create perfectly curved arcs.

Tip: Working with the Pen tool is a lot (a *whole* lot) less intuitive than working with the other Flash drawing tools. Because you can easily whip out a triangle with the Line tool or a perfect circle with the Oval tool, save the Pen tool for when you're trying to draw a more complex shape—such as a baby grand piano—and need more control and precision than you can get free-handing it with the Pencil or the Brush.

As you can see in the Tools panel shown in Figure 2-12, the Pen tool icon looks like the old-fashioned nib of a fountain pen.

To draw a straight line with the Pen tool:

1. **Select the Pen tool.**

   Your cursor changes into a miniature pen nib.

2. **Click the Stage, move your cursor an inch or so to the right, and click again.**

   Two anchor points appear, connected by a straight segment.

3. **Move the cursor again, stopping where you want to anchor the line and change direction again.**

   Figure 2-12 shows the results of several clicks. Flash keeps connecting each anchor point every time you click the Stage. To break a line and start a new one, double-click the Stage where you want to end the first line.

To draw a curve with the Pen tool:

1. **Select the Pen tool.**

   Your cursor changes into a miniature pen nib.

2. **Click the Stage once and then move your cursor an inch or so to the right.**

   A single anchor point appears.

Note: Flash lets you change the way it displays anchor points as well as the way your cursor appears when you're using the Pen tool. You can even tell Flash to preview line segments for you, much as it previews curves. To change any of these preferences, select Edit → Preferences. Then, in the Preferences window, select the Drawing category. The Pen tool preferences appear at the top of the Preferences window.

3. **Click again; but this time, *without letting go of the mouse button,* drag the cursor around.**

   Your cursor turns into an arrow, and Flash displays a preview curve and a temporary (straight) line to show you the angle of the curve you'll create if you let go of the mouse button. You can see an example in Figure 2-13 (top).

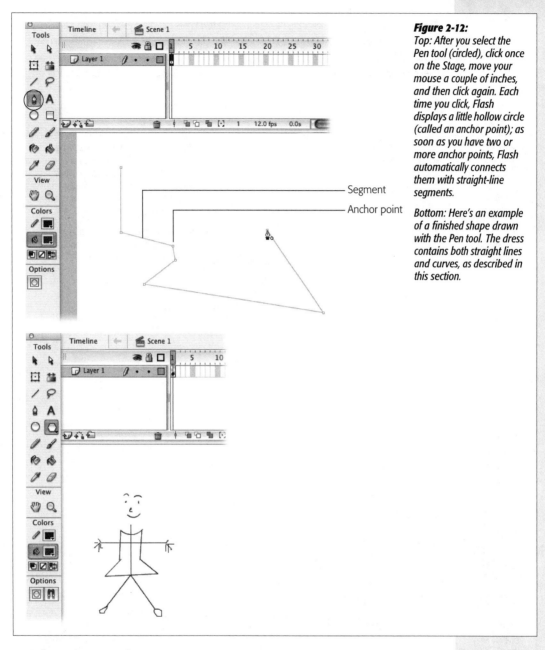

Figure 2-12:
Top: After you select the Pen tool (circled), click once on the Stage, move your mouse a couple of inches, and then click again. Each time you click, Flash displays a little hollow circle (called an anchor point); as soon as you have two or more anchor points, Flash automatically connects them with straight-line segments.

Bottom: Here's an example of a finished shape drawn with the Pen tool. The dress contains both straight lines and curves, as described in this section.

Segment

Anchor point

4. **Release the mouse button.**

Your curve appears on the Stage, as shown in the umbrella curve in Figure 2-13 (bottom).

Tip: Trying to draw a curve with the Pen tool the first few times can drive you nuts; you can't just start a new curve every time you feel like it, because each time you click the Stage, Flash appends the new curve to your old one. To start a new curve, click the Selection tool (or any other tool on the Tools panel) and then click the Pen tool again. *Then* move your cursor back to the Stage and begin your new curve.

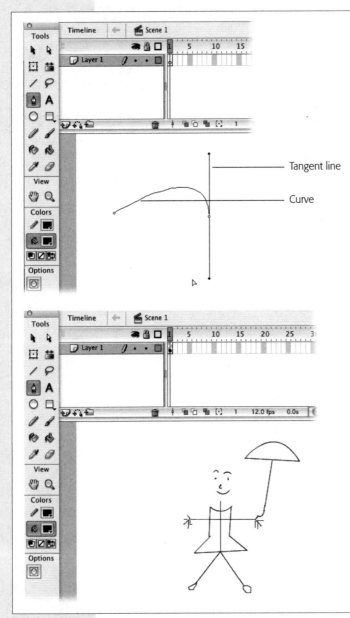

Tangent line

Curve

Figure 2-13:
Top: To create a curve using the Pen, click the Stage to begin the curve. Then move your cursor an inch or so, click again, and drag. While you're dragging, Flash displays a temporary line (a slope guide, or tangent line) to help you gauge the angle of your curve.

Bottom: As soon as you let up on your mouse button to finish the curve, the temporary line disappears.

Brush tool

You use the Brush tool to create freeform drawings, much like the Pencil tool described on page 59. The differences between the two are:

- **You can change the shape and size of the Brush tool.** You can choose a brush tip that's fat, skinny, round, rectangular, or even slanted. (You can't change either the size or the shape of the Pencil.)

- **You create fills using the Brush tool.** You create strokes using the Pencil. This distinction becomes important when it comes time to change the color of your drawings (see page 72).

To use the Brush tool:

1. **On the Tools panel, click the Brush tool (the little paintbrush icon).**

   Flash displays your Brush options, including Brush size and shape, in the Options section of the Tools panel.

2. **From the Brush Size drop-down menu (Figure 2-14), select the smallest brush size.**

   The larger brushes let you paint great sweeping strokes on the Stage. But in this example, you'll be drawing tiny little hairs on your stick figure, so a modest brush size is more appropriate. Your cursor changes to reflect your choice (you see this change if you mouse over the Stage).

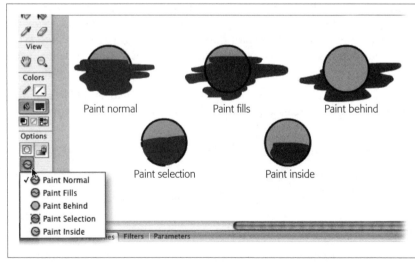

Figure 2-14:
Here you get an idea of how the different brush modes work. The same circle (a fill surrounded by a stroke) is scribbled on using the Brush tool; the only difference is that a different mode (Paint Normal, Paint Fills, and so on) was applied before brushing each circle.

Tip: Whenever you make a mistake, or simply want to wipe out the very last thing you did in Flash, select Edit → Undo.

---

3. **From the Brush Shape drop-down menu, choose the round brush shape.**

Each brush shape gives you a dramatically different look. To draw hair, as you do in this example, you choose round because it most closely approximates the results you get with a real brush. Once again, your cursor changes to reflect your choice.

4. **Click the down arrow next to Brush Mode and then, from the pop-up menu that appears, make sure the checkbox next to Paint Normal is turned on.**

Here's a rundown of all the brush modes you can choose from:

Paint Normal. Flash uses this mode unless you tell it otherwise. If you brush over an existing object on the Stage using Paint Normal, your brush stroke appears on top of the shape.

Paint Fill. If you brush over an existing object on the Stage using Paint Fill, your brush stroke appears on top of the fill portion of the object, behind the stroke, and on the Stage.

Paint Behind. If you brush over an existing object on the Stage using Paint Behind, your brush stroke always appears behind the object.

Paint Selection. If you brush over an existing object on the Stage using Paint Selection, your brush stroke only appears on the parts of the shape that are both fills and that you've previously selected (using one of the selection tools described on page 56).

Paint Inside. If you brush over an existing object on the Stage using Paint Inside and begin *inside* the stroke outline, your brush stroke only appears inside the lines of an object (even if you color outside the lines). If you begin *outside* the lines, your brush stroke only appears outside (even if you try to color inside them).

5. **Click on the Stage just about where your stick person's hair should be and drag your mouse upward; release the mouse button when the "hair" is the length you want it.**

Your paintbrush stroke appears on the Stage.

6. **Repeat to create additional hairs.**

You should see a result similar to the one shown in Figure 2-15.

Shape tools: Oval, Rectangle, and PolyStar

Flash gives you three quick ways to create basic shapes: the Oval tool, which lets you draw everything from a narrow cigar shape to a perfect circle; the Rectangle tool, which lets you draw (you guessed it) rectangles, from long and skinny to perfectly square; and the PolyStar tool, which you can use to create multisided polygons (the standard five-sided polygon, angled correctly, creates a not-too-horrible side view of a house) and star shapes.

Figure 2-15:
*Ms. Stick Person again, this time sporting hair applied using the
Brush tool. Notice the flowing curves of the brush strokes, in
contrast to the straight no-nonsense lines of the body and dress
(which were produced using the Line and Pen tools,
respectively).*

You see the Oval, Rectangle, and PolyStar tools in Figure 2-16; Figure 2-17 shows
you how to configure the PolyStar tool.

Note: You can always create a circle or a square or a star using one of the other drawing tools, such as
the Pencil or the Line tool. But most people find the shape tools quicker and easier.

To create a shape:

1. **Click the shape tool you want (choose from Oval, Rectangle, or PolyStar, as
   shown in Figure 2-16).**

   Your cursor changes into a cross.

2. **Click on the Stage where you want to start your shape and then drag your cursor to form the shape. When you're satisfied with the way your shape looks,
   release your mouse button.**

   Flash displays your shape on the Stage.

Tip: To create a perfectly round circle or a perfectly square square, simply hold down the Shift key while
you drag to create your shape.

Aligning Objects with the Align Tools

Sometimes dragging stuff around the stage and eyeballing it works just fine; other
times, you want to position your graphic elements with pinpoint precision. Using

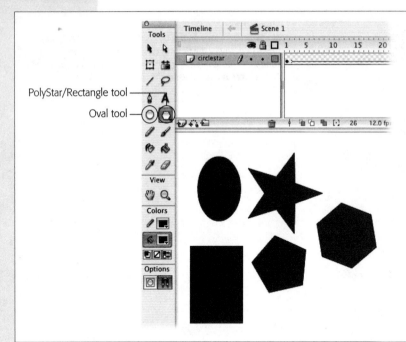

Figure 2-16:
The Oval, Rectangle, and PolyStar tools offer quick ways to create basic shapes. Because normal people don't draw polygons as often as circles or squares, Flash tucks the PolyStar tool out of the way until you need it. To display it, click the down arrow you see next to the Square tool.

PolyStar/Rectangle tool

Oval tool

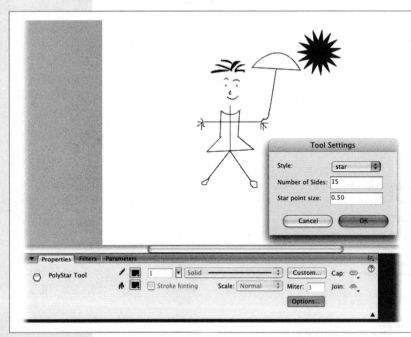

Figure 2-17:
Because the PolyStar tool does double-duty, if you want to create anything besides the five-sided polygon that Flash assumes you want—if, for example, you want to create a 15-point star to serve as the sun in your stick-figure drawing—you need to change the PolyStar tool settings. To do so, select the PolyStar tool; then head to the Property Inspector and click Options. In the Tool Settings window that appears, you can choose a style (polygon or star) and tell Flash how many sides you want your shape to have.

the Align panel, you can align graphic elements based on their edges (top, bottom, right, left) or by their centers. And you can base this alignment on the objects themselves (for example, you can line up the tops of all your objects) or on the

Stage (useful if you want to position, say, the feet of several stick people precisely at the bottom of the Stage, as shown in Figure 2-18). You can even distribute objects evenly with respect to each other.

To display the Align panel, select Window → Align or press Ctrl+K (Windows) or ⌘-K (Mac).

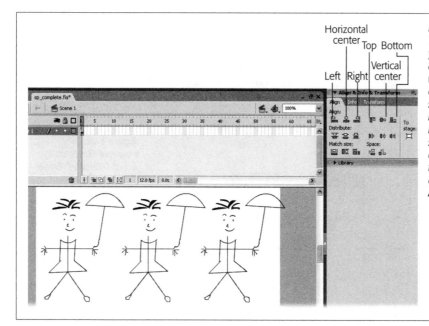

Horizontal center
Top Bottom
Vertical center
Left Right

Figure 2-18:
The Align panel gives you the opportunity to align a single object (or whole groups of selected objects) along the left side of the Stage, the right side, the top, the bottom, and more. Make sure you select the objects you want to align first; then click the alignment icon from the Align panel.

Erasing Mistakes with the Erase Tool

Only in the digital realm does an eraser work so effectively. Try erasing a goof on paper or canvas, and you not only have shredded eraser everywhere, you're also left with ghostly streaks of paint, lead, or charcoal.

No so in Flash. Using the Eraser tool (Figure 2-19), you can effectively wipe anything off the Stage, from a little speck to your entire drawing.

Figure 2-19:
Here the Eraser tool is rubbing out the PolyStar shape. Erasing in Flash isn't useful just for fixing mistakes; you can create cool effects (like patterns) by erasing, too. If you happen to start erasing the wrong thing, no problem; just click Edit → Undo Erase.

Note: Using the Eraser tool is similar to selecting Edit → Undo, but not identical. The difference: Edit → Undo tells Flash to work sequentially backward to undo your last actions or changes, last one first. The Erase tool, on the other hand, lets you wipe stuff off the Stage regardless of the order in which you added it.

To use the Erase tool:

1. **In the Tools section of the Tools panel, click the Eraser tool to select it.**

   Your cursor changes to the size and shape of eraser Flash assumes you want. To make your eraser larger or smaller, head to the Options section of the Tools panel and, from the Eraser Shape pop-up menu (Figure 2-20), select the eraser size and shape you want. (You want a nice fat eraser if you have a lot to erase, or a skinny one if you're just touching up the edges of a drawing.)

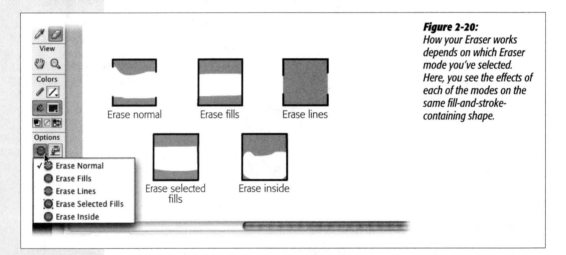

Figure 2-20:
How your Eraser works depends on which Eraser mode you've selected. Here, you see the effects of each of the modes on the same fill-and-stroke-containing shape.

2. **On the Stage, click where you want to begin erasing and drag your cursor back and forth.**

   Flash erases everything your cursor touches (or not, depending on the erase mode you've chosen—see the following section for details).

Tip: To erase a line or a fill in one fell swoop, click the Faucet tool (shown in Figure 2-20). Then click the line or fill you want to erase.

Configuring the Eraser

Flash offers a ton of Eraser modes you can use to control how the Eraser tool works (and what it erases). To see them, click the down arrow next to the Options icon (Figure 2-20) and then, from the pop-up menu that appears, select one of the following modes:

Note: The Eraser tool works only on editable objects. It doesn't work on grouped objects or symbols.

- **Erase Normal.** Flash uses this mode unless you tell it otherwise. If you erase over an existing object on the Stage using Erase Normal, Flash erases everything, fill and stroke included.

- **Erase Fill.** If you erase over an existing object on the Stage using Erase Fill, only the fill portion of the object disappears.

- **Erase Lines.** If you erase over an existing object on the Stage using Erase Lines only the stroke portion of the object disappears.

- **Erase Selected Fills.** If you erase over an existing object on the Stage using Erase Selected Fills, you erase only those parts of the object that are both fills and that you've previously selected (using one of the selection tools described on page 56).

Note: Oddly enough, if you configure your erase to Erase Selected Fills and then rub your virtual eraser over *non*-selected fills, Flash pretends to erase them—until you let up on your mouse, when they pop right back onto the Stage.

- **Erase Inside.** If you erase over an existing object on the Stage using Erase Inside, Flash erases the inside (fill) of the object as long as you begin erasing inside the stroke outline; if you begin erasing outside the line, it only erases outside the line.

Copying and Pasting Drawn Objects

Copying graphic elements and pasting them—either into the same frame, into another frame, or even into another document—is much faster than drawing new objects from scratch. It's also the most familiar. If you've ever copied text in a word processing or spreadsheet document and pasted it somewhere else, you know the drill.

A simple copy-and-paste is the best way to go when you're experimenting: for example, when you want to see whether the blue-eyed wallaby you drew for one animation looks good in another. But if you're trying to keep your animation's finished file size as small as possible, or if you plan to include more than one copy of that wallaby, copying and pasting *isn't* the best way to go. Instead, you'll want to look into symbols (page 205).

To copy and paste an image:

1. **On the Stage, select the image you want to copy.**

   Page 56 gives you an overview of the selection tools. In Figure 2-21, the butterfly is selected.

Choose Edit → Copy (or press Ctrl+C in Windows; ⌘-C on the Mac). Then select the keyframe into which you want to paste the image.

You can paste the image in the keyframe you're in, or you can select another one. Flash doesn't restrict you to the document you currently have open; you can open another document to paste the image into.

Choose one of the Paste commands. Your options include:

Edit → **Paste in Center.** Tells Flash to paste the image in the center of the Stage.

Edit → **Paste in Place.** Tells Flash to paste the image in the same spot it was on the original Stage. (If you choose this option to paste an image to the same Stage as the original, you'll need to drag the pasted copy off the original to see it.)

Edit → **Paste Special.** (Windows only) Displays a Paste Special dialog box that lets you paste an image as a device-independent bitmap (an uneditable version of your image with a fixed background the size and shape of the selection box).

Flash pastes your image based on your selection, leaving your original copy intact.

Tip: If all you want to do is make a quick copy of an image on the same Stage as the original, Flash gives you an easier way than copying and pasting. Select Edit → Duplicate (or press Ctrl+D in Windows; ⌘-D on the Mac). When you do, Flash pastes a copy of the image just a little below and to the right of your original image, ready for you to reposition as you see fit.

Adding Color

The Colors section of the Tools panel lets you choose the colors for your strokes and fills. Before you click one of the drawing icons to begin drawing (or afterward, to change existing colors) you can click either of the Stroke or Fill icons in the Color Section to bring up a color palette, as you see in Figure 2-22. Choose a color from the color palette, and Flash applies that color to the Stage as you draw.

Changing the Color of a Stroke (Line)

One of the best things about drawing in Flash is how easy it is to change things around. If you draw a bright orange line using the Pencil tool, for example, you can change that line an instant later to spruce, chartreuse, or puce (and then back to orange again) with just a few simple mouse clicks.

Note: In Flash, all lines are made up of strokes. The Flash drawing tools that produce strokes include the Pencil, the Pen, the Line, and the shape tools (Oval, Rectangle, and PolyStar).

Flash gives you two different ways to change the color of a stroke: the Property Inspector and the Ink Bottle tool.

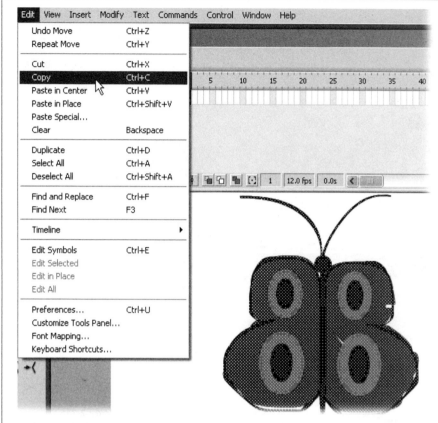

Figure 2-21:
Copying and pasting is the easiest way to try out a look. If you're copying a complex image, as shown here, you may want to group the selected image first by choosing Modify → Group. (There's much more detail on grouping objects on page 156 in Chapter 5.) For additional copies, simply choose Edit → Paste in Center or Edit → Paste in Place again.

Coloring strokes with the Property Inspector

Changing the color of a stroke using the Property Inspector is best for situations when you want to change the color of a single stroke or when you want to change more than just the color of a stroke (for example, you want to change stroke thickness or the color of the fill inside the stroke).

To change the color of a stroke using the Property Inspector:

1. **On the Stage, select the stroke you want to change.**

    A Property Inspector similar to the one in Figure 2-23 appears.

2. **In the Property Inspector, click the Stroke Color icon.**

    A Color Picker appears.

3. **Click to choose a new color for your selected stroke.**

    The Color Picker disappears, and Flash redisplays your stroke using the color you chose.

Figure 2-22:
Before you begin drawing with the Pen or Pencil tools (both of which let you create strokes), you can choose the color Pen or Pencil you want to use by clicking the Stroke Color icon and then selecting a color from the palette that appears. If you want to change the color that appears when you use the Brush tool (which creates fills), you need to click the Fill Color icon (and select a color) before you click the Brush tool and begin to draw.

Stroke color

Fill color

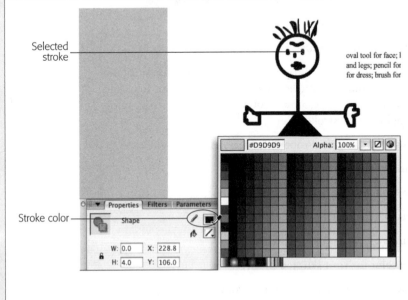

Figure 2-23:
Using the Property Inspector is a quick and easy way to change the color of a single stroke. First, select the stroke you want to recolor; then, in the Property Inspector that appears, click the Stroke Color icon. When you do, the Color Picker appears, complete with any custom color swatches you've added to it (if any). The instant you choose a color, the Color Picker disappears and the selected stroke(s) change to the new color. Notice here that the Fill Color icon has a slash through it, meaning that no fill is currently selected.

Selected stroke

Stroke color

Coloring strokes with the Ink Bottle tool

The Ink Bottle tool is great for situations when you want to apply the same color to a bunch of different strokes all in one fell swoop.

To change the color of a stroke (or several strokes) using the Ink Bottle tool:

1. **In the Tools panel, select the Stroke Color icon (Figure 2-24, top).**

   The Color Picker appears, and as you mouse over the different colors, you notice your cursor looks like a tiny eyedropper.

2. **Click a color to choose it.**

   The Color Picker disappears, and Flash redisplays the Stroke Color icon using the color you just selected.

3. **On the Stage, select the stroke(s) you want to recolor.**

   Flash highlights the selected strokes.

4. **In the Tools panel, click the Ink Bottle tool (Figure 2-24, bottom).**

   As you mouse over the stage, you notice your cursor looks like a little ink bottle.

5. **Click the selected strokes.**

   Flash recolors the selected strokes, as shown in Figure 2-24 (bottom).

Tip: If all you want to do is change the color of one stroke, you don't need to select it first. Just click the Ink Bottle tool and then, on the Stage, click the stroke to recolor it.

Changing the Color of a Fill

If you change your mind about the color of any of the fills you add to the Stage, no problem. Flash gives you two different ways to change the color of a fill: the Property Inspector and the Paint Bucket tool.

Note: The Flash drawing tools that produce fills include the Brush tool and all of the shape tools (Oval, Rectangle, and PolyStar).

Coloring fills with the Property Inspector

Using the Property Inspector to change the color of a fill is great for situations when you want to change more than just fill color: for example, you want to change both fill color and the color of the stroke outline surrounding the fill.

To change the color of a fill using the Property Inspector:

1. **On the Stage, select the fill you want to change.**

   A Property Inspector similar to the one in Figure 2-25 appears.

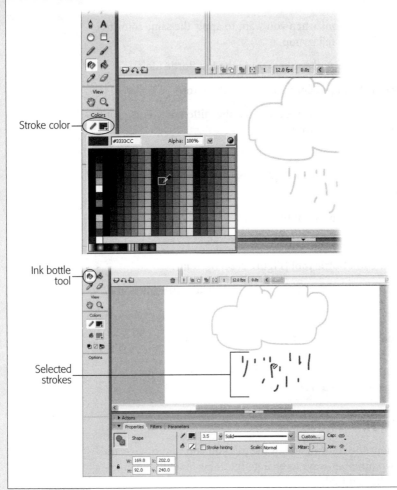

Stroke color

Ink bottle
tool

Selected
strokes

Figure 2-24:
*Top: Clicking the Stroke Color
icon displays the Color
Picker. Here, you can change
not just the hue, but also the
transparency you want. To
do so, click the arrow next to
the Alpha box and drag the
slider anywhere from 0%,
(completely transparent) to
100% (completely opaque).*

*Bottom: After you select one
or more strokes, click the Ink
Bottle tool to change the
color of all of the selected
strokes. To change the color
of strokes one by one, you
don't need to select them
first; simply click them with
the Ink Bottle tool.*

2. **In the Property Inspector, click the Fill Color icon.**

   The Color Picker appears.

3. **Click to choose a new color for your selected fill.**

   As soon as you let go of your mouse, the Color Picker disappears, and Flash
   redisplays your fill using the color you chose.

Tip: To change the color of a bunch of fills quickly, select the fills you want to recolor first; then select the
Fill Color icon and choose a new color. When you do, Flash automatically redisplays all your selected fills
using your new color.

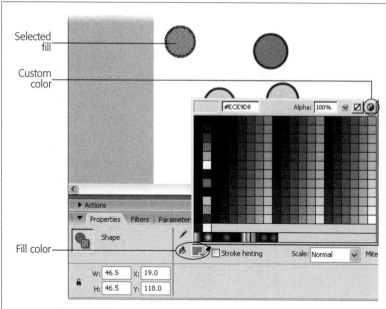

Selected fill

Custom color

Fill color

Shape

Figure 2-25:
When you select a fill-containing shape (here, the inside of a circle), the Property Inspector automatically appears. In the Property Inspector, you see the Fill Color icon. Click it to display the Color Picker and then click to choose a new color for your fill. If you don't see the exact color you want, you can click the Custom Color icon to blend your own custom shade. And while you're here in the Property Inspector, you can also change the stroke outline of the shape, if you like.

Coloring fills with the Paint Bucket tool

The Paint Bucket tool is great for situations where you want to apply the same color to one or more fills on the Stage, either one fill at a time or all at once.

To change the color of a fill using the Paint Bucket tool:

1. **In the Tools panel, select the Fill Color icon (Figure 2-26, top).**

    The Color Picker appears, and as you mouse over the different colors, you notice your cursor looks like a tiny eyedropper.

2. **Click a color to choose it. (If you know the hexadecimal number of a specific color you want, you can type it into the field next to the preview window.)**

    The Color Picker disappears, and Flash redisplays the Fill Color icon using the color you just selected.

3. **On the Stage, click the fill(s) you want to recolor.**

    Flash recolors each fill you click, as shown in Figure 2-26 (bottom).

Tip: If you don't have a completely closed outline around your fill, Flash might not let you apply a fill color. To tell Flash to ignore small gaps (or medium gaps, or even relatively large gaps) surrounding your fill: in the Options section of the Tools panel (Figure 2-26, bottom), click Gap Size. Then, from the pop-up menu that appears, turn on the checkbox next to Close Small Gaps, Close Medium Gaps, or Close Large Gaps. Then try to modify your fill again. (If you're unsuccessful, you may want to consider closing the gap yourself using one of Flash's drawing tools.)

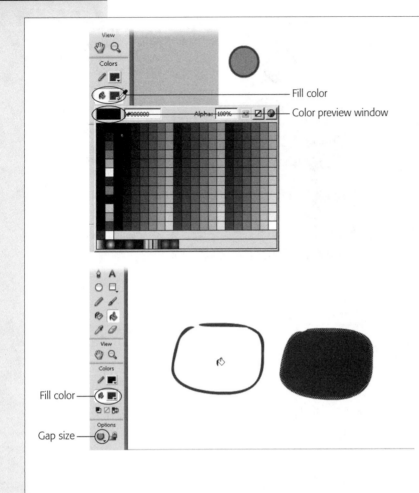

Fill color

Color preview window

Fill color

Gap size

Figure 2-26:
Top: Click the Fill Color icon to choose a new color for your fills. As you move your cursor around the Color Picker, you notice the Preview Window displays the color your cursor happens to be over at any given time.

Bottom: After you select a new fill color, apply it to the fills on Stage by clicking the Paint Bucket and then clicking each fill. If you're adding a fill for the first time and you find that Flash doesn't add your fill color, make sure your fill is perfectly enclosed. If it's not—if there's so much as a tiny gap in the outline surrounding your fill—Flash won't be able to tell where your fill stops and the Stage begins, so your new color won't take. Fortunately, you can tell Flash to ignore the gap and change your fill color as best it can. To do so, click the Gap size option (shown here) and, on the pop-up menu that appears, turn on the checkbox next to Close Small (or Medium, or Large) Gaps.

Animating Your Drawings

Animation is what Flash is all about. Sure, Flash offers tons of drawing and special-effect tools, but these are all means to an end: a series of slightly different drawings that you can string together to create the illusion of movement.

In the old days, animators had to create each drawing, or *frame*, by hand—a daunting process when you consider that your average feature presentation clicks by at 24 frames per second. (That's 1,440 drawings *per minute* of onscreen animation. Expensive? Hoo boy.)

To keep those costs down, animation companies did what all self-respecting companies do: They figured out how to separate the highly skilled labor from the less-skilled labor. They figured out that there are key drawings (called *keyframes*) that show big changes in the finished animation, and a certain number of less-detailed, *in-between* drawings (regular frames) they could assign to lower-paid workers. For example, say you're a producer working on an animation showing a cartoon kangaroo jumping up into the air. If you get a skilled animator to draw the kangaroo-on-the-ground, kangaroo-midway, and kangaroo-at-the-top frames, you can hand these keyframes off to a low-paid tweener. All the tweener has to do is copy the keyframes and make a few adjustments, and bingo: You've got yourself a finished animation at a bargain-basement price.

Flash, like the animation studios of old, gives you the opportunity to use tweening to slash the time it takes to produce a finished animation. In this chapter, you see both approaches: frame-by-frame (still the best choice when you need to create highly complex, tightly controlled animations) and tweening (wherein Flash serves as your very own low-paid illustrator).

Frame-by-Frame Animation

An *animation* is nothing more than a series of framed images displayed one after the other to create the illusion of motion. When you create an animation by hand in Flash, you create each frame yourself—either by using Flash's drawing and painting tools (Chapter 2), or by importing images or movie clips that someone else has created (Chapter 8).

The best way to gain an understanding of frames, keyframes, and Flash's animation tools is to start animating by hand, frame by frame. Most of the time, though, you'll use tweening (page 91) to save time and frustration. For more advice on when to use either technique, see the box below.

UP TO SPEED

To Tween or Not to Tween

The great thing about creating an animation frame by frame is that it gives you the most control over the finished product. If you're looking for a super-realistic effect, for example, you're probably not going to be satisfied with the frames Flash generates when you tell it to tween (page 91). Instead, you're going to want to lovingly handcraft every single frame, making slight adjustments to lots of different objects as you go.

Say, for instance, you're creating an animation showing an outdoor barbecue. Over the course of your animation, the sun's going to move across the sky, which is going to change the way your characters' shadows appear. Bugs are going to fly across the scene. When one character opens his mouth to speak, the other characters aren't going to remain static: Their hair's going to ripple in the breeze, they're going to start conversations of their own, they're going to drop pieces of steak (which the host's dog is going to come streaking over and wolf down). You can't leave realistic, director-level details like this to Flash; you've got to create them yourself.

On the downside, animating by hand is understandably time-intensive. Even though most Web-based Flash animations run at a modest 12 *fps* (frames per second), that's a whole lot of frames. And compared to tweening, creating individual frames adds substantially to the file size of your movie, too—a big consideration if you intend to put your finished animation up on the Web. (Big files tend not to play so well over the Web, thanks to uncontrollable variables such as Internet traffic and the connection speed of the folks viewing your animation. You can find tips for optimizing your finished animation's file size in Chapter 14.)

In other words, with frame-by-frame animation, you get more control—but it's going to cost you in time and hassle, and (potentially) it's going to make your finished animation harder for folks to view. The choice is yours.

Frames and Keyframes

Flash recognizes two different types of frames: *keyframes*, and plain old *frames*. Although in frame-by-frame animations most of the frames you create are keyframes, if you want to tell Flash to hold a particular image for effect, you'll need both:

• **Keyframes** are the important frames—the frames you designate to hold distinct images.

- **Frames** in a Flash animation contain whatever image you associated with the last keyframe; their purpose is to mark time. You use them to pace the action of your animation by telling Flash to skip a beat in the action here and there.

As you see on in the following section, you add both keyframes and frames to an animation using the Timeline.

Creating a Frame-by-Frame Animation

To build a frame-by-frame animation, you can use Flash's drawing tools to draw the content of each frame on the Stage, or you can import (page 243) existing images created in another program. Either way, you must place an image in each keyframe you create.

Here are the steps to creating a frame-by-frame animation:

1. **Open a blank Flash document.**

   As the Property Inspector in Figure 3-1 shows, Flash starts you out in Layer 1, Frame 1. (If you don't see the Property Inspector, select Window → Properties → Properties.)

Tip: You'll learn how to add more layers to your animation later in this chapter. When you've got more than one layer, you must click a layer name in the Timeline to select the layer you want to animate.

---

2. **Drag the playhead and release it over the frame in which you want to begin your animation.**

   Flash displays the red playhead rectangle over the frame you chose. In most cases—as in Figure 3-1—the frame you want to begin your animation in is Frame 1.

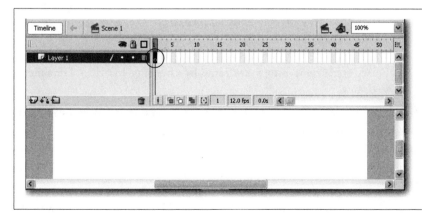

Figure 3-1:
Most things begin at the beginning; when you create a new Flash document, as shown here, Flash automatically designates Frame 1 as a blank keyframe. You can tell that Frame 1 contains a blank keyframe by the little hollow circle Flash displays in Frame 1 (and by the fact that there's nothing on the Stage).

3. **Using Flash's paint and drawing tools, draw an image on the Stage.**

   Figure 3-2 shows an example drawing of a frog with a tempting fly overhead.

Note: If you have an existing image stored on your computer, you can bring it onto the Stage. Select File → Import → Import to Stage and then, in the Import window that appears, type in (or browse to) the name of the file you want to pull in. When you finish, click OK. (Chapter 8 covers importing files in more detail.)

Figure 3-2:
Flash associates the selected keyframe with all the images you place on the Stage—whether you draw them directly on the Stage using the drawing and painting tools, drag them from the Library, or import them from previously created files. Here, Flash associates the frog-and-fly drawing with the keyframe in Frame 1.

4. **Click to select another frame further out on the Timeline.**

   Which frame you select depends on how long you want Flash to display the content associated with your first keyframe. Since Flash usually plays at a rate of 12 frames per second, selecting Frame 2 would tell Flash to display the two images so quickly that all you'd see is smooth, fast motion. For practice, so you can clearly see each frame of your work-in-progress, try Frame 10. Flash highlights the frame you select, as you see in Figure 3-3.

Note: Although Flash has a frame rate of 12 fps (frames per second) out of the box, you can change this setting. Learn how on page 295.

5. **Turn the selected frame into a keyframe by choosing Insert → Timeline → Blank Keyframe.**

   Flash moves the playhead to the selected frame (Frame 10 in Figure 3-4), inserts a keyframe icon, and clears the Stage.

6. **Draw a second image on the Stage.**

   The second keyframe in Figure 3-4 shows the frog with a thought balloon instead of a fly. But if your two images are fairly similar, you can avoid having to completely redraw the image for your second keyframe, as you'll see in the next step.

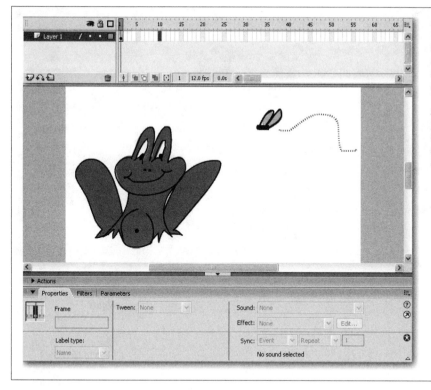

Figure 3-3:
*When you click a
frame in the Timeline,
Flash highlights it with
a tiny blue rectangle,
as shown in Frame 10.
The Property Inspector
starts out blank since
you haven't yet added
a keyframe (or a
regular frame) at
Frame 10.*

7. **Click further out in the Timeline (Frame 20, say), and choose Insert → Timeline → Keyframe.**

   Just as when you chose Insert → Timeline → Blank Keyframe, Flash still moves
   the playhead and inserts a keyframe icon; but instead of clearing the Stage, Flash
   carries over the content from the first keyframe, all ready for you to tweak and
   edit.

8. **Repeat the previous step to create as many keyframes as you want.**

To get the hang of frame-by-frame animation, adding two or three keyframes is
plenty. But when you're building an actual animation, you'll likely need to add
dozens or even hundreds of keyframes (or even more, depending on the length
and complexity you're shooting for).

Note: You can examine this sample animation to check your work. Simply download frame_by_frame.fla
from the "Missing CD" page.

GEM IN THE ROUGH

Making the Timeline Easier to Read

You can't create an animation—frame-by-frame or tweened—without the Timeline. The Timeline serves as a kind of indispensable thumbnail sketch of your animation, showing you at a glance which frames contain unique content (the keyframes) and which don't (the regular frames), how many layers your animation contains (page 89), which sections of your animation contain tweens (page 91), and so on.

Unfortunately, with its tiny little squares and cryptic symbols, the Timeline can be pretty hard to read. And the more keyframes you add to your animation, the harder it is to remember which image you put in which keyframe.

You can always click a keyframe (or drag the playhead over a keyframe) to tell Flash to display the image associated with that keyframe on the Stage—but there's an easier way.

You can tell Flash to expand the Timeline and show miniature versions of each of your keyframes. In the Timeline, click the Options menu you see in the upper-right corner; then, from the pop-up menu that appears, turn on the checkbox next to Preview.

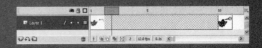

Figure 3-4:
Here, the playhead is over the second keyframe, which tells Flash to place the content on the Stage in the second keyframe (Frame 10). Flash displays only new content in the finished animation when it detects a new keyframe, so Frames 2–9 carry forward the content from Frame 1 (the first keyframe). You can verify this behavior by dragging the playhead (scrubbing) from Frame 10 back to Frame 1.

Testing Your Frame-by-Frame Animation

You have two choices when it comes to testing your animation, and both of them are simple:

- **Control → Play.** The quickest, easiest approach is to test your animation inside the Flash development environment. Select Control → Play (or press Enter). When you do, Flash runs your animation right there on the Stage. So, for example, if you create an animation containing just two keyframes (similar to the

example on page 81), Flash displays the content for the first keyframe, followed
by the content for the second keyframe.

Note: When you select Control → Play, Flash starts your animation beginning at whatever frame your
playhead happens to be over—even if that's at the end of your animation. To tell Flash to begin at the
beginning, drag the playhead to Frame 1 before you select Control → Play.

- **Control → Test Movie.** Selecting Control → Test Movie *exports* your Flash document (compiles the .fla document into an executable .swf file) and automatically loads the .swf file into the built-in Flash Player. Figure 3-5 shows an
example.

Testing your animation this way takes a bit longer, but it's more accurate:
You're actually seeing what your audience will eventually see, from beginning to
end. (In some cases—for example, if you've added a motion guide path as
described on page 103 to your animation—selecting Control → Play shows a
slightly different result than selecting Control → Test Movie does.)

Figure 3-5:
*The first time you run your
animation in Flash Player, Flash
assumes you want to run it over
(and over, and over, and over).
Fortunately, you can disabuse
Flash of this annoying
assumption. From the player
main menu, select Control and
then turn off the checkbox next to
Loop. Other useful options you
find on the player's Control menu
include stopping your animation,
rewinding it, and even stepping
through it frame by frame.
Chapter 13 covers animation
testing in-depth.*

Editing Your Frame-by-Frame Animation

It's rare that your first crack at any given animation will be your last. Typically,
you'll start with a few keyframes, test the result, add a few frames, delete a few
frames, and so on until you get precisely the look you're after.

This section shows you how to perform the basic frame-level edits you need to take
your animation from rough sketch to finished production: inserting, copying,
pasting, moving, and deleting frames.

Selecting frames and keyframes

Selecting a single frame or keyframe is as easy as zipping up to the Timeline and clicking the frame (or keyframe) you want to select, as shown in Figure 3-6.

But if you want to select multiple frames, Flash gives you four additional selection alternatives:

- **To select multiple contiguous frames.** Click the first frame you want to select and then drag your mouse to the last frame you want to select. Alternatively, click the first frame you want to select and then Shift-click the last frame you want to select.

Note: Click-dragging to select multiple frames can be highly annoying. Flash lets you move frames by selecting a series of frames and then dragging it to somewhere else on the Timeline, so you may well end up moving frames when all you wanted to do was select them.

- **To select multiple noncontiguous frames.** Ctrl-click (on the Mac, ⌘-click) each frame you want to select.

Note: Oddly enough, Ctrl-clicking (or, on the Mac, ⌘-clicking) the last frame in a frame span *deselects* all the selected frames (except for the last frame).

- **To select an entire frame span.** Double-click any frame in the *frame span*. A frame span consists of all the frames between one keyframe (including that keyframe) and the next keyframe. So, for example, if you have a keyframe in Frame 15 and another keyframe in Frame 30, double-clicking *any* frame from Frame 15 through Frame 29 automatically selects *every* frame from Frame 15 through Frame 29.

- **To select all the frames on a layer.** Click the name of the layer. In the example in Figure 3-6, clicking "Fly" would automatically select all the frames in the Fly layer; clicking "Frog" would automatically select all the frames in the Frog layer.

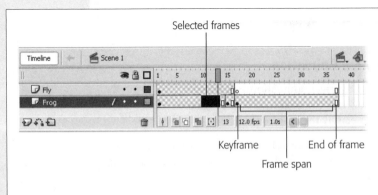

Selected frames

Keyframe   End of frame

Frame span

Figure 3-6:
To select a single frame (including a keyframe), simply click the frame; to select multiple frames, click-drag or choose one of Flash's other two multiple-frame-selection options. A frame span comprises a keyframe, an end frame, and all the frames between the keyframe and end frame. If you've added multiple layers to your animation, make sure you select frames from the correct layer.

No matter which alternative you use, Flash highlights the frames to let you know you've successfully selected them.

Inserting and deleting keyframes and frames

The smoothness of your finished animation depends on the number of keyframes and regular frames you've included. This section shows you how to add and delete both to an existing animation.

Inserting keyframes. Typically, you'll start with a handful of keyframes and need to insert additional keyframes to smooth out the animation and make it appear more realistic (less herky-jerky).

For example, say you're working on an animation showing a dog wagging its tail. You've got a keyframe showing the tail to the left of the dog; one showing the tail straight behind the dog; and a final keyframe showing the tail to the right of the dog. You test the animation and it looks okay, but a little primitive.

Inserting additional keyframes showing the dog's tail in additional positions (just a bit to the left of the dog's rump, a little bit further to the left, a little further, and *then* all the way to the left) will make the finished sequence look much more detailed and realistic.

Note: Technically speaking, you don't actually insert a keyframe in Flash; you turn a regular frame into a keyframe. But Flash-ionados speak of inserting keyframes, and so does the Flash documentation, so that's how this section presents it.

To insert a keyframe into an existing animation:

1. **In the Timeline, select the regular frame you want to turn into a keyframe.**

   If you want to add a keyframe midway between Frame 1 and Frame 10 on Layer 1, for example, click in Layer 1 to select Frame 5, as shown in Figure 3-7.

   Flash moves the playhead to the frame you selected.

2. **Select Insert → Timeline → Keyframe (to tell Flash to carry over the content from the previous keyframe so that you can edit it) or Insert → Timeline → Blank Keyframe (to tell Flash to clear the Stage).**

   On the Stage, Flash either displays the image associated with the previous keyframe or, if you inserted a blank keyframe, displays nothing at all.

3. **Using the drawing and painting tools, add content for your new keyframe to the Stage.**

   If you've already created drawings in another program, you can import them as described on page 243.

Inserting frames. Regular frames in Flash act as placeholders: They simply mark time while the contents of the previous keyframe display. So it stands to reason that

---

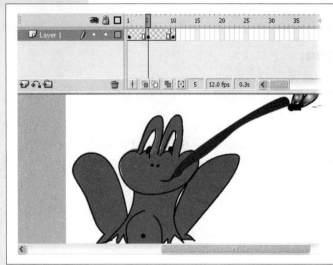

Figure 3-7:
Technically, you don't always add a keyframe in Flash (unless you're positioned over an existing keyframe or the very last frame in a layer); instead, when you're positioned over a regular frame, you turn that regular frame into a keyframe. As you can see here, Flash displays its usual icons to show the results: The selected frame, Frame 5, is now a keyframe (you can tell by the solid black dot in Frame 5), and Frame 4 is the end frame, or the last frame that'll display the contents of the previous keyframe, Frame 1 (you can tell this by the hollow rectangle in Frame 4).

you want to insert additional frames when you want to slow down the action a little. In fact, inserting frames is sort of like having a director yell, "Hold camera!" with the contents of the last keyframe remaining onscreen while the camera's holding.

To insert a frame into an existing animation:

1. **On the Timeline, click to select the frame** *before which* **you want to add a frame. (Make sure the frame you select appears on the Timeline** *after* **the keyframe you want to hold onscreen.)**

    Flash moves the playhead to the frame you selected.

2. **Select Insert → Timeline → Frame (or press F5).**

    Flash inserts a new frame *after* the frame you selected, bumping up the total number of frames in your animation by one.

Deleting keyframes. Technically speaking, a keyframe is just a regular frame to which you've added unique content. So to delete a keyframe, you first need to turn it back into a regular frame; then you need to delete the frame altogether.

To clear a keyframe and turn it back into a regular frame (page 89 shows you how to delete a frame):

1. **On the Timeline, click to select the keyframe you want to clear.**

    The playhead appears over the keyframe.

2. **Right-click the selected keyframe and then, from the pop-up menu that appears, choose Clear Keyframe.**

    Flash removes keyframe status from the frame and whisks the associated image off the Stage.

Tip: Because you can't tie a drawing to a regular frame, clearing a keyframe means *you lose anything you've drawn or imported to the Stage for that keyframe*. To get the contents of the Stage back—perhaps you'd like to save your drawing as a reusable symbol or save it off in its own separate file, as shown in Chapter 7, before you delete it from this frame—select Edit → Undo Clear Frame.

Deleting frames. Deleting frames—like inserting them—lets you control the pace of your animation. But instead of padding sections of your animation the way inserting frames does, deleting frames squeezes together the space between your keyframes to speed up sections of your animation. When you delete a frame, you're actually shortening your animation by the length of one frame.

For example, say you're working on the animation showing a frog catching a fly. You've created three keyframes: one showing the frog noticing the fly, one showing the frog actually catching the fly, and one showing the frog enjoying the fly. If you space out these three keyframes evenly (say, at Frame 1, Frame 15, and Frame 30), all three images spend the same amount of time onscreen. That's perfectly serviceable—but you can create a much more realistic effect by shortening the number of frames between the second and third keyframes (in others words, by deleting a bunch of frames between Frame 15 and Frame 30 to speed up this portion of the animation).

To delete frames:

1. **On the Timeline, select the frame (or frames) you want to delete.**

   Flash highlights the selected frame(s) and moves the playhead to the last selected frame.

2. **Select Edit → Timeline → Remove Frames.**

   Flash deletes the selected frames (including selected keyframes, if any) and shortens the Timeline by the number of deleted frames.

Adding Layers to Your Animation

Imagine you're creating a complex animation in Flash. You want to show a couple of characters carrying on a conversation, a car speeding by in the background, and some clouds floating across the sky.

Theoretically, you *could* draw all of these elements together, in one *layer* (one set of frames). In the first frame, you could show the characters greeting each other, the car entering from stage left, and the first cloud drifting in from the right. In the second frame, the characters might begin speaking and waving their hands, the car might advance just a bit, more clouds might appear from the right, and so on.

Now imagine that your spec changes. It's not a car you need in the background, but a galloping dog. A relatively simple change, conceptually—but because you've drawn all the graphic elements on a single set of frames, you now need to redraw *every single frame*. You need to slice away the car where it touches the other elements, and then you need to draw in the dog. And because the dog needs to appear behind the two chatting characters, you can't even take advantage of Flash's motion tweening (which you can learn how to do on page 91), or even copying and pasting to speed up the animation process (page 71).

Fortunately, Flash gives you an alternative: *layers*. Layers in Flash are virtual, clear plastic sheets that you stack on top of each other to create composite frames. So you can draw each element of your animation on a separate layer: the clouds, the car, the first character, and the second character. When you stack the layers together, your animation's complete.

Then, when you need to replace the car with a dog, all you need to do is delete the car layer and create a dog layer. You're working with a single object on your dog layer, so you can copy and paste and even create motion and shape tweens, all without affecting any other part of your animation. And if you decide you want the dog to gallop in *front* of your characters instead of behind, you can make that change simply by restacking (reordering) your layers with the dog layer on top.

Creating Layers

When you create a new document, Flash starts you out with one layer, called Layer 1, in the Layers area of the Timeline (Figure 3-8).

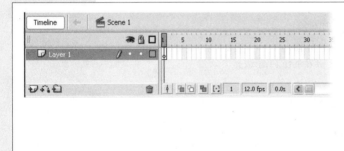

Figure 3-8:
A layer is nothing more than a set of frames, which is why Flash displays layers to the left of the Timeline (that way, you can easily spot which frames belong to which layer). When you create a new document in Flash, Flash names your first set of frames Layer 1. At some point, replace it with a more meaningful name that describes the content of the layer. See the tip on page 104.

To create an additional layer:

1. On the Timeline, click the name of the layer you want to add a layer *above*.

   If you're starting out in a new Flash document, there's only one layer to select—Layer 1.

2. Still on the Timeline, right-click the layer name—in this example, Layer 1—and then, from the pop-up menu that appears, select Insert Layer.

Flash creates a new layer, named Layer 2, and places this new layer above the existing layer, as shown in Figure 3-9.

Note: Flash gives you two additional ways to create layers: by clicking the Insert Layer icon (Figure 3-9) and by selecting Insert → Timeline → Layer.

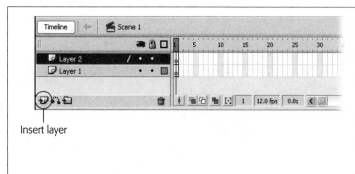

Figure 3-9:
To create a new layer, select an existing layer and then click the Insert Layer icon. Flash immediately creates a new layer, names it (here, Layer 2), and places it above the selected layer. The fact that Flash places the new layer above (and not below) the existing layer is important because each layer's position determines how Flash displays your frames' contents. Change your layers' orders by dragging them. If you can't see all the layers in the Layers window, just click the bottom of the Layers window and then drag to resize it.

Animating Automatically (Tweening)

When you create a frame-by-frame animation, it's up to you to create every single keyframe and frame. And in cases where you want absolute control over every single image that appears in your finished animation, frame-by-frame animation is the way to go.

Often, however, you can get by with a little less control. If you want to create a scene of a ball rolling across a lawn, for example, you can create one keyframe showing a ball on the left side of the lawn, another keyframe showing the same ball on the right side of the same lawn, and tell Flash to create a *tween*, or all the keyframes in between. Bingo—scene done.

Tip: You can combine frame-by-frame animation with tweening. In fact, that's what a lot of professional animators do: Take care of the complex stuff themselves, and rely on Flash to fill in the spots that aren't as critical.

Tweening saves you more than just time and effort; when you go to publish your animation, it also saves you file size. That's because Flash doesn't save every single frame of a tweened animation the way it does with a frame-by-frame animation. Instead, for tweened animations, Flash saves only the keyframes you create, plus the information it needs to generate the tweened frames from your keyframes. And smaller file sizes are a good thing—especially if you're planning to put your finished animation up on a Web site. (You can find out more about file sizes, including tips for optimization, in Chapter 14.)

Dividing Your Animation into Layers: The Common Sense Approach

When it comes to divvying your animation up into layers, there's no hard and fast rule. Some animators like to put every single element on its own separate layer; others take a more conservative approach. In general, the more layers you have, the more control you have over your animation, because you can change and position the content on each layer independently.

But on the downside, the more layers you have, the more organizational overhead and potential confusion you have—and at the end of the day you may find you don't actually need all that control.

While this is one of those areas that's more art than science, here are a few questions to ask yourself when you're trying to decide whether (and how) to break up your animation into layers.

- **What's most likely to change?** If you know going into a Flash project that a particular design idea might change (for example, your team's still arguing over whether the ad you're developing should feature two people talking to each other or one person talking into a cell phone), by all means put those two people on their own layers so you can switch them out easily if you need to.

- **What moves independently of the objects nearest it?** Any moving object that you position on or near other objects needs to live in its own layer. Eyes and mouths are good examples; you want to be able to fine-tune eye and mouth movement to create different expressions on your characters without having to redraw the entire face every time. Same with characters' legs (you want to leave yourself the option of changing your characters' stroll to a sprint without having to redraw their bodies every time).

- **What do you want to tween?** You can't place more than one tween on a layer. (Well, technically, you *can*, but you don't want to: Flash generates unreliable results for multiple tweens on a single layer.) So if you know you want to create a specific motion tween—a star streaking across the sky, for example—place the tweened star on its own layer, whether or not it's positioned near any other objects on any other layers.

In this section, you see examples of both types of tweening Flash offers: shape tweening and motion tweening.

Shape Tweening (Morphing)

Shape tweening—sometimes referred to as *morphing*—lets you create an effect that makes one object appear as though it's slowly turning into another object. All you have to do is draw the beginning object and the ending object, and Flash does all the rest.

For example, say you create a keyframe containing a circle. Then, 10 frames along the Timeline, you create another keyframe containing a star. You apply a shape tween to the frame span, and Flash generates all the incremental frames necessary to show the circle slowly—frame by frame—transforming itself into a star when you run the animation.

When to Use a Motion Tween (and When to Use a Shape Tween)

There seems to be a lot of overlap between motion tweening and shape tweening. If I can tween motion with a shape tween and size, color, and rotation with either one, what's the real difference between the two? When should I use one over the other?

It's true, there's a lot of overlap between shape and motion tweens. Using both, you can tween straight-line motion (position), color and gradient, transparency, and transforms (scale, rotation, and skew).

The important differences between the two are: *Shape tweens* work only on editable shapes; *motion tweens* work only on symbols, grouped objects, and text blocks. Motion tweens are the only way you can tween nonlinear motion (for example, if you want to show an object moving in an arc, a squiggle, or a curlicue).

So here's the bottom line: You must use a shape tween when you want to work with an editable object or when you want to show a shape change, from a simple square-to-circle redraw to a step-by-step morphing effect from, say, an acorn to a tree. You must use a motion tween when you want to show motion that doesn't follow a straight-line path (for example, an object that spins, swoops, or shrinks and expands).

In all other cases, the choice is yours.

Note: Shape tweens work only on editable graphics. If you want to tween a symbol (Chapter 7), you need to use a motion tween. If you want to tween a group of objects or a chunk of text, you need to ungroup the objects (Chapter 5), break apart the text (Chapter 6), or use a motion tween.

Shape tweening lets you change more than just an object's shape over a series of frames. Using a shape tween, you can also change an object's size, color, transparency, position, scale, and rotation.

To create a shape tween:

1. **Select the frame where you want your tween to begin (for example, Frame 1).**

   Flash highlights the selected frame.

2. **On the Stage, draw the shape you want to begin your tween.**

   In Figure 3-10, the beginning shape's a raindrop.

3. **If the selected frame isn't a keyframe (if you don't see a dot in the frame), turn it into a keyframe by selecting Insert → Timeline → Keyframe.**

   Flash displays a dot in the frame to let you know it's a keyframe.

4. **Select the frame where you want your tween to end (for example, Frame 10).**

   Flash highlights the selected frame.

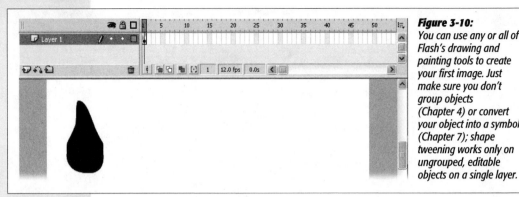

Figure 3-10:
You can use any or all of Flash's drawing and painting tools to create your first image. Just make sure you don't group objects (Chapter 4) or convert your object into a symbol (Chapter 7); shape tweening works only on ungrouped, editable objects on a single layer.

5. **Insert an ending point for your tween (and a clean, fresh Stage on which to draw your ending shape) by selecting Insert → Timeline → Blank Keyframe.**

   The Stage clears, the playhead moves to the selected frame, and Flash displays a hollow dot in the selected frame to let you know it's a keyframe.

Tip: As explained on page 87, you can carry over your beginning image from the first keyframe and make changes to it by choosing Insert → Timeline → Keyframe (instead of Insert → Timeline → Blank Keyframe).

---

6. **On the Stage, use Flash's drawing and painting tools to draw the shape you want to end your tween.**

   Your ending shape can differ from your first shape in terms of position, color, transparency, rotation, skew, and size, so go wild. In Figure 3-11, the ending shape's a puddle.

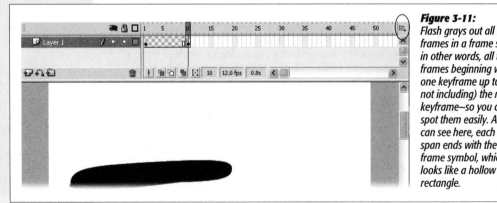

Figure 3-11:
Flash grays out all the frames in a frame span—in other words, all the frames beginning with one keyframe up to (but not including) the next keyframe—so you can spot them easily. As you can see here, each frame span ends with the end frame symbol, which looks like a hollow rectangle.

7. **On the Timeline, click to select any frame in the frame span.**

   Flash highlights the selected frame and the Property Inspector appears, as shown in Figure 3-12. (If you don't see it, select Window → Properties and then, from the pop-up menu that appears, turn on the checkbox next to Properties.)

To create a shape tween, from the Tween drop-down box, select Shape. (If the Tween drop-down appears grayed out, you haven't selected a frame; make sure that you're clicking in a frame and not just above, where Flash lists the frame numbers.)

8. **In the Property Inspector, head to the Tween drop-down box (Figure 3-12) and select Shape.**

   Flash turns the frame span a nice lime color and inserts an arrow to let you know you've successfully added a shape tween. And in the Property Inspector, shape-related tween options (Ease and Blend) appear.

Note: If you have Tinted Frames turned off, Flash doesn't turn your frame span green to let you know you've successfully added a shape tween; instead, Flash applies a gray crosshatch pattern and turns the tween arrow blue. To turn on Tinted Frames, click the Options menu (the tiny icon you see on the far right of the Timeline, just after the frame numbers, as shown in Figure 3-11); then turn on the checkbox next to Tinted Frames.

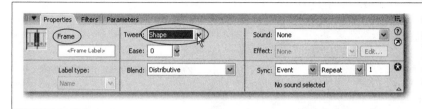

Figure 3-12:
As soon as you click a frame in your frame span, Flash displays the Property Inspector for frames.

9. **If you like, set the Ease and Blend shape-tween options (Figure 3-13).**

   Ease tells Flash to speed up (or slow down) the tween. If you want your tween to start out normally but speed up at the end, click the drop-down arrow next to Ease and drag the slider that appears until a positive number appears. To tell Flash to start your tween normally but slow down at the end, drag the Ease slider until a negative number appears. (Zero means that when you play your animation, the tween appears to be the same speed throughout.)

   Blend tells Flash how picky you want it to be when it draws its in-between frames. If you want to preserve the hard angles of your original shape, click on the Blend drop-down box and select Angular; if you want Flash to smooth out the hard edges so that the tween appears smoother, select Distributive.

10. **Test your shape by selecting Control → Play.**

    Flash plays your shape tween on the Stage (Figure 3-14).

Shape Hints

Flash does a bang-up job when it comes to tweening simple shapes: circles, squares, stars, rain drops. But the more complicated the images you want to tween, the harder Flash has to work to calculate how to generate the in-between images.

WORKAROUND WORKSHOP

When Bad Things Happen to Good Tweens

You can apply a shape tween only to an editable shape. You *can't* apply a shape tween to a grouped object, a symbol, or a block of text.

But if you try, Flash won't exactly put itself out to let you know what's happening. Instead, when you test your tween, Flash mutely displays your beginning image, then a blank Stage (instead of tweened images), followed by your ending image. Clearly, something's not working—but *what?*

Flash does offer a couple of hints, but you have to know where to look for them.

- In the Timeline, check to make sure the tween arrow appears in your frame span. If a dashed line appears instead, you know that Flash recognizes your tween but doesn't approve of it (although you still don't know why).

- In the tween section of the Property Inspector, check to see whether Flash is displaying a warning icon (a little yellow triangle with an exclamation point). If you see one, click it to display a somewhat-helpful pop-up message like the one shown here, which warns you that you're trying to tween a non-editable object.

The fix? Do one of the following and then test your animation again:

- If your object is grouped, select it and then choose Modify → Ungroup to ungroup it. (Unfortunately, Flash has problems applying multiple shape tweens to the same *layer;* it gets confused trying to figure out which shape you want to morph into which other shape. So if you're trying to morph an image made up of several different shapes, you need to place each ungrouped shape on a separate layer [Chapter 8] and tween them all separately.)

- If your object's a symbol (this includes a block of text), you need to change it into an editable object. To change it, select your object and then choose Modify → Break Apart.

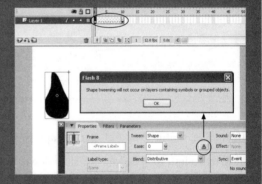

And if you think about it, that difficulty makes sense. Because complex beginning-and-ending images like a stylized acorn and tree (Figures 3-15 and 3-16) contain a bunch of editable lines, shapes, and colors, Flash has to guess at which elements are most important and how you want the morph to progress from the first keyframe to the last.

Sometimes, Flash guesses correctly; other times, you need to give it a few hints. Adding *shape hints* to your tweens tells Flash how you want it to create each in-between frame, with the result that your finished tween appears more realistic— more how *you* want it to be.

In short, shape hints give you more (but not complete, by any means) control over the shape-tweened sections of your animation.

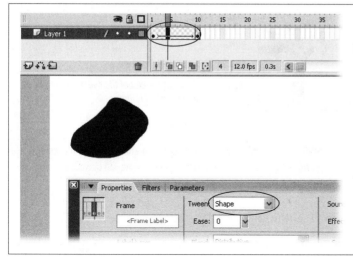

Figure 3-13:
You know you've successfully applied a shape tween when Flash displays an arrow in your frame span like the one shown here. You'll also notice that shape-related tweening options appear in the Property Inspector: namely, Ease (to speed up or slow down your tween) and Blend (to tell Flash to preserve hard corners and angles from frame to frame or smooth them out). To preview the in-between frames Flash generated for you, just select any frame in the frame span.

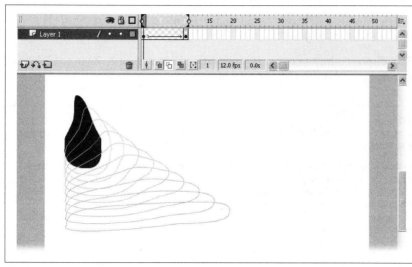

Figure 3-14:
When you run your animation, your beginning image appears to morph into your ending image, thanks to the in-between frames Flash generates when you create your shape tween. Here—because the pages of a book can't show motion—onion skin outlines (page 115) attempt to represent the animated tween you see on the Stage.

Figure 3-15:
Top: The original acorn drawing: so far, so good.

Middle: Flash's first attempt at generating an in-between frame is a little scary.

Bottom: Clearly, the acorn is changing and growing, but that's about all you can say for this generated image.

Figure 3-16:
Left: You can almost make out the outline of a tree now.

Middle: This one's getting there…

Right: And finally, at the end of the tween, Flash makes it to your original ending image.

Note: Shape hints are especially valuable when you're working on an animation that moves at a relatively slow frame rate; in other words, in situations when each separate frame will be visible to your audience's naked eye.

To add shape hints to a shape tween:

1. **Select the first frame of your tween.**

   Flash highlights the selected frame.

2. **Choose Modify → Shape → Add Shape Hint (or press Ctrl+Shift+H [Windows] or Shift-⌘-H [Mac]).**

   Flash displays a hint (a red circle containing a letter from A–Z) in the center of your shape, as shown in Figure 3-17 (top).

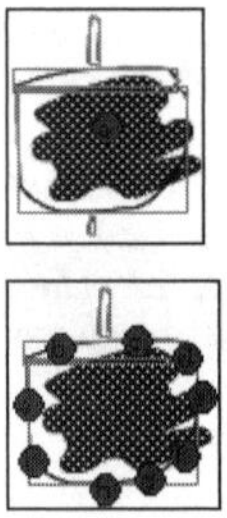

Figure 3-17:
Top: When you add a shape hint, Flash places it at the center of your object. All you have to do is drag it to the edge of your object.

Bottom: The more shape hints you use (and the more accurately you place them around the edge of your object), the more closely Flash attempts to preserve your shape as it generates the tween frames. Make sure you place the hints in alphabetical order as you outline your shape. If you find after several tries that Flash doesn't seem to be taking your hints, your shapes might be too complex or too dissimilar to tween effectively. In that case, you'll want to create additional keyframes or even consider replacing your tween with a frame-by-frame animation.

3. **Drag the hint to the edge of your shape.**

   Figure 3-17 (bottom) shows the result of dragging several hints to the edge of your shape.

4. **Repeat as many times as necessary, placing hints around the outline of the object in alphabetical order.**

   The bigger or more oddly-shaped your object, the more hints you'll need. Placing a hint at each peak and valley of your object tells Flash to preserve the shape of your beginning object as much as possible as it morphs toward the shape of your ending object.

5. **Test your animation by clicking Control → Play.**

The tweened frames of your animation conform, more or less, to the hints you provided. Figures 3-18 and 3-19 show you an example.

Figure 3-18:
Left: The original acorn is the same here as it was in Figure 3-15.

Middle: Compare this attempt at generating a first in-between frame to the one in Figure 3-15. It's not exactly a prize pig, but it's better.

Right: Already, you can see the form of the tree taking shape.

Figure 3-19:
Top: Here, the already-pretty-well-shaped tree looks as though it's about to burst out of the acorn outline.

Middle: Compared to tweening without shape hints (see Figure 3-16), this tween appears much smoother; you don't see the Flash-generated squiggly lines that you see in Figure 3-16.

Bottom: The final frame of any tween appears the same, whether or not you use shape hints.

Motion Tweening

Motion tweening is similar to shape tweening: To create both types of tweens, all you need to do is create a beginning image and an ending image and then tell Flash to generate all the "in-between" frames to create an animated sequence. And you can create a lot of the same effects using both types of tweens: You can create a series of frames that, when run, show an object changing size, position, color and gradient, transparency, rotation, and skew.

But beyond that, there are two important differences between shape tweening and motion tweening:

- **Tweenable objects.** While shape tweening works only on editable objects, motion tweening works only on noneditable objects: symbols, grouped objects (page 156), and text. And motion tweening, unlike shape tweening, limits you to one object per layer. (The single object can be a grouped object or a symbol containing multiple shapes; it just has to be a single object as far as Flash is concerned.)

- **Nonlinear paths.** With motion tweening, you can create a series of frames that show an object moving across the Stage in a nonlinear fashion: for example, swooping, diving, arcing, rotating, or pulsing. You can't do that with shape tweening.

To create a basic (linear) motion tween:

1. **Select the frame and layer where you want your tween to begin (for example, Frame 1 in Layer 1).**

   Flash highlights the selected frame.

Note: Flash won't let you create a motion tween if you have more than one object (one symbol, one grouped object, or one text element) on the Stage. To motion tween multiple objects, you need to distribute each object to its own layer and then tween them all separately. The box on page 122 shows you how.

---

2. **On the Stage, draw the shape (or create the text) you want to begin your tween.**

   In Figure 3-20, the beginning shape is a fly on the right side of the Stage.

3. **Convert the drawing to a noneditable form by selecting all the elements of your drawing and then choosing either Modify → Group (to flatten all the elements into a single group) or Modify → Convert to Symbol (to convert the editable drawing into a reusable symbol).**

Tip: For a quick refresher on symbols, see page 19. For the full story, see Chapter 7.

   Flash displays a box around the entire drawing to show that it's now a single, noneditable entity (Figure 3-20).

4. **If the selected frame isn't a keyframe (if you don't see a dot in the frame), turn it into a keyframe by selecting Insert → Timeline → Keyframe.**

   Flash displays a dot in the frame to let you know it's a keyframe.

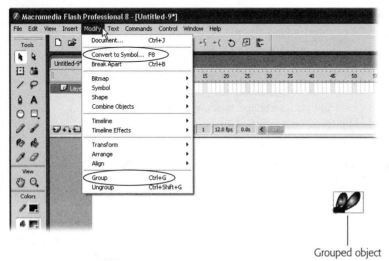

Figure 3-20:
You can't motion tween an editable object; you have to use a symbol, a grouped object, or a block of text. This restriction might seem capricious, but it's actually practical. If you drew a complex object consisting of seven different shapes and didn't flatten it into a symbol or a group, Flash wouldn't know which shape to move where.

Grouped object

5. Select the frame where you want your tween to end (for example, Frame 10).

   Flash highlights the selected frame.

6. Insert an ending point for your tween by selecting Insert → Timeline → Keyframe.

   The playhead moves to the selected frame, and Flash displays a solid dot in the selected frame to let you know it's now a keyframe, as shown in Figure 3-21.

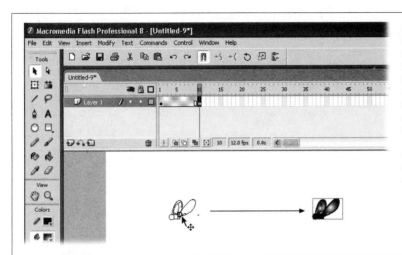

Figure 3-21:
Here, you see a symbol being dragged from the left side of the Stage to the right side. Moving a symbol is the quickest way to create a motion tween, but it's certainly not the only way. Using the Properties, Color Mixer, and Transform panels, you can create a tween that morphs an object's color, transparency, rotation, scale, and skew.

7. On the Stage, drag the object to somewhere else on the screen.

   You can most easily create a motion tween by carrying over your beginning image from the first keyframe and moving it, but you can create a much more sophisticated motion tween. To change the color, transparency, or size of your ending object, you can use the Properties, Color Mixer, and Transform panels.

8. Select any frame in the frame span.

   Flash highlights the selected frame and the Property Inspector appears, as shown in Figure 3-22.

9. In the Property Inspector, click the Tween drop-down box (Figure 3-22) and then, from the menu that appears, select Motion.

   Or, to tell Flash to do this step for you, right-click the selected frame and choose Create Motion Tween from the context menu that appears.

   Flash turns the frame span bluish-purple and inserts an arrow (Figure 3-23) to let you know you've successfully added your motion tween. And in the Property Inspector, motion-related tween options appear: Scale, Ease (Edit), Rotate, Orient to path, Sync, and Snap.

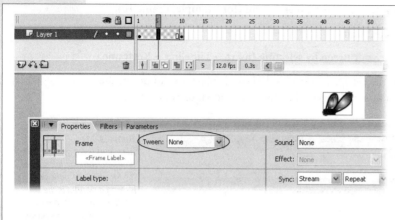

Figure 3-22:
Clicking in the frame span tells Flash to display the Property Inspector associated with that frame span. If you don't see the Property Inspector, select Window → Properties and then, from the pop-up menu that appears, turn on the checkbox next to Properties. Finally, click the Tween drop-down box (circled) and, from the menu that appears, change None to Motion.

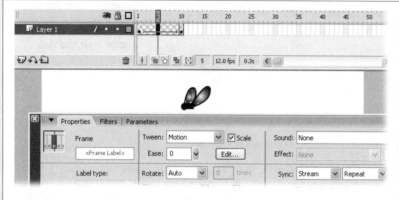

Figure 3-23:
Flash adds a motion tween automatically (the instant you select Motion from the Tween drop-down box), so depending on the frame you selected to display the Property Inspector, the content on the Stage might change. For example, here, Frame 5 is selected, so the contents of Frame 5 (a tweened image of the fly halfway across the Stage) appear.

Tip: If you see a dashed line in the frame span (instead of an arrow), that's Flash telling you your motion tween is broken. Check to make sure you're tweening noneditable objects (symbols, grouped objects, or text blocks) and that you've created both a beginning and an ending keyframe for your tween.

---

10. **If you like, set the Ease option.**

   Ease tells Flash to speed up (or slow down) the tween. If you want your tween to start out normally but speed up at the end, click the drop-down arrow next to Ease and then drag the slider that appears until a positive number appears. To tell Flash to start your tween normally but slow down at the end, drag the Ease slider until a negative number appears. (Zero means that when you play your animation, the tween appears to be the same speed throughout.)

   If you're running Flash Professional, you can create a custom speed that varies throughout the tween. (Perhaps you're tweening a scene of a mouse running past a gauntlet of cats and want your mouse to speed up every time it passes a cat and slow down in-between.) To do so, click Edit. Then, in the Custom Ease

In/Ease Out window that appears, drag the diagonal tween line to specify the relative speed for each frame of your frame span. When you finish, click OK.

Note: Because the other motion tween–related options are useful only in the context of specific motion-related effects, "Orient to path" and Snap are described beginning on page 105; Scale and Rotate in Chapter 5; and Sync in Chapter 8.

---

11. **Test your motion tween by selecting Control → Play.**

    Flash plays your motion tween on the Stage.

Motion guide layers (moving along a nonstraight path)

The previous section shows you how to create a straight-line motion tween, where an object appears to move from one point on the Stage to another. This section takes motion tweening a little further by explaining how you can use a motion guide layer to create a nonlinear motion tween.

Note: In Flash, there are other kinds of layers besides the generic ones you learned to create earlier in this chapter. There are also *guide layers* to help you position objects precisely on the Stage (Chapter 4), *mask layers* to hide and display specific portions of your images (Chapter 6) for a peek-a-boo effect, and *motion guide layers* to create a nonlinear motion tween (these are the layers you get acquainted with in this section).

Using a motion guide layer to create a nonlinear motion tween is surprisingly easy. All you have to do is create a regular straight-line motion tween, as described on page 100. Then, you create a special type of layer called a motion guide layer. On the motion guide layer, you draw the path you want your object to follow. You can draw a twisty line, a curve, or whatever you like. Then you drag your objects to the beginning and the end of the path, respectively. That's it—dead simple. You see a step-by-step example below.

Note: You don't see the actual path when you run your animation; you see it only when you're editing your animation and testing it. You can think of a path as a kind of guideline that "shows" your objects how to move along a motion tween.

To create a tween along a nonlinear path using a motion guide layer:

1. **Create a basic, straight-line motion tween.**

   The steps for creating one begin on page 100.

2. **On the Timeline, select the keyframe that begins your tween.**

   Flash highlights the selected keyframe as well as the name of the layer you're working in (the *active* layer). In Figure 3-24, the active layer is Layer 1.

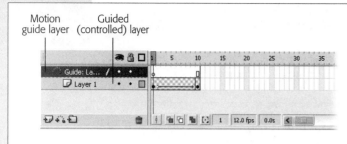

Motion   Guided
guide layer   (controlled) layer

Figure 3-24:
*When you create a motion guide layer,
Flash places it directly above the active
layer–and indents the active layer– to
give you a visual reminder that the
motion guide layer controls the active
layer. As you see in the following steps,
the path you draw on your motion guide
layer determines how the objects on your
active layer behave during a motion
tween.*

Tip: You can rename a layer from Flash's unimaginative Layer 1, Layer 2, and Layer 3 to something more
meaningful, like Fly Motion. (Doing so will help you remember what each layer contains–especially useful if you create animations with multiple layers.) To rename a layer: On the Timeline, double-click the
name of the layer you want to rename. In the editable name field that appears, type a new name and then
press Enter.

3. **On the Timeline, click Add Motion Guide (the icon that looks like a slinky, as
   in Figure 3-24).**

   If you prefer, you can right-click the active layer and then, from the context
   menu that appears, select Add Motion Guide.

   Flash creates a motion guide layer, selects it, and places it directly above the
   active layer (Figure 3-24).

4. **With the motion guide layer still selected, draw a *path* (the line you want your
   motion tween to follow) on the Stage.**

   The Pencil is an easy tool to use for this task—especially with the Smooth
   option turned on, as described on page 60. But you can use any of Flash's drawing tools to draw your path. Figure 3-25 shows you an example.

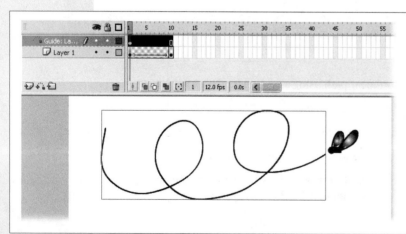

Figure 3-25:
*You can use any drawing or
painting tool you like to
create your path. If the path
you create is a closed shape
(like a circle) Flash will
decide which direction the
tween should go.*

Tip: Some folks find it hard to concentrate on drawing a path with objects in the way. To temporarily hide the objects on the Stage: On the Timeline next to your *non*–motion guide layer, click the Show/Hide All Layers icon (the icon that looks like an eye, as shown in Figure 3-24). After you finish drawing your path, click the Show/Hide All Layers icon again to redisplay the objects on the Stage.

5. **In the non–motion guide layer, click to select the beginning keyframe for your animation.**

   Flash highlights the selected keyframe.

6. **Click the center of your image to select it and then drag the image until the center "snaps" onto one end of your path.**

   Flash displays a little circle in the center of your image to help you center the image directly onto your path, as shown in Figure 3-26.

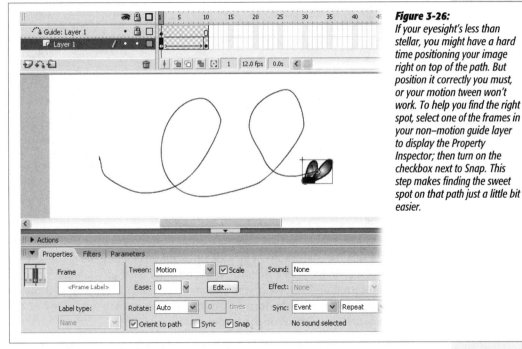

Figure 3-26:
If your eyesight's less than stellar, you might have a hard time positioning your image right on top of the path. But position it correctly you must, or your motion tween won't work. To help you find the right spot, select one of the frames in your non–motion guide layer to display the Property Inspector; then turn on the checkbox next to Snap. This step makes finding the sweet spot on that path just a little bit easier.

Note: If you don't position the center circle of your image precisely on the path, your motion tween won't work. (Your image doesn't have to be at the very *end* of the path, but it *does* have to be exactly *on* the path.) If you have trouble positioning your image, make sure you're selecting it by clicking in its center (that helps Flash position its helpful circle). If that doesn't help, select the first keyframe in your animation and then, in the Property Inspector that appears, turn on the checkbox next to Snap. Doing so tells Flash to widen the center circle it displays on your image when you move it near the path so that you know when to let go of the mouse.

7. **Select the ending keyframe for your animation.**

   Flash highlights the selected keyframe.

8. **On the Stage, click the center of your image to select it and then drag the image until the center "snaps" onto the other end of your path.**

   Again, as you drag your image, Flash displays a little circle in the center of your image to help you position it directly onto your path.

9. **Test your guided motion tween by selecting Control → Play.**

   Flash plays your motion tween on the Stage, moving your object along the path you defined in step 4. Figure 3-27 shows you an example.

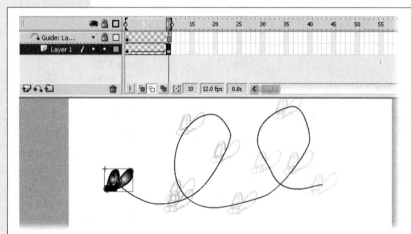

Figure 3-27:
Here you see the effect of a motion guide layer: The fly buzzes along according to a nonlinear, loopy path–much more realistic and interesting than a straight shot from right to left. But notice that the fly always faces straight ahead, even when it's upside down. If this isn't the effect you want in your motion tweens, check out the "Orient to path" section coming up next.

Orient to path

If you've created a nonlinear path using a motion guide layer (page 103), you may have noticed that the object stays right-side up as it moves along the path—even if the path's a loop-de-loop, like the one in Figure 3-27. That effect might be what you want. If it isn't, and you want your object to turn to face the path as it moves along, you can do so easily by turning on the "Orient to path" checkbox in the motion tween section of the Property Inspector (Figure 3-28).

You see the effect of turning on the "Orient to path" checkbox in Figure 3-28.

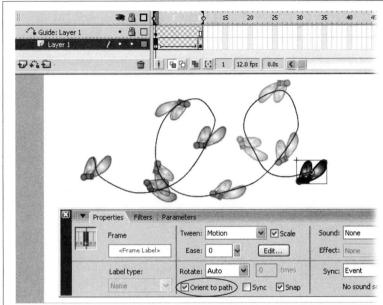

Figure 3-28:
Turning on "Orient to path" in the Property Inspector (click any frame in your non-motion guide layer to view Frame properties in the Property Inspector) tells Flash to turn the object as it moves along the path. You get a much more realistic motion tween.

Part Two:
Advanced Drawing and Animation

2

Organizing Frames and Layers

Part 1 of this book gets you started launching Flash, creating your own drawings, and transforming them into moving animations. Most animation work, though, takes place after you've got all the frames and layers in place. Like a film director slaving away in the cutting room, as an animator you spend most of your time testing, editing, and retesting your movie.

This chapter is your crash course in Flash animation editing. Here you'll see how to reorganize your animation horizontally (over time) by cutting, pasting, and rearranging frames on the Timeline. You'll also see how to reorganize your animation vertically by shuffling and restacking the layers you've added to it.

Working with Frames

When you create an animation, you build it from frames and keyframes. Editing your document is a simple matter of moving, cutting, and pasting those frames until they look good and work well. You can perform these operations on individual frames or on multiple frames by combining them into groups, as you'll see at the end of this section.

Copying and Pasting Frames

Copy and paste are the world's favorite computer commands with good reason. These functions let you create a piece of work once (a word, line, shape, drawing, or what have you) and then quickly recreate it to build something even more complex with a minimum of effort. Well, Flash lets you cut, copy, and paste not just the content of your frames but your frames themselves, from one part of your Timeline to another.

Copying and pasting frames is a great way to cut down on your development time. Here's how it works. Say you have a series of frames showing a weasel unwrapping a stick of chewing gum. It's a gag scene, one you want to repeat throughout your animation for comic effect. Instead of having to insert all the keyframes and regular frames every time you want to slip in the weasel gag, all you need to do is copy the weasel frames once and then paste them onto your Timeline wherever you want them to go.

Furthermore, copying and pasting isn't just useful for those times when you want a carbon copy of a scene. If you want to change something in each pasted scene—the brand of chewing gum the weasel's unwrapping, for example—you can do that, too, after you've pasted the frames.

Copying and pasting frames works almost exactly like copying and pasting words or drawn objects—with a few twists. Here are some points to keep in mind:

- As usual, you must select what you're going to copy before you set off the command. You select frames in the Timeline (see page 34 for a refresher).

- If the frames you're selecting contain layers, make sure you select all the layers in each frame, as shown in Figure 4-1.

- If you're copying a series of tweened frames, beware: While Flash displays tweened frames as separate, distinct images, they're not. As you learned in Chapter 3, only keyframes contain distinct images. So if you copy a series of tweened frames beginning with a frame (as opposed to beginning with a keyframe), you get an unexpected result when you go to paste those frames. Instead of the contents of your first frame, Flash begins pasting with the content of the *previous keyframe.*

- Flash doesn't limit you to pasting within the same document. After you copy, you can open any other Flash animation and paste the frames right in.

Note: Although Cut, Copy, and Paste usually travel as a threesome, in Flash things work a little differently. The Cut Frames command on the Edit → Timeline submenu doesn't actually cut *frames*; instead, it cuts the *contents* of the selected frame. To get rid of the frame itself, you need to use Edit → Timeline → Remove Frames, as described in the box on page 115.

The process of copying and pasting frames follows the same basic steps every time:

1. **On the Timeline, select the frames you want to copy.**

   You probably want to make sure that the set of frames you choose begins with a keyframe, as described in the third bullet point above. Either way, Flash highlights the selected frame(s) and moves the playhead to the last selected frame.

2. **Choose Edit → Timeline → Copy Frames (or press Ctrl+Alt+C on Windows; Control-⌘-C on The Mac). Select the keyframe where you want to begin pasting the copied frames.**

   In other words, select the frame after which you want to add the copied frames.

You can paste copied frames into the document you currently have open or into another document (select File → Open to open another Flash document). If the frames you copied contain multiple layers, make sure the keyframe you select contains the same number of multiple layers.

3. **Select Edit → Timeline → Paste Frames.**

Flash pastes the copied frames, replacing the currently selected keyframe with the first copied frame. If you pasted frames into the middle of a Timeline, Flash repositions your existing frames *after* the last pasted frame.

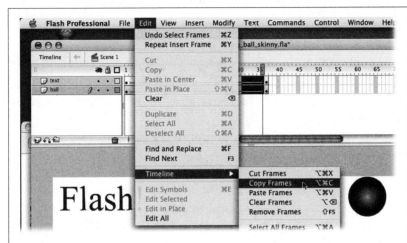

Figure 4-1:
To select multiple frames, click the first frame of the series you want to select; then Shift-click the last frame. Flash automatically selects all the frames in between. If you know you're going to be copying and pasting frames in the same document, you can speed up the process by pressing the Alt key (Windows) or the Option key (Mac) while you drag a copy of the selected frames from their original location to where you like on the Timeline.

Moving Frames (Keyframes)

The Timeline is serial: When you run your animation, Flash displays the content in Frame 1, followed by the content in Frame 2, followed by the content in Frame 3, and so on. If you change your mind about the order in which you want frames to appear, all you need to do is move them.

Simple in theory—but moving frames in Flash isn't quite as cut and dried as you might think. As you may recall if you've had a chance to read through Chapter 3, only keyframes can contain actual images; regular frames contain either tweened or "held over" copies of the images placed in the previous keyframe. So whether you move a frame or a keyframe, you end up with a keyframe. Here's how it works:

- **Moving a keyframe.** When you move a keyframe, what Flash actually moves is the keyframe's content and keyframe designation; Flash leaves behind a regular frame in the original keyframe's place. (And that regular frame may or not be empty, depending on whether or not a keyframe precedes it on the Timeline.)

- **Moving a regular frame.** Flash moves the regular frame, but turns the moved frame into a keyframe. (If you move a series of regular frames, Flash just turns the first moved frame into a keyframe.)

Tip: There's another way to change the order in which Flash plays frames: by creating an ActionScript action, as described in Chapter 10. Creating an action lets you tell Flash how to play your frames: backwards, for example, or by rerunning the first 10 frames three times and then moving on. You want to use ActionScript (as opposed to moving frames) when you want to give your audience the choice of viewing your animation in different ways.

To move frames, you simply select and then drag them. The process is the same whether you're moving frames, keyframes, or both, and all the usual rules of frame selection described earlier in this chapter still apply.

Here are the steps in detail:

1. **On the Timeline, select the frame(s) you want to move.**

   Flash highlights the selected frame (or frames) and moves the playhead to the last selected frame.

2. **Drag the selected frame(s) to the frame *after* which you want to place the selected frames.**

   As you drag the selected frames, Flash displays a gray box above your cursor to help you position them (Figure 4-2).

Tip: If you begin to drag your selected frames and see Flash highlighting the Timeline, which tells you it's selecting additional frames (instead of displaying a neat gray box, which tells you it's moving the selected frames), stop right there and start the whole process over. When your cursor is above the frame after which you want to move the selected frames, let go of your mouse button.

   Flash deletes the selected frames from their original position, and inserts them in their new location.

Tip: If dragging your frames isn't working, you can always copy and paste the frames you want to move (page 111). Then use Edit → Timeline → Remove Frames to delete them from their original location (page 115).

Editing Multiple Frames

Imagine you've just completed a 250-frame animation showing a character in a red t-shirt demonstrating your company's latest product, an electronic egg slicer. Suddenly, your boss comes in and declares that red's out. (Red's the color your competitor's using for *their* egg slicer launch.) You have, your boss declares, until the end of the day to change all 250 frames.

Now, if you had to change all 250 frames by hand, you'd never be able to get it done in time; and even if you did, you'd probably make a few mistakes along the way, like accidentally repositioning the t-shirt in a couple of frames or missing a few frames altogether. But it's precisely this kind of en masse editing job that Flash's multiple frame editing capability was designed to handle.

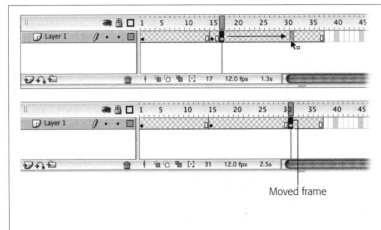

Figure 4-2:

Top: Click the frame you want to move and then let go of your mouse. Drag the frame you just selected. If Flash displays a gray selection-sized box above your cursor, you're gold: Drag to the point in the Timeline where you want to insert the moved frame (here, Frame 30) and then drop it. (If you don't see a gray box, you need to start the process over.)

Bottom: Here, you can tell the move succeeded because the keyframe and end frame indicators have disappeared from their original locations (Frames 16 and 17) and reappeared in their new locations (Frames 29 and 30).

Moved frame

Remove vs. Cut vs. Clear

Flash offers several commands you can use to get rid of your frames (and the content associated with those frames): remove, cut, and clear. Unfortunately, it's not immediately clear which command does what.

Here's what these commands do to selected frames:

- **Edit → Timeline → Remove Frames.** Removing a frame deletes that frame from the Timeline—*unless* the frame happens to be a keyframe that's not followed either by another keyframe, or by nothing. If you attempt to remove a keyframe followed by a regular frame, Flash deletes the frame immediately to the right of the keyframe instead (go figure). To be safe, if you want to remove a keyframe—in other words, if you want to delete a keyframe from the Timeline—you first want to *clear* the keyframe (strip the frame of its keyframe status); *then* you can remove the frame itself.

- **Edit → Timeline → Cut Frames.** Cutting a frame deletes the content on the Stage associated with that frame (in other words, turns the frame into a blank keyframe). If the immediately succeeding frame is a regular frame, Flash turns that succeeding frame into a keyframe. Flash stores the contents of the cut frames on the Clipboard, so that you can restore them by choosing Edit → Timeline → Paste Frames.

- **Edit → Timeline → Clear Frames.** Clearing frames is identical to cutting them, with one difference: Flash doesn't store the contents of the cleared frames (so you can't restore them).

Using a technique called *onion skinning*, you can see the contents of several different frames all at once. The currently selected frame appears on Stage it always does; the other frames you've told Flash using *onion markers* that you want to see appear grayed out, so you can tell which is which. Onion skinning lets you quickly identify (and change) the frames containing red t-shirts.

Onion skinning is also useful for those times when you want to hand-draw an "in-between" frame because you can see both the preceding and succeeding frames on the Stage at the same time.

Note: Technically speaking, when you edit multiple frames in Flash, you're actually editing multiple *keyframes*. Keyframes are the only frames that contain unique, editable art. (Regular frames just "hold over" the contents of the previous keyframe, and Flash stores tweened frames not as editable images, but a bunch of calculations.)

To edit multiple frames using onion skinning:

1. **In the Timeline, click the Edit Multiple Frames icon.**

    Flash displays multiple frames on the Stage and adds onion markers to the frame display (Figure 4-3, top). These beginning and ending onion markers tell Flash which frames you want it to display on the Stage.

2. **Click the Modify Onion Markers icon.**

    Flash displays a pop-up menu.

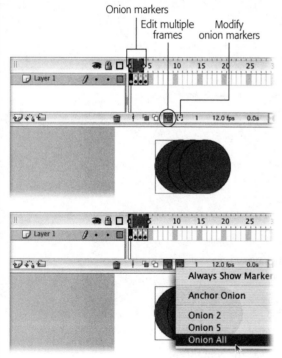

Onion markers
Edit multiple frames
Modify onion markers

Figure 4-3:
Top: When you click Edit Multiple Frames, Flash shows the content of a bunch of frames on a single Stage. Unfortunately, Flash might miss a frame or two. To tell Flash to show the content of all your frames, click Modify Onion Markers and then, from the pop-up menu that appears, select Onion All. (You can also drag the onion markers separately to enclose a different subset of frames.)

Bottom: Here you see the result of selecting Onion All. The onion markers surround the entire frame span (Frame 1 through Frame 4) and all four images appear on the same Stage, ready for you to edit en masse.

3. **From the pop-up menu, select Onion All (Figure 4-3, bottom).**

   Flash displays onion markers from the beginning of your Timeline's frame span to the end, and shows the contents of each of your frames on the Stage. (If you don't want to edit all the frames in your animation, you can drag the onion markers independently to surround whatever subset of your frame span you want.)

4. **Edit the frames.**

   Because you can see all the content on a single Stage, you can make your edits more easily than having to hunt and peck individually through every frame in your animation. In Figure 4-4, all four frames' contents are first recolored and then moved in one fell swoop.

5. **Click Edit Multiple Frames again.**

   Flash returns to regular one-frame-at-a-time editing mode and displays only the contents of the current frame on the Stage.

Note: You can't edit multiple frames on a locked layer (page 128). In fact, when you click Edit Multiple Frames on a locked layer, Flash doesn't even show you the content of the unselected frames (not even in onion skin form).

Adding Content to Multiple Layers

A layer is nothing more than a named sequence of frames. So you won't be surprised to learn that, after you create a couple of layers as described in Chapter 3, you need to fill up each layer's frames with content. This section shows you how.

When you're working with a single layer, adding content to frames is easy because you don't have to worry about which layer you're working with: You simply click a keyframe and use Flash's drawing and painting tools to create an image on the Stage.

But when you're working with multiple layers—for example, when you're creating a composite drawing by adding a background layer, a foreground layer, and a separate layer for your sound clips—you may find adding content a bit trickier because you have to be aware of the layer to which you're adding your content. Fortunately, as you see in the steps below, the Timeline's Show/Hide icon helps you keep track of which content you've placed on which layers.

Here's how to add content to multiple layers:

1. **Open the file multiple_layers.fla.**

   You can find this file (and all the other examples files for this book) on the "Missing CD" page at *www.missingmanuals.com/cds*.

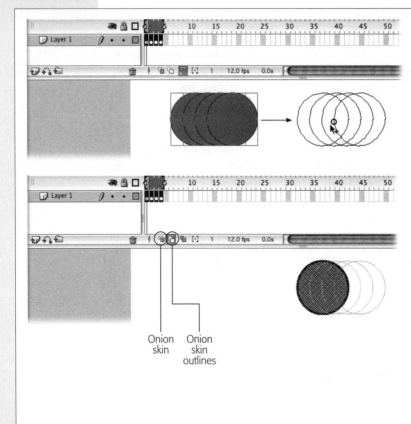

Figure 4-4:
Top: You can work with multiple images just as easily as single images. For example, you can select several (or all of them) and apply whatever edits you like—moving them, coloring them, reshaping them, and so on.

Bottom: If you need to differentiate between the content in the selected frame and the content in the other frames, click Edit Multiple Frames and then click Onion Skin Outlines. All the non-selected frames appear in outline form, as shown here. (Clicking Onion Skin shows the content of non-selected frames in semi-transparent form). With onion skinning turned on, you can see multiple frames, but you can edit only the content of the selected frame; click Edit Multiple Frames to return to multiple-frame editing mode.

Onion skin   Onion skin outlines

2. **Click the first keyframe in Layer 1.**

   Flash highlights the selected frame, as well as the layer name. You also see a little pencil icon that lets you know this frame's now ready for editing.

3. **Use Flash's drawing and painting tools to draw a fence on the Stage.**

   Your fence doesn't have to be fancy; a quick "wooden" fence, like the one in Figure 4-5, is fine.

4. **Hide Layer 1 by clicking the Show/Hide icon next to Layer 1.**

   The content on the Stage temporarily disappears. Flash replaces the Show/Hide icon with an X and draws a slash through the pencil icon next to Layer 1 to let you know this layer is no longer editable (Figure 4-5).

   Note: Technically, you don't *have* to hide the contents of one layer while you're working with another; in fact, in some cases, you *want* to see the contents of both layers on the Stage at the same time (page 120). But for this example, hiding is the best way to go.

Editing Multiple Frames with Find and Replace

Another way to edit the content of multiple frames is to use Flash's "Find and Replace" function. Similar to the find-and-replace you've undoubtedly used in word processing programs, this function lets you search every frame of your animation for a specific bit of text (or even a certain color or bitmap file) and either replace the occurrences yourself, or tell Flash to replace them for you using the text (or color or bitmap file) you tell it to use.

To use this function, select Edit → Find and Replace. Then, in the "Find and Replace" window that appears, head to the For drop-down menu and select the item you want to find. Your choices include Text, Font, Color, Symbol, Sound, Video, and Bitmap.

To change the occurrences yourself, click Find Next or Find All (and then make your changes on the Stage). To tell Flash to change the occurrences, add a Replace With option (for example, the color or text you want to insert) and then click Replace or Replace All.

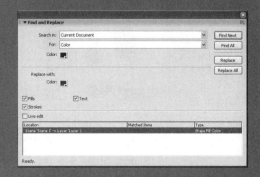

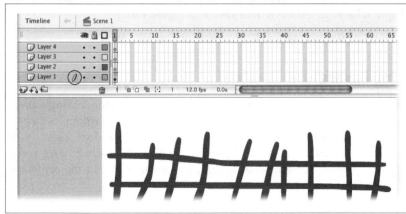

Figure 4-5:
You can tell at a glance which layer's active (editable) by the pencil icon next to the layer's name. Here, Layer 1 is active.

5. **Click the first keyframe in Layer 2.**

   Flash highlights the selected frame, as well as the layer name (Layer 2). Now the pencil icon's next to Layer 2.

6. **Use Flash's drawing and painting tools to draw a few flowers on the Stage.**

   Your workspace should look like the one in Figure 4-6.

7. **Hide Layer 2 by clicking the Show/Hide icon next to Layer 2.**

   The content on the Stage temporarily disappears. Flash replaces the Show/Hide icon with an X and draws a slash through the pencil icon next to Layer 2 to let you know that this layer is no longer editable.

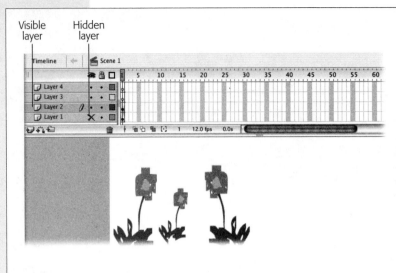

Figure 4-6:
Sometimes you want to see the frame contents of two or more layers at the same time, like when you're trying to line up objects in multiple layers. But sometimes seeing all those different objects on the same Stage—some of which you can edit and some of which you can't, since Flash only lets you edit one layer at a time—is just plain confusing. Here, the fence in the first frame of Layer 1 is hidden (you can tell by the big X in the Show/Hide column) so that you can focus on the contents of Layer 2 (the flowers).

8. Repeat Steps 4–6 for Layers 3 and 4, adding some gray clouds to Layer 3 (Figure 4-7, top) and some flying birds to Layer 4 (Figure 4-7, bottom).

9. To see the content for all four layers, click to uncheck the Show/Hide icon next to Layer 3, Layer 2, and Layer 1, as shown in Figure 4-8.

Flash displays the content for all four layers on the same Stage.

Viewing Layers

This section shows you how to use Flash's layer tools (including locking/unlocking and hiding/showing) to keep from going crazy when you're editing content in multiple layers. (Two layers isn't so bad, but if you need to add six, eight, 10, or even more layers, you'll find it's pretty easy to lose track of which layer you're working in.) Then, in the following section, you see how to edit the content in your layers.

Showing and Hiding Layers

Whether or not you want Flash to show the contents of your layered frames on the Stage depends on the situation. Typically, when you're creating the content for a new layer, you want to hide all the other layers so that you can focus on what you're drawing without any distractions. But after you've created a bunch of layers, you're probably going to want to see them all at once so that you have an idea of what your finished animation looks like and make adjustments as necessary.

Flash shows all layers until you tell it otherwise.

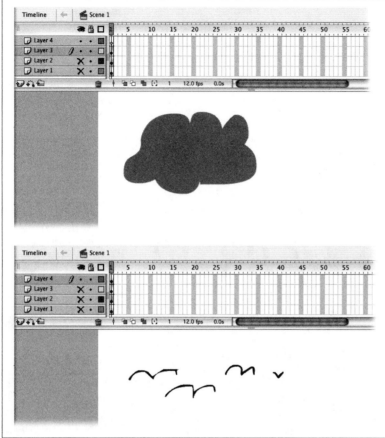

Figure 4-7:
Top: Creating separate layers for different graphic elements gives you more control over how each element appears in your finished animation.

Bottom: In this example, the images are static, but you can place everything from motion and shape tweens to movie clips, backgrounds, actions, and sounds on their own layers. Hiding layers affects only what you see on the Stage; when you select Control → Test Movie to test your animation, Flash displays all layers, whether or not you've checked them as Hidden.

Tip: You can tell Flash to show (or hide) *all* your layers by clicking the Show/Hide All Layers icon you see in Figure 4-6. Click the icon again to turn off showing (or hiding).

To hide a layer

On the Timeline, click the dot (the Show/Hide) icon next to the layer you want to hide (Figure 4-9, top). When you do, Flash redisplays the dot as an X and temporarily hides the contents of the layer (Figure 4-9, bottom).

To show a layer

On the Timeline, click the X (the Show/Hide icon) next to the layer you want to show (Figure 4-9, bottom). When you do, Flash redisplays the X as a dot and displays the contents of the layer on the Stage (Figure 4-9, top).

Figure 4-8:
Here's what the composite drawing for Frame 1 looks like: the fence, the flowers, the cloud, and the birds, all together on one Stage. Notice the display order: The flowers (Layer 2) appear in front of the fence (Layer 1), and the birds (Layer 4) in front of the cloud (Layer 3). Flash automatically displays the layer at the bottom of the list first (Layer 1), followed by the next layer up (Layer 2), followed by the next layer (Layer 3), and so on. But you can change this stacking order, as you see on page 127.

GEM IN THE ROUGH

Distribute to Layers

If you have a bunch of graphic elements on one layer that you want to put on separate layers (because, for example, you want to be able to tween them all), you can save time by telling Flash to do the work for you. First, select the objects you want to put on different layers and then select Modify → Timeline → Distribute to Layers.

Unfortunately, like any automatic process, this approach may not create the precise results you want. Flash can't possibly know that you want both an eye and an eyebrow to go

on the same layer, for example. And this trick *doesn't* break apart bitmaps, symbols, or grouped objects.

If you want to distribute the elements of a bitmap or symbol to individual frames, you first need to break up that bitmap, symbol, or grouped object by selecting it and then choosing Modify → Break Apart or Modify → Ungroup, respectively.

To hide (or show) all layers except the one you're currently editing

On the Timeline, Alt-click (Windows) or Option-click (Mac) the Show/Hide icon next to the layer you're editing. Flash immediately hides (or shows) all the layers except the one you're editing.

Note: *If you try to edit a hidden layer by drawing on the Stage, Flash displays a warning dialog box that gives you the opportunity to show (and then edit) the layer. Not so if you try to drag a symbol to the Stage—Flash just refuses to let you drop the symbol on the Stage. Oddly enough, however, Flash does let you add a keyframe to a locked layer.*

Why Layer?

In addition to making it much, much easier for you to change your animations, working with layers gives you the following benefits:

You can create multi-tweened animations. Flash lets you create only one tween (Chapter 3) per layer. So if you want to show two baseballs bonking a parked car—one ball sailing in from the right, and one from the left—you need to either draw the entire animated sequence for each ball by hand, or use two separate layers, each containing one tween.

You can create more realistic effects. Since you can shuffle layers, putting some layers behind others and even adjusting the transparency of some layers, you can add depth and perspective to your drawings. And because you can distribute your drawings to layers at whatever level of detail you want, you can create separate layers that give you independent control over, say, your characters' facial expressions and arm and leg movements.

You can split up the work. TV and movie animators use layers (technically, they use transparent sheets of plastic called *cels*, but it's the same concept) to divvy up their workload, and so can you. While you're crafting the dog layer, one of your teammates can be working on the cloud layer, and another two can be working on the two character layers. When you're all finished, all you need to do is copy everyone's layers and paste them onto a single Timeline, and bingo—instant animation.

You can organize your animations. As you begin to create more sophisticated animations that may include not just images and animated effects, but symbols (Chapter 7), sounds (Chapter 8), and actions (Chapter 9), you quickly realize you need to organize your work. Layers help you get organized. If you get into the habit of putting all your animation's actions into a single layer (called *actions*), all the sounds into a single layer (called *sounds* or *soundtrack*), all the text into a single layer (called *text*), and so on, you can quickly spot the element you're looking for when it comes time to edit your animation.

Working with Layers

The more layers you have, the more important it is to keep them organized. In this section, you see how to give your layers meaningful names, so that you can remember which images, sounds, or actions you placed in which layers. You also see how to order your layer so that your composite images appear just the way you want them and to copy and paste your layers (to cut down on the work you have to do to create similar layered effects).

Renaming Layers

The names that Flash gives the layers you create—Layer 1, Layer 2, Layer 3, and so on—aren't particularly useful when you've created 20 layers and can't remember which layer contains the ocean background you spent 10 hours drawing. Get into the habit of renaming your layers as soon you create them, and you'll have an easier time locating the specific elements you need when you need them.

This section builds on the example you created in "Adding Content to Multiple Layers" earlier in this chapter. If you haven't had a chance to work through that section, you can download flowers.fla from this book's "Missing CD" Web page and use it instead.

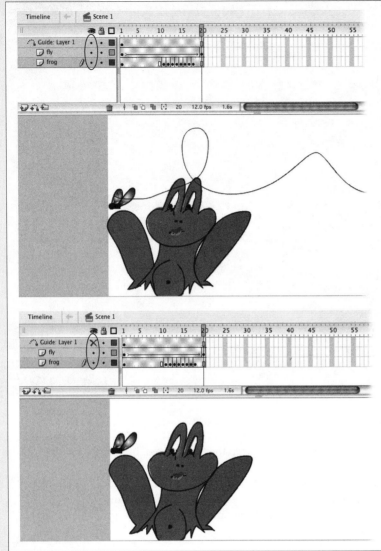

Figure 4-9:
Top: This animation contains three layers: one containing a motion tween of a buzzing fly; one containing the path the fly takes as it buzzes around the frog's head; and one containing the highly interested frog. In some situations, showing all layers is fine, but here it's confusing to see all those images on the Stage at the same time.

Bottom: Hiding the motion guide layer lets you focus on the two main elements of this animation: the frog and the fly.

To rename a layer:

1. **Open the file flowers.fla.**

   If you created your own Flash document when you worked through "Adding Content to Multiple Layers" (page 117), you can use that document instead.

2. **Double-click the name Layer 4.**

   Flash redisplays the layer name in an editable text box (Figure 4-10). On the Stage, you see the content for this layer (the birds) selected.

Layer Properties

Flash gives you two different ways to change the properties associated with your layers: for example, the name of your layer, whether you want to show the content of a layer on the Stage or hide it, whether you want to lock a layer or leave it editable, and so on.

One way is clicking the icons in the Layers window. (That's the approach described in this chapter.) The other way is by using the Layer Properties dialog box.

To display the Layer Properties dialog box, click to select a layer; then do *one* of the following:

- Double-click the layer icon you find just to the left of the layer name). Right-click the layer name and, from the shortcut menu, choose Properties.

- Select Modify → Timeline → Layer Properties

The Layer Properties dialog box lets you change any or all of the following layer properties in one fell swoop:

- **Name.** Type a name in this text box to change the name of your layer.

- **Show.** Turn on this checkbox to show the contents of this layer on the Stage; turn it off it to hide the contents of this layer.

- **Lock.** Turn on this checkbox to prevent yourself (or anyone else) from editing any of the content in this layer; turn it off it to make the layer editable once again.

- **Type.** Click to choose one of the following layer types:

  - **Normal.** The type of layer described in this chapter.

  - **Guide.** A special type of layer that you use to position objects on a guided layer, and which doesn't appear in the finished animation (Chapter 3).

  - **Guided.** A regular layer that appears below a guide layer (Chapter 3).

  - **Mask.** A type of layer you use to carve out "portholes" through which the content on an underlying masked layer appears (Chapter 6).

  - **Masked.** A regular layer that appears below a mask layer (Chapter 6).

  - **Folder.** Not a layer at all, but a container you can drag layers into to help you organize your animation (page 129).

- **Outline color.** Click to choose the color you want Flash to use when you turn on the checkbox "View layer as outlines."

- **View layer as outlines.** Turning on this checkbox tells Flash to display the content for this layer on the Stage, but to display it as outlines (instead of the way it actually looks, which is the way it appears when you run the animation). Find out more on page 129.

- **Layer height.** Click the arrow next to this drop-down list to choose a display height for your layer in the Timeline: 100% (normal), 200% (twice as big), or 300% (three times as big). You may find this option useful for visually setting off one of your layers, making it easy for you to spot quickly.

After you make your changes, click OK to tell Flash to apply your changes to your layer.

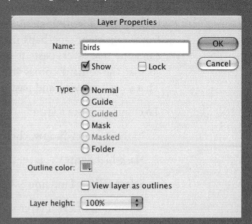

Note: Instead of double-clicking the layer name, you can use the Layer Properties dialog box to rename your layer. Check out the box on page 125 for details.

3. **Click inside the text box and then type** *birds*; **then click anywhere else in the workspace.**

   Flash displays the new name for your layer.

4. **Repeat steps 1 and 2 for Layers 3, 2, and 1, renaming them** *cloud, flowers,* **and** *fence,* **respectively.**

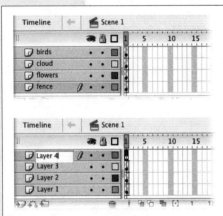

Figure 4-10:
Top: The Layers area of the Timeline isn't particularly big, so make sure you keep your layer names short and sweet. (Even if you tell Flash to expand the layer, as described in the box on page 125, the space for the layer name doesn't increase.)

Bottom: If you can't remember what a particular layer contains, check the Stage: When you double-click a layer name to rename it, Flash automatically highlights the content associated with that layer.

Copy and Paste a Layer

Earlier in this chapter, you saw how to copy and paste individual series of frames. But Flash also lets you copy and paste entire layers—useful when you want to create a backup layer for safekeeping, or when you want to create a duplicate layer to change slightly from the original.

For example, if you want your animation to show an actor being pelted with tomatoes from different angles, you can create a layer that shows a tomato coming in from stage right—perhaps using a motion or shape tween (Chapter 3). Then you can copy that layer, paste it back into the Layers window, rename it, and tweak it so that the tomato comes from stage left. Maximum effect for minimum effort: That's what copying and pasting gives you.

To copy and paste a layer:

1. **In the Layers window, click the name of the layer you want to select.**

   Flash highlights the layer name, as well as all the frames in the layer.

2. **Select Edit → Timeline → Copy Frames.**

   If you don't have a layer waiting to accept the copied frames, create a new layer now before going on to the next step.

3. In the Layers window, select the name of the destination layer. Then choose
   Edit → Timeline → Paste Frames.

Flash pastes the copied frames onto the new layer, beginning with the first
frame. It also pastes the name of the copied layer onto the new layer.

Reordering (Moving) Layers

Flash always draws layers from the bottom up. For example, it displays the contents of the bottom layer first; then, on top of the bottom layer, it displays the contents of the next layer up; then, on top of both of those layers, it displays the
contents of the third layer up; and so on. Figure 4-11 shows you an example.

Figure 4-11:
*Flash treats layers the same
way you treat a stack of
transparencies: The image
on the bottom gets covered
by the image above it,
which gets covered by the
image above it, and so on.
Stacking isn't an issue if
none of your images
overlap. But when they do,
you need to decide which
layers you want in front and
which behind. Here, for
example, the cloud's
covering up both the flowers
and the fence, so it needs to
be reordered.*

Because Flash always displays layers from the bottom up, if you want to reorder
your layers, you need to reorder their position in the layers list. Doing so is simple:
All you have to do is click the name of a layer to select it and then—without letting up on your mouse—drag the layer to reposition it. Figure 4-12 shows you an
example.

Delete a Layer

Flash gives you three different ways to delete a layer:

- In the Layers window, right-click the layer you want to delete and then, from
  the shortcut menu that appears, choose Delete Layer.

- Drag the layer you want to delete to the Trash can (see Figure 4-13).

Figure 4-12:
Moving a layer is easy: Just click to select a layer and then drag it to reposition it (and change the order in which Flash displays the content of your frames). Here, the cloud layer has been moved to the bottom of the list, so it now appears behind the other images. The birds layer is in the process of being moved; you can tell by the thick gray line you see beneath the cursor.

- Click the layer you want to delete to select it (or Shift-click to select several layers) and then click the Trash can.

Whichever method you choose, Flash immediately deletes the layer or layers (including all the frames associated with that layer or layers) from the Layers window.

Tip: If you delete the wrong layer by mistake, choose Edit → Undo Delete Layer.

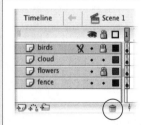

Figure 4-13:
The quickest way to dispose of a layer is to select it and then click the Trash can. All Flash animations must contain at least one layer, so you can't delete the last layer. If you try, Flash doesn't display any error—it just quietly ignores you.

Locking and Unlocking Layers

Working with layers can be confusing, especially at first. So Flash lets you lock individual layers as a kind of safeguard, to keep yourself from accidentally changing content you didn't mean to change:

- **To lock a layer,** click the Unlocked icon (the dot in Figure 4-14) next to the layer you want to lock. When you do, Flash turns the dot into a little padlock icon and deselects any objects that you'd selected on the Stage in that layer. If you locked the active layer, Flash draws a red slash through the pencil icon next to the layer's name as a visual reminder that you can't edit it.

- **To unlock a layer,** click the Locked icon (the padlock you see in Figure 4-14) next to the layer you want to unlock. Instantly, the padlock turns into a dot, Flash reselects your objects, and you can edit them once again on the Stage.

- **To lock (or unlock) all of your layers all at once,** click the Lock/Unlock All Layers icon. Click the icon again to return to unlocked (or locked) layers.

- **To lock all layers** *except* **the one you're currently editing,** Alt+click (Windows) or Option-click (Mac) the unlocked icon next to the layer you're editing.

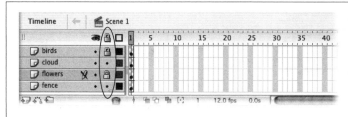

Figure 4-14:
Here, the cloud and fence layers are unlocked, and the birds layer (and the selected flowers layer) are locked. Some people get into the habit of locking all the layers they're not currently editing. That way, they can't possibly add a shape or a tween to the wrong layer.

Note: If you try to edit a locked layer, Flash displays a warning dialog box that gives you the opportunity to unlock (and then edit) the layer.

Organizing Layers

Flash gives you a couple of options that help you organize your layers both in your finished animation and in Flash. The *outline view* helps you tweak the way the content of your layers appears in your finished animation. You use the outline view to help position the objects on one layer with respect to the objects on all the other layers. *Layer folders* help you organize your layers on the Timeline so that you can find and work with them more easily.

Outline View

To help you fit your layers together just the way you want them, Flash lets you display the contents of your layers in outline form. Looking at your layer content in outline form (Figure 4-15) is useful in a variety of situations: for example, when you want to align the content of one layer with respect to the content of another.

Tip: To display the content of *all* your layers as outlines, click the Show All Layers As Outlines icon. (Clicking it again redisplays your layers normally.) Or, to outline the contents of every layer *except* the one you're working on, Alt-click (Windows) or Option-click (Mac) the outline icon for that layer.

- **To show layer content in outline form,** in the Layers widow, click the Non-Outline icon (the filled square in Figure 4-15) displayed next to the layer. When you do, Flash changes the filled square to a hollow square (the Outline icon) and displays your layer content in outline form on the Stage.

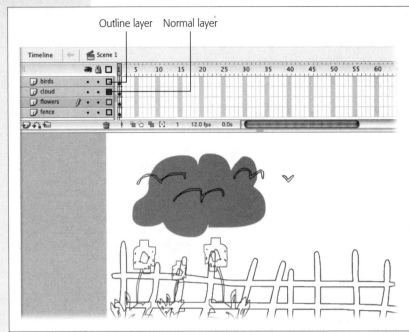

Outline layer   Normal layer

Figure 4-15:
Depending on the visual effect you're going for, you might want to align the centers of your flowers with the crosspieces of your fence. But when you look at the content normally, it's hard to see the alignment, because both your flowers and your fence are opaque. Here, Flash displays the birds, flowers, and fence layers in outline form so that you can concentrate on shape and placement without being distracted by extraneous details.

- **To return your layer to normal**, click the Outline icon (the hollow square) next to the layer.

Tip: You can change the color that Flash uses to sketch your outlined content. For example, you can change the color from light to dark so that you can see the outline easier against a light background or so that there's more contrast between two overlapping outlines. To change the outline color for a layer, first select the layer; then, select Modify → Timeline → Layer Properties. From the Layer Properties dialog box that appears, click the Outline Color swatch and then select a color from the Color Picker that appears.

Organizing Your Layers with Layer Folders

When your animation contains only a handful of layers, organization isn't such a big deal. But if you find yourself creating 10, 20, or even more layers, you'll want to use layer folders to keep your layers tidy (and yourself from going nuts).

A *layer folder* is simply a folder you can add to the Layers window. Layer folders aren't associated with frames; you can't place images directly into them. (If you try, you see the error message shown in Figure 4-16.)

Instead, layer folders act as containers to organize your layers. For example, you might want to put all the layers pertaining to a certain drawing (such as a logo or character) into a single layer folder, and name the folder *logo* or *Ralph*. That way, you don't have to scroll through a bunch of layers to find the one image you're looking for.

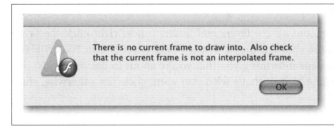

Figure 4-16:
If you try to draw on the Stage when you've selected a folder instead of a layer, Flash lets you know in no uncertain terms. (An interpolated frame's a tweened frame; as you learn in Chapter 3, you can't place images in a tweened frame, either.)

Note: As you might expect, showing, hiding, locking, unlocking, and outlining a layer folder affects every layer inside that folder.

Creating layer folders

When you start working with layer folders, you may want to drag to increase the size of the Timeline so that you can see all your layers. Then proceed as follows:

1. **Click the name of a layer to select it.**

   It doesn't much matter which layer you select since you'll be moving layers as well as the layer folder.

2. **Click the Insert Layer Folder icon in Figure 4-17. (If you prefer, you can choose Insert → Timeline → Layer Folder or right-click the layer and, from the shortcut menu that appears, choose Insert Folder.)**

   Flash creates a new layer folder named Layer Folder 1 and places it above the layer you selected, as in Figure 4-17.

3. **Drag files onto the layer folder.**

   The files appear beneath the layer folder, and the layer folder icon changes from collapsed to expanded.

Tip: You can place layer folders inside other layer folders, but don't go wild; the point is to organize your layers so that you can find them easily, not to see how few folders you can display in the Layers window.

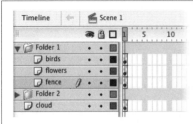

Figure 4-17:
Newly created layer folders appear expanded, like Folder 1 here (note the down arrow). Clicking the down arrow collapses the folder and changes the down arrow to a right arrow (Folder 2). When you drag layers onto an open folder (or expand a collapsed folder), the layers appear beneath the folder. You rename a layer folder the same way you rename a layer: by double-clicking the existing name and then typing in one of your own. You can move layer folders around the same way you move layers around, too: by dragging.

Deleting a layer folder

To delete a layer folder *and all the layers and folders inside*, right-click the layer folder and then, from the shortcut menu that appears, select Delete Folder. Flash pops up a warning message informing you that you're about to delete not just the folder, but also everything in it. If that's what you want, click Yes; otherwise, click Cancel.

Advanced Drawing and Coloring

Chapter 2 shows you how to create a simple drawing using Flash's drawing and painting tools. But in real life—whether you're pounding out Flash animations for your boss or for your own personal Web site—you're rarely going to be satisfied with a simple drawing. For each keyframe of your animation, you're going to want to start with a basic sketch and then play with it, changing its color, moving a line here and there, adding a graphic element or two, and repositioning it until it looks exactly the way you want it to look.

This chapter shows you how to take a drawing from simple to spectacular. Here, you get acquainted with Flash's *selection* tools—the tools you use to tell Flash which specific part of a drawing you want to change. Then you apply Flash's editing tools from basic (copying, pasting, and moving) to advanced (scaling, rotating, stacking, grouping, and more).

There's also more you can do with color in Flash drawings than you saw in Chapter 2. After a quick background in color theory, this chapter covers applying color effects like brightness and transparency, and even creating your own custom colors.

Selecting Graphic Elements

With few exceptions, before you can modify an object on the Stage, you first have to *select* the object. It's just as in a word processor, where you have to highlight a word with your cursor before you can edit or delete it. Since Flash deals with more complex objects than words, it gives you a variety of selection tools for different purposes. The Tools panel (Figure 5-1) has three different selection tools. Each is good for selecting different types of objects.

There are a couple of exceptions to this rule: specifically, modifying fill color using the Paint Bucket tool (page 77) and reshaping lines and curves using the Selection tool (below). But in general, you need to select stuff in Flash before you can work with it.

Tip: To select everything on the Stage, choose Edit → Select All.

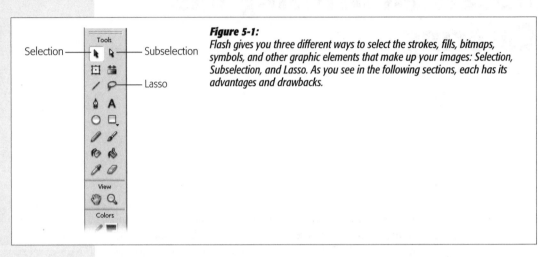

Selection —

Subselection

Lasso

Figure 5-1:
Flash gives you three different ways to select the strokes, fills, bitmaps, symbols, and other graphic elements that make up your images: Selection, Subselection, and Lasso. As you see in the following sections, each has its advantages and drawbacks.

- **Selection.** Clicking with the black arrow selects entire strokes, fills, shapes, and objects (such as bitmaps and symbols), as well as individual portions of those strokes, fills, shapes, and objects.

- **Subselection.** The white arrow lets you select the individual points that make up lines and curves.

- **Lasso.** This tool, which looks like a miniature lasso, is great for selecting groups of objects, oddly shaped objects, or portions of objects. When objects are close together on the Stage, you can use the lasso to carefully select around them.

The following sections describe each of these three tools in detail.

Note: The selection tools behave differently depending on whether you've drawn your objects on the Stage using object drawing mode or chosen to stick with merge drawing mode (which Flash assumes you want until you tell it differently). This chapter shows the selection tools in object drawing mode. (Page 56 explains the differences between the two modes.)

The Selection Tool

The aptly named Selection tool is the workhorse of Flash's selection tools; with it, you can select individual graphic elements such as strokes, fills, shapes, symbols, text blocks, and grouped objects. You can also use the Selection tool to select a portion of any object, as shown in Figure 5-2, or to move or reshape an object (a process sometimes referred to as *transforming* an object).

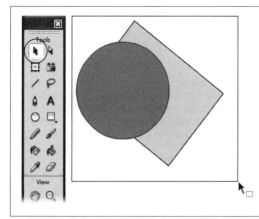

Figure 5-2:
Using the Selection tool is the easiest way to select just about any object, whether it's a shape, a stroke, a bitmap, a fill, or a text block. To use the Selection tool: In the Property panel, click the tool; then, on the Stage, click the object you want to select. To select groups of objects, you have a choice: You can either Shift-click each object, or click outside the group and drag until Flash displays a selection box around your group.

Selecting a graphic element

The most common thing you're going to want to do with the Selection tool is select an entire graphic element—a circle, a line, a block of text, a bitmap, a hand-drawn kangaroo—so that you can apply color to it, copy it, skew it, or make some other modification to it.

Note: To deselect a selected object (regardless of which tool you used to select it), simply click any blank spot on the Stage.

To select an entire graphic element (or groups of elements) using the Selection tool:

1. **In the Tools panel, click the Selection tool.**

   Flash highlights the Selection tool, and Selection-specific options appear in the Options section of the Tools panel (Figure 5-3). When you mouse over the Stage, Flash displays a tiny gray selection box just below your cursor.

Note: You use the "Snap to Objects" option to help you align an object you've selected using the Selection tool. You'll find out more about this option on page 159.

2. **Either click the object you want to select, or (best for lines and groups of objects) click near the object and drag your cursor until the selection box surrounds the object.**

Tip: You can also select groups of objects with the Selection tool when you Shift-click each object you want to select.

   Flash highlights the selected object either by displaying a selection box around the object as shown on the left in Figure 5-3 or covering the selected area with the selection pattern on the right. Either way, the Property panel changes to reflect the object you've selected.

Note: When you select a straight line, you may find it tough to see the selection box because Flash draws it so closely around the line that it almost looks like part of the line itself.

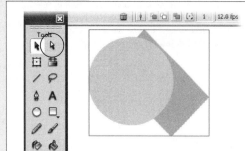

Figure 5-3:
Flash displays a selection box around grouped objects (like the circle and rectangle shown here), symbols, and text blocks to let you know you've successfully selected them. To let you know you've successfully selected an ungrouped fill or stroke, Flash displays the subtle pattern shown here on top of the freeform Brush-drawn fill and part of the Pencil-drawn stroke.

Note: If you use the Selection tool to select a line or shape, Flash displays the Straighten and Smooth options (check out the Options section of the Tools panel). These options let you tweak your lines and shapes—useful if you've got a shape almost the way you want it, but not quite (and you don't want to have to start over and redraw the whole thing). To incrementally straighten a curved line, with the line selected, click the Straighten option. To incrementally turn a series of straight-line angles into a curve, with the line selected, click the Smooth option.

With the object selected, you can make any modifications you want to the object using the main menu options, Flash's color or transform tools (pages 72 and 147) or any of the panels, such as the Property Inspector.

Selecting part of a graphic element

Sometimes you want to carve a chunk off an object to work with it separately: to apply a gradient effect, to cut it out of your image entirely, or whatever strikes your fancy. Using the Selection tool, you can drag a rectangle anywhere over an object to tell Flash to select just that portion of the object.

Note: If you want to select a freeform portion of an object—for example, you've drawn a jungle scene and you want to cut the shape of a baboon's head out of it—you need the Lasso tool (page 141). The Selection tool allows you to select only a rectangular shape.

To select just a portion of an ungrouped graphic element using the Selection tool:

1. **In the Tools panel, click the Selection tool.**

   Flash highlights the Selection tool.

2. **Click near the object and then drag your cursor until the selection box surrounds just the portion of the object you want to select (Figure 5-4).**

3. **Let go of the mouse.**

Flash highlights the selected portion of the object as in Figure 5-4, right.

Note: Flash doesn't let you select a portion of a grouped object, a bitmap, or an object created using object drawing mode. To select a portion of a grouped object (or a single object created in object drawing mode), you need to ungroup it first (Modify → Ungroup). To select a portion of a bitmap, you need to break it apart first (Modify → Break Apart). To learn how to draw an object using merge drawing mode, check out page 51.

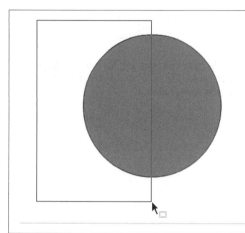

Figure 5-4:
The Selection tool lets you select using only a rectangular selection box. You can make it a large rectangle or a small one, but it's still a rectangle. If you need to select an irregular portion of an object, you need the Lasso tool. If Flash insists on selecting the entire shape (or bitmap) when all you want to do is select a piece of it, ungroup the shape (or break apart the bitmap).

Moving and reshaping (transforming) with the Selection tool

The Selection tool does double-duty: It lets you select objects and portions of objects, as described in the preceding section, but it also lets you move and reshape, or *transform*, them. This double-duty is great—as long as you know what to expect. (Many's the budding Flash-ionado who's sat down to select part of an image and been totally dismayed when the object suddenly, inexplicably, developed a barnacle-like bulge.)

Note: Whether or not Flash treats your shape as a single cohesive entity (for example, an outlined circle) or a combination of independent elements (the circle's outline plus the circle's fill) depends on whether you drew that shape in object or merge drawing mode.

Here's how it works. If you click the Selection tool and then position your cursor directly over an unselected fill or stroke, Flash displays, next to your cursor, one of three icons: a hooked cross, a curve, or an angle.

- **Moving (hooked cross).** The hooked cross (Figure 5-5) tells you that you can click to move the object directly beneath your cursor.

- **Reshaping (curve).** When you see the curve icon shown in Figure 5-6, dragging reshapes the line beneath your cursor (in other words, it lets you add a curve).

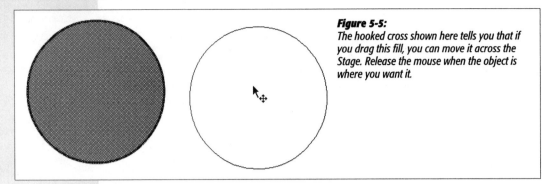

Figure 5-5:
The hooked cross shown here tells you that if you drag this fill, you can move it across the Stage. Release the mouse when the object is where you want it.

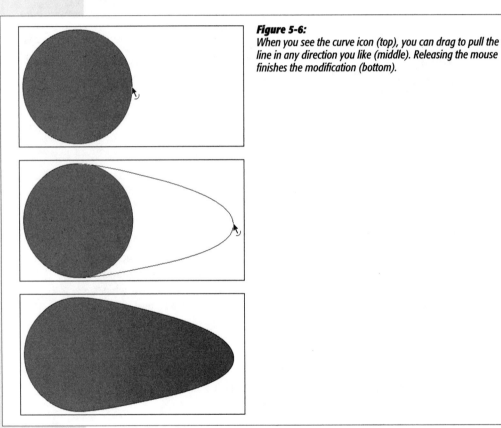

Figure 5-6:
When you see the curve icon (top), you can drag to pull the line in any direction you like (middle). Releasing the mouse finishes the modification (bottom).

Tip: To add an angle rather than a curve, when you see the curve icon, press Alt (Windows) or Option (Mac) before dragging.

- **Reshaping (angle).** Dragging the angle icon (Figure 5-7) lets you reshape one of the corners of your object.

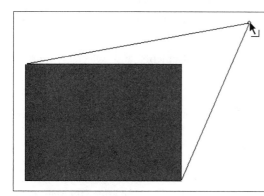

Figure 5-7:
When you mouse over an object's corner and see the angle icon shown here, dragging lets you pull the corner in any direction to reshape it. Releasing the mouse finishes the modification. Here, the upper-right corner of a rectangle is being reshaped.

The Subselection Tool

When you want to modify the individual points and segments that make up your shapes, use the Subselection tool.

As shown in Figure 5-8, the Subselection tool (the white arrow) lets you redisplay shapes as a series of points and segments. You can drag any point to modify it (as well as the attached segments) or drag the tangent handle (temporary slope guide) for a curve to adjust the curve. You can also move a shape—both its outline strokes and inside fill—using the Subselection tool.

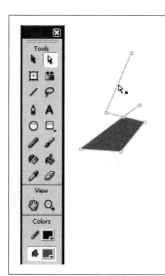

Figure 5-8:
If you click the Subselection tool and then click an object you've created using any drawing tool (Pen, Pencil, Brush, Line, or shape), Flash redisplays the line as a series of segments and points. Click any segment (Flash displays a tiny black square as you mouse over a segment), and Flash lets you move the entire object. Click a point (a hollow square) instead, and Flash lets you change the object's shape.

To use the Subselection tool to move an object:

1. **In the Tools panel, click the Subselection tool (Figure 5-8).**

   Flash highlights the Selection tool.

2. **Click the object you want to work with (or click near the object and drag your cursor until the selection box surrounds the object).**

   Flash redisplays the object as a series of segments and selectable points (Figure 5-8).

3. **Mouse over any of the segments in the object.**

   Flash displays a black square.

4. **Drag to move the object. When you're satisfied, let go of the mouse.**

   Flash displays your moved object. Figure 5-8 shows an example.

To use the Subselection tool to modify a point (and, by association, the segments attached to that point):

1. **In the Tools panel, click the Subselection tool (Figure 5-9, left).**

   Flash highlights the Subselection tool.

2. **Click the object you want to work with (or click near the object and then drag your cursor until the selection box surrounds the object).**

   Flash redisplays the object as a series of segments and selectable points (Figure 5-9, middle).

3. **Mouse over the point you want to modify.**

   Flash displays a hollow square.

4. **Click once and then drag the point to reshape your object. When you're satisfied, let go of the mouse.**

   Flash displays your modified object. You see an example in Figure 5-9, right.

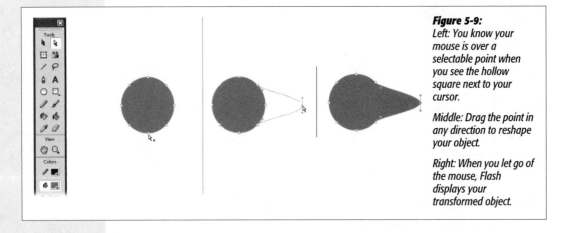

Figure 5-9:
Left: You know your mouse is over a selectable point when you see the hollow square next to your cursor.

Middle: Drag the point in any direction to reshape your object.

Right: When you let go of the mouse, Flash displays your transformed object.

Tip: If the point defines a curve (in other words, if you see a hollow square at the end of a curved line), clicking the point tells Flash to display a temporary slope guide, or *tangent handle*. You can click either end of the tangent handle and drag to adjust the curve.

The Lasso Tool

Say you want to select just part of an object to work with: to cut, recolor, and so on. The Selection tool (page 134) works just fine if your objects are nicely spread out on the Stage with lots of room around each one. But if your Stage is jam-packed with images, you can't select the image you want with the Selection tool without inadvertently selecting parts of images you *don't* want. Figure 5-10 shows an example.

Note: The Lasso tool only lets you select portions of objects if those objects are either ungrouped lines or fills or broken-apart bitmaps. You create ungrouped shapes by using merge drawing mode, but you can also ungroup them after the fact by choosing Modify → Ungroup. To break apart a bitmap, select it and then choose Modify → Break Apart.

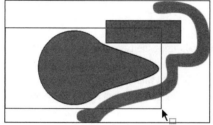 

Figure 5-10:
Selecting an object that "overhangs" other objects on the Stage (left) doesn't work with the Selection tool, which only offers you a one-size-fits-all selection rectangle. If you try it, you end up selecting portions of other, nearby objects. Use the Lasso tool (right) for pinpoint control over the objects and portions of objects you select.

You can also use the Lasso tool to select nonrectangular portions of objects both by drawing freehand and by pointing and clicking.

Freehand selecting with the Lasso

Depending on how steady your hands are, drawing a freehand lasso around an object (or around the portion of an object you want to select) is the quickest way to select what you want. Straight out of the box, this is how the Lasso works.

To use the Lasso tool to select objects (and portions of objects) freehand:

1. **In the Tools panel, click the Lasso tool (Figure 5-11, left).**

   Flash highlights the Lasso tool; and in the Options section of the Tools panel, the Lasso-related options appear.

2. **Click near the object you want to select, and drag your mouse to encircle the object.**

    Figure 5-11 (right) shows you an example.

3. **When you've completely encircled your object, let go of the mouse.**

    Flash selects everything inside the loop you drew with the Lasso tool.

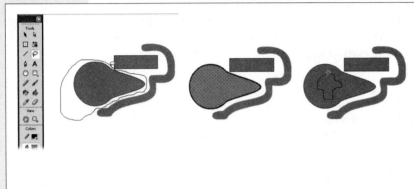

Figure 5-11:
Left: To use the Lasso tool, click near the object and drag your mouse to draw a circle around the object.

Middle: When you let go of the mouse, Flash highlights (selects) everything you lassoed.

Right: Use the Lasso tool to select portions of objects, too (or portions of multiple objects).

Tip: You can have a tricky time describing a precise loop using the Lasso, especially if you're using a mouse instead of a graphics tablet. Fortunately, Flash has got your back; if you don't completely close the loop, Flash closes it for you, using a straight line. If this action isn't what you want, just select Edit → Undo Lasso and then start over. If you're still having trouble, try using the Zoom tool to enlarge the Stage or try the Lasso's Polygon mode, described in the following section.

Pointing and clicking with the Lasso

At times, you may find you need to select an object that's *really* close to another object on the Stage. Or you may find you need to select a very precise portion of an object, such as a perfect triangle.

In these cases, freehand just doesn't cut it; one slip, and you have to start over. You're better off taking advantage of the Lasso tool's Polygon Mode, which lets you click to surround an area. (Flash takes care of filling in the straight lines between your clicks so you don't have to.)

To use the Lasso tool to select objects (and portions of objects) by pointing and clicking:

1. **In the Tools panel, click the Lasso tool.**

    Flash highlights the Lasso tool. In the Options section of the Tools panel, the Lasso-related options appear.

2. **Click the Polygon Mode option (Figure 5-12). Then, using a series of clicks,
   enclose the object you want to select.**

   Flash automatically connects your clicks with straight-line segments.

3. **When you've completely enclosed your object, let go of the mouse.**

   Flash selects everything inside the loop you drew with the Lasso tool.

Tip: You may find the Lasso—especially in Polygon Mode—doesn't want to quit when you do. In other words, when you go to use the main menu or a panel or another drawing tool, you find you can't because Flash keeps insisting you need to draw another lasso. Normally, to deactivate a tool, all you have to do is click the Selection tool. If this doesn't work, on the Stage, right-click the Lasso and then click the Selection tool.

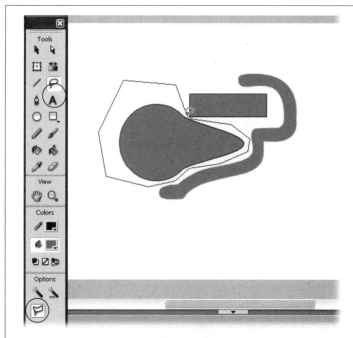

Figure 5-12:
Drawing a lasso freehand around the curvy shape on the left side of the Stage is harder than it looks: one slip, and you've selected part of the rectangle right next to it. Fortunately, the Lasso's Polygon Mode combines precise control with automatic help. To use the Lasso tool in Polygon mode, click near the object you want to select and then click again (and again and again) around the area you want. As you click, Flash connects your clicks for you, letting you create an enclosing shape quickly and easily.

Selecting ranges of color in bitmaps with the Magic Wand

Flash treats *bitmaps*—the GIF, JPEG, and other image files that you can pull into a Flash document, as you see in Chapter 8—differently from the way it treats the images you create using its drawing tools. And if you take a look at Figure 5-13, you see why.

While you can't manipulate bitmaps in Flash anywhere near as easily or as completely as you can manipulate the shapes and lines you draw directly onto the

Figure 5-13:
Top: The drawing is clearly composed of three shapes, each of which you can click to select separately.

Bottom: The bitmap image is much more complex, with no easily identifiable shape outlines. When you click to select the image on the bottom, Flash highlights the entire rectangular image; it makes no distinction between the colors and shapes inside.

Stage, Flash does offer a special tool specifically for selecting ranges of colors in bitmaps: the Magic Wand. After you select color ranges, you can then recolor them or cut them out of the bitmap completely.

To select color ranges in a bitmap using the Magic Wand:

1. **On the Stage, select the bitmap with which you want to work.**

   Flash displays a light-colored border around the selected bitmap.

2. **Choose Modify → Break Apart.**

   Flash redisplays the bitmap as a selected fill.

3. **From the Tools panel, select the Lasso. Then, in the Options section of the Tools panel, click the Magic Wand (Figure 5-14, top).**

   As you mouse over the Stage, your cursor turns into a tiny magic wand.

Figure 5-14:
Top: The first time you click the Magic Wand, Flash notes the color you choose.

Bottom: The second (and subsequent) times you click the Magic Wand, Flash selects the bits of color nearby that match your first selection. Selecting colored areas of bitmaps with the Magic Wand can be slow going. Don't expect the precision you enjoy when you're working with primitive shapes, such as squares and circles. Still, depending on the effect you're after, the Magic Wand can be useful. Here, most of the background was selected with the Magic Want tool and then deleted. A few swipes with the Eraser tool (page 69) and the shirt area will be primed for repainting.

4. **Click the bitmap to select a color range.**

   Flash highlights bits of selected color.

5. **Click the bitmap again (click a similarly colored area).**

   Flash highlights the bits of color that precisely match your first selection.

You can modify the highlighted bits of fill color as you go (cut them, recolor them using the Eyedropper tool described in Chapter 5, and so on), or continue to click the bitmap as you did in step 6 to add to the selection.

In Figure 5-14 (bottom), the designer first selected and then cut (Edit → Cut) the pixels to make the selected areas easier to see.

Manipulating Graphic Elements

Flash offers you a gazillion tools to modify the drawings that make up your animations. You can stack, rearrange and reposition each individual graphic element, transform (shrink and squish) them, move them, apply color effects, and more until you're completely satisfied with the way they look. It's a cliché, but it's true: When it comes to drawing in Flash, you're pretty much limited only by your imagination.

This section acquaints you with the most powerful tools Flash offers for modifying the lines, shapes, bitmaps, symbols, and other graphic elements you add to your drawings.

Modifying Object Properties

Flash's Property Inspector is a beautiful thing. Select any element on the Stage, and the Property Inspector responds by displaying all the characteristics, or *properties*, that you can change about that element.

In Figure 5-15, for example, you see several graphic elements on the Stage: a painted fill, a bitmap of a frog, a line of text, and a star. When you select the star, the Property Inspector shows all the properties associated with the star: the color, width, and type of outline, the fill color, and so on. When you select the text, the Property Inspector changes to reflect only text properties.

Note: If you don't see the Property Inspector, choose Windows → Properties and, in the pop-up menu that appears, turn on the checkbox next to Properties. If you still don't see it, check to see whether you've expanded your Stage and pushed it out of the way or collapsed the Property Inspector.

You can change any of the object properties you see in the Property Inspector. For example, in the Property Inspector on the left side of Figure 5-15, you can change the color, width, or style of the star's outline color. (You can change all these properties by using Flash's selection and drawing tools, too, of course, but using the Property Inspector is a lot quicker for most changes.)

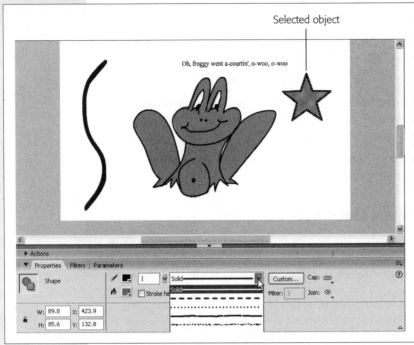

Selected object

Figure 5-15:
Selecting an object tells Flash to display that object's properties right there at the bottom of the work area in the Property Inspector. Here, the star shape's selected, so the properties all relate to this particular star. As long as the property isn't grayed out, you can change it in the Property Inspector.

Moving, Cutting, Pasting, and Copying

After you have an object on the Stage, you can move it around, cut it (delete it), paste it somewhere else, or make copies of it.

Tip: All the things you can do to an object—cutting, pasting, copying, and moving—you can also do to a *piece* of an object. Instead of selecting the entire object, just select whatever portion of the object you want to work with and go from there.

Moving

To move an object, simply select it (page 133) and then drag it around the Stage. Figure 5-16 shows an example of using the Selection tool to select a group of objects and move them together.

Cutting

To cut an object, select the object (page 133) and then choose Edit → Cut. Flash deletes the object from the Stage and enables the Paste functions (see below).

Note: Choosing Edit → Clear deletes the select object, too, but doesn't enable the Paste functions. In other words, after you choose Edit → Clear, it's gone, baby, gone (unless you quickly choose Edit → Undo Delete).

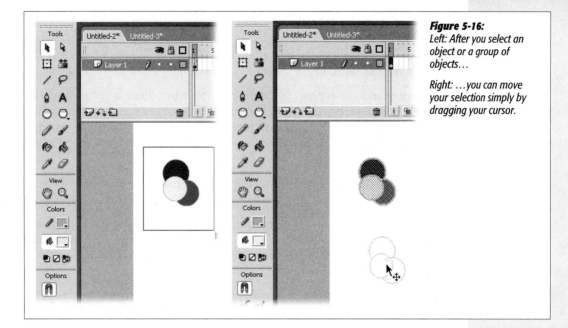

Figure 5-16:
Left: After you select an object or a group of objects...

Right: ...you can move your selection simply by dragging your cursor.

Copying

To copy an object, select the object and then choose Edit → Copy. Flash leaves the object on the Stage and enables the Paste functions (see below).

Tip: You can perform a quick copy-and-paste operation by selecting an object and then choosing Edit → Duplicate. Flash displays a movable copy of the selected object just above the selected object.

Pasting

To paste an object that you've either cut or copied, choose one of the following:

- **Edit → Paste in Center.** Tells Flash to paste the cut (or copied) object smack in the middle of the Stage's visible area, on top of any other image that happens to be there.

- **Edit → Paste in Place.** Tells Flash to replace the cut object, or to put the copied object square on top of the original.

Transforming Objects (Scaling, Rotating, Skewing, Distorting)

In the graphics world, *transforming* an object doesn't just mean changing the object; transforming means applying very specific shape and size changes to the object. These changes—called *transforms*—include:

- **Scaling.** Among graphic designers, *scaling* means resizing. You can scale (shrink or enlarge) a selected shape based on its width, height, or both.

- **Rotating.** You can *rotate* (turn) an object as far as you want, in any direction. (When you rotate an object 180 degrees, it's called *flipping*.)

- **Skewing.** A limited kind of distortion, *skewing* means slanting an object either horizontally or vertically.

- **Distorting and enveloping.** You *distort* an object by pulling it out of shape: in other words, by repositioning one or more of the object's angles. The *envelope* transform is similar, but it doesn't preserve the lines of the shape the way distortion does; instead, it allows you to pull any angle, line, or curve out of shape to create fantastic effects.

You have three choices when it comes to applying a transform to a selected object (or group of objects):

- You can click the Free Transform tool (Figure 5-17), choose the appropriate option from the Options section of the Tools panel and then, on the Stage, drag your selection to apply the transform. This approach is described in the following sections.

- You can type information (for example, the number of degrees you want to rotate an object) directly into the Transform panel.

- You can choose Modify → Transform and, from the pop-up menu that appears, turn on the checkbox next to the transform you want to apply.

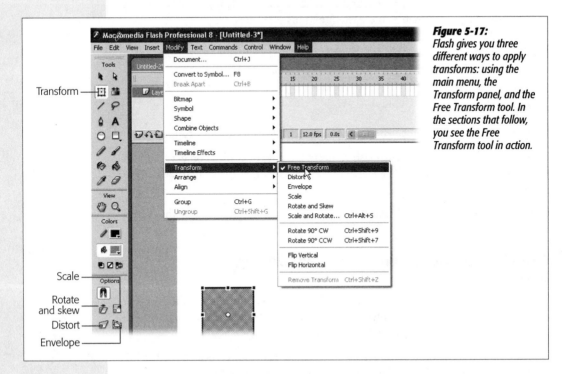

Figure 5-17:
Flash gives you three different ways to apply transforms: using the main menu, the Transform panel, and the Free Transform tool. In the sections that follow, you see the Free Transform tool in action.

Scaling objects

To resize a drawn object, first select the object on the Stage, then proceed as follows:

1. **Select the Free Transform tool's Scale option (Figure 5-17).**

   Black squares appear at the corners and sides of your selection.

2. **Position your cursor over one of the black squares.**

   Your cursor turns into the double-headed *scale arrow*.

3. **Drag to scale the selection (Figure 5-18, top).**

   As you drag outward, the selection gets larger; as you drag inward, the selection gets smaller. You see an example of a scaled object in Figure 5-18 (bottom).

Rotating objects

To rotate a drawn object around its axis, first select the object on the Stage, then proceed as follows:

1. **Select the Free Transform tool's "Rotate and Skew" option (Figure 5-17).**

   Flash displays a black bounding box around your selection.

2. **Position your cursor over one of the black squares you see at the corners of your selection.**

   Your cursor turns into a circular *rotation arrow* (Figure 5-19, top).

3. **Drag to rotate the selection (Figure 5-19, top).**

   If you drag your cursor to the right, the entire selection rotates right; if you drag your cursor to the left, the selection rotates to the left. There's a rotated object in Figure 5-19 (bottom).

Tip: You can most easily rotate a selected object 180 degrees (upside down or left-to-right) by selecting Modify → Transform → Flip Vertical or Modify → Transform → Flip Horizontal.

Skewing objects

To give your drawing a slanted shape, first select the object on the Stage, then proceed as follows:

1. **Select the Free Transform tool's Rotate and Skew option (Figure 5-17).**

   Flash displays a black bounding box around your selection.

2. **Position your cursor over one of the black squares at the sides of your selection (Figure 5-20, top).**

   Your cursor turns into a *skew arrow* (Figure 5-20, top).

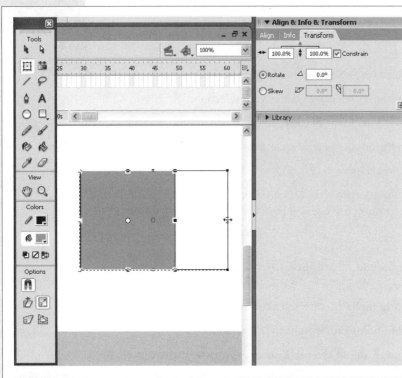

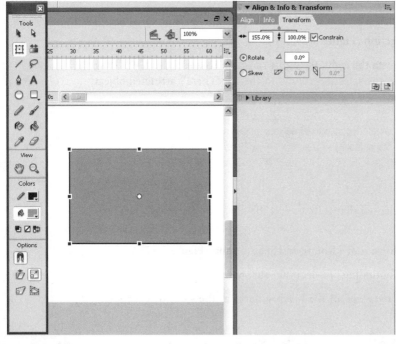

Figure 5-18:
Top: Mousing over any of the black squares on the sides and at the corners of your object displays a scale arrow. By dragging a square, you can scale an object vertically, horizontally, or both. Notice that before the scaling begins, the Transform panel displays the original width/height dimensions as 100% and 100%.

Bottom: Flash automatically plugs the new dimensions into the Transform panel on the bottom. Instead of dragging the object to scale it, you can also type the scale dimensions into the Transform panel yourself.

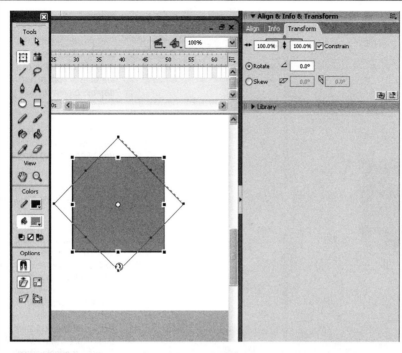

Figure 5-19:
Top: After you select the "Rotate and Skew" option, mousing over any of the black squares at the corners of your object displays a rotation arrow. Notice that before the rotation begins, the Transform panel displays the original rotation degrees as 0.0%. Drag to rotate the object on its center axis (its transformation point).

Bottom: After you let go of your mouse, Flash automatically records the rotation degrees into the Transform panel on the right. Instead of dragging the object to rotate it, you can also type the rotation degrees into the Transform panel yourself.

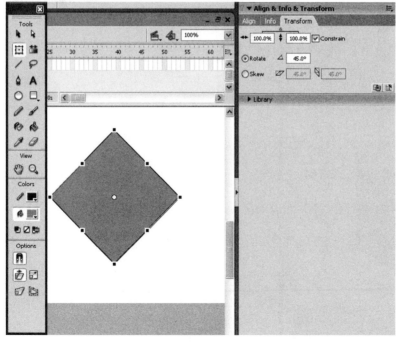

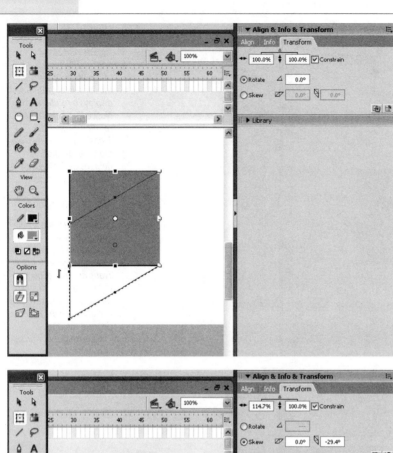

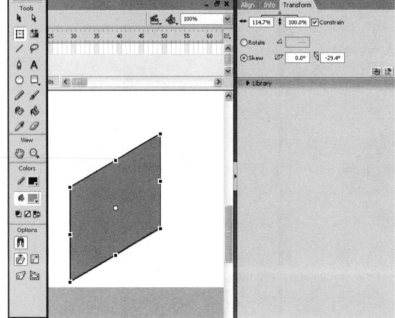

Figure 5-20:
Top: After you select the "Rotate and Skew" option, mousing over any of the black squares at the sides of your object displays a skew arrow. Notice that before the skew begins, the Transform panel shows the Skew radio button turned off. Drag to skew the object.

Bottom: After you let go of your mouse, check the Transform panel: Flash automatically turns on the Skew button and logs the horizontal and vertical skew degrees. Instead of dragging the object to skew it, you can also turn on the Skew button and type the horizontal and vertical skew degrees into the Transform panel yourself.

3. **Drag to skew the selection.**

Dragging slants the selection along one of its axes (the one marked by the skew arrow you clicked) in the direction you're dragging. Figure 5-20 (bottom) shows a skewed object.

Distorting objects

For more freedom than simple skewing, you can distort your drawn objects in any way or direction:

1. **First, select the object you want to distort and then select the Free Transform tool's Distort option (Figure 5-17).**

   Flash displays black squares around the sides and corners of your selection.

2. **Position your cursor over one of the black squares.**

   Your cursor turns into a tailless *distortion arrow* (Figure 5-21, top).

3. **Drag to distort the selection.**

   As you drag outward, the shape bulges outward; drag inward, and the shape dents inward. Figure 5-21 (bottom) shows a distorted object.

Tip: Shift-dragging a corner point lets you *taper* a shape; that is, move that corner and the adjoining corner apart from each other an equal distance.

Applying an envelope transform

As discussed on page 148, an envelope transform is the most radical distortion. It gives you more distortion points than the regular Distort option, and also gives you finer control over the points by letting you drag inward or outward to create rounded bulges or dents (not just pointy ones). Here's how to use the Envelope distortion.

1. **Click the Free Transform tool.**

   The Free Transform options appear in the Options section of the Tools panel.

2. **Select the object you want to distort.**

   Flash highlights the selected object with a black bounding box and tiny black squares.

3. **Click the Envelope option.**

   The selected object appears surrounded by a series of black squares and circles.

4. **Position your cursor over one of the black squares or circles (*distortion points*).**

   Your cursor turns into a tailless *distortion arrow* (Figure 5-22, left).

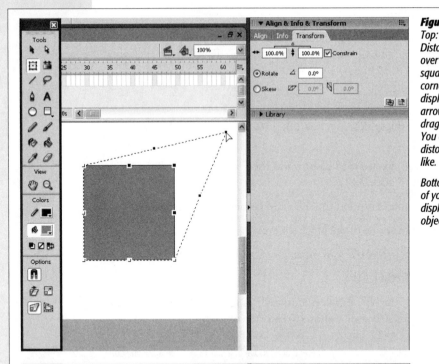

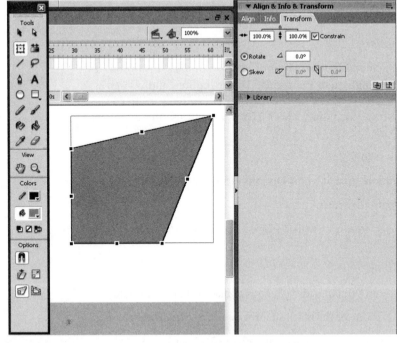

Figure 5-21:
Top: After you select the Distort option, mousing over any of the black squares at the sides and corners of your object displays a distortion arrow, which you can drag to distort the object. You can drag as many distortion points as you like.

Bottom: After you let go of your mouse, Flash displays the distorted object.

5. **Drag to pull the selection into a new shape (Figure 5-22, middle).**

You'll notice that the envelope transform gives you a lot more distortion points to choose from than the distort transform; it also gives you finer control over the points you choose to distort (by dragging inward or outward).

You see the results of modifying several distortion points in Figure 5-22 (right).

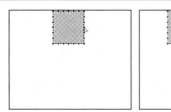 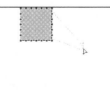 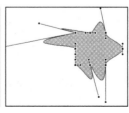

Figure 5-22:
Left: After you select the Envelope option, mousing over any of the black squares or circles at the sides and corners of your object displays a distortion arrow.

Middle: Drag to distort the object. You can drag as many distortion points as you like.

Right: After you let go of your mouse, Flash displays the modified object. Here, you see the results of modifying several distortion points.

Stacking Objects

In Chapter 4, you learned how to stack objects to create composite drawings using *layers*. But you don't need layers to place one item on top of another. You can overlap two or more objects on the same layer—as long as you don't need to tween them separately. The instant you create two or more overlapping shapes on the Stage, though, you need to think about *stacking*, or arranging, those shapes. Stacking tells Flash which shape you want to appear in front of the other.

Note: You can't stack ungrouped objects, which includes any lines and fills you've created in merge drawing mode. See the box on page 156 for details.

In Figure 5-23 (top), for example, you see three shapes: a rectangle, a circle, and a star. When you drag the rectangle and drop it on top of the star (Figure 5-23), Flash displays the rectangle *behind* the star. Then, when you drag the circle and drop it on top of both the rectangle and the star, Flash displays the circle *behind* the rectangle and the star. If that's the effect you want, great; if not, you can change the stacking order of all three shapes.

WORKAROUND WORKSHOP

Safety in Groups

If you plan to move your graphic elements around a lot—stack them, unstack them, and reposition them on the Stage—make sure you create them in object drawing mode (page 51), which tells Flash to group each object individually. If you want to stick with merge drawing mode (because it's the only way Flash let you draw pre-Version 8 and you're used to it, for example), draw your objects on a fresh, clean corner of the Stage and then group them individually yourself.

Here's why. Say you're working in merge drawing mode and you create a rectangle on the Stage using Flash's Rectangle drawing tool. What you've really created are two separate animals: a rectangular fill, and a rectangular outline, or stroke. If you want to select the entire rectangle, outline and all, you need to drag the Selection tool to surround the entire rectangle—which is a problem if you didn't draw your rectangle on a fresh part of the Stage and your rectangle happens to be sitting on top of another shape.

Selection is no problem, you say? Well, try dragging your selected (ungrouped) rectangle and dropping it onto another ungrouped shape, such as a circle. When you go to move the circle, you see that it's no longer a circle at all: Flash has taken a pair of scissors to it.

Here's one last reason to group your objects before you begin rearranging or moving them: Flash uses a different automatic stacking order depending on the type of objects you drag on top of each other. Whichever way Flash stacks your objects, you can change the stacking order to suit yourself—with one exception. *Flash doesn't let you place an ungrouped object on top of a grouped object or a symbol—no way, no how.*

If you need to place an ungrouped object on top of a grouped object (or on top of a symbol), either group the ungrouped object and then restack it (to group a selected object, choose Modify → Group), or move the ungrouped object to a separate layer (page 117).

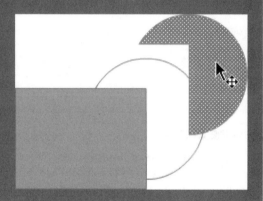

To stack objects on the Stage:

1. **Select the object you want to rearrange (either to push behind or pull in front of another object).**

   In Figure 5-24 (top), the circle's selected.

2. **Choose Modify → Arrange and then, from the pop-up menu that appears, change the object's stacking order.**

   Here are your options:

   Bring to Front. Pulls the selected object all the way forward until it's on top of all the other objects.

   Bring Forward. Pulls the selected object forward in front of just one other object.

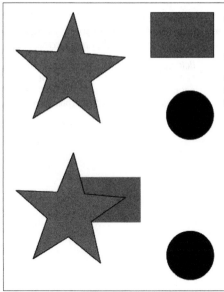

Figure 5-23:
Top: Stacking isn't an issue when your objects don't touch each other. The instant you drag one object on top of another, though, you have to decide which object you want to appear on top, and which behind.

Bottom: Flash stacks objects differently depending on the kind of objects involved. Here, Flash places the third grouped object behind the other two.

Send Backward. Pushes the object back behind just one other object.

Send Back. Pushes the selected object all the way back, until it's behind all the other stacked objects.

Figure 5-24 (bottom) shows you an example of choosing Bring Forward with the circle selected.

Converting Strokes to Fills

As you saw in Chapter 2 (page 52), Flash treats lines and fills differently when you're working in merge drawing mode. For example, take a look at Figure 5-25, which shows a line drawn with the Pencil and a line drawn with the Brush.

If you click the Selection tool and then click to select the Pencil-drawn line, Flash highlights just one stroke of the line (Figure 5-25, top). But performing the very same operation on the similar-looking Brush-drawn line selects the *entire* Brush-drawn line (Figure 5-25, bottom).

When you convert a line into a fill, Flash lets you interact with the line just as you would with any other fill. This technique is especially useful when you're working with shapes, no matter which drawing mode you're using. That's because when you create a shape using one of Flash's shape tools—a star, say, or a circle—Flash actually creates two separate elements: the inside of the shape (a fill), and the outline of the shape (a stroke). If you want to change the color of the entire shape, you need to use two tools: the Paint Bucket tool (which lets you change the color of fills), and the Ink Bottle tool (which lets you change the color of strokes). When you convert the outline to a fill, Flash lets you manipulate both the outside and the inside of the shape in the same way using the same tools. Converting also lets you

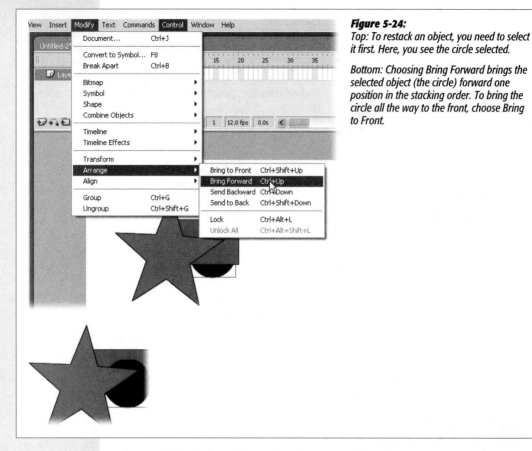

Figure 5-24:
Top: To restack an object, you need to select it first. Here, you see the circle selected.

Bottom: Choosing Bring Forward brings the selected object (the circle) forward one position in the stacking order. To bring the circle all the way to the front, choose Bring to Front.

create scalable shapes (images that shrink evenly) and nice straight corners (thick strokes appear rounded at the corners; thick fills shaped like lines don't).

To convert a line into a fill:

1. **Select the line (or outline) you want to convert into a fill.**

    Flash highlights the selected line.

2. **Choose Modify → Shape → Convert Lines to Fills.**

    Flash redisplays the line as a fill, and the Property Inspector changes to display fill-related properties (as opposed to line-related properties).

Aligning Objects

In Chapter 2 (page 50), you saw how to use Flash's grid, guides, and rulers to help you eyeball the position of objects as you drag them around on the Stage. You also see how to use the Alignment panel to line up objects with respect to each other or to one of the edges of the Stage.

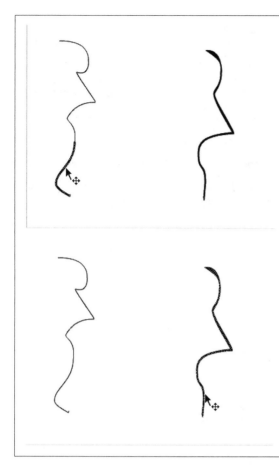

Figure 5-25:
Top: When you're working with ungrouped objects (which is what you create in merge drawing mode), the Selection tool behaves differently. Here, you see the results of clicking the Pencil-drawn line: Flash selects only a portion of the line (a single stroke).

Bottom: Clicking the Brush-drawn line, on the other hand, selects the entire line. This behavior is just one example of the different way Flash treats strokes and fills.

Both these approaches are useful—but Flash doesn't stop there. Snapping and guide layers give you even more control over where you place your objects with respect to each other on the Stage.

Snapping

Snapping is one of those features you're going to either love or hate. When you turn snapping on, you tell Flash to help you out when you're moving an object around by giving you a visual cue when you start to get too close to (or actually touch) a gridline, a guideline, or another object.

For example, in Figure 5-26, you see a circle being dragged across the Stage. Because Snap Align is turned on, Flash displays a faint dotted line (top) when the circle's dragged within range of the other object on the Stage (in this case, a bitmap image). And because "Snap to Objects" is turned on, Flash displays a thick *o* at the very center of the object as it's dragged over the edge of the bitmap (Figure 5-26, bottom).

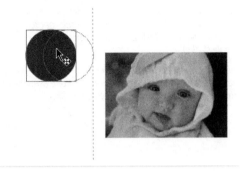

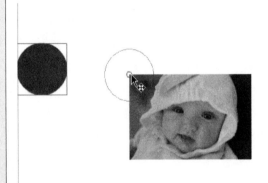

Figure 5-26:
*Top: When you turn on snapping, Flash gives you a visual
cue when you drag one object close to another object: a
gridline or a guideline. Here, Snap Align's turned on, so
Flash displays a dotted line when the circle's dragged near
the bitmap. You tell Flash how close is close enough using
the Horizontal and Vertical Object Spacing fields of the Edit
Snapping window, which you display by choosing View →
Snapping → Edit Snapping and then, in the Edit Snapping
window that appears, clicking Advanced.*

*Bottom: In this example, Snap to Objects is turned on, too,
so if you continue dragging past the dotted line, you see
another helpful hint: Flash displays a circle when you center
the circle directly over the bitmap's edge.*

Tip: For snapping to work, you can't speed around the Stage; if you do, you'll miss Flash's cues. Instead,
drag your objects slowly.

To turn on snapping, select View → Snapping and then, from the context menu
that appears, choose one of the following:

- **Snap Align.** Displays a dotted line when you drag an object within a certain
  number of pixels (you see how to change this number in the box on the next
  page) of another object or of any edge of the Stage.

- **Snap to Grid.** Displays a small, thick circle in the middle of your object when
  you drag that object close to a gridline (page 51).

- **Snap to Guides.** Displays a small, thick circle in the middle of your object when
  you drag that object close to a guideline (page 51).

- **Snap to Pixels.** Useful only if you want to work at the single-pixel level (your
  Stage must be magnified to at least 400 percent for this option to work), this
  option prevents you from moving an object in any increment less than a whole
  pixel. (To magnify your Stage by 400 percent, select View → Magnification →
  400%; when you do, a single-pixel grid appears.)

- **Snap to Objects.** Displays a small, thick circle in the middle of your object when you drag that object close to another object on the Stage.

The next time you move an object on the Stage, Flash displays the snapping behavior you chose.

Object Snapping: How Close Is Too Close?

Everybody says Snap Align is so great, but I'm not sure why I'd use it or how close I should set the snapping range.

Whether or not you'll find Snap Align useful depends entirely on you (some folks prefer to freewheel it, while others appreciate hints and advice) and what you're trying to create on the Stage. Snap Align is most useful in situations where you're trying to custom-position objects down to the pixel. For example, say you've drawn a row of different-sized flowers, and you're trying to position a row of bees, one bee at a time, exactly 25 pixels above the flowers. You can use the Align panel for a lot of basic alignment tasks, but this kind of custom alignment isn't one of them: Snap Align's your best option.

Flash assumes a buffer zone of 10 pixels around objects and 18 pixels around each edge of the Stage. (In other words, when you drag an object within 10 pixels of another object or 18 pixels from the edge of the Stage, Flash displays a snap guideline.) To change either of these buffer zones:

1. Choose View → Snapping → Edit Snapping. The Edit Snapping window appears.

2. In the Edit Snapping window, click Advanced to display expanded Edit Snapping options.

3. In the Object Spacing fields, type the buffer zone you want in pixels (you can specify both horizontal and vertical).

Edit Snapping

☑ Snap Align
☐ Snap to Grid
☐ Snap to Guides
☑ Snap to Pixels
☐ Snap to Objects

OK
Cancel
Save Default
Basic

Snap align settings
    Stage border: 18 px
Object spacing:
    Horizontal: 20 px
    Vertical: 20 px
Center alignment:
    ☐ Horizontal center alignment
    ☐ Vertical center alignment

Guide layers

If you've ever traced a drawing onto a piece of onionskin paper, you understand the usefulness of guide layers in Flash.

A *guide layer* is a special kind of layer that doesn't appear in your finished animation, but that you can hold beneath your Stage while you're drawing to help you position objects on the Stage. Say, for example, you want to align objects in a perfect circle, or on a perfect diagonal, or you want to arrange them so that they match a specific background (say, an ocean scene). You create a guide layer and, on it, draw your circle or diagonal or ocean scene. Then, when you create your "real" layer, your guide layer shows through so you can position your objects the way you want them. When you go to run your animation, though, you don't see your guide layer at all; it appears only when you're editing on the Stage.

Note: Technically speaking, a guide layer is a motion guide layer (just without the motion). You learned more about motion guide layers in Chapter 3.

To create a guide layer:

1. **On the Stage, draw your guide shapes, lines, or images.**

   In Figure 5-27 (top), the guide's a diagonal line.

2. **Position your cursor over the name of the layer you want to turn into a guide layer and then right-click.**

   Flash displays a pop-up menu.

3. **From the pop-up menu, select Guide.**

   Flash displays a little T-square just before the layer name, as in Figure 5-27 (bottom).

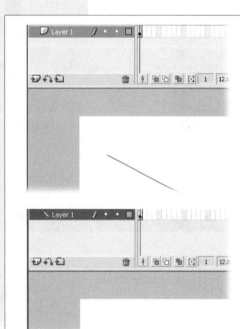

Figure 5-27:
Top: First, draw your guide. You can import a bitmap (useful if you want to display a background image as your guide) or use any of Flash's drawing tools. Here, the guide's a simple diagonal line.

Bottom: To tell Flash that this layer's going to be a special, only-see-it-while-you're-editing guide layer, right-click the layer name and then, from the menu that appears, select Guide. After you do, Flash designates a guide layer by displaying the little T-square icon in front of the layer name (here, Layer 1).

4. With the guide layer still selected, create a new, regular layer for your objects by choosing Insert → Timeline → Layer.

Flash creates a new layer and places it above the guide layer, as in Figure 5-28 (top).

Tip: Working with layers—especially guide layers—can be confusing if you're not used to it (and, frankly, it can be confusing even if you *are* used to it, especially if you're working with a lot of layers). To make sure you don't inadvertently modify your guide layer, you can *lock* it (tell Flash not to let you edit it temporarily). To lock your guide layer, click to select it and then turn on the checkbox beneath the Lock/Unlock column. Then, when you click to select your regular layer, you can align away without worrying about accidentally changing your (locked) guide layer.

---

5. Select View → Snapping and, in the context menu that appears, turn on the checkbox next to "Snap to Objects." You've turned snapping on.

Turning snapping on helps you position your objects on your guide layer.

6. With the regular layer selected, draw your objects.

You can then drag each object to your guideline (or guide object, or guide background) as shown in Figure 5-28 (bottom).

Adding Text to Your Drawing

Just as Flash offers tools for adding shapes and lines to your drawings, it offers a tool specifically designed to let you add text to your drawings—the Text tool.

To use the Text tool:

1. In the Tools panel, select the Text tool (Figure 5-29, top).

Flash highlights the Text tool; when you mouse over to the Stage, your cursor changes to crosshairs accompanied by a miniature letter A.

2. Click the Stage where you want your text to begin.

Flash displays a squished-up empty text box, and the Property Inspector displays text-related properties.

3. Drag the box a few inches.

Flash widens the text box.

4. If you like, in the Property Inspector, change the font size, color, or any other text-related property:

Text Type (Static, Dynamic, Input). *Static text* is the text you add directly to your drawing, as shown in Figure 5-29; *dynamic text* is a placeholder for text that changes when your finished animation plays (for example, the current date or stock prices); *input text* is a text placeholder into which your audience can type text (and which you can then manipulate) when your finished animation runs. Find out more about static and dynamic text in Chapter 11.

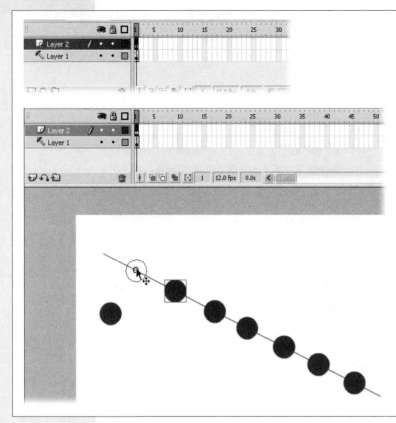

Figure 5-28:
Top: Flash designates a "regular" layer using an icon of a little page turning.

Bottom: Here you see a handful of circles being aligned on the diagonal. Although the diagonal line appears to be on the same Stage as the circles, it's not; it's safely tucked away in the guide layer. When you run your animation, all you see are your objects; the guide layer doesn't appear at all in your finished animation.

You get the following options for Dynamic text only: Line Type (tells Flash to accept multiple lines of text or a single line); Selectable (tells Flash whether or not you want your audience to be able to select the dynamic text at runtime); "Render Text as HTML" (tells Flash to interpret any HTML code it encounters in the dynamic text instead of just displaying it); Show Border Around Text (tells Flash to display a border around the dynamic text to set it off from the rest of the content in that frame); and Var (tells Flash what variable name you want to use for this dynamic text input field when you're accessing the contents of the field using ActionScript).

Selection Width and Height. Type pixels to change the size of the text box.

Selection X Position and Y Position. Type pixels to reposition the text box.

Font. Click to select from a long list of text fonts.

Letter Spacing. Drag the slider to squish letters together (or pull them apart), a process called *manual kerning*.

Character Position. Choose from Normal, Superscript (raised slightly), or Subscript (lowered slightly).

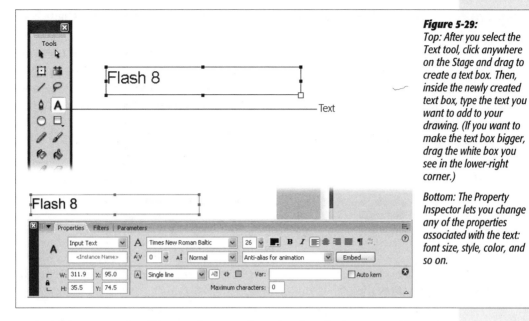

Figure 5-29:
Top: After you select the Text tool, click anywhere on the Stage and drag to create a text box. Then, inside the newly created text box, type the text you want to add to your drawing. (If you want to make the text box bigger, drag the white box you see in the lower-right corner.)

Bottom: The Property Inspector lets you change any of the properties associated with the text: font size, style, color, and so on.

Font Size. Drag the slider to choose a font size from 8 (super-small) to 96 (gigantic).

Text Color. Click the color picker to choose a new color for the text.

Bold, Italic, Align Left, Align Center, Align Right, Justify. Click these toggle buttons to apply bolding, italics, and alignment options to your text.

Edit Format Options. Click to change indent, line spacing, and margins for your text.

Change Orientation of Text. Flash assumes Horizontal, but you can click to choose Vertical, Left to Right or Vertical, Right to Left.

Font Rendering Method. Click to choose from Use Device Fonts, Bitmap Text (No Anti-Alias), Anti-Alias for Animation, Anti-Alias for Readability, and Custom Anti-Alias. (Applying one of the first two options to fonts from 12 to 24 points can make the text appear a bit crisper.)

Auto Kern. Turn on this checkbox to make your font look as natural as possible. (Turn it off if you prefer to kern manually; see the Letter Spacing option above.)

URL Link. Type a URL (such as *www.missingmanuals.com*) to display text in your finished animation as a clickable link.

Target. Useful only if you're creating nested objects in Flash, this option lets you specify precisely where in the hierarchy you want to load the URL specified in URL Link.

5. In the text box, type the text you want to add to your drawing (**Figure 5-29, top**).

Flash displays your text based on the properties you set in the Property Inspector.

Tip: To change the properties of individual letters, simply select the letters you want to work with and then, in the Property Inspector, make the changes you want. If you want to apply other, non–Properties panel effects to individual letters, though (for example, if you want to skew or flip certain letters and not others, or apply a *gradient*), you first need to break the text apart. To break text, select the text box; then choose Modify → Break Apart *twice*. (Choosing Modify → Break Apart once breaks text into individual text boxes; choosing the text a second time turns the text into a fill.)

---

6. **Click a blank part of the Stage to exit text-editing mode.**

Flash removes the bounding box, and the text properties disappear from the Property Inspector. At this point you can move your text, resize it, and reshape it just as you can any other object. To change the text itself, though, you need to double-click the text box to get back into text-editing mode and redisplay the text properties.

Tip: If you're using Flash Professional 8 (as opposed to Flash Basic 8), you can apply *filters* (special effects) such as Drop Shadow, Blur, and Glow to your text by using the Filters panel (Window → Properties → Filter). Check out page 233 for details.

Advanced Color and Fills

Color is one of the most primitive, powerful communicative devices at your disposal. With color, a skillful animator can engender anxiety or peacefulness, hunger or confusion. She can jar, confuse, delight, soothe, entertain, or inform—all without saying a word.

Color theory is too large a topic to cover completely here. What you *do* find in this chapter is a quick introduction to basic color theory, as well as tips on how to work with color in Flash. You'll see how to change the colors of the shapes, lines, and images you create with Flash's drawing tools; how to create and reuse custom color palettes (especially useful if you're trying to match the colors in your Flash animation to those of a corporate logo, for example, or to a specific photo or piece of art); and how to apply sophisticated color effects including gradients, transparency, and bitmap fills.

Color Basics

The red you see in a nice, juicy watermelon—or any other color, for that matter—is actually made up of a bunch of different elements, each of which you can control using Flash's Color panel:

- **Hue** is what most people think of when someone says *color*. Red, orange, yellow, green, blue, indigo, and violet are all hues. Out of the box, Flash offers 216 different hues. You can also blend your own custom hues by mixing any number of these basic 216 hues.

- **Saturation** refers to the amount of color (hue) you apply to something. A light wash of red, for example, looks pink; pile on more of the same color and you get a rich, vibrant red.

- **Brightness** determines how much of any given color you can actually see. A lot of light washes out a color; too little light, and the color begins to look muddy. At either end of the spectrum, you have pitch black (no light at all) and white (so much light that light is all you can see). In between these two extremes, adding light to a hue creates a *tint*. For example, if you add enough light to a rich strawberry-ice-cream pink, you get a delicate pastel pink.

- **Transparency** refers to how much background you can see through a color, from all of it (in which case the color is completely transparent, or invisible) to no background at all (in which case the color is *opaque*). In Flash, you set the transparency (technically, the *opacity*) for a color using the Alpha field.

RGB and HSB

Color doesn't exist in a vacuum. The colors you get when you mix pigments aren't the same as the colors you get when you mix different colored lights (which is how a computer monitor works). Artists working in oil paint or pastel use the red-yellow-blue color model, for example, and commercial printers use the cyan-magenta-yellow-black color model. In the world of computer graphics and animation, though, the color model you use is *red-green-blue*, or *RGB*.

This model means that you can tell Flash to display any color imaginable just by telling it precisely how much red, green, and blue to display. But if you don't happen to know how much red, green, and blue makes up, say, a certain shade of lilac, Flash gives you three more ways to specify a particular color:

- **HSB.** You can tell Flash the hue, saturation, and brightness you want it to display.

- **Hexadecimal.** You can type the hexadecimal number for the color you want Flash to display. Because hexadecimal notation is one of the ways you specify colors in HTML, you can use hexadecimal numbers to match a Web page color precisely to a color in Flash.

- **Selection.** In the Color Panel, you can drag your cursor around on the Color Mixer tab's Color Picker (Figure 5-30) until you find a color you like. This option's the easiest, of course, and the best part is, after you decide on a color, Flash tells you the color's RGB, HSB, and hexadecimal numbers (all of which come in handy if you want to create a color precisely, either in another Flash animation or in another graphics program altogether).

In the next section, you see how to specify a custom color using Flash's Color panel.

The Six Commandments of Color

Whether you're using Flash to create an interactive tutorial, an animated art short, a slick advertisement, or something else entirely, you need to be aware of color and how it supports (or detracts from) the message you're trying to get across. Color is at least as important as any other design element, from the fonts and shapes you choose to the placement of those shapes and the frame-by-frame timing of your finished animation.

Although the psychology of color is still in its relative infancy, a few color rules have stood the test of time. Break them at your own risk.

1. **Black text on a white background is ubiquitous for a reason.** Any other color combination produces eyestrain after as little as one sentence.

2. **Color is relative.** The human eye perceives color in context, so the same shade of pink looks completely different when you place it next to, say, olive green than it does when you place it next to red, white, or purple.

3. **For most animations, there's no such thing as a Web-safe color.** *Web-safe colors*—the handful of colors that supposedly appear the same on virtually all computers, whether they're Mac or Windows, laptop or desktop, ancient or new—were an issue in the old days. If you chose a non-Web-safe color palette, your audiences might have seen something different from what you intended (or might have seen nothing at all, depending on how their hardware and software were configured). But time marches on, and any computer newer than a few years old can display the entire range of colors that Flash lets you create. Of course, if you know for a fact that your target audience is running 15-year-old computers (as a lot of folks in other countries and in schools are), or if you suspect they might have configured their monitor settings to display only a handful of colors (it happens), you probably do want to play it

safe and stick to the Web-safe colors that Flash offers. (To display Web-safe colors, choose Window and, in the pop-up menu that appears, turn on the checkbox next to Color Swatches. In the Color panel, click the Options menu and then, from the pop-up menu that appears, select Web 216. The Color Swatches tab displays 216 Web-safe colors.)

4. **Contrast is at least as important as color.** *Contrast*—how different or similar two colors look next to each other—affects not just how your audiences see your animation, but whether or not they can see it at all. Putting two similar colors back-to-back (putting a blue circle on a green flag, for instance, or red text on an orange background) is unbearably hard on your audience's eyes.

5. **Color means different things in different cultures.** In Western cultures, black is the color of mourning; in Eastern cultures, the color associated with death and mourning is white. In some areas of the world, purple connotes royalty; in others, a particular political party; in still others, a specific football team. In color, as in all things Flash, knowing your audience helps you create and deliver an effective message.

6. **You can never completely control the color your audience sees.** Hardware and software calibration, glare from office lighting, the amount of dust on someone's monitor—a lot of factors affect the colors your audience sees. So unless you're creating a Flash animation for a very specific audience in which you know precisely what equipment and lighting they'll be using to watch your masterpiece, don't waste a lot of time trying to tune your colors to the nth degree.

Creating Custom Colors

Out of the box, Flash offers 216 Web-safe colors. But if you can't find the precise shade you want among those 216 colors, you're free to mix and match your own custom colors using the Flash's Color panel.

Here's how:

1. **Select Window → Color Mixer.**

   The Color panel shown in Figure 5-30 appears with the Color Mixer tab selected.

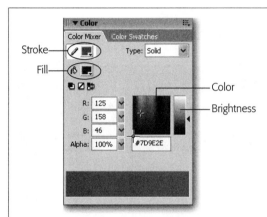

Stroke
Fill
Color
Brightness

Figure 5-30:
Flash packs a lot of power into the tiny Color Mixer tab. But most of the time, you can safely ignore everything except the Stroke and Fill icons (one of which you need to choose before you begin working with the Color Mixer) and the Color and Brightness windows, which you use to select a custom color. Out of the box, Flash lets you specify red, green and blue values, as shown here; if you'd prefer instead to specify hue, saturation, and brightness, check out Figure 5-31.

2. **On the Color Mixer tab, click either the Fill icon or the Stroke icon, depending on whether you plan to apply your custom color to a fill or a stroke (page 57 gives you the lowdown on the difference between the two).**

3. **Select a custom color. You can do this one of four ways:**

   You can drag around on the Color Picker until you see a color you like in the Preview window (Figure 5-30).

   If you know them, you can type values for the red, green, and blue color components of the color you want. (See the box on page 170.)

   You can type a hexadecimal value in the Hexadecimal Color Designator box. (Hexadecimal, or base 16, values can only contain the following digits: 0-9 and A-F. Folks who spend a lot of time writing HTML code are usually comfortable with hex numbers; if you're not one of them, you can safely skip this option.)

   You can type values for hue, saturation, and brightness. Click the Options menu and then, from the pop-up menu that appears, turn on the checkbox next to HSB. The Color Mixer tab changes to displays fields for Hue, Saturation, and Brightness, as shown in Figure 5-31.

Figure 5-31:
Clicking the Options menu and turning on the checkbox next to HSB results in this version of the Color Mixer tab, which lets you specify a color by typing in values for hue (in degrees), saturation (as a percentage), and brightness (also as a percentage).

UP TO SPEED

Specifying Common RGB Colors

RGB is a funky system based not on the way humans think, but on the way computers think. So the numbers you type in the Color Mixer to describe the red, green, and blue components of a color need aren't in percentages, as you might expect, but instead need to range from 0 (no color at all) to 255 (pure color).

Here are a handful of common colors expressed in RGB terms:

Red	Green	Blue	Result
0	0	0	Black
255	255	255	White
255	0	0	Red
0	255	0	Green
0	0	255	Blue
255	255	0	Yellow
0	255	255	Cyan
255	0	255	Magenta

4. **To customize your color even further, you can also specify one of the following:**

   Color type. Choose from Solid (most of the time, you want this), Linear (a type of gradient effect described on page 173), Radial (another type of gradient described on page 173), and Bitmap (lets you color an object using an image rather than a hue, as on page 172).

   Transparency (opacity). You can tell Flash to make your color more or less transparent, so that the images and backgrounds you put behind the color show through (Figure 5-32). Click the arrow next to Alpha and then drag the slider that appears. Zero percent tells Flash to make your color completely transparent (see-through); 100 percent tells Flash to make your color completely opaque.

Tip: Invisible color sounds like an oxymoron, but zero percent opacity actually has a place in your bag of Flash tricks. As you see in Chapter 6, you can create a nifty appearing/disappearing effect using see-through color and a shape tween.

Brightness. To tint a color (in other words, to add light, or brightness), click the Brightness window (Figure 5-32) and then drag until you see the exact shade you want in the Preview window.

5. **In the Tools panel, select a drawing tool and then begin drawing on the Stage.**

Your strokes (or fills, depending on which icon you selected in step 1) appear in your brand-new custom color.

Tip: You don't have to create a custom color before you draw an object. You can draw an object first, select it and then create a custom color. When you create a color, Flash automatically changes the object's color to your new custom color.

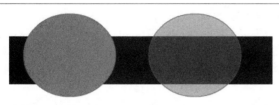

Figure 5-32:
When you use a transparent color, background objects and the Stage itself show through, giving the appearance of a different color altogether. Here, the two ovals are actually the same color, but they don't look like it: The selected oval on the right is 50 percent opaque, while the oval on the left is 100 percent opaque.

Saving Color Swatches

After you go to all the hard work of creating a custom color as described in the preceding section, you're probably going to want to save that color as a virtual *swatch* so that you can reuse it again without having to try to remember how you mixed it.

To save a custom color swatch, first create a custom color as described in the preceding section. Then follow these steps:

1. **In the Color panel, select the Color Swatches tab.**

(If you don't see the Color panel, choose Window and then, from the drop-down menu that appears, turn on the checkbox next to Color Swatches.)

Flash displays the Color Swatches tab in Figure 5-33.

2. **Move your cursor over the bottom half of the panel, anywhere below the color chart.**

Your cursor turns into a miniature paint bucket.

3. **Click anywhere below the color chart.**

Flash adds your new custom swatch to the bottom of the color chart on the left.

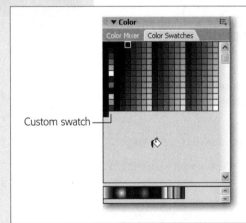

Figure 5-33:
Saving a specific color as a color swatch—whether it's one you custom-mixed or a standard color you found on the palette and liked—is kind of like saving the empty paint can after you paint your kitchen. The next time you want to use that particular color, all you have to do is grab the swatch (instead of relying on your memory or spending hours trying to recreate the exact shade). If you work with color a lot, swatches can make your life a whole lot easier.

Custom swatch

After you've saved a custom swatch, you can use it to change the color of a stroke or a fill, as you see in the following sections.

Using an Image as a Fill "Color"

Instead of choosing or blending a custom color, you can select an image to use as a fill "color." You can select any image in Flash's Library panel (page 30) or anywhere on your computer and apply that image to any size or shape of fill to create some pretty interesting effects.

As you can see in the following pages, the result depends on both the size and shape of the fill and the image you choose.

To use an image as a fill color:

1. **Select all the fills you want to "color."**

   Figure 5-34 (bottom) shows an example of two files: a star, and a freeform fill created using the Brush.

2. **In the Color Mixer tab of the Color panel, click the arrow next to Type (the Fill Style field) and, from the drop-down list that appears, choose Bitmap.**

   Flash displays the "Import to Library" window (Figure 5-34, top).

Note: To import additional image files to use as fills: in the Color Mixer tab of the Color panel, click the button marked Import (Figure 5-34, bottom). Then, with the fill on the Stage selected, click the image you want to use.

3. **In the "Import to Library" window, select the image file you want and then click Open.**

   Flash displays the image in the bottom of the Color Mixer panel, as well as next to the Fill icon, and "paints" your fills with the image. If your fill's larger than your image, Flash tiles the image, as shown in Figure 5-35.

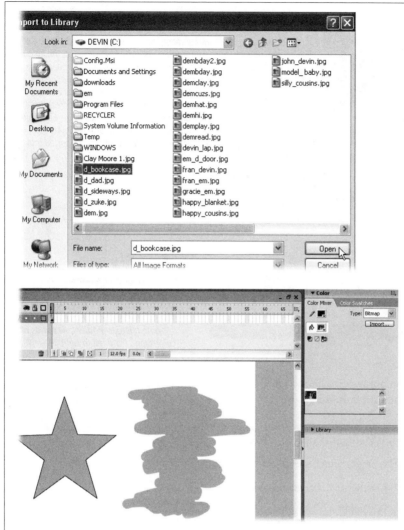

Figure 5-34:
Top: The first time you head to the Color Mixer tab of the Color panel and, in the Fill Style field, select Bitmap (see below), Flash pops open this Import to Library window. Despite the name of the Fill Style selection (Bitmap), Flash lets you import JPEG and other types of image files; you're not limited to .bmp files. Browse your computer for the image file you want and then click Open.

Bottom: The result: You get a custom "color" that consists of your image file. You apply this image to a fill (such as the star or freeform fill you see here) just as you do any other color.

Tip: If you apply the new fill "color" to an image by clicking the Paint Bucket icon and then clicking the fill, Flash tiles super-tiny versions of the image inside the fill to create a textured pattern effect.

Applying a Gradient

A *gradient* is a fill coloring effect that blends bands of color into each other. Flash offers *linear gradients* (straight up-and-down, left-to-right bands of color) and *radial gradients* (bands of color that begin in the center of a circle and radiate outward).

By applying a gradient to your fills, you can create the illusion of depth and per-spective. For example, you can make a circle look like a sphere, a line that looks like it's fading, and text that looks like it's reflecting light (Figure 5-36).

Figure 5-35:
How Flash applies your image to your fill depends on the size of your fill and the size of your image (and whether you select the fill and then change the Style Type to Bitmap, or vice versa). Here, the star is smaller than the image imported into Flash, so Flash shows a single image framed by the star's outline. Because the freeform fill is larger than the image, Flash tiles the image inside the freeform fill. Note, too, that Flash sticks the image you imported into the Library panel.

Figure 5-36:
Applying one of the preset radial gradients that Flash provides turns this circle into a ball, and makes this text look so shiny that it's reflecting light. The thin rectangle beneath the text is sporting a linear gradient; its bands of color blend from left to right.

You can apply a gradient swatch to your fills, or you can create your own custom gradients in Flash, much the same way you create your own custom colors (page 169).

To apply a gradient swatch to an object:

1. **On the Stage, select the object to which you want to add a gradient.**

   Flash highlights the selected object.

2. **Click the Fill Color icon.**

   Flash displays the Color Picker (Figure 5-37).

3. **From the Color Picker, choose one of the six gradient swatches that come with Flash.**

   Flash automatically redisplays your object using the gradient swatch you chose. Figure 5-37 shows a red radial gradient applied to a plain circle to create a simple 3-D effect.

To create a custom gradient:

1. **On the Stage, select the object to which you want to apply a custom gradient.**

   Flash highlights the selected object.

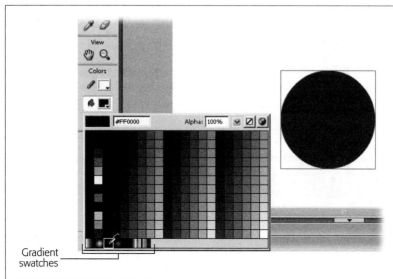

Figure 5-37:
Applying a gradient swatch is just as easy as applying a color. Flash comes with four radial gradient swatches (white, red, green, and blue) and two linear gradient swatches (blue/orange and rainbow). If one of these creates the effect you want, great. If not, you can change any of them to create your own custom gradient effects, as you see in the next section.

Gradient swatches

2. **Apply a gradient swatch to the object (see page 173).**

   If you like, change the color of the gradient, as described next.

3. **In the Color Mixer tab of the Color panel, double-click the first Color Pointer to select it.**

   Flash displays a Color Picker.

4. **In the Color Picker, click to select a color.**

   In your selected object, Flash turns the color at the center (for a radial gradient) or at the very left (for a linear gradient) to the color you chose. Repeat these two steps for each Color Pointer to change the color of each band of color in your gradient.

   If you like, change the thickness and definition of your gradient's color bands, as described next.

5. **In the Color Mixer tab of the Color panel, drag the first Color Pointer to the right.**

   The farther to the right you drag it, the more of that color appears in your custom gradient. The farther to the left you drag it, the less of that color appears in your custom gradient. Repeat this step for each band of color in your gradient.

   Next, if you like, you can add a new band of color to your custom gradient.

6. **In the Color Mixer tab of the Color panel, click anywhere on the Gradient Edit Bar.**

   Flash creates a new Color Pointer (see Figure 5-38), which you can edit as described in step 3. You can add as many Color Pointers (new bands of color) to your gradient as you like.

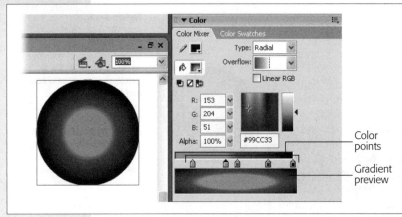

Figure 5-38:
Creating a custom gradient is more art than science. As you create new color bands, adjust the colors, and widen and thin each band using the Color Points, keep an eye on the Gradient Preview Window and on your selected object, too; Flash updates both as you edit your gradient, so you can see at a glance whether you like the effects you're creating.

For even more excitement, apply one or more *gradient transforms* to your object, as described next.

7. **In the Tools panel, click the Gradient Transform tool.**

   Flash displays a rotation arrow, a stretch arrow, and a reposition point.

   You can drag the *rotation arrow* to rotate the gradient; drag the *stretch arrow* to stretch the bands of color in your gradient, as shown in Figure 5-39 (top); or drag the *reposition point* to reposition the center of the gradient, as shown in Figure 5-39 (bottom).

Importing a Custom Color Palette

Depending on the type of animation you're creating in Flash, you might find it easier to import a custom color palette than to try to recreate each color you need.

For example, say you're working on a promotional piece for your company, and you want the colors you use in each and every frame of your animation to match the colors your company uses in all its other marketing materials (its brochures, ads, and so on). Rather than eyeball all the other materials or spend time contacting printers and graphics teams to try and track down the RGB values for each color, all you need to do is import a GIF file into Flash that contains all the colors you need: a GIF file showing your company's logo, for example, or some other image containing the colors you need to match.

To import a custom color palette:

1. **In the Color Swatches tab of the Color panel, click the Options menu.**

   A pop-up menu appears.

2. **From the pop-up menu, select Clear Colors.**

   Flash clears out the entire color palette on the Color Swatches tab, leaving just two swatches: black and white (Figure 5-40, right).

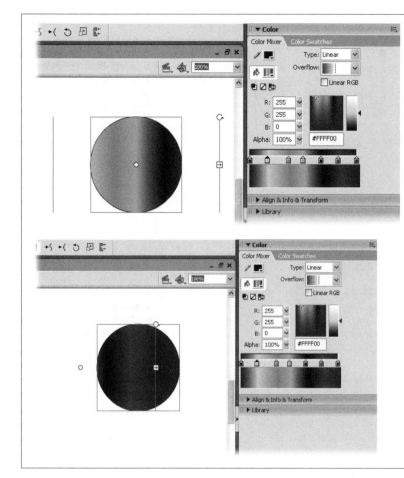

Figure 5-39:
*Top: Just as regular
transforms let you poke and
prod regular images to create
interesting effects, gradient
transforms let you
manipulate gradients (with
respect to the shapes you
originally applied them to) to
create interesting effects.
Here, dragging the stretch
arrow pulls the bands of
color, widening the bands at
the center and discarding the
bands at the edges. You see
the result of the stretched
gradients in the Color Mixer
panel.*

*Bottom: When you drag the
reposition point, you move
the center of the gradient
away from the center of the
object. This effect is especially
useful when you're working
with radial gradients because
it lets you create the illusion
that the object is reflecting
light streaming in from a
different angle.*

3. Once again, click the Options menu.

   The pop-up menu reappears.

4. **From the pop-up menu, select Add Colors.**

   Flash displays the Import Color Swatch window (Figure 5-40, left).

5. **In the Import Color Swatch window, click to choose a GIF file and then click
   Open.**

   Flash imports the custom color palette, placing each separate color in its own
   swatch in the Color Swatches tab (Figure 5-41).

Note: To restore the standard Flash color palette: From the Color Swatch tab, click the Options menu
and then, from the pop-up menu that appears, select Load Default Colors.

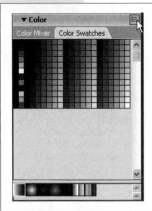
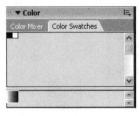

Figure 5-40:
Left: Here's what the typical Color Swatches tab looks like before you clear it (by clicking the Options menu and selecting Clear Colors). Think twice before you clear the palette: You can get back Flash's basic color palette, but you lose any custom color swatches you've saved in this document.

Right: After you clear the color palette, you're left with just two swatches: black and white.

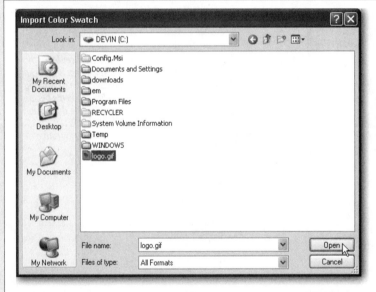

Figure 5-41:
When you head to the Color Mixer panel, click the Options menu and then choose Add Colors to import a custom color palette, Flash displays an Import Color Swatch window that should look pretty familiar if you've ever had occasion to open a file on a computer. Here, you click to browse the files on your computer. When you find the GIF file containing your custom color palette, click Open. Flash returns you to your Color Mixer panel, where you'll see that Flash has pulled in each separate color in your GIF file as a separate swatch, ready for you to use.

Copying Color with the Eyedropper

Tying color elements together is a subtle—but important—element of good design. It's the same principle as accessorizing: Say you buy a white shirt with purple pinstripes. Add a pink tie, and you're a candidate for the Worst Dressed list. But a purple tie that matches the pinstripes somehow pulls the look together.

In Flash, you may find you've created a sketch and colored it just the right shade of green, and you want to use that color in another part of the same drawing. Sure, you could slog through the Color panel, write down the hexadecimal notation for the color and then recreate the color. Or, if you know you're going to be working a lot with that particular color, you could create a custom color swatch (page 171).

But if you want to experiment with placing bits of the color here and there on the fly, the Eyedropper tool's the way to go. The Eyedropper tool lets you click the color on one image, and apply it instantly to another color on another image.

Note: The Eyedropper tool lets you transfer color only from a bitmap or a fill to a fill, and from a stroke to another stroke. If you want to transfer color *to* a bitmap, you need the Magic Wand (Lasso).

To copy color from one object to another:

1. **Select Edit → Deselect All.**

   Alternatively, you can press Ctrl+Shift+A (Windows) or Shift-⌘-A (Mac) to deselect everything on the Stage.

2. **From the Tools panel, click to select the Eyedropper tool.**

   As you mouse over the Stage, your cursor appears as an eyedropper while it's over a blank part of the Stage; an eyedropper and a brush when it's over a fill (as shown in Figure 5-42, top); and an eyedropper and a pencil when it's over a stroke.

3. **Click the bitmap, fill, or stroke color you want to copy** *from* **(imagine sucking the color up into your eyedropper).**

   If you click to copy from a fill or a bitmap, your cursor turns immediately into a paint bucket, as shown in Figure 5-42 (bottom); if you click to copy from a stroke, the cursor turns into an ink bottle.

Note: You can copy from a stroke, a fill, or a bitmap using the Eyedropper tool; you *can't* copy from a symbol or a grouped object.

---

4. **Click the bitmap, fill, or stroke you want to copy** *to* **(imagine squeezing the color out of your eyedropper). If you copied color from a bitmap or a fill, you need to click a fill; if you copied color from a stroke, you need to click a stroke.**

   Flash recolors the to stroke, fill, or bitmap you click on, applying the *from* color to the *to* color as shown in Figure 5-42, bottom.

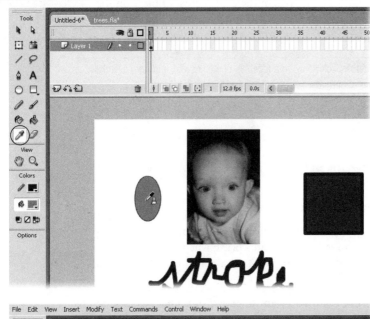

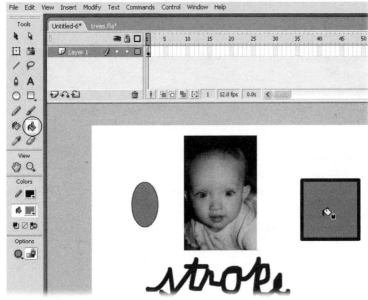

Figure 5-42:
Top: After you click the Eyedropper tool, your cursor changes to remind you what it's passing over. If it's over a fill or a bitmap, you see a little brush next to the eyedropper; it it's over a stroke, you see a little pencil next to the eyedropper. Here, the Eyedropper tool is selecting a fill (the oval).

Bottom: Here, the paint bucket icon lets you know you need to click a fill.

Adding Special Effects

One of the first things you want to do when you start working with Flash is create cool animated effects. Some effects require a hefty chunk of work on your part. For example, if you want to create a complex custom effect such as a superhero dipping and diving across the screen while his cape flutters behind him and sparks shoot out of his fingertips, you need to roll up your sleeves and apply the tweening and frame-by-frame animation techniques in Chapter 3.

But if all you want to do is apply a basic, run-of-the-mill animated effect to an object on the Stage, Flash offers an alternative—*Timeline effects.* These effects handle things like text that starts out tiny and grows, so that it looks like it's coming straight at the audience, a heart that appears to be beating, or a line that looks like it's drawing itself on the screen. Using Timeline effects, you can click an object on the Stage, tell Flash which effect you'd like to apply, and sit back and relax while Flash cranks out the frames to make it so.

This chapter describes the built-in Timeline effects you can use, along with tips and hints for incorporating them into more complex animations. It also shows you an additional animated effect you can create (by hand) using a special type of layer called a mask layer.

Note: Timeline effects are a boon to folks who are new to Flash, of course, because they deliver maximum animation punch for a minimum investment of time and know-how. But they're useful and sophisticated enough that even seasoned pros have been known to use them. Hey, if all you need is a straightforward effect, why reinvent the wheel?

Built-in Timeline Effects

Flash comes with a handful of Timeline effects, including Distributed Duplicate, Blur, Expand, Explode, Transition, and Transform. As you see in the following sections, all you have to do to apply a Timeline effect is select an object on the Stage, click a button to display the effect wizard (basically, a settings window) and then fill out a few bits of information describing how you want Flash to apply the effect to this particular object. When you finish, Flash generates all the drawings, symbols, and tweened frames necessary to create the animated effect and then sticks them in their own layer on the Timeline. (As a bonus, Flash sticks the symbols it creates during the generation process into the Library for you to inspect or reuse as you please.)

You can apply a Timeline effect to any kind of object: editable lines and shapes, grouped objects, text blocks, symbols, or bitmaps.

Note: Flash offers two additional Timeline effects that don't involve animation and so aren't covered here: Drop Shadow, which applies a drop shadow effect similar to the Drop Shadow filter described on page 233 and Copy to Grid, which lets you copy a single object and position the copies in evenly aligned rows and columns.

There's only one catch: You can't modify a Timeline effect by hand. If you want to tweak the effect, you have to remember to use the same effects wizard you used to create it in the first place. If you don't, you risk breaking or even removing the effect. (See the box on page 183.)

Distributed Duplicate (Tumbling)

The Distributed Duplicate effect lets you copy an object and then paste copies of that object on the Stage in a straight line. You get to choose the angle of the straight line; you also get to tell Flash how close you want the copies to appear to each other and whether or not you want the copies in different colors.

If you like, you can spread the effect out over a series of frames and add rotation, as you see in the following steps, to turn a static diagonal line of copies into an animated sequence that looks as if the object's tumbling.

Note: You can download the Flash document in this example (dd_begin.fla), a working copy (dd.fla), and all the other examples in this chapter from the "Missing CD" page at *www.missingmanuals.com/cds*.

To apply a Distributed Duplicate Timeline effect:

1. **Open the file dd_begin.fla. Then, on the Stage, select the die (Figure 6-1).**

   Make sure you see the blue selection box around the die. If you don't select an object first, Flash doesn't let you choose a Timeline effect.

2. **Select Insert → Timeline Effects → Assistants → Distributed Duplicate.**

   Up pops the Distributed Duplicate window in Figure 6-2.

No Such Thing as a Free Lunch

When you apply a Timeline effect, it's Flash that does all the grunt work, so it's Flash that gets to decide how to organize and name the layers and symbols it creates—not you.

If you go back later and change the names of the layers and symbols, Flash renames them the instant you modify the effect (page 187).

Flash does let you edit both the instance of the single-frame graphic symbol it generates as part of the effect process and the single-frame graphic symbol itself. But if you try to edit the multiframe graphic symbol or make any changes directly to the Timeline—in other words, if you try to edit the effect by hand—Flash either removes the effect immediately or displays this error message:

Click OK in the error message, and you can't modify the effect using the effects window (the wizard) ever again. If you try, you find the Modify → Timeline Effects → Edit Effect menu option appears grayed out.

The best strategy: Take advantage of the point-and-click ease of Timeline effects, but don't edit them by hand unless you have to. And even then, wait until you're absolutely, positively sure you won't need to edit them through the wizard again. (You'd also be wise to make a backup copy of your document first.)

> You are trying to edit a symbol that has an effect applied. If you choose to proceed, you will lose the ability to edit its settings. Do you want to continue?
>
> ☐ Don't warn me again.
>
> (Cancel) (OK)

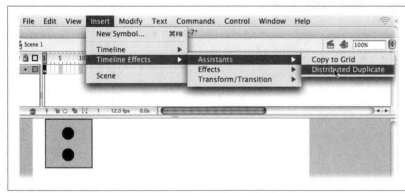

Figure 6-1:
In this example, the die's a grouped object, but you can apply Timeline effects to ungrouped graphics, bitmaps, or symbols. Just keep in mind that Flash turns your object into a symbol as part of the Timeline effect process, and you can't edit that symbol without breaking your effect.

Next, you'll change the settings to create a tumbling effect.

3. **Click the Offset Rotation box and then type *25*. Click the Offset Start Frame box and then type *10*. Then, turn off the checkbox next to Change Color.**

   You can preview the effect by clicking the Update Preview button. Flash displays the results of your changes in the preview area of the Distributed Duplicate window (Figure 6-3).

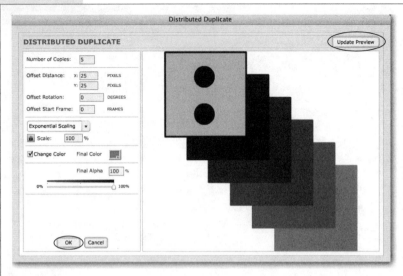

Figure 6-2:
In the preview area, you see Flash's best guess at how you want your effect to appear. If it's not what you want (and it rarely is), you can change any of the settings on the left side of the Distributed Duplicate window. Click Update Preview frequently to see the effects of your changes. When you're satisfied, click OK to return to your workspace.

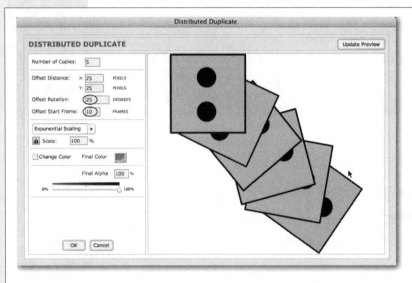

Figure 6-3:
You want to get in the habit of using the Update Preview window to preview your effects—it's much, much quicker than clicking OK—and then testing your animation the usual way, by selecting Control → Test Movie. Here you see the results of changing a couple of settings (circled). But by changing different settings, as described below, you can create a number of surprisingly different looks.

4. **Click OK to save your effect and return to your workspace.**

   The Distributed Duplicate window disappears. On the Timeline, you see a 50-frame graphic symbol. You also notice that Flash has placed the 50-frame graphic symbol (in this example, named Distributed Duplicate 6) in the Library, along with a single-frame graphic symbol named effectSymbol (Figure 6-4).

Tip: The full story on graphic symbols comes in the next chapter.

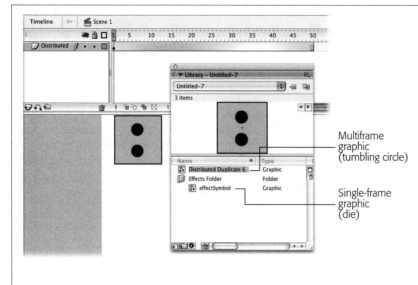

Figure 6-4:
In this example, the Number of Copies was set to 5 and the Offset Start Frame (the number of frames between copies) was set to 10, so Flash generated a total of 50 frames in the layer it named Distributed Duplicate 6. It also saved a copy of the one-frame die symbol (effectSymbol) it created from the original grouped object and a copy of the 50-frame graphic symbol (Distributed Duplicate 6) it placed on the Timeline and put them both in the Library for you to reuse as you see fit.

Multiframe graphic (tumbling circle)

Single-frame graphic (die)

Here's a rundown of all the settings you can change in the Distributed Duplicate window:

- **Number of Copies.** Tells Flash how many copies of your original object to display.

- **Offset Distance.** Tells Flash how far apart (in pixels) you want it to place each copy, and in what direction. You can type individual numbers for horizontal distance (X) and vertical distance (Y). For example, typing *0* for X and *50* for Y tells Flash to display the copies straight up and down; typing *50* for X and *0* for Y tells Flash to display copies horizontally.

- **Offset Rotation.** Tells Flash how far to rotate each copy with respect to the previous copy. If you type 0 for this setting, Flash doesn't rotate the copies at all.

- **Offset Start Frame.** Tells Flash how slowly you want it to display the new copies, with larger numbers resulting in slower displays. For example, if you type *5*, Flash places five frames in between the frames containing each copied object; if you type *10*, Flash places 10 frames in between; and so on. If you type *0* for this setting, Flash creates a single-frame, static effect.

- **Exponential Scaling/Linear Scaling, Lock icon, and Scale.** You can tell Flash to shrink or expand each copy it displays, based either on the previous copy (Exponential Scaling) or the original object (Linear Scaling). Clicking the Lock icon lets you type individual scaling percentages for the horizontal (X) and vertical (Y) dimensions of your object; clicking it again locks the scaling to a single, overall, uniform percent (Scale). For example, typing in an overall Scale of *50* with Exponential Scaling turned on tells Flash to shrink each copy in half compared to the previous copy; typing in an overall Scale of *200* tells Flash to expand each copy to twice the size of the previous copy.

• **Change Color, Final Color, and Final Alpha.** Turning on the Change Color checkbox tells Flash to display each copy in a slightly different color, starting with the color and transparency of the original object and ending with the color and transparency you choose using the Final Color color picker and the Final Alpha slider, respectively.

Blur

The Blur effect lets you change the transparency, position, and scale of an object to create a blurring, or smudging, effect. You get to tell Flash how hard or soft you want the effect, along with whether you want it to move your object horizontally, vertically, or both. If you choose both, as in the following example, the object appears to recede into the distance, creating smudgy trails as it disappears.

To apply a Blur effect:

1. **Open the file blur_begin.fla.**

   You can find this file on the Missing Manuals CD, along with a working copy of the example called blur.fla.

2. **On the Stage, select the bitmap you want to blur. Then choose Insert → Timeline Effects → Effects → Blur.**

   The Blur window in Figure 6-5 appears. In the preview area, Flash displays the selected image and then immediately begins showing you the effect.

Figure 6-5:
Technically, you can apply a blur effect to any object. You'll want to experiment, of course, but in general, single-colored objects don't produce as interesting an effect as multicolored objects with nice fat streaks of contrast, like this bitmap.

3. **Change the intensity of the blur by clicking the Resolution box and then typing in 55 (instead of 15); then click Update Preview.**

   In the preview area, you see the results of the change: a much more intense, almost abstract effect (Figure 6-6).

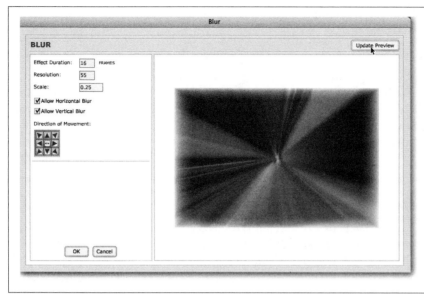

Figure 6-6:
Here you see the results of the blur. Click OK, and Flash returns you to your workspace, where you find the Timeline filled with auto-generated frames and the Library with auto-generated symbols. Flash recreates and renames symbols and layers each time you make a change in the Blur window and click Update Preview. If you've experimented a bit, don't be surprised to find names like Blur 10 and Blur 11.

4. **Click OK to save your changes and return your workspace.**

The Blur window disappears. On the Timeline, you see a 16-frame graphic symbol in its own layer. If you open the Library panel, you see that Flash has placed two symbols in the Library: the multiframe graphic symbol and a single-frame graphic symbol. (For the skinny on symbols and instances, check out Chapter 7.)

Tip: To preview your effect on the Stage, drag the playhead along the Timeline.

Here's a list of all the different settings you can change in the Blur window to create different effects:

- **Effect Duration.** How long you want this effect to last; in other words, the number of frames you want this effect to span. (Flash assumes 16 unless you tell it otherwise.)

- **Resolution.** The number of copies of your image you want Flash to display, to create the blurring effect. The larger the number you type in this box, the more abstract the effect (and the harder Flash—and your computer—have to work to produce it; type *500* or so, and you may have time to go out for coffee while you wait for Flash to render your preview).

- **Scale.** The size of the image you want Flash to begin with before it starts blurring expressed as a percentage of the size of your original. For example, 0.25 tells Flash to begin with a copy of your image one-quarter the size of the original and *then* begin the blur.

- **Allow Horizontal Blur.** Turn on this checkbox to let Flash move your object left and right.

- **Allow Vertical Blur.** Turn on this checkbox to let Flash move your object up and down.

- **Direction of Movement.** Click one of the nine arrows in this box to tell Flash which direction to blur your image. (If you want to click an arrow that appears grayed out, turn on the checkboxes next to Allow Horizontal Blur and Allow Vertical Blur.) Clicking the two tiny arrows in the middle of the box, as in the example in Figures 6-5 and 6-6, tells Flash to blur in all directions simultaneously to create a coming-straight-at-you effect.

Expand

Using the Expand effect, you can make a bunch of letters, shapes, or other objects appear to stretch apart (expand) or squeeze together (contract). You can also make a single object appear to expand and contract, as you see in the following example.

To apply the Expand effect:

1. **Open the file expand_begin.fla.**

   You can download this file from the "Missing CD" page.

2. **On the Stage, select the grouped object (the heart). Then choose Insert →
   Timeline Effects → Effects → Expand.**

   The Expand window in Figure 6-7 appears. In the preview area, the heart shape's bouncing from side to side.

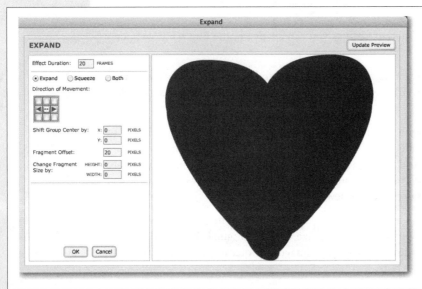

Figure 6-7:
If you were applying the Expand effect to a chunk of text, the preview Flash shows you would actually make sense: You'd see the letters stretch apart. Not so when you're trying to apply the effect to a single object. You have to change the numbers in the Fragment Offset and Change Fragment Size by boxes before you see the object expand.

3. **In the Expand window, turn on the checkbox next to Both. Click the Fragment Offset box. and then type *0*. Click the Change Fragment Size by (Height) box and then type *50*. Finally, click the Change Fragment Size by (Width) box and then type *50*.**

Test your changes by clicking the Update Preview button: A pulsing heart should appear in the preview area.

4. **Click OK to save your changes and return to your workspace.**

The Expand window disappears. On the Timeline, you see a 20-frame graphic symbol stretched out in its own layer. If you open the Library panel, you see the same symbol. (With its Flash-assigned name, it's hard to miss.) If you like, you can drag a few more instances of your beating heart onto the Stage and view the results by choosing Control → Test Movie.

Here's a list of all the settings you can change in the Expand window:

- **Effect Duration.** How long you want this effect to last; in other words, the number of frames you want this effect to span. (Flash assumes 20 unless you tell it otherwise.)

- **Expand.** Tells Flash to move multiple objects apart and to stretch single objects.

- **Squeeze.** Tells Flash to push multiple objects together and to compress single objects.

- **Both.** Tells Flash to alternate expanding and squeezing (see above).

- **Direction of Movement.** Click one of the three arrows in this box to tell Flash which direction to expand (or contract) your images: left, from the center out, or right.

- **Shift Group Center by (X, Y).** Expands or contracts horizontally (X) or vertically (Y), based on the direction you chose above.

- **Fragment Offset.** Tells Flash how far apart to position the objects during expansion (or contraction) with respect to each other.

- **Change Fragment Size by (Height, Width).** Tells Flash to stretch or compress the objects themselves (height-wise, width-wise, or both) during expansion or contraction. Flash assumes 0 in both cases; you can type negative numbers (to compress objects) or positive numbers (to expand them).

Explode

Applying the standard Explode effect to a graphic element makes the element appear to burst apart, with each piece gradually turning transparent as it spins and arcs away from ground zero.

The Explode effect is pretty effective on a single bitmap or shape, as you see in the steps below. But it also works well on grouped objects, such as the letters in a block of text.

To apply the Explode effect:

1. **Open the file explode_begin.fla.**

   You can download the file (along with a working copy of the example, explode.fla), from *www.missingmanuals.com/cds*.

2. **On the Stage, select the star (Figure 6-8, left). Then choose Insert → Timeline Effects → Effects → Explode.**

   The Explode window in Figure 6-8 (right) appears. In the preview area, you see the star breaking apart into transparent, arcing little pieces. Next, why not make the effect a little more pronounced?

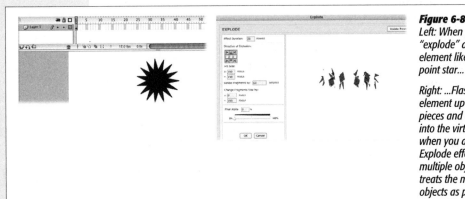

Figure 6-8:
Left: When you "explode" a single element like this 15-point star...

Right: ...Flash breaks the element up into little pieces and tosses them into the virtual air. But when you apply the Explode effect to multiple objects, Flash treats the multiple objects as pieces; it doesn't break them down further.

3. **Click the Arc Size (Y) box and then type *350*. Then, click the Change Fragments Size by (X) box and then type *100*.**

   Click the Update Preview button to see the results of your changes. In the preview area, you see the larger pieces (fragments) that explode higher.

4. **To save your changes and return to your workspace, click OK.**

   The Explode window disappears.

On your Timeline, spanning the first 20 frames, you see the graphic symbol Flash created. Flash renamed your layer, too. In Figure 6-9, the layer name is *Explode 13*. (Flash adds 1 to the name each time you preview *any* effect, beginning with the last time you launched the program.) In the Library, you see that Flash has been busy, indeed, organizing 16 single-frame movie clip symbols and one multiframe graphic symbol into two folders.

Here's a list of all the settings you can change in the Explode window to create different exploding effects:

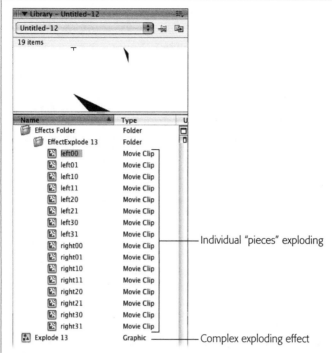

Figure 6-9:
You can drag instances of any of these symbols onto the Stage to create your own effects, if you like, and even change the color, transparency, position, or skew of the instances, but you can't edit the symbols. If you try—by double-clicking the name of one of the movie clip symbols, for example— Flash immediately erases the frames on the Timeline, thereby removing your effect.

Individual "pieces" exploding

Complex exploding effect

- **Effect Duration.** How long you want this effect to last; in other words, the number of frames you want this effect to span. (Flash assumes 20 unless you tell it otherwise.)

- **Direction of Explosion.** Click one of the six arrows in this box to tell Flash which direction you want the explosion to move.

- **Arc Size (X, Y).** Click the X box and then type a number to tell Flash how far (in pixels) you want the pieces to fly horizontally; click the Y box and then type a number to tell Flash how far (in pixels) you want the pieces to fly vertically.

- **Rotate Fragments by.** Click the box and then type a number to tell Flash (in degrees) how far to rotate each of the pieces.

- **Change Fragments Size by (X, Y).** Tells Flash how much to stretch (or shrink) each piece (in pixels) during the explosion sequence. You can specify a number for width (X), for height (Y), or both. A number over 100 tells Flash to stretch the pieces; a number under 100 tells Flash to shrink them.

- **Final Alpha.** Tells Flash how transparent you want the pieces to be at the end of the explosion sequence. Flash initially assumes 0% (completely transparent), but you can type any number you want up to 100% (completely opaque).

Note: Flash doesn't let you apply more than one Timeline effect to the same object in the same layer. If you want to apply multiple effects–for example, you want an object to spin *and* explode–you need to copy the object to multiple layers and then apply one effect per layer.

Transform (Shape Tween)

The Transform effect lets you create a simple shape tween quickly and easily. (As you may recall from Chapter 3, a *shape tween* is a Flash-generated animated sequence that shows an object being scaled, rotated, recolored, faded, and/or repositioned.)

Note: You can create a lot of different effects with the Transform effect. Some of the most useful include spinning, fading in and out, flying on and off, and changing color.

Compared to creating a shape tween by hand, the Transform effect is a sweet deal indeed. Instead of having to hunt around in a bunch of panels to choose the effect you want, you have to deal with only one dialog box; and instead of having to test your tween by choosing a menu option or dragging the playhead, all you have to do when you apply the Transform effect is click a button to instantly preview your tween.

The downside, of course, is the same as it is for any Timeline effect. When you apply an effect, Flash generates symbols, and you can't change those symbols by hand without breaking the effect. Not so if you create your tween effect by hand. (See the box on page 80.) Another difference: You can't distort or skew an object using the Transform effect. (You *can* if you create a shape tween by hand.)

To see how it works, download the example file transform_color_begin.fla from the "Missing CD" page. Then, to apply the Transform effect:

1. **Select the first keyframe in the *apple* layer.**

   Flash highlights the fill (the green body of the apple).

2. **Select Insert → Timeline Effects → Transform/Transition → Transform.**

   The Transform window in Figure 6-10 appears. Here's where you create the color tween.

3. **Turn on the checkbox next to Change Color. Click the Final Color swatch and then, from the Color Picker that appears, choose a nice bright shade of red. Drag the Motion Ease slider all the way to the left, until the Motion ease box contains the number –100.**

   Test your changes by clicking the Update Preview button. In the preview area, the green apple slowly turns red.

4. **Click OK to save the effect and return to your workspace.**

You notice that Flash has renamed the apple layer; now its name is Transform (followed by the number of times you've previewed an effect since you last launched Flash). You also notice that Flash has placed two graphic symbols—a single-frame graphic symbol and a 30-frame graphic symbol—in the Library. (If you don't see the Library panel, select Window → Library.)

5. **Select Control → Test Movie to view the completed animation.**

In the test window, you see the apple redden; the stem and blossom (the frames on the stem layer) aren't affected. (You can find a completed, working example on the "Missing CD" page—transform_color.fla.)

Note: Because Flash keeps the frames and symbols it creates when it generates Timeline effects neatly organized in their own separate layers, you can add your own layers without worrying about getting stuff mixed up.

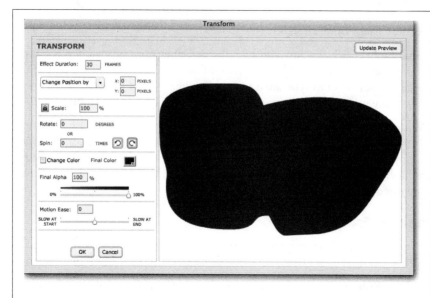

Figure 6-10:
Depending on the settings you change in this window, you can create completely different effects. For example, to move an object in a straight line, type numbers for Change Position by/ Move Position by (X is horizontal, Y is vertical). To make an object rotate, type a number for Spin. And to make an object disappear, type 0 in the Final Alpha box. You can combine effects, if you like, to make an object appear to spin across the screen and then disappear.

Here's a list of all the settings you can change in the Transform window:

- **Effect Duration.** How long you want this effect to last; in other words, the number of frames you want this effect to span. (Flash assumes 30 frames unless you tell it otherwise.)

- **Change Position by/Move to Position (X, Y).** Tells Flash to create a straight-line motion tween. Select "Change Position by" to type the number of pixels you want Flash to move the object based on the object's original position; click "Move to Position" if you want to type a fixed position on the Stage. (X is horizontal; Y is vertical.)

- **Lock/Scale (X, Y).** You can tell Flash to shrink or expand the width or height (or both) of the object. Clicking the Lock icon lets you type individual scaling percentages for the horizontal (X) and vertical (Y) dimensions of your object; clicking it again locks the scaling to a single, overall, uniform percent (Scale).

- **Rotate or Spin and Left/Right.** You can rotate an object once, or spin it as many times as you like. Click the Rotate box and then type the number of degrees you want Flash to rotate the object. (If you type a number greater than 360, Flash just assumes you want to spin the object and fills in the Spin box accordingly.) Or click the Spin box and type the number of times you want Flash to spin the object. Click Left to rotate (or spin) the object to the left; click Right to rotate (or spin) the object to the right.

- **Change Color.** Turn on this checkbox to create a color tween.

- **Final Color.** Click this swatch and then, from the Color Picker that appears, choose the color into which you want Flash to morph the original color (or colors) of your object. Flash ignores the Final Color swatch unless you've turned on the Change Color checkbox (see above).

- **Final Alpha.** Click this box and type the percentage of transparency you want your object to transition to. Flash assumes an Alpha of 100 percent (fully opaque), but you can type any number you like from *0* (fully transparent) to *100*. If you prefer, you can drag the slider instead of typing in a number.

- **Motion Ease.** Click this box and then type a number to tell Flash how uniformly you want it to apply the effect. For example, zero applies the effect evenly; a negative number tells Flash to start slow and speed up; and a positive number tells Flash to start fast and slow down. Instead of typing in a number, you can drag the slider.

Transition (Fade/Wipe)

The Transition effect lets you create two classic transitions you're probably familiar with if you've ever had to sit through any kind of computer-based presentation:

- **Fade in/Fade out.** An object appears transparent at first and then gradually becomes more opaque (a *fade-in*) or appears opaque at first and then gradually becomes transparent (a *fade-out*).

- **Wipe.** An object appears onscreen bit by bit, as though it's being drawn as you watch.

Although you can certainly use the Transition effect to create presentation- or slideshow-like animations, in which one image-filled frame fades or wipes after another, you don't have to stop there. You can apply multiple Transition effects—in other words, tell Flash to create multiple transition layers—to create composite images that fade or wipe piece by piece. You can also create an effect that looks like text is typing itself across the screen, as shown in the steps below.

To try it out, download transition_begin.fla from the "Missing CD" page. Then, to apply the Transition effect:

1. **On the Stage, select the text block.**

   Flash displays a blue selection box around the text.

2. **Select Insert → Timeline Effects → Transform/Transition → Transition.**

   The Transform window in Figure 6-11 appears.

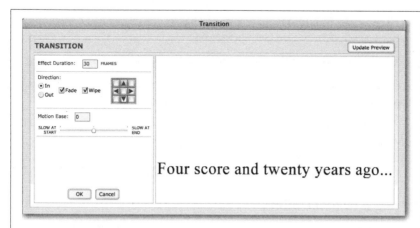

Figure 6-11:
The Transition effect is one of the simplest to apply. All you have to do is tell Flash whether you want to fade an object in (or out) or wipe the object in (or out). To create an even more artistic effect, slice your image into pieces and distribute each piece to a separate layer; then apply a different Transition effect to each piece.

Your mission: Change the settings to make the text look as though it's being typed onto the screen, one letter at a time.

3. **Turn off the Fade checkbox. In the Direction box, click the right arrow.**

   Take a look at your changes by clicking Update Preview.

4. **Click OK to save your effect and return to your workspace.**

   Flash renames your layer, fills the first 30 frames with a multiframe graphic symbol, and places a reusable copy of the symbol (as well as reusable copies of the single-frame symbols it generated) in the Library.

Tip: Flash complains if you try to add a keyframe to the transition layer it created, even if the keyframe you're adding comes *after* the frame span of the effect. So if you want to create a slideshow-type animation (where images wipe, or fade, in and out one after another) and still be able to modify each Transition effect through the settings window, you need to place each image on its own separate layer, and apply the Transition effect to each image separately.

You may want to create a different transition effect. To do so, you need to change one or more off the settings you find on the Transition window:

- **Effect Duration.** How long you want this effect to last: in other words, the number of frames you want this effect to span. (Flash assumes 30 frames unless you tell it otherwise.)

- **In/Out.** Turning on the In checkbox tells Flash to begin with a transparent version of the object and slowly fade (or wipe) it in. Turning on the Out checkbox tells Flash to begin with the object as is and slowly fade (or wipe) it out.

- **Fade.** Tells Flash to add transparency (or opacity) to the object, depending on whether you select In or Out (see above).

- **Wipe.** Tells Flash to make the object appear or disappear, little by little.

- **Direction Arrows.** Click one of the four arrows to make the effect move from left to right, right to left, top to bottom, or bottom to top.

- **Motion Ease.** Click this box and then type a number (or drag the slider) to tell Flash how uniformly you want it to apply the transition. For example, 0 applies the transition evenly; a negative number tells Flash to start slow and speed up; and a positive number tells Flash to start fast and slow down.

Modifying a Timeline Effect

You can't modify a Timeline effect the way you can modify a tween you've created by hand. In other words, you can't modify a Timeline effect by clicking on the Timeline and creating keyframes, adding or deleting frames, or editing the symbols Flash placed on the Stage. (If you do, you break—or even remove—the effect. See the box on page 183, "No Such Thing as a Free Lunch," for details.)

Instead, to modify an effect, you need to change the effect settings with the same dialog box you used to create the effect.

There's a file all set up with a wipe effect you can modify for practice. Download wipe2.fla from the "Missing CD" page. Then do the following:

1. **Click to select the first keyframe in layer Transition 16.**

    In the Layers window, Flash displays the pencil icon next to Transition 16 to let you know you've activated this layer. On the Stage, you see the symbol's registration point and a selection line.

2. **Choose Modify → Timeline Effects → Edit Effect.**

    Flash displays the settings window for the Transition effect. You see the *wipe in* effect (wiping left) in the preview area.

Note: Another way to redisplay the effects setting window is to right-click the symbol on the Stage and then, from the shortcut menu that appears, chose Timeline Effects → Edit Effect.

---

3. In the Transition window, head to the Direction box and click the right arrow; then click Update Preview to see the result of your changes.

In the preview area, the image now wipes right.

4. Click OK to save your change and return to the workspace.

Flash renames your layer.

5. Test the animation by choosing Control → Test Movie.

In the test window, you see four pieces of a single image, all wiping in from different directions to form a spiral drawing effect.

Deleting a Timeline Effect

Deleting a Timeline effect deletes the graphic symbols and movie clip symbols Flash created when it applied the effect. It also deletes all of the additional instances of those symbols that you've created (if any).

To delete a Timeline effect:

1. On the Stage, select the symbol from which you want to delete the effect.

Because Flash always changes your graphic element into a symbol when you apply a Timeline effect, you'll always be removing an effect from a symbol.

2. Choose Modify → Timeline Effects → Remove Effect (or right-click the symbol on the Stage and then, from the shortcut menu that appears, select Timeline Effects → Remove Effect).

Flash removes everything related to the effect, including the frames and images it placed on the Timeline, the symbols it placed in the Library, and any instances of the symbols you may have placed by hand in any layer in the current document. Flash also changes your layer name back to its original name, and the symbol on the Stage back into the form it was in (for example, editable object or bitmap) when you applied the effect.

Tip: You can remove multiple Timeline effects from multiple layers at the same time. On the Stage, select all the symbols from which you want to delete the effects. (When you do, Flash highlights all the related layers.) Then choose Modify → Timeline Effects → Remove Effect.

Spotlight Effect Using Mask Layers

Imagine placing a sheet of red construction paper containing a cutout of a star over a piece of green construction paper. The result you see, when you look at the two sheets stacked on top of each other, is a green star on a red background.

That's the concept behind *mask layers*, a special type of layer that lets you create shaped "portholes" through which content in an underlying (*masked*) layer appears.

As you may have noticed, mask layers are horribly misnamed. In real life, masks *hide* stuff. In Flash, masks *reveal* stuff. Still, if you can keep the difference straight in your mind, they're easy to use. And when you apply a motion tween to the "porthole," you can create an effect that looks like a spotlight playing over an image—mighty cool, indeed.

Here's how you go about it:

1. **Open the file mask_begin.fla.**

   You can download this file, a working example of the file (mask.fla), and all the other examples shown in this chapter from the "Missing CD" page at *www.missingmanuals.com/cds*.

2. **Click Layer 1 to select it.**

   In the example file for this section (mask.fla), Layer 1 contains a bitmap image.

3. **Click the Insert Layer button.**

   Flash creates a new layer named Layer 2 and places it above Layer 1.

4. **Double-click the layer icon next to Layer 2.**

   The Layer Properties window appears.

5. **In the Layer Properties window, turn on the checkbox next to Mask and then click OK.**

   Flash displays the mask icon next to Layer 2 (Figure 6-12).

6. **Double-click the layer icon next to Layer 1.**

   The Layer Properties window appears again.

7. **This time, turn on the checkbox next to Masked and then click OK.**

   Flashed displays the masked icon next to Layer 1 (Figure 6-12).

Tip: Flash gives you a bunch of ways to create masks and masked layers (by right-clicking an existing layer and choosing Mask or Masked, for example), but one thing doesn't change: Masked layers must appear directly below mask layers in the Layers window for the effect to work. If you create a mask layer and a masked layer in the wrong order, just drag the mask layer above the masked layer, and you're all set.

---

8. **Click to select the first keyframe in Layer 2 (the mask layer).**

9. **On the Stage, click the Oval tool and then draw a circle in the upper-left corner of the Stage (Figure 6-13).**

   The oval can be any color you choose, since it won't appear in the finished effect; instead, it'll act as a see-through portal.

Mask layer
Masked layer

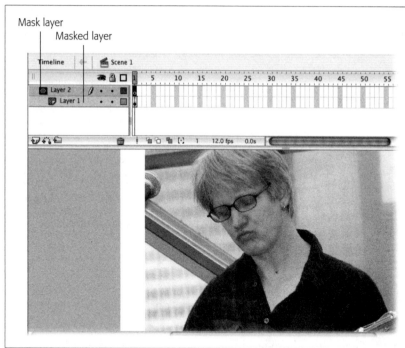

Figure 6-12:
The difference between mask layers and masked layers can be confusing. It helps to remember that the mask layer, just like a piece of red construction paper containing a cutout of a star, always goes on top of a masked layer (the green construction paper background)—both conceptually and in the Layers window. Notice also that Flash indents the masked layer, to remind you that it's attached to the mask layer directly above it. Here, the masked layer contains a bitmap image.

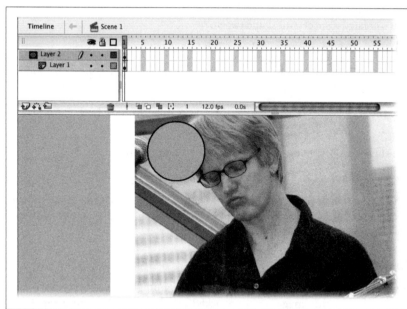

Figure 6-13:
The shape you use as a portal must be either a fill (like the circle shown here) or a symbol. Because the Brush tool creates fills, you can use the Brush to draw a freehand-shaped portal. (Strokes on the mask layer have no effect.)

10. In Layer 2, click Frame 20 and then select Insert → Timeline → Keyframe.

Flash inserts a keyframe in Frame 20. On the Stage, the bitmap image disappears so that all you see is the circle you drew in step 8.

11. Click the Select tool; then drag the circle to the lower-right corner of the Stage (Figure 6-14).

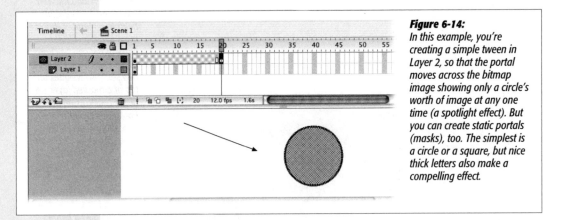

Figure 6-14:
In this example, you're creating a simple tween in Layer 2, so that the portal moves across the bitmap image showing only a circle's worth of image at any one time (a spotlight effect). But you can create static portals (masks), too. The simplest is a circle or a square, but nice thick letters also make a compelling effect.

12. In Layer 2, click Frame 2.

The circle jumps back into the upper-left corner of the Stage, and the Property Inspector appears.

13. From the Tween drop-down box in the Property Inspector, choose Shape.

Flash displays an arrow in Layer 2 from Frame 2 through Frame 19, showing you it's created a successful shape tween.

14. In Layer 1, click Frame 20 and then select Insert → Timeline → Keyframe.

Flash inserts a keyframe. On the Stage, the bitmapped image appears behind the circle (Figure 6-15).

15. Click the lock icon you see above the layers once to lock both Layer 1 and Layer 2.

Flash shows you the mask effect on the Stage (Figure 6-16).

16. Run the animation by choosing Control → Test Movie.

In the test window, you see the circle move in a diagonal line, revealing the bitmap beneath just as though you were looking through a tube sweeping diagonally across the image.

Adding a Motion Path to a Mask

In the previous section, you saw an example of an animated mask that moves in a straight line across the image on the masked layer. Wouldn't it be great if you could add a motion path to the mask to make the spotlight dip and weave and wiggle its way around the image?

Well, you *can*—but not in the usual way.

Figure 6-15:
At Frame 20 (notice the position of the playhead), the bitmapped image appears on Stage along with the circle. At this point, testing the animation by choosing Control → Test Movie shows you the mask effect. But to see the mask effect on the Stage, in edit mode, you need to lock both the mask and masked layers.

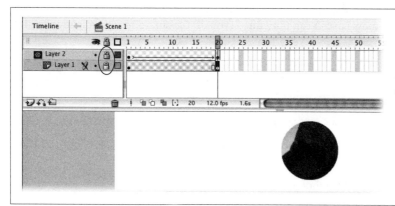

Figure 6-16:
Here you see the effect at Frame 20: a circle's worth of bitmap, just like that cutout star showing the green construction paper underneath. You can test the effect quickly on the Stage by dragging the playhead backward, from Frame 20 to Frame 1.

Flash doesn't let you apply a motion guide layer (Chapter 3) to a mask layer. (Selecting a mask layer and clicking the Add Motion Guide icon has no effect, and right-clicking a layer and then trying to choose Add Motion Guide from the shortcut menu doesn't work, either: The Add Motion Guide option appears grayed out.)

But you *can* add a motion path to a mask indirectly, by using an animated movie clip symbol as the mask shape. It's a simple matter of creating the mask shape, then converting it to a movie clip symbol before applying your motion tween. (You can learn a lot more detail about movie clip symbols on page 222 in the next chapter.)

Note: You can find a copy of the example shown in this section, at the "Missing CD" page. Look for spotlight_begin.fla (ready for you to begin the exercise) and spotlight.fla (a completed, working example).

Here's how to animate a mask layer, step by step:

1. **Open the file spotlight_begin.fla. Click the first keyframe of a new document and add the image or drawing you want on the masked layer (Layer 1).**

   As you can see in Figure 6-17, the background image for this example file is a guitarist.

2. **Choose Insert → Timeline → Layer.**

   Flash creates a new layer named Layer 2 and places it just above Layer 1.

3. **Double-click the layer icon next to Layer 2.**

   The Layer Properties window appears.

4. **In the Layer Properties window, turn on the checkbox next to Mask and then click OK.**

   Flash displays the mask icon next to Layer 2.

5. **Double-click the layer icon next to Layer 1.**

   Once again, the Layer Properties window appears.

6. **This time, turn on the checkboxes next to Masked and Lock and then click OK.**

   Flash displays the masked icon next to Layer 1; there's also a little padlock that lets you know Layer 1 can't be edited (you don't want to modify it inadvertently).

7. **Click the first keyframe in Layer 2.**

   Flash highlights the selected keyframe.

8. **Use the Oval tool to draw a circle on the Stage.**

   So far, these are the same steps you take to create a straight-line motion tween.

9. **Select the entire circle (including its outline) and then choose Modify → Convert to Symbol.**

   The Convert to Symbol dialog box appears.

10. **In the Convert to Symbol dialog box, turn on the radio button next to Movie Clip and then click OK.**

    The dialog box disappears.

11. **On the Stage, double-click the circle symbol.**

    Flash pops you into symbol editing mode: The content you placed in the masked layer appears grayed out, the name of your symbol appears in the Edit bar, and you see a fresh, clean Timeline (the symbol's timeline) containing just one layer.

12. On the Stage, select the entire circle again (including its outline) and then choose Modify → Convert to Symbol.

    The Convert to Symbol dialog box appears.

13. Leaving the Movie Clip radio button selected, click OK.

    The dialog box disappears. Flash places a copy of this second symbol into the Library. On the Stage, a selection box appears around the circle and a center point appears at the center's circle.

14. Click in Frame 20 and then select Insert → Timeline → Keyframe.

    Flash inserts a keyframe into Frame 20.

15. Click to select Layer 1 and then click the Add Motion Guide icon.

    Flash creates a guide layer and places it directly above Layer 1.

16. In Guide: Layer 1, click Frame 1 (the first keyframe). Then use the Pencil tool to draw a line (a motion path) on the Stage.

    The motion path you draw can be curved, circular, jagged—anything you like. Figure 6-17 shows an example.

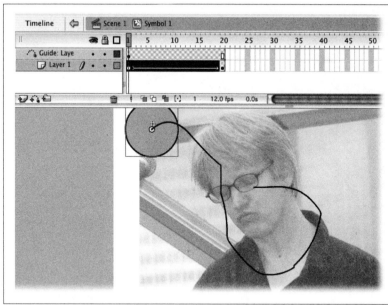

Figure 6-17:
Here's a motion path superimposed on the guitar player background (the masked layer). When you finish the steps in this example, the mask (the circle) will "shine a spotlight" on the guitar player following the curved motion path.

17. In Layer 1, click Frame 1. Using the Selection tool, drag the circle until its center snaps to the first end of the motion path (Figure 6-17). Click Frame 20 and then drag the circle until its center snaps to the second end of the motion path.

    You've just created the beginning and end points for the spotlight animation. Now you can tween it, as described next.

18. In Layer 1, click Frame 2. In the Property Inspector, from the Tween drop-down box, choose Motion. Then select Edit → Edit Document.

Flash saves the movie clip symbol and returns you to your main Timeline.

The movie clip symbol takes up just one frame (Frame 1) of the mask layer, which is Layer 2. You know it's a symbol because you see the cross and circle that are the symbol's registration point and center point, respectively; you know it's in the first frame because when you click the first frame of Layer 2, Flash displays a selection box around the symbol, as shown in Figure 6-18.

You can test the effect by choosing Control → Test Movie. In the test window, the "spotlight" should move along the motion path you drew.

Figure 6-18:
When you've finished adding the movie clip symbol to the mask layer, this is what you see: the selected symbol on top of the Layer 1 background. (You know it's the mask layer—Layer 2—that contains the selected symbol because you can see that Layer 2's highlighted.)

Reusable Flash: Symbols and Templates

The secret to productivity is to work smarter, not harder. And the secret to smart work is to avoid doing the same thing more than once. Flash understands. The program gives you ways to reuse bits and pieces of your animations—everything from simple shapes to complex drawings, multiframe sequences, and even entire animations. Create something once, reuse it as many times as you like.

Reusing animation elements can save you more than just time and effort—Flash lets you store pieces of animation as reusable master copies that can actually whittle the size of your finished animation file. That's great news if you plan to put your animation up on a Web site or shoot it out to handhelds. The smaller your file size, the faster it downloads, which makes *you* less likely to lose your audience to impatience.

Finally, if your work requires you to create animations that are so many variations on a theme, you can save documents as templates. Flash has templates representing many common document sizes like banner ads and cellphone screens so that you don't have to start from scratch. You can also save templates containing the pictures, logos, and other elements that appear in just about all your documents.

Note: Flash gives you two additional reuse options that are useful only in certain situations, and so are covered elsewhere in this book. You can export and import images (and animated clips) that you've created in either Flash or some other program (Chapter 8), and you can use layers to reuse chunks of composite drawings (Chapter 4).

Symbols and Instances

Copying and pasting is the most obvious way to reuse something you've created, but while that time-honored technique saves *time*, it doesn't save *space*. Say, for example, you need to show a swarm of cockroaches in the Flash advertisement you're creating for New and Improved Roach-B-Gone. You draw a single cockroach, then copy and paste it a hundred times. Congratulations: You've got yourself a hundred cockroaches…and one massive Flash document.

Instead, you should take that first cockroach and save it in Flash as a *symbol*. Symbols help keep your animation's finished file size down to a bare minimum. When you create a symbol, Flash stores the information for the symbol, or master copy, in your document as usual. But every time you create a copy (an *instance*) of that symbol, all Flash adds to your file is the little bit of information it needs to keep track of where you positioned that particular instance.

Then, to create the illusion of a swarm, you drag a hundred instances of the symbol onto the Stage (and a hundred more for each frame of the animated sequence showing the swarm). Instead of swelling your document with all the kilobytes it would take to draw thousands of individual roaches in your running animation, all Flash has to do is increase your file size by the kilobytes it takes to draw *one* roach (plus a little extra, for the thousands of instances pointing to the one "real" roach). You can even vary the roach instances a little for variety and realism (so important in a pesticide ad) by changing their color, position, size, and even their skew.

If symbols offered only file optimization, they'd be well worth using. But symbols give you two additional benefits:

- **Consistency.** By definition, all the instances of a symbol look pretty much the same. You can change certain instance characteristics—color and position on the Stage, for example—but you can't redraw them; Flash simply doesn't allow it. (You can't turn a roach into a ladybug, for example.) For situations where you really need basic consistency among objects, symbols help save you from yourself.

- **Instantaneous update.** You can change an instance without affecting any other instances or the symbol itself. (You can turn one roach light brown, for example, without affecting any of the dark brown roaches.) But when you edit the symbol, Flash automatically updates all the instances of that symbol.

So, for example, say you create a symbol showing the packaging for Roach-B-Gone. You use dozens and dozens of instances of the symbol throughout your animation, and *then* your boss tells you the marketing team has redesigned the packaging. If you'd used copy-and-paste to create all those boxes of Roach-B-Gone, you'd have to find and change each one manually. But with symbols, all you need to do is change the symbol. Flash automatically takes care of updating all the symbol's instances for you.

- **Nesting.** Symbols can contain other symbols. Sticking symbols inside other symbols is called *nesting* symbols, and it's a great way to create unique, complex-looking images for a fraction of the file size you'd need to create them individually.

Flash lets you create three different types of symbols: graphic symbols, movie clip symbols, and button symbols. As you see in Figure 7-1, Flash stores all three types of symbols in the Library.

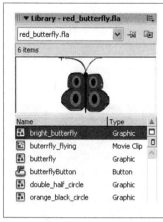

Figure 7-1:
The Library is your one-stop shop for symbols; from this panel, you can create symbols, edit them, and drag instances of them onto the Stage. Note the icons and descriptions that tell you each symbol's type–graphic, button, or movie clip. If you don't see the Library panel, select Window, and then turn on the checkbox next to Library. To display all the information in the Library panel, move your cursor over the bottom-right corner of the panel until your cursor turns into a diagonal two-headed arrow; then drag to resize the panel.

Note: The button symbol is nothing more than a specialized form of the movie clip symbol. For example, you can add an instance of a movie clip symbol to a single frame in a button symbol to create a button that plays an animation when you mouse over it. You'll learn how to add this kind of interactivity to your animations in Part 3.

Graphic Symbols

You can tell Flash to turn everything from a simple shape (such as a circle or a line) to a complex drawing (such as a butterfly) into a symbol. You can nest graphic symbols. For example, you can combine circle and lines symbols to create a nested butterfly symbol (Figure 7-2).

A graphic symbol isn't even limited to a static drawing. You can save a series of frames as a *multiframe* graphic symbol that you can add to other animations.

Note: Another kind of symbol that contains multiple frames is a movie clip symbol (page 222). But there are two big differences between the two, as described in the box on page 208.

Flash gives you two different options for creating a graphic symbol:

- **You can create a regular image on the Stage and then convert it to a graphic symbol.** This is the best approach for those times when you're drawing an image (or a multiframe animated scene) and suddenly realize it's so good that you want to reuse it.

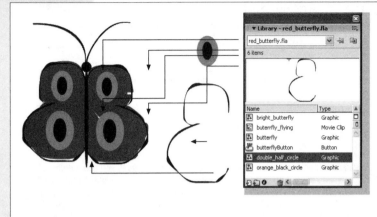

Figure 7-2:
If you're really serious about paring down the size of your animation file, consider nesting your symbols. Here, a couple of basic graphic symbols (double_half_circle and orange_black_circle) combine to form a more complex graphic symbol (bright_butterfly). Flash allows you to flip, resize, and recolor symbol instances, so you can create surprisingly different effects using just a few basic shapes—all while keeping your animation's file size as small as possible.

FREQUENTLY ASKED QUESTION

Multiframe Graphic Symbol vs. Movie Clip

A movie clip symbol is a series of frames, but a graphic symbol can have multiple frames, too. So what's the difference between the two?

Leave it to the Flash development team (the people who let you add motion to a shape tween and manipulate shapes with a motion tween) to refer to a multiframe animation clip as a *graphic* symbol (instead of a movie clip symbol). The truth is, there are two big differences between a multiframe graphic symbol and a movie clip.

- **A multiframe graphic symbol has to match the animation to which you add it, frame for frame.** For example, if you add a 15-frame graphic symbol to an animation containing 20 frames, you're essentially replacing 15 of your original frames, similar to a straight cut-and-paste operation (but without all the file size overhead associated with a real cut-and-paste operation). A movie clip symbol, on the other hand, does *not* have to match the animation you add it to frame by frame because movie clips have their own Timelines. So if you add that same 15-frame movie clip symbol to your original 20-frame animation, you're replacing only *one*

frame, not 15. Here's another way to look at it: If you put a 25-frame graphic symbol onto a 10-frame Timeline, only the first 10 frames of the multiframe graphic symbol play. But if you put a 25-frame movie clip onto a 10-frame Timeline, the movie clip plays all 25 frames and then some. (It'll loop until it encounters either a keyframe or an ActionScript statement telling it to stop playing.)

- **A multiframe graphic symbol can't include sound or interactivity; a movie clip symbol can.** Movie clip symbols take up just one frame in the main Timeline, so you can drop instances of them into button symbols and other movie clip symbols to create interactive nested symbols. Because they're not tied frame-for-frame to the animation you drop them into, they're able to hang fire while your animation plays and spring into action only when an audience member clicks them.

Chapters 8 and 10 show you how to add sounds and ActionScript actions to your symbols, respectively.

- **You can create your symbol from scratch using Flash's symbol editing mode.** If you know going in that you want to create a reusable image or series of frames, it's just as easy to create it in symbol editing mode as it is to create it on your main animation's Stage and Timeline—and you get to save the conversion step.

The following sections show you both approaches.

Converting an existing image to a graphic symbol

If you've already got an image on the Stage that you'd like to turn into a symbol, you're in luck: The process is quick and painless.

To convert an existing image on the Stage to a graphic symbol:

1. **On the Stage, select the image (or images) you want to convert.**

   Flash's selection tools are described on page 133. Converting a grouped or editable image into a graphic symbol is quick and easy. Figure 7-3 shows three separate images selected that, all together, form a star.

 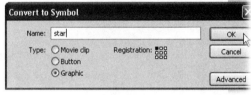

Figure 7-3:
Don't worry about clicking one of the little squares you see to specify a new registration point for your symbol; clicking them is only useful if you'll be working extensively with ActionScript and need to specify a registration point other than the perfectly serviceable 0,0.

2. **Select Modify → Convert to Symbol.**

   The "Convert to Symbol" dialog box in Figure 7-4 appears.

3. **In the Name text box, type a name for your symbol.**

   Because you'll be creating a bunch of instances of this copy over the course of the next several hours, days, or weeks (and because you may end up with dozens of symbols before you're finished with your animation), you want a unique, short, descriptive name.

4. **Turn on the radio button next to Graphic and then click OK.**

   Flash creates the new graphic symbol, places it into the Library, and automatically replaces the selected image on the Stage with a selected instance of the symbol (Figure 7-4). Notice the instance's single bounding box (the original three images in this example had three).

Registration Point vs. Center Point

Flash associates two different points with each symbol you create: a center point and a registration point. They both define the symbol's position, but in quite different ways. Here's the scoop:

- The symbol's *center point* is the little circle Flash displays in the center of the symbol. Flash uses the symbol's center point when you transform a symbol—for example, when you rotate it. You can change the center point while you're in transform mode (which you do by selecting the symbol on the Stage and then clicking the Free Transform tool) by dragging it; double-clicking tells Flash to put it back the way it was, dead center.

- The symbol's *registration point* appears as a little cross on the symbol. The registration point is the set of coordinates Flash uses to refer internally to an instance of a symbol. For example, say you plan to use ActionScript (Chapter 9) to make a symbol move automatically when your audience clicks a button. To tell Flash where you want it to reposition the symbol, you must give it (in your ActionScript) the

coordinates of where to move the symbol's registration point. Flash assumes a registration point of 0,0 (which translates to "upper-left corner") unless you tell it otherwise, either by clicking a square in the Convert to Symbol dialog box or by dragging your symbol on the Stage in Symbol Editing mode so that the little cross appears somewhere other than the upper-left corner of the symbol.

- The upshot: Unless you're planning to write some heavy-duty ActionScript code that refers to the symbol's position, you don't have to think twice about the registration point. Let Flash put it in the upper-left corner and leave it there.

Figure 7-4:
You can tell that Flash has converted your image on the Stage to an instance of the newly created symbol two ways: the cross in the upper-left corner of the instance (the instance's registration point) and the little round circle (the instance's center point). Flash uses the center point if you decide to transform the instance, as described in Chapter 5. You'll learn more about these points in the box above.

Tip: If you're already poking around the Library panel, you can create a new graphic symbol quickly by clicking the Library panel's New Symbol button (Figure 7-1) or by clicking the Library panel's Options menu and then, from the pop-up menu that appears, selecting New Symbol. Either way tells Flash to display the Create New Symbol dialog box.

Creating a graphic symbol in symbol editing mode

If you want to create a symbol from scratch without going through the conversion step described above you can use Flash's symbol editor—the same symbol editor you use to edit, or modify, your symbols.

To create a graphic symbol in symbol editing mode:

1. **Make sure you have nothing on the Stage selected by choosing Edit → Deselect All.**

   You want to make sure nothing is selected because you don't want to accidentally convert an existing image to a symbol. If Edit → Deselect All is grayed out, you're good to go—nothing on your Stage is selected.

2. **Select Insert → New Symbol.**

   The Create New Symbol dialog box shown in Figure 7-5 (top) appears.

3. **In the Name text box, type a name for your symbol.**

   Shoot for unique, short, and descriptive.

4. **Turn on the radio button next to Graphic, and then click OK.**

   Flash displays the symbol editing workspace shown in Figure 7-5 (bottom). The symbol editing workspace looks very much like an animation workspace, even down to the color of the animation Stage. The key differences to look for that tell you you're in symbol editing mode:

   The name of the symbol you're currently editing appears in the Edit bar. To see the Edit bar, select Window → Toolbars, and then turn on the checkbox next to Edit Bar.

   A cross (the registration point for the symbol you're about to create) appears in the middle of the symbol editing Stage. Technically, you can position your symbol anywhere you like with respect to the registration point. But if you don't have a good reason for doing otherwise, go ahead and center your symbol over the registration point. (See the box on page 210 for more details on the registration point.)

   The Back arrow and current scene icons in the Edit bar (Figure 7-5, bottom) appear clickable, or active.

5. **On the symbol editing Stage, create a graphic symbol.**

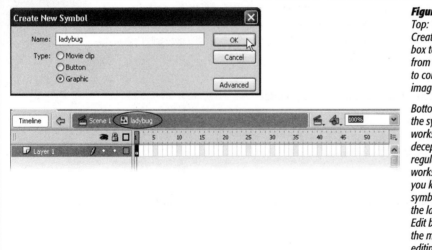

Figure 7-5:
Top: You use the same Create Symbol dialog box to create a symbol from scratch as you do to convert an existing image to a symbol.

Bottom: Here, you see the symbol editing workspace, which looks deceptively similar to the regular animation workspace. The only way you know you're in symbol editing mode is the ladybug icon in the Edit bar and the cross in the middle of the symbol editing Stage (not shown here).

You can use Flash's drawing tools, instances of other symbols, or even an imported image (Chapter 8), just as you can on the main Stage. As you draw, Flash displays a thumbnail version of your symbol in the Library preview window (Figure 7-6). Note that the *use count* is zero. (A use count is the number of instances of this particular symbol that have been dragged onto the main animation Stage. To tell Flash to keep a running total, click the Library's Options menu and then, from the pop-up menu that appears, turn on the checkbok next to Keep Use Counts Updated.)

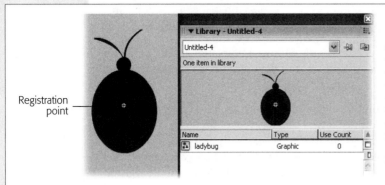

Registration point

Figure 7-6:
The ladybug symbol here has just been finished, so it's not surprising that the Library's showing a use count of 0. You don't have to center your symbol directly over the registration point as shown here, but if you don't have a good reason to do otherwise, centering is a choice you won't regret later.

6. **When you're finished creating your symbol, head to the Edit bar, and then click the Back arrow or select Edit → Document.**

   Flash returns you to your main animation workspace.

In the Mode

It's astonishingly easy to get confused about where you are when you're working in symbol editing mode. If you think you're in your main animation when you're actually in symbol mode, for example, you get frustratingly unexpected results when you try to test your animation by selecting Control → Play or Test → Movie. (In fact, when you're working with graphics symbols, Control → Play appears grayed out.)

You can most easily tell where you are when you make sure the Edit bar's visible (select Window → Toolbars and then turn on the checkbox next to Edit Bar). If your symbol's name appears in the Edit bar, you're in symbol editing mode; if it doesn't, you're not.

Using a graphic symbol (creating an instance of a graphic symbol)

After you've created a symbol, you use it by creating an instance of that symbol, and then placing the instance somewhere in your animation. You can easily create a symbol, as the steps below demonstrate.

To create an instance of a graphic symbol:

1. **Make sure the Library panel containing the graphic symbol you want is visible. If it isn't, select Window and turn on the checkbox next to Library.**

   Flash displays the Library panel.

2. **On the Timeline, click to select the keyframe and layer where you want to put the instance.**

   Flash highlights the selected keyframe.

3. **In the Library panel, click the name of the symbol you want to use.**

   A thumbnail version of the symbol appears in the Library's preview window.

4. **Drag the thumbnail onto the Stage (Figure 7-7).**

   Flash creates an instance of the symbol and places it on the Stage. You can transform or recolor this instance, as shown in the following section, without affecting any other instances or the symbol itself.

Tip: You can always convert an instance of a graphic symbol back into an editable image. You lose the file optimization benefits that an instance gives you, but on the other hand, you get to rework the graphic using Flash's drawing and painting tools. To convert an instance of a graphic symbol back into an editable image, first select the instance; then choose Modify → Break Apart. If your instance contains nested instances, you need to choose Modify → Break Apart once for each level of nested instance to convert the entire symbol into editable pixels.

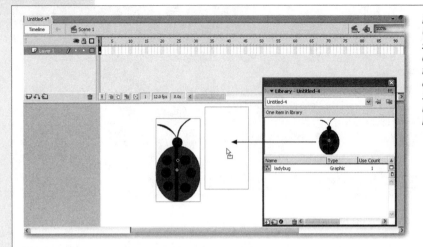

Figure 7-7:
*Creating an instance of a
symbol is as easy as
dragging the symbol
from the Library and
dropping it onto the
Stage. Flash has bumped
up the use count for the
ladybug symbol to 1.*

Editing an instance of a graphic symbol

The whole point of graphic symbols is to help you reuse images (and to help Flash keep down file size while you're doing it). So it should come as no surprise that you can't completely rework the instances you create. You can't, for example, create an instance of a ladybug, erase it, draw a toad in its place, and expect Flash to consider that toad an instance of the ladybug symbol.

But while you can't use Flash's drawing and painting tools to change your instance, you *can* change certain characteristics of an instance, including color, transparency, tint, and brightness, which you change using the Property Inspector; and scale, rotation, and skew using the Properties and Transform panels.

Note: When you transform or recolor an instance, only that instance changes; the other instances you've added to your animation aren't affected, and neither is the symbol itself. If you want to change multiple instances en masse, you need to edit the symbol itself (page 215).

You can also edit an instance by swapping one instance of a graphic symbol for another. Say, for example, that you've created a nature backdrop using multiple instances of three symbols: a tree, a bush, and a flower. If you decide you'd rather replace a few trees with bushes, Flash gives you a quick and easy way to do that, as shown in the following steps:

1. **On the Stage, select the instance you want to replace.**

   Flash redisplays the Property Inspector to show instance-related properties. (If you don't see the Property Inspector, choose Window → Properties → Properties to display it.)

2. **In the Property Inspector, click Swap (Figure 7-8, top).**

   The Swap Symbol dialog box in Figure 7-8 (bottom) appears.

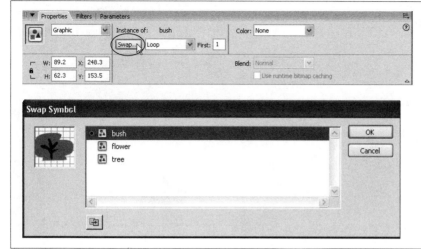

Figure 7-8:

Top: The Swap button's active only when you have a single instance selected on the Stage.

Bottom: The Swap Symbol dialog box is misnamed; it should be called the Swap Instance dialog box. That's because you use it to replace an instance of one symbol with an instance of another symbol; the symbols themselves don't change.

3. **In the Swap Symbol dialog box, click to select the symbol with which you'd like to replace the original. When you finish, click OK.**

   On the Stage, Flash replaces the selected instance with an instance of the symbol you chose in the Swap Symbol dialog box.

Editing a graphic symbol

Recoloring or transforming an instance changes only that instance, but editing a symbol changes *every single instance* of that symbol, immediately, wherever you've placed them in your animation.

The good news about editing symbols, of course, is that it can save you a boatload of time. Say you've added hundreds of instances of your company's logo to your animation and the brass decides to redo the logo. Instead of the mind-numbing chore of slogging through your animation finding and changing each instance by hand, all you have to do is edit one little image—your logo symbol. The minute you do, Flash automatically ripples your changes out to each and every instance of that symbol.

The bad news, of course, is that you might edit a symbol by mistake, thinking you're editing an instance instead (page 214). Editing a symbol is for keeps. You can select Edit → Undo if you realize your mistake in time, but once you close your Flash document and Flash erases your Undo history, it's all over but the crying: You're stuck with your edited symbol, for better or for worse.

Tip: If the thought of editing a symbol makes you leery—say you've got 500 instances of your symbol scattered around your animation and you don't want to have to redraw it if you goof up the edit job—play it safe and make a duplicate of the symbol before you edit it. In the Library panel, click the Options menu. Then, from the pop-up menu that appears, select Duplicate. When you do, Flash displays the Duplicate Symbol window, which lets you give your backup copy a unique, descriptive name (like logo_backup).

Exchanging Symbols Between Documents

Flash puts all the symbols you create in a Flash document—as well as all the bitmaps, sound files, and other goodies you import into that document—into the Library panel, which you display by choosing Window → Library.

Technically speaking, the stuff you put in the Library is good only for that Flash document or project (unlike the Common Libraries, which you access by choosing Window → Common Libraries, and which always list the same pre-installed files, no matter which document you have open).

But you can pull a symbol from one document's library and put it into another by copying and pasting. To do so:

1. Open the two documents between which you want to exchange symbols (File → Open).

2. Open the Library panel from which you want to copy a symbol (Window → Library), and then choose the document from the drop-down list in the Library panel.

3. In the Library panel, right-click the name of the symbol you want to copy and then, from the pop-up menu that appears, choose Copy.

4. Above the Timeline, click the tab displaying the name of the other document.

5. In the new document, click to select the keyframe where you want to paste the symbol.

6. Choose Edit → Paste in Center. Flash pastes a copy of the other document's symbol on the Stage.

To open a document's library without having to open the document itself: Select File → Import → Open External Library, choose the document whose symbols you want to copy, and then click Open. When you do, Flash opens the document's Library (but not the document).

Flash gives you two ways to edit symbols: in place, and in a new window.

- **Editing in place** lets you edit a symbol right there on the Stage, surrounded by any other objects you may have on the Stage. (Flash grays out the other objects; they're just for reference. The only thing you can edit in this mode is the symbol.)

This option's right up there with the most confusing features the Flash design team has ever come up with. As you can see in Figure 7-9, mixing the symbol editing mode with the appearance of the main Stage makes it incredibly easy to assume you're changing an *instance* of a symbol (instead of the symbol itself) with frustrating results.

Note: One man's meat is another man's poison. If you absolutely have to see your symbol in context (surrounded by all the other stuff on the Stage) to be able to edit it properly, editing in place is just what you want.

Figure 7-9:
It's hard to tell that the large ladybug (the one that's not grayed out) is a symbol and not just an instance of a symbol. (Your one clue: the symbol name ladybug Flash displays above the timeline.) Editing a symbol when you mean to edit an instance can have pretty serious consequences, so if you find yourself second-guessing, stick to editing in a new window, as described below.

Double-clicking a symbol on the Stage and selecting Edit → Edit in Place (from the main menu or from the pop-up menu that appears when you right-click an instance on the Stage) all tell Flash that you want to edit in place.

• **Editing in a new window** as shown in Figure 7-10 is your best bet, and this book demonstrates that method.

Figure 7-10:
When you edit your symbol in its very own window, there's no ambiguity: You know you're editing a symbol (and not merely an instance). You edit a symbol using the same tools and panels you use to edit any other image. As you make your changes, Flash automatically updates the symbol in the Library, as well as all the instances of that symbol, wherever they may be in your Flash document

To tell Flash you want to edit a symbol in a new window, do any of the following (in the Library panel):

- Double-click the symbol, either in the list or in the preview window.

- Select a symbol from the list and then click the Options menu. From the pop-up menu that appears, choose Edit.

- Right-click a symbol in the list. From the pop-up menu that appears, choose Edit.

- On the Stage:

- Select Edit → Edit Symbols.

- Select an instance of the symbol and then choose Edit → Edit Selected.

- Right-click an instance of the symbol and then, from the pop-up menu that appears, choose Edit or Edit in New Window.

- In the Edit Bar (Window → Toolbars → Edit Bar), click Edit Symbols (the icon that looks like a jumble of shapes).

No matter which method you choose—editing in place or editing in a new window—you get out of symbol editing mode and return to the main Stage the same way: by selecting Edit → Document.

Deleting a graphic symbol

You can delete the graphic symbols you create. Just remember that when you do, *Flash automatically deletes all the instances of that symbol,* wherever you've placed them in that document.

To delete a graphic symbol:

1. **In the Library panel, click to select the graphic symbol you want to delete.**

   Flash highlights the selected symbol's name and type.

2. **Right-click the graphic symbol icon and then, from the pop-up menu that appears, choose Delete.**

   Flash removes the graphic symbol from the Library panel. It also removes all the instances of that symbol from your animation.

Multiframe Graphic Symbols

Multiframe graphic symbols are a kind of hybrid symbol halfway between single-frame graphic symbols and movie clip symbols. Multiframe graphic symbols can't contain sounds or actions the way movie clip symbols can, but they *can* contain multiple frames (which regular single-frame graphic symbols can't).

Much like a standard copy-and-paste operation, multiframe graphic symbols must be tied frame-for-frame to the animation in which you place them, as you see in the following section.

Creating a multiframe graphic symbol

Flash gives you the same two options for creating multiframe graphics symbols as it does for single-frame graphic symbols: You can create a series of frames as usual and then convert it into a reusable symbol, or you can use Flash's editing mode to create a multiframe graphic symbol from scratch and save yourself the conversion step. This section demonstrates both approaches.

To convert a series of frames to a multiframe graphic symbol:

1. **On the Timeline, select the frames you want to convert.**

   You can easily select a series when you click at one end of the series and then Shift-click at the other end. Flash automatically selects all the frames in between.

2. **Choose Edit → Timeline → Copy Frames (or press Ctrl+Alt+C in Windows, or Option-⌘-C on the Mac). Then choose Insert → New Symbol.**

   The Create New Symbol dialog box appears.

3. **In the Create New Symbol dialog box, turn on the Graphic radio button. Type a short, descriptive name for your symbol, and then click OK.**

   The name of your symbol appears in the Library panel and in the Edit bar above your Stage to let you know you're in symbol editing mode. In addition, Flash replaces your animation Stage with the symbol editing Stage. You can recognize the symbol editing Stage by the cross (your symbol's registration point) that appears in the middle of the symbol editing Stage.

4. **In the symbol Timeline, click to select the first keyframe (Frame 1).**

   Flash highlights the selected keyframe.

5. **Select Edit → Timeline → Paste Frames.**

   Flash pastes the copied frames in the symbol's Timeline. The Library panel's preview window shows you the contents of your new symbol's first keyframe (along with a mini-controller, as shown in Figure 7-11).

6. **Preview your symbol by clicking the mini-controller's Play button.**

   Flash runs a thumbnail version of the symbol in the preview window.

7. **Get out of symbol editing mode by choosing Edit → Edit Document.**

   Flash hides the symbol editing Stage and returns you to your main animation's Stage and Timeline.

Figure 7-11:
Get into the habit of previewing your multiframe graphic symbols in the Library before you add instances of each symbol to your animation. If you do, you'll save the hassle that can result from incorporating instances of a symbol that doesn't run properly. To preview your symbol, click the Play button as shown. Flash displays the contents of each frame of your symbol, one after the other, in the Preview window.

To create a multiframe graphic symbol from scratch in symbol editing mode, follow the steps you see on page 211 ("Creating a Graphic Symbol in Symbol Editing Mode"), adding the content for as many frames as you need in step 5.

Creating an instance of a multiframe graphic symbol

Creating an instance of a multiframe graphic symbol is like creating an instance of a movie clip symbol, but it's not identical. Because multiframe graphic symbols (unlike movie clip symbols) need to be tied frame-for-frame to your main animation, you need to make sure you have room in your main animation for your multiframe graphic symbol. The following steps show you how.

To create an instance of a multiframe graphic symbol:

1. **In your main animation, click to select the keyframe where you want to place an instance of a multiframe graphic symbol.**

    Only keyframes can contain new content (see page 80 for the skinny on keyframes). So if you try to place a symbol in a regular frame, Flash "backs up" and places your symbol in the keyframe immediately preceding the selected frame anyway.

2. **Make sure you have exactly as many frames *after* the selected keyframe as you need for this instance.**

    If you're creating an instance of a symbol that contains 10 frames, make sure 10 frames exist after the selected keyframe. If the symbol contains 20 frames, make sure 20 frames exist. To add frames after your selected keyframe, choose Insert → Timeline → Frame (or press F5) once for each frame you want to add.

Warning: If you forget this step and add a multiframe graphic symbol to a Timeline that *doesn't* contain exactly as many frames as the symbol, Flash doesn't issue any warnings. Instead, it matches as many of the instance frames to your Timeline frames as it can. If you don't have enough room on your Timeline, Flash quietly snips off the instance frames that don't fit. If you have too *much* room, Flash repeats the instance frames until all your main animation's frames are filled.

3. **In the Library, click to select the multiframe graphic symbol of which you want to create an instance.**

   You can either click the symbol's icon from the list or click the symbol's thumbnail in the preview window. The Library lists the Type of both single and multiframe graphics the same—Graphic—but you can always tell a multiframe graphic by the mini-controller that appears along with the symbol's content in the Library's preview window.

4. **Drag the symbol to the Stage.**

   Flash creates an instance of the symbol and places it in the keyframe you selected in step 1. As you see in Figure 7-12, Flash colors your frames a nice solid gray to let you know they now contain content. But Flash *doesn't* display the individual keyframes of your instance in your main Timeline. (By the same token, if your symbol contains multiple layers, you don't see those on your main Timeline, either. This visual simplification is one of the benefits of using symbols, as opposed to just copying and pasting frames.) To preview your instance, select Control → Test Movie.

Note: You can also test an instance of a multiframe graphic symbol by choosing Control → Play, or by dragging the playhead on the main Timeline.

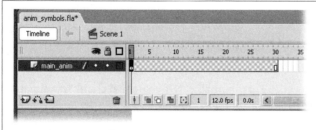

Figure 7-12:
The solid gray bar you see beginning with the keyframe (Frame 1) lets you know that Frames 1–30 now contain content: in this case, an instance of a multiframe graphic symbol. If testing your animation yields an unexpected result, check to make sure that the frame span to which you've added the symbol matches your symbol frame for frame. Also check to make sure that your frame span doesn't contain any keyframe other than the initial keyframe adding an instance of a symbol to your Timeline doesn't overwrite keyframes.

Editing an instance of a multiframe graphic symbol

If you need the flexibility to change each keyframe of a multiframe graphic instance individually, you're out of luck.

Flash allows you to change the contents of the first keyframe of your instance, just the way you can an instance of a single-frame graphic (page 211). But Flash automatically applies those changes to the contents of *every* keyframe in your instance. Skew the frog in your first keyframe and turn it blue, for example, and every image in every frame of your instance appears skewed and blue.

Editing a multiframe graphic symbol

You edit a multiframe graphic symbol the same way you edit a single-frame graphic symbol: by switching to symbol editing mode (page 211). In both cases, Flash immediately applies the changes you make to the symbol to all the instances of that symbol.

Deleting a multiframe graphic symbol

You delete a multiframe graphic symbol the same way you delete any other symbol in Flash: through the Library panel. Just remember that when you delete a symbol, *Flash automatically deletes all the instances of that symbol*, wherever you've placed them.

To delete a graphic symbol:

1. **In the Library panel, click to select the graphic symbol you want to delete.**

   Flash highlights the selected symbol's name and type.

2. **Right-click the graphic symbol icon and then, from the pop-up menu that appears, choose Delete.**

   Flash removes the graphic symbol from the Library panel. It also removes all the instances of that symbol from your animation.

Movie Clip Symbols

A *movie clip* symbol (Figure 7-13) is a reusable, self-contained chunk of animation you can drop into a single frame in another animation.

Unlike multiframe graphic symbols, you can add sounds (Chapter 8) and actions (Chapter 9) to movie clip symbols. Also unlike multiframe graphic symbols, movie clip symbols run independently from the animations to which you add them.

So movie clips give you the opportunity to create nonsequential effects such as repeating, or *looping*, scenes, as well as interactive graphics—for example, buttons, checkboxes, and clickable images that tell Flash to display something different, depending on what your audience clicks.

As you see in the following section, movie clip symbols have their very own Time-lines, so an instance of a movie clip symbol always takes up just one frame in the animation to which you add it, no matter how many frames the movie clip actually contains.

Figure 7-13:
When you select a movie clip symbol in the Library, the Library panel's preview window shows you the first frame of the symbol, as well as a mini-controller you can use to play (and stop) the movie clip right there in the Library before you go to all the trouble of dragging an instance of the movie clip to the Stage. (You see this same mini-controller when you select a multiframe graphic in the Library.)

Creating a movie clip symbol

Creating a movie clip symbol in Flash is similar to creating a multiframe graphic symbol (page 218). You can either create a series of frames (including sounds and actions, if you like) and convert it into a movie clip symbol, or you can use Flash's editing mode to create a movie clip symbol from scratch and save yourself the conversion step.

In fact, as the following steps show, only one minor but important difference exists between creating a multiframe graphic symbol and creating a movie clip symbol, and that's turning on a radio button in step 4.

Warning: Modify → Convert to Symbol works only when you're converting an image to a single-frame graphic symbol; it *doesn't* let you convert a series of frames into a movie clip symbol. But if you try it, Flash won't give you an error. Instead, it'll chug along happily, pretending it's creating a movie clip symbol. But in reality, the symbol you create this way contains just one frame—the last keyframe in your series.

To convert a series of existing frames to a movie clip symbol:

1. **On the Timeline, select the frames you want to convert.**

   It's easy to select a series of frames. Click at one end of the series, and then Shift-click at the end of the series. Flash automatically selects all the frames in between. If your frames contain layers, make sure you select all the layers in each frame.

2. Choose Edit → Timeline → Copy Frames (or press Ctrl+Alt+C on Windows, or Option-⌘-C on Mac).

3. Choose Insert → New Symbol.

The Create New Symbol dialog box appears.

4. In the Create New Symbol dialog box, make sure the Movie Clip radio button is turned on.

If it's not, click to select it.

5. Type a name for your movie clip symbol and then click OK.

The name of your movie clip symbol appears in the Library panel and in the Edit bar above your Stage, to let you know you're in symbol editing mode. Another tip-off that you're in symbol editing mode is the cross, or registration point, that appears in the middle of the symbol editing Stage.

6. In the symbol Timeline, click to select the first keyframe (Frame 1).

Flash highlights the selected keyframe.

7. Select Edit → Timeline → Paste Frames.

Flash pastes the copied frames onto the symbol's Timeline and displays the first keyframe of the new symbol (along with a mini-controller) in the Library panel's preview window.

8. In the Library panel, preview your symbol by clicking the mini-controller's Play button.

Flash runs a thumbnail version of the movie clip symbol in the preview window.

9. Get out of symbol editing mode by choosing Edit → Edit Document.

Flash returns you to the workspace and your main animation.

To create a movie clip symbol from scratch in symbol editing mode, follow the steps on page 211 ("Creating a Graphic Symbol in Symbol Editing Mode"), adding the content for as many frames as you need in step 5.

Creating an instance of a movie clip symbol

Because movie clip symbols have their own timelines, they're completely self-contained. You don't have to worry about matching your movie clip symbol to your main animation's Timeline the way you do with a multiframe graphic symbol (page 219); movie clip instances live on a single frame in your main animation, no matter how many frames the instances themselves contain. As a matter of fact, as you see next, creating an instance of a movie clip symbol is as easy as dragging and dropping.

To create an instance of a movie clip symbol:

1. **In your main animation, click to select the keyframe where you want to place an instance of a multiframe graphic symbol.**

   Only keyframes can contain new content. So if you try to place a symbol in a regular frame, Flash "backs up" and places your symbol in the keyframe immediately preceding the selected frame anyway.

2. **In the Library, click to select the movie clip symbol of which you want to create an instance.**

   You can either click the symbol's icon from the list or click the symbol's thumbnail in the preview window.

3. **Drag the symbol to the Stage.**

   Flash creates an instance of the symbol and places it in the keyframe you selected in step 1, as shown in Figure 7-14.

4. **To preview your instance, select Control → Test Movie.**

You'll notice that even if you turn looping off in the Control panel (which you do by selecting Control and then, from the pop-up menu that appears, turning off the checkbox next to Loop) your movie clip instance continues to loop. The movie clip behaves this way because it's running on its own Timeline (not the Timeline Flash associates with your main animation). One way to tell Flash to stop looping your movie clip instance is to add a keyframe (blank or otherwise) to your Timeline *after* the keyframe that contains your movie clip instance.

Note: Flash automatically *loops* the movie clip instance (plays it over and over again) until it encounters the next keyframe on the Timeline, or until it encounters an ActionScript statement that tells it to stop (such as *stop()* or *goToAndStop()*). You see an example of controlling playback with ActionScript in Chapter 10.

Editing a movie clip symbol

You edit a movie clip symbol the same way you edit a single-frame graphic symbol: by switching to symbol editing mode (page 211). In both cases, Flash immediately applies your changes to all the instances of that symbol.

Editing an instance of a movie clip symbol

Similar to multiframe graphic symbols, Flash lets you change the contents of the first keyframe of your movie clip instance, just the way you can an instance of a single-frame graphic (page 215). But Flash automatically applies those changes to the contents of *every* frame in your instance. So, for example, if you apply a sepia tint to the first keyframe, your entire movie clip instance looks old-timey.

If you're running Flash Professional, you can also apply filters (page 227) to movie clip instances, including buttons. (Button symbols, as discussed on page 226, are nothing more than specialized movie clip symbols.)

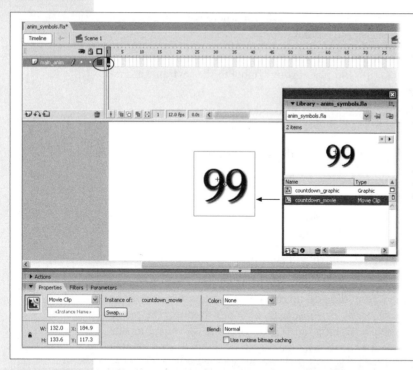

Figure 7-14:
Dragging a movie clip symbol from the Library to the Stage tells Flash to create an instance of the symbol. No matter how many frames (or layers) your movie clip instance contains, it takes up only one frame on your animation (circled), which makes movie clips perfect for creating animated buttons.

Reuse Deluxe: Repurposing Symbols

When you think about it, it's the simple, classic shapes you use most often in drawing.

Sure, it's great to have a sun, flower, or cockroach symbol hanging around in the Library, but it's the ovals, wedges, and sweeps that you find yourself coming back to again and again. And because Flash lets you resize, reposition, and recolor each instance, you can create radically different drawings using the same handful of simply shaped graphic symbols. You optimize the size of your finished animation, and, as a bonus, you get to focus on design at the graphic element level. (Even accomplished animators can find fresh ideas by limiting themselves to a handful of shapes.)

Expand and flip a raindrop symbol and add a tail, for example, and you've got yourself a whale.

Button Symbols

The easiest way to make your animation interactive is to add a button someone can click at runtime to perform a task, such as replaying your entire animation, choosing which of several scenes to play, loading a Web page, and so on.

To make creating a button easy, Flash offers button symbols. A *button symbol* is a specialized form of movie clip symbol (Figure 7-15) that contains four frames:

- **Up.** In this frame, you draw the button as you want it to appear *before* your audience mouses over it.

- **Over.** In this frame, you draw the button as you want it to appear *after* your audience mouses over it.

- **Down.** In this frame, you draw the button as you want it to appear when your audience clicks it.

- **Hit.** In this frame, you draw the active, or "clickable," area of your button. In most cases, you want the active area to be identical to the button itself. But in other cases—for example, if you want to create a bullseye-shaped button that responds only when your audience clicks the tiny red dot in the center—you draw that center dot here, in the fourth frame (the Hit frame).

Of course, you can always create your own interactive button from scratch and save it as a movie clip symbol (page 222). But the better way to go is to create a button symbol. When you do, Flash automatically gives you the four Up, Over, Down, and Hit frames—all you have to do is plug in your drawings and go. As you see in the following section, Flash also gives you a handful of built-in graphic effects, called *filters*, which you can apply to your buttons to get professional-looking results.

Note: To get your button to actually *do* something when someone clicks it—to display a different section of the Timeline, for example, or some dynamic text—you need to tie a snippet of ActionScript code to your button. Chapter 11 shows you how.

Figure 7-15:
Because button symbols are nothing more than specialized movie clip symbols, you see the same mini-controller in the Library's preview window when you click a button symbol as you see when you select a movie clip or multiframe graphic symbol. Clicking Play cycles through the button symbol's four frames, so you get to see how the button looks: 1) before a cursor mouses over it, 2) after a cursor mouses over it, 3) after a cursor mouses over the active (clickable) portion of the button, and 4) when a mouse actually clicks the active portion. When you create a button symbol, Flash spots you the four frames; all you have to do is customize them, as shown in the following sections.

Creating a button symbol

When you create a button symbol, you start out basically as if you're creating any graphic symbol from scratch (page 207), but since button symbols have those four possible states, you can create up to four different graphics. When you choose Button in the New Symbol dialog box, Flash gives you a separate frame to hold each drawing so that you won't get confused.

In this example, you'll create a round, red button that turns yellow when your audience mouses over it and green when your audience clicks it.

1. **Click Insert → New Symbol.**

   The Create New Symbol dialog box appears.

2. **In the Name text box, type** *bullseye.* **Make sure the radio button next to Button is turned on. Then click OK.**

   When you create a new button symbol, Flash gives you four named frames (Figure 7-16). It's up to you which frames you want to modify, but at the very least, you need to add a drawing to the Up frame, to show the button before it's clicked. For a more sophisticated button, you'll also add a drawing to the Over frame (as shown below) to let someone know when his mouse is over the button.

Tip: Flash comes with a blue million button symbols already spiffed up and ready for you to drop into your animations. So before you get too carried away drawing your own button, choose Window → Common Libraries → Buttons to see if Flash already has a button symbol that fits your bill. (You still have to add ActionScript code to the prebuilt button symbol to tell Flash what you want it to do when your audience clicks your button, of course; Flash isn't a mind reader. Find out how in Chapter 11, page 217.)

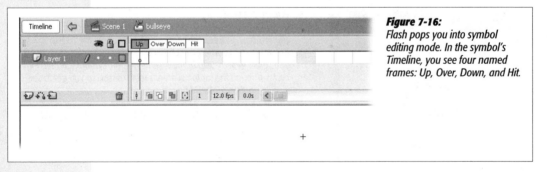

Figure 7-16:
Flash pops you into symbol editing mode. In the symbol's Timeline, you see four named frames: Up, Over, Down, and Hit.

3. **Draw your button as you want it to appear initially by using the Oval tool to add a red circle to the first keyframe (the Up frame).**

   Center your circle as much as possible on the registration point (the cross) on the symbol editing Stage. When you finish, your workspace should look similar to the one in Figure 7-17.

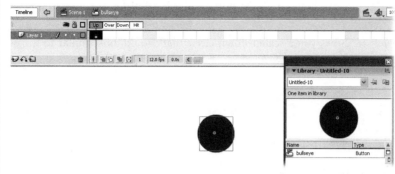

Figure 7-17:
Your button doesn't have to look like a button; it can be an image, a shape, a line—anything you like. But most people are used to circular buttons, so a circle's a good place to start. Notice that as you create your image, Flash automatically updates the Library's preview window.

4. **Right-click Frame 2 (the Over frame) and then, from the pop-up menu that appears, select Insert → Keyframe.**

   Flash displays a hollow circle in Frame 2 to let you know you've successfully added a keyframe. On the Stage, you see a copy of the button you drew in Frame 1.

5. **Here's how you make the button change when a cursor passes over it: On the Stage, select the circle. In the Property Inspector, click the Fill Color icon; then, from the color picker that appears, choose a yellow swatch.**

   Flash recolors the circle yellow. If you don't see the Property Inspector, select Window → Properties and then, from the pop-up menu that appears, turn on the checkbox next to Properties. If you still don't see it, make sure you've selected the circle on the Stage.

6. **Right-click Frame 3 (the Down frame) and then, from the pop-up menu that appears, select Insert → Keyframe.**

   Flash displays a hollow circle in Frame 3 to let you know you've successfully added a keyframe (and, therefore, can change the content of the frame).

7. **Here's how you draw the button as you want it to appear when a cursor clicks it: Select the button. In the Property Inspector, click the Fill Color icon once again; then, from the color picker that appears, choose a green swatch.**

   Flash recolors the circle green.

8. **Right-click Frame 4 (the Hit frame) and then, from the pop-up menu that appears, select Insert → Keyframe.**

   Flash displays a hollow circle in Frame 4 to let you know you've successfully added another keyframe. As you can see on the Stage, Flash assumes you want the entire button to respond to a mouse click—and in a lot of cases, that's exactly what you do want. But you can make the clickable portion of your button smaller or larger. To do so:

9. **On the Stage, click the circle to select it. Then choose Window → Transform to display the Transform panel.**

In the Transform panel, type *50* into the Width and Height boxes, and then press Return.

Figure 7-18 shows you a scaled-down circle that should look similar to the one you see on your workspace.

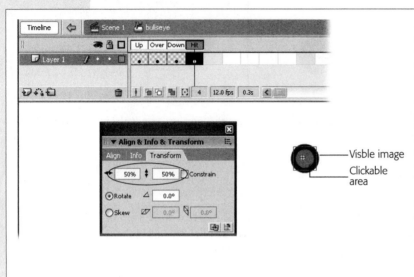

Figure 7-18:
Normally, you want to draw the same size shape in the Hit frame as you do in the other frames so that the entire button responds to mouse clicks. Drawing a smaller (or even different-shaped) image for the Hit frame allows you to create more sophisticated buttons: clickable images, for example, or invisible buttons that let the content of your frame itself appear to respond to mouse clicks (see the box on page 231). Here, the clickable portion of the button is exactly half the size of the visible portion.

Visble image
Clickable area

10. Return to your animation by choosing Edit → Document.

Flash hides your symbol editing workspace and displays your animation workspace.

Using a button symbol (creating an instance of a button symbol)

To create an instance of a button symbol:

1. Click to select the first keyframe (Frame 1) in your animation.

   Flash highlights the selected frame.

2. In the Library panel's preview window, drag your button symbol's thumbnail onto the Stage.

   On the Stage, Flash creates an instance of the button symbol and surrounds it with a selection box.

3. Test your button instance. To do so, choose Control → Test Movie.

   A red circle appears in the middle of the test window (Figure 7-19).

Oddly Shaped (and Invisible) Buttons

Why would I want to make my Hit frame smaller than the button itself? Won't that just make it harder for people to click?

One popular situation in which you might want to make the hit frame *smaller* than the button itself (as shown in Figure 7-18) is when you're creating a hotspot. For example, say you're creating an interactive Web-based game for kids. On the Stage, you've drawn several different animals: a pig, a duck, and a lamb. The audio file you've attached to your animation tells the player which specific part of each animal to click: the duck's bill, for instance, or the pig's tail. In this case, you want to limit the clickable portion of the image to the bill (or tail).

A situation in which you might consider making the hit frame *larger* than the button is when you want to give your audience a larger target. Instead of making someone center her cursor precisely over a teeny-tiny button, for example, you can let her click as soon as her cursor comes anywhere close to the button. (Obviously, this strategy works best when you have only a few buttons on the Stage and they're not near each other.)

Finally, you can create *invisible* fill-only buttons by applying an Alpha value of zero percent to your button's fill in the Up, Over, and Down states. (If your button contains a line, you need to erase it, since Flash doesn't let you apply an Alpha value of zero percent to a line.) Invisible buttons are useful if, for example, you plan to give discounts to site visitors who've read your paper catalog (and thus know that they can get a discount by clicking the unmarked bottom portion of your order form).

Tip: To test your button instance on the Stage, select Control → Enable Simple Buttons. When you do, your button responds to mouse movement and clicking right there on the Stage.

---

4. **In the test window, drag your mouse over the red circle.**

   When your mouse nears the center of the red circle, your arrow cursor turns into a pointing finger, and the red circle turns yellow.

5. **With your pointing-finger cursor, click the yellow circle.**

   The yellow circle turns green.

Note: Chapter 11 shows you how to add an action to your button so that clicking it does something useful.

Editing an instance of a button symbol

You can't change the individual frames of your button instance individually. But Flash *does* let you apply the same changes to *all* the frames of your button instance.

Page 228 shows you the steps you can take to apply color, transparency, and transforms to your button instances. (The steps are identical to those you take to edit a single-frame graphic instance.) But you can also apply *filters*, or visual effects, to your buttons. Filters can turn even a plain oval button into something that looks like you spent hours tweaking it.

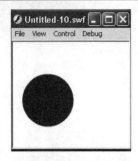

Figure 7-19:

Top: Whatever you drew in Frame 1 (the Up frame) appears first.

Middle: As soon as a cursor moves into the area defined in Frame 4 (the Hit frame), Flash changes the cursor's shape to show it's over an active (clickable) button and displays the contents of Frame 2 (the Over frame).

Bottom: Clicking the active button displays the contents of Frame 3 (the Down frame). The animation contains only a button, but because a button instance is just another graphic element, you can place it on top of an image or symbol to create a more sophisticated effect.

Note: Filters aren't just for buttons. You can also apply filters to text blocks (Chapter 5, page 163) and movie clip instances.

To apply a filter to a button instance:

1. **On the Stage, select the button instance.**

   Flash draws a blue selection box around the instance.

2. **In the Property Inspector, click the Filters tab.**

   You can also display the Filters panel when you choose Window → Properties, and then, from the pop-up menu that appears, turn on the checkbox next to Filters. Either way, the Filters panel appears.

3. **Click the Add Filter icon (the + sign).**

   A pop-up menu appears (Figure 7-20) listing the following options, each of which Figure 7-21 demonstrates.

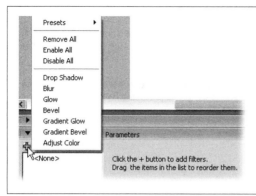

Figure 7-20:
When you click the Add Filter icon (the + sign) in the Filters tab, this pop-up menu appears, showing you all the effects you can add to your button instance.

Drop Shadow. Displays a shadow on the right and bottom edges of the button.

Blur. Redraws the surface of the button so that it appears soft and blurred.

Glow. Redraws just the outline of the button so that it appears soft.

Bevel. Applies brightness and shadow on opposite sides of the button to create a 3-D effect.

Gradient Glow. Similar to Glow (above), but lets you specify bands of different colors (instead of just one color).

Gradient Bevel. Similar to Bevel (above), but lets you choose bands of different colors for the brightness and shadow.

Adjust Color. Lets you individually adjust the brightness, contrast, saturation, and hue of your button.

4. **From the menu, select Glow.**

   A red glowing effect appears around your button, and the Filter panel displays the Glow properties (Figure 7-22).

5. **Click the down arrow next to Blur X and then drag the slider to 40.**

   On the Stage, the glow diffuses.

6. **Click the Shadow Color icon and then, from the color picker that appears, click the black swatch.**

   On the Stage, the glow turns from red to black, yielding a subtle 3-D effect.

7. **Test your newly edited button by selecting Control → Test Movie.**

   In the test window that appears, you see your button with the Glow effect applied.

8. **In the test window, drag your mouse over your button.**

   Flash applies filters to the entire instance (not just the contents of the keyframe to which you apply them), so the Glow effect remains even when you mouse over the button.

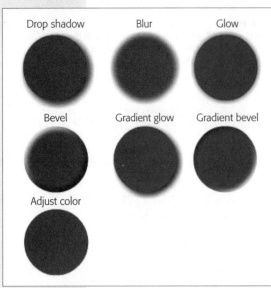

Drop shadow   Blur   Glow

Bevel   Gradient glow   Gradient bevel

Adjust color

Figure 7-21:
With filters, you can quickly make a button instance look both unique and spiffy. Flash lets you change the properties of your filters—for example, you can change the size of a blur or the color of a drop shadow—so the drop shadow you apply to one instance doesn't have to look the same as the drop shadow you apply to another instance of the same symbol.

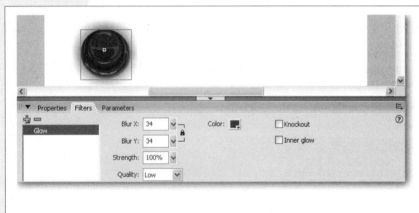

Figure 7-22:
When you apply a Glow filter to a button, you can change the horizontal and vertical width of the glow (Blur X and Blur Y), the density of the blur (Strength), and how far out the blur extends (Quality). You can also choose a different color for your blur or apply a Knockout effect (which leaves the blur but erases the button) or Inner Glow (which erases the blur and then uses the blur color to repaint the surface of the button).

To remove a filter you've applied: In the Filter panel, select the filter you want to remove, and then click the Remove Filter icon (the – sign).

Tip: Applying a filter isn't an either/or proposition. You can add multiple filters to the same instance to create different effects: For example, you can add both a Glow and a Drop Shadow. Flash applies filters in top-down order, so adding a Glow and a Drop Shadow yields a different result than adding a Drop Shadow and *then* a Glow. (To change the order of your filters, simply drag them to reposition them in the Filter panel.) You can even add the same filter more than once to compound the effect.

Editing a button symbol

You edit a multiframe graphic symbol the same way you edit a single-frame graphic symbol: by switching to symbol editing mode (page 211). In both cases, Flash immediately applies the changes you make to the button symbol itself, as well as all the instances of that button symbol.

DESIGN TIME

Organizing Your Symbols

If you do a lot of work in Flash, chances are you're going to create a lot of symbols. But in Flash as in life, if you can't see what you've already got, you're apt to recreate it, or else go without—both of which lose you the benefits of reuse that you're using symbols for in the first place.

The answer? Organize your symbols into folders.

Flash lets you create folders inside the Library. You can use these folders to organize your symbols. For example, you might want to keep all your movie clip symbols in one folder, all your graphic symbols in another, and so on. Or you might want to keep all the symbols related to a composite drawing (such as a cartoon character or a corporate logo) in a separate folder. Use whatever organization makes sense to you; you can always reorganize your files and folders later.

To create a folder in the Library:

1. In the Library, click the Options menu. From the pop-up menu that appears, choose New Folder.

   A folder named *untitled folder 1* appears in the Library beneath your symbols.

2. Click the folder name, and then replace it by typing in a new, more meaningful name, such as *logo*, *spaceman*, or *intro_scene*.

3. Drag all the logo-related symbols into the logo folder, all the spaceman-related symbols into the spaceman folder, and so on.

If you need more levels of organization, you can place folders inside folders.

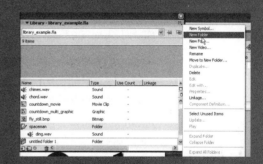

Templates

While symbols let you reuse images and series of frames, *templates* let you reuse entire Flash documents.

Templates are useful when you find yourself cranking out animations that look and behave similarly. For example, say you create marketing animations for display on your corporate Web site. You may find that your animations share a lot of the same elements: your company's logo somewhere on the background, a copyright notice, the same sound clips of your CEO speaking, the same color palette, the same size Stage, and the same intro and credit scenes.

Using a template, you can create all these basic elements just once. Then, the next time you're tapped to do a marketing spot, you can load the template and just add the new content you need. You've not only saved yourself a lot of time, but you've also ensured consistency among your animations (highly important in certain corporate circles).

In this section, you see how to create and use your own templates. You also see how to take advantage of Flash's prebuilt templates.

Using a Prebuilt Template

Flash comes with a bunch of templates all ready for you to customize. While they're obviously not specific to your particular company or project, they *can* save you time on a lot of basic animations, including banner ads, slideshows, and presentations. Here's a quick rundown of the templates you find in Flash (Figure 7-23):

- **Advertising.** Pop-up, skyscraper (skinny vertical), banner (skinny horizontal), and full-page ads.

- **Form applications.** Data input forms that you need to hook up to a server on the back end.

- **Global phones.** Stages targeted for certain (Symbian) phones.

- **Japanese phones.** Stages targeted for Japanese phones.

- **PDAs.** Stages targeted for Nokia, Motorola, Sony, and other personal digital assistants (handhelds).

- **Photo Slideshows.** For Flash animations showing drawings or bitmaps overlaid with Forward and Back controls.

- **Presentations.** Automatic (noninteractive) slideshows, similar to PowerPoint presentations.

- **Quiz.** Simplified data input forms that let your audience page through multiple screens and answer yes/no questions.

- **Slide Presentations.** Similar to Photo Slideshows, but with nontraditional buttons and decorative graphics.

Note: Flash's templates are useful—*if* you can figure out what they're supposed to do and how to customize them. To see what few hints the Help system offers, select Help → Flash Help, and then, in the window that appears, type *using templates* and click Search. A better option: Check out one of the Flash developer support sites listed in the Appendix.

To use one of the prebuilt templates that come with Flash:

1. **Select File → New.**

   The New Document window appears.

2. **In the New Document window, click the Templates tab.**

   The New from Template window in Figure 7-23 appears.

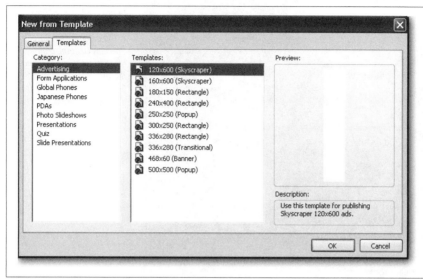

3. **In the Category box, click to select Photo Slideshows.**

   Modern Photo Slideshow appears selected in the Templates box. You see a thumbnail of the first keyframe in the preview window and, below the preview window, a short description of this template.

4. **Click OK.**

   Flash opens the Modern Photo Slideshow (Figure 7-24).

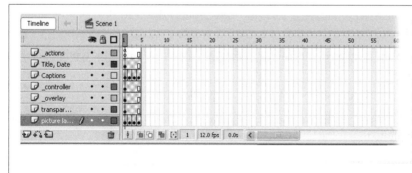

Figure 7-24:
Clicking the bottom of the Timeline and dragging downward expands the Timeline so you can see all the layers. Other than a few vague hints in the Flash Help, these layer names are your only clues for understanding what you need to do to customize this template.

5. **Select Control → Test Movie to preview the template. It's always a good idea to preview a template before you begin to customize it.**

   A test window similar to the one in Figure 7-25 appears.

Figure 7-25:
Notice the title (My Photo Album), the screen number (1 of 4), the photo itself (an ocean cliff), and the caption ("The elegant seashore"). You can customize all these items while keeping the nifty controller that lets you scroll forward and back through the photos.

6. **In the test window, select File → Close.**

   The test file closes, and Flash returns you to the template workspace.

   Next, change the title of the slideshow.

7. **Change the title of the slideshow. To do so:**

8. **On the Timeline, click to select the first keyframe in the Title, Date layer.**

   On the Stage, you see a selection box around the text "My Photo Album" (Figure 7-26).

9. **Click the text box, and then replace "My Photo Album" by typing *Custom Slideshow*.**

   Next, replace the photos that appear in the slideshow.

10. **Click the first keyframe in the layer named "picture layer". On the Stage, click the photo to select it and then choose Edit → Cut.**

    The photo disappears.

11. **Click the Oval tool; then click the Stage and drag your cursor to create a red circle.**

    This example shows a circle for simplicity's sake in demonstrating the Modern Photo Slideshow template, but after reading Chapter 8 you may prefer to add a scanned-in photo of your own to the Stage (page 243).

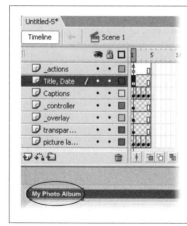

Figure 7-26:
This template was set up to make customization easy: Its creators placed every element you can edit—from the slideshow title to the caption for each picture— on its own separate, appropriately named layer.

12. Repeat the previous step for the second and third keyframes of the picture layer.

    Insert a square and a star, respectively. There's one more keyframe, which you're going to remove.

13. Click the fourth keyframe of the picture layer. On the Stage, right-click the photo and then, from the pop-up menu that appears, select Cut.

    Flash removes the solid black dot that indicates a filled keyframe and replaces it with a hollow dot that indicates an empty keyframe.

    Next, change the captions for your three new images.

14. Click the first keyframe in the layer named Captions.

    On the Stage, a selection box appears around the text "The elegant seashore". (You may need to scroll down the Stage to see the text.)

15. Click the text box and then replace "The elegant seashore" by typing *Circle*.

    Repeat Steps 10 and 11 for the second and third keyframes of the Captions layer, replacing the existing captions with *Square* and *Star*, respectively.

16. On the Timeline, click to select the fourth frame in the "_actions layer". Then Shift-click in the fourth frame of the "picture layer".

    Flash highlights the fourth frame of all seven layers, as shown in Figure 7-27.

17. Right-click the selected frames and then, from the pop-up menu that appears, select Remove Frames.

    Flash deletes the fourth frame of every layer.

18. Test your customized template by selecting Control → Test Movie.

    You should see something similar to Figure 7-28.

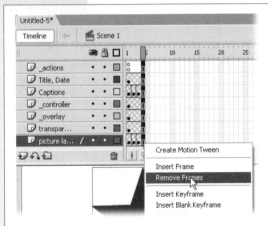

Figure 7-27:
This template displays the slide number (1 of 4, 2 of 4, 3 of 4, and so on) based on how many frames the Timeline contains. So because in this example you're only replacing content for three of the frames, you want to remove the fourth frame of each layer so that the template (technically, the template's ActionScript code) can calculate and display the correct number of frames.

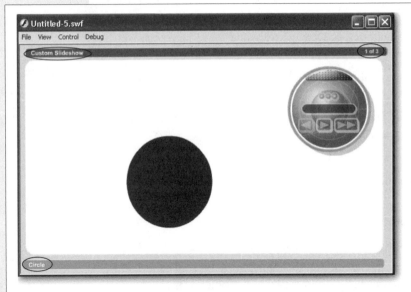

Figure 7-28:
Note the changes you made: the title (now Custom Slideshow), the number of pages (now 1 of 3), the content of the frame itself (a basic circle), and the caption (Circle). When you click the Next button, you step through your remaining frames containing the square and the star. You've got a professional-looking, fully functional, completely customized slideshow—all for just a few minutes' effort. That is the power of templates.

Creating and Using Your Own Custom Template

You create a custom template the same way you create a regular Flash document—with one exception, as you see in the steps below.

To create a custom template:

1. **Create a new Flash document. Add to it the images, frames, and layers you want your template to have.**

    Because you know you (or your colleagues) will be reusing this template, you need to think about reuse as you're deciding which graphic elements and effects to add. The box on page 241 gives you some ideas.

DESIGN TIME

Building a Better Template

Sometimes, you'll find yourself creating a template almost by accident. For example, imagine that you're hard at work on one animation when your boss comes in, peeks over your shoulder, and tells you to create another one "just like that one" for another client. Choose File → Save As Template, continue with the instructions you find on page 240, and you're on your way.

But if you know *beforehand* that you're creating a template, you can plan for reuse. And planning always results in a more useful template. Here are a few planning tips for creating a template you'll use over and over again:

- **Include only reusable stuff.** If you save a working animation as a template (complete with company-specific elements), you'll need to delete any unusable elements each time you reuse the template. Consider up front which elements apply across the board, and include only those in your template.

- **Name your layers.** Giving your layers meaningful names that describe what each layer contains (such as

actions, sounds, background, buttons, and so on) is always a good idea. But it's even more important when you're creating a template, because it gives you (or your colleague, or whoever's reusing the template two weeks from now) an easy way to find and change the elements that need to be changed.

- **Document, document, document.** Have pity on the person who tries to reuse your template a month from now, and tell him up front what the template's for (a product demonstration combined with an order form, for example) and what needs to be changed (the company logo, demo movie clip, and three form fields). The quickie description you type when you create your template (below) is rarely enough. Instead, attach a script to the first frame and use ActionScript comments to document the template. Or—better yet—add documentation text to the first frame, where the person reusing your template can't miss it (but can easily delete it before putting the template into action).

2. **Save your template. To do so, choose File → Save As Template.**

   The Save As Template window in Figure 7-29 appears, complete with a thumbnail preview of the first keyframe of your template.

3. **In the Name field, type a short, descriptive name for your template. Then, from the Category pop-up menu, choose a category.**

   The categories listed are the same categories you see when you use one of Flash's built-in templates: Advertising, Form Applications, Global Phones, Japanese Phones, PDAs, Photo Slideshows, Presentations, Quiz, and Slide Presentations. If none of these categories seems appropriate for your template, you can type your own category into the Category box.

4. **In the Description box, type a complete, concise description of your template and then click Save.**

   Flash saves your document as a template.

You use a custom template the same way you use one of Flash's prebuilt templates. To use (open) a custom template:

1. **Select File → New.**

   The New Document window appears.

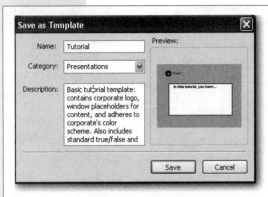

Figure 7-29:
Choosing File → Save As Template displays the window you see here, which lets you type a name (not a file name, but an actual human-readable name), a category (to let you group your templates), and a description (to help remind you which features you added to this template and which situations it's most appropriate for). Be sure to add as complete a description as you can in the 255 characters Flash gives you. The few minutes you spend now will pay off in the future, when you don't have to keep opening the template over and over again just to remind yourself what it does.

2. **In the New Document window, click the Templates tab.**

   Your custom template appears in the "New from Template" window listed in the category you selected for it in step 5 above. Figure 7-30 shows you an example.

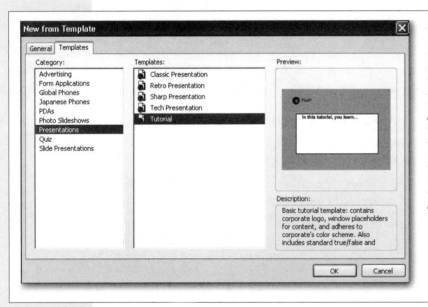

Figure 7-30:
The next time you go to open a template, you see your template listed in the category you selected for it, complete with a preview and the description you typed in when you saved it. Click OK to create a document from this template just as though it were one of Flash's prebuilt templates.

Incorporating Non-Flash Media Files

Flash gives you a ton of drawing and painting tools you can use to create original artwork, as you saw in Chapters 2 and 5. But if you've already got some cool logos or backgrounds that you've created in another program (like Adobe Illustrator or Macromedia Freehand), you don't have to redraw them in Flash. All you have to do is pull them into Flash—*import* them. Once you do, you can work with them nearly as easily as you do the images you create directly on the Stage. You can also add sound clips, video clips, and scanned-in photos to your animations.

This chapter introduces you to the different types of media files with which Flash lets you work. It also gives you tips for working with imported files: You'll see how to apply effects to bitmap graphics, edit video clips, and synchronize (match) sound clips to specific animated sequences.

Note: After you've incorporated non-Flash media into your animation, you can control that media using ActionScript. For more details, flip to Chapter 11.

Incorporating Graphics

Theoretically, you can cut or copy graphic elements from any other program you have open, paste them into Flash, and tweak them. For example, say you've created a drawing in Microsoft Paint. In Microsoft Paint, you can choose Edit → Copy. Then, in Flash, you can choose Edit → Paste in Center to transfer the image from Microsoft Paint to your Stage and edit it using Flash's drawing and painting tools.

Unfortunately, you can get hit-or-miss results by using the system clipboard in this way. Flash may decide to flatten (group) the drawing, limiting your ability to edit it. Flash may also decide to ignore certain effects (such as transparency and gradients) so that the image you paste onto your Stage doesn't quite match the image you cut or copied.

A much safer alternative: In your non-Flash program, save your graphic elements as separate files, and then import those files into Flash. Flash lets you import virtually all graphics file formats, including the popular .jpg, .gif, .bmp, and .eps formats (see Table 8-1 for a complete list).

Table 8-1. *Graphics File Formats You Can Import into Flash*

File Type	Extension	Note
Adobe Illustrator	.eps, .ai, .pdf	Instead of automatically pulling these files in as flat, rasterized bitmaps, Flash lets you set import settings that help preserve the original images' layers and editable text.
AutoCAD DXF	.dxf	
Windows Bitmap	.bmp, .dib	If you're running a Mac, you need to have QuickTime 4 (or later) installed on your computer to import Windows bitmap files into Flash.
Enhanced Windows Metafile	.wmf	Only works on Windows.
Macromedia Freehand	.fh7, .fh8, .fh9, .fh10, and .fh11	Instead of automatically pulling these files in as flat, rasterized bitmaps, Flash lets you set import settings that help preserve the original images' layers and editable text.
Graphic Interchange Format (including animated GIF)	.gif	
Joint Photographic Experts Group	.jpg	
Portable Network Graphic	.png	Instead of automatically importing PNG files created in Macromedia Fireworks in as flat, rasterized bitmaps, Flash lets you set import settings that help preserve the original images' layers, editable objects, and editable text.
Flash and FutureSplash (pre-Flash) players	.swf, .spl	

Table 8-1. *Graphics File Formats You Can Import into Flash (continued)*

File Type	Extension	Note
MacPaint	.pntg	You have to have QuickTime 4 installed before you can import MacPaint files into Flash.
Portable Document Format (Adobe Acrobat)	.pdf	Instead of automatically pulling these files in as flat, rasterized bitmaps, Flash lets you set import settings that help preserve the original images' layers and editable text.
Photoshop	.psd	You have to have QuickTime 4 installed before you can import Photoshop files into Flash.
PICT	.pct, .pict	You have to have QuickTime 4 installed before you can import PICT files into Flash.
QuickTime Image	.qtif	You have to have QuickTime 4 installed before you can import QuickTime Image files into Flash.
Silicon Graphics Image	.sgi	You have to have QuickTime 4 installed before you can import Silicon Graphics Image files into Flash.
Targa	.tga	You have to have QuickTime 4 installed before you can import Targa files into Flash.
Tagged Image File	.tif, .tiff	You have to have QuickTime 4 installed before you can import TIFF files into Flash.
Windows metafile	.wmf	Only works on Windows.

Note: If you're looking for places to find third-party graphics files to import into Flash, check out the box on page 257.

Importing Graphics Files

Flash lets you import graphics files that you've created with another image-editing program (such as Adobe Photoshop) and then stored on your computer. After you import a graphics file, you can either edit the image it contains using Flash's tools and panels or just add it directly to your animation.

Note: Table 8-1 shows you a complete list of all the different graphics file formats you can import into Flash.

Flash/QuickTime Cross-Pollination

Since the good old days of Flash 4, Flash has enjoyed a symbiotic relationship with Apple's QuickTime. Back then, you could import a QuickTime movie into Flash, and then add some Flash content (for example, buttons that Web surfers can press to start and stop the QuickTime movie). And you can still import QuickTime movies into Flash 8 and link the two together, as you see on page 269.

But the relationship between Flash and QuickTime goes beyond video integration—it also affects your ability to import media files into Flash. If you have QuickTime installed on your computer, for example, Flash lets you import more types of graphic file formats than it does if you don't have QuickTime installed (see Table 8-1 for details).

Fortunately, QuickTime's easy to install. It's free, too. To download a copy, visit *www.apple.com/quicktime/download*.

As you see in the steps below, after you've imported a graphics file, Flash stores a copy of the image in the Library panel (page 30) so you can add as many instances of the image to your animations as you like.

Of course, there's no such thing as a free lunch. Depending on the format of your graphics file (Table 8-1), Flash either pulls the image in as a collection of editable shapes and layers—which you can work with just as you work with any image in Flash—or as a flattened bitmap, which limits your editing choices a bit. "Editing bitmaps" on page 250 gives you tips for working with flattened bitmaps.

To import a graphics file into Flash:

1. **Choose File → Import → Import to Stage.**

   The Import dialog box you see in Figure 8-1 appears.

2. **In the "File name" field, type the name of the file you want to import (or, in the file window, click the file to have Flash fill in the name for you).**

   To see all the different types of files you can import, click the drop-down box next to "Files of type."

3. **Click Open.**

   The Import dialog box disappears. Flash places a copy of the image both on the Stage and in the Library (Figure 8-2)—*unless* you chose to import a file with one of the following extensions: .ai, .eps, .pdf, .png, or .fh*.

   When you import one of those five file types, Flash displays an extra Import settings window that lets you tell it how much editability you want to preserve: whether you want it to convert the original frames into Flash frames or Flash scenes, whether you want Flash to pull in all the frames or just a few, whether you want it to include invisible layers or not, and so on. For example, Figure 8-3 shows you the Import settings windows you see when you import files created with Adobe Illustrator, Fireworks, and Freehand.

Figure 8-1:
You can import a graphic to the Stage and to the Library, as you see in the numbered steps, or just to the Library (by choosing Edit → Import to Library). Either way, you first have to tell Flash which file contains the graphic you want to import—and that's exactly what you do here, in the Import dialog box.

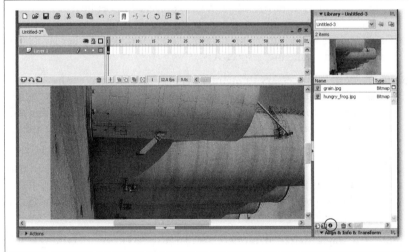

Figure 8-2:
After you import a bitmap, Flash throws a backup copy of the image into the Library as a convenience so that you can drag another copy onto the Stage if you want to (without having to go through all the trouble of importing the file again). To see the properties of your newly imported bitmap, click the information icon you see here.

4. **If you see one of the Import settings windows (Figure 8-3), click to select one or more of the following options, and then click OK.**

   Convert pages to: Scenes/Keyframes. Tells Flash to map multiple pages in the graphics file either to individual scenes in Flash (see Chapter 10) or to keyframes. In most cases, keyframes are your best bet.

   Convert layers to: Layers/Keyframes/Flatten. Tells Flash to keep the layering structure of the original file intact, to place the content of each layer in a separate keyframe, or to flatten the content of all layers onto a single Flash layer, respectively.

Which pages to import (All/From/To). Tells Flash to import the graphic elements on all the pages of a multipage file, or only those elements on the specific pages you specify.

Include invisible layers. Tells Flash to try to import all layers, including those marked as hidden in the original editing program.

Include Background Layer. Tells Flash to import the layer that, in the original drawing program, is the equivalent of the Stage.

Maintain text blocks. Tells Flash to keep the text blocks that it imports editable.

Rasterize everything. Tells Flash to flatten all of the elements in the graphics file into bitmap images on one layer, no matter how many layers the file contains. Choosing this option gives you the best shot at importing something that looks close to what it looks like in the original drawing program, although obviously you're sacrificing the ability to edit the image.

Rasterization resolution. Only available if you chose "Rasterize everything" (see above), this option tells Flash how high-quality a bitmap you want it to create from the graphics file. Your options are 72, 144, and 300 (the higher the number, the higher the quality).

File structure: Import as movie clip and retain layers/Import into new layer in current scene. Tells Flash either to import the graphics file into a new movie clip Timeline or to place it in a single Flash layer on top of any other layers that happen to be in the Timeline, respectively.

Objects: Rasterize if necessary to maintain appearance/Keep all paths editable. Tells Flash either to flatten all images onto a single layer so they can't be edited separately or to try to preserve the editability of objects. (Flash may not be able to keep objects editable after it imports them, but you can tell it to do its best.)

Text: Rasterize if necessary to maintain appearance/Keep all paths editable. Tells Flash either to flatten all text blocks so that individual letters can't be edited separately, or to try to preserve the editability of the text blocks. (Flash may not be able to keep text blocks editable after it imports them, depending on factors such as the fonts used, but you can tell it to try.)

Import as a single flattened bitmap. Similar to "Rasterize everything," this option tells Flash not to preserve the editability of any part of the graphics file and just pull the whole thing in as a single, nonlayered entity.

The Import settings window disappears. Flash places a copy of the graphics in the graphics file both on the Stage (or in multiple frames and layers, based on the options you selected above) and in the Library, as shown in Figure 8-2.

Importing Unimportable Graphics

Don't expect perfection when you're importing complex graphics—especially if you're trying to preserve the ability to edit your graphics in Flash. Flash does the best it can, but there are an awful lot of variables involved, from the specific effects you applied to the graphics to the specific version of the program you used to create them.

If the graphics you import into Flash don't look or behave the way they do in the original program, try one or more of the following:

- **Ungroup the imported image** by selecting it on the Stage and then choosing Modify → Ungroup.

- **Try using the Clipboard.** First, choose Edit → Preferences (Windows) or Flash → Preferences (Mac) to display the Preferences window. In the Category list,

click Clipboard. Then adjust the settings based on what you're trying to import. For example, if you're trying to import an image containing a gradient effect, click the Gradient Quality drop-down list and then choose Best. If you're trying to import a Free-Hand file, turn on the checkbox next to "Maintain as blocks." Then, in the original program, copy your image. Return to Flash and choose Edit → Paste in Center.

- **Return to the original program and see if you can simplify the image.** Reduce the number of colors you're using, as well as the number of layers, and flatten (group) as much of the image as you can. Then try the import process again.

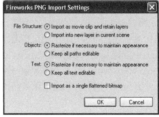

Figure 8-3:

Top Left: When you try to import certain types of vector files into Flash, Flash lets you specify how much editability you're willing to sacrifice for good-quality images. Here, you see the dialog box Flash displays when you try to import a PostScript file created with Adobe Illustrator.

Top Right: This settings window appears when you try to import a file created with Macromedia Fireworks. You'll notice that the options you can set here are very similar to those you can set in the other two.

Bottom: These are the settings Flash offers when you try to import a file created with Macromedia FreeHand. In a perfect world, Flash would do exactly what you tell it, settings-wise; but in real life, Flash isn't always able to import externally created files perfectly in terms of either graphic effects or editability.

Editing Bitmaps

Depending on the graphic file format you import into Flash, you may be able to edit the edited image using Flash's tools, or you may not. If Flash recognizes the image as a *vector* image, with distinct strokes and fills, you're good to go. Just open the Tools panel, choose a selection, drawing, or painting tool, and get to work.

But if the image comes through as a bitmap, you need to do a bit of finagling, because Flash treats bitmaps as big blobs of undifferentiated pixels. (See the box on page 253 for more details.)

With bitmaps, Flash's selection tools don't work as you might expect. Say, for instance, you import a scanned-in photo of the Seattle skyline. Flash treats the entire photo as a single entity. When you click the Space Needle, Flash selects the entire scanned-in image. When you try to use the Lasso tool to select the half of the image that contains Mount Rainier, Flash selects the entire image. When you try to repaint the sky a lighter shade of gray, Flash repaints (you guessed it) the entire image.

Fortunately, Flash gives you a few options when it comes to working with bitmaps: You can break them apart, you can turn them into vector graphics, or you can turn them into symbols. The following sections describe each option.

Turning bitmaps into fills

Breaking apart a bitmap image transforms the image from a homogenous group of pixels into an editable fill. You still can't click the Space Needle and have Flash recognize it as a distinct shape (you can only do that with vector art), but you *can* use the Selection, Subselection, and Lasso tools to select the Space Needle and then either cut it, copy it, move it, repaint it, or otherwise edit it separately from the rest of the scanned-in image.

To break apart a bitmap:

1. **On the Stage, select the bitmap image you want to break apart.**

    Flash displays a selection box around the image.

2. **Choose Modify → Break Apart.**

    Flash covers the image with tiny white dots to let you know it's now a fill.

At this point, you can use the Selection, Subselection, and Lasso tools to select portions of the image (something you *couldn't* do before you broke the bitmap apart).

Turning bitmaps into vectors

Tracing a bitmap transforms a bitmap into a vector graphic. You can check out the box on page 253 for a rundown of the differences between the two; but basically, turning a bitmap into a vector gives you three benefits:

• It produces a cool, stylized, watercolor effect.

- It reduces the file size associated with the image (but only in cases where the image doesn't contain a lot of different colors or gradients).

- It turns a nonscalable image into a scalable image—one you can "zoom in" on without it turning all fuzzy on you.

Note: The less colors your bitmap contains, the more faithful your bitmap-turned-vector is likely to be to the original. Tracing a bitmap of a hand-drawn sketch done in black charcoal, for example, is going to result in a vector graphic that resembles the original bitmap much more closely than a bitmap trace of a scanned-in photo. (Even photos that look to the naked eye as though they only contain a handful of colors usually contain many, many more at the pixel level.)

To trace a bitmap, select the bitmap you want to turn into a vector graphic, and then select Modify → Bitmap → Trace Bitmap. Figure 8-4 shows you an example.

Turning bitmaps into symbols

You can't change the color, brightness, or transparency (*alpha*) of an imported bitmap, but you *can* change them for a symbol. So if all you want to do is tint or fade a bitmap, you can use a quick and easy fix, and transform it into a symbol.

To turn a bitmap into a symbol:

1. **Select the bitmap, and then choose Modify → Convert to Symbol.**

   The Convert to Symbol dialog box appears.

2. **In the Convert to Symbol dialog box, turn on the radio box next to Graphic and then click OK.**

   In the Property Inspector, click the drop-down list next to Color to set the symbol's brightness, tint, and alpha (transparency) settings.

Note: For the skinny on symbols, check out Chapter 7; for more on color, brightness, and transparency, see Chapter 5.

Importing a Series of Graphics Files

At times, you may have a series of graphics files you want to import into Flash. Say, for example, you have a series of images you took with a digital camera showing a dog leaping through the air to catch a tennis ball. If you import all these images into Flash, one per frame, you've got yourself an animation. (How herky-jerky or smooth the animation appears depends on how many images you have; the more images, the smoother the animation.)

If you give your graphics files sequential names such as dog_01.gif, dog_02.gif, dog_03.gif, and so on, Flash is smart enough to recognize what you're trying to do, and it imports the entire series in one fell swoop.

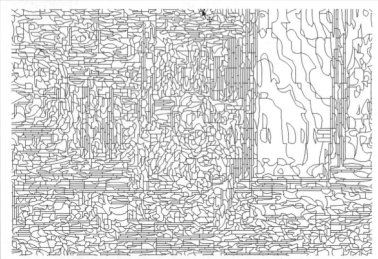

Figure 8-4:
Top: Here's the way a scanned-in image looks as a bitmap.

Bottom: This is how it looks after Flash has traced it (turned it into vector art). With photos, the effect is more arty than realistic, which might be just what you're looking for. Even though the image is now a vector, you can't click to select individual objects—such as the child or the open book—because Flash doesn't recognize meaningful shapes. Instead, it works off pockets of color saturation.

To import a series of graphics:

1. Make sure the names of the files you want to import end with sequential numbers; for example, file1.bmp, file2.bmp, and file3.bmp.

2. Choose File → Import → Import to Stage.

   The Import dialog box you see in Figure 8-5 (top) appears.

3. In the Import dialog box, click to select the first file in the series, and then click Import.

   The confirmation dialog box you see in Figure 8-5 (bottom) appears.

4. Click Yes.

   The confirmation dialog box disappears, and Flash imports the series of files. On the Timeline you see one image (and one keyframe) per frame.

Vector vs. Bitmap Images

Flash lets you import and work with two different types of graphics files: vector and bitmap. You can't tell by looking at the image—the difference is in the structure of the information that makes up the image. Here are the main points:

Computer programs, including Flash, store vector graphics (such as the original artwork you create on the Stage) as a bunch of formulas. Vector graphics have the advantage of being pretty modest in size compared to bitmaps, and they're scalable. In other words, if you draw a tiny blackbird and then decide to scale it by 500 percent, your scaled drawing will still look like a nice, crisp blackbird, only bigger.

In contrast, computer programs store *bitmap*, or *raster*, graphics (such as a scanned-in photo) as a bunch of pixels. Bitmap graphics doesn't refer just to files with the Windows bitmap (.bmp) extension; it refers to all images stored in bitmap format, including .eps, .ai, .gif, .jpg, and .png. (You can find a complete list of the file formats Flash lets you import on page 248.)

The good thing about bitmap graphics is that they let you create super-realistic detail, complete with complex colors, gradients and subtle shadings. On the downside, bitmaps typically take up a whopping amount of disk space, and they're *not* particularly scalable: If you scale a photo of a blackbird by 500 percent, it appears blurry because all Flash can do is enlarge each individual pixel: It doesn't have access to the formulas it would need to draw the additional pixels necessary to keep the detail crisp and sharp at five times the original drawing size.

Why do you care whether a graphics file is a vector or bitmap? Because you work with imported bitmap files differently in Flash than you do with imported or original vector files. As you see on page 250, you need to break bitmap images apart before you can crop them in Flash. You also need to optimize the bitmaps you import into Flash if you're planning to reduce the size of your finished animation. (Chapter 14 shows you how.)

If you check the Library panel (Window → Library), you see that Flash has placed each of the image files in the Library.

Incorporating Sound

Flash lets you score your animations much the same way a filmmaker scores a movie. You can add a soundtrack that begins when your animation begins and ends when it ends. Or you can tie different sound clips to different *scenes* (series of frames) of your animation. For example, say you're creating an instructional animation to demonstrate your company's egg slicer. You can play music during the opening seconds of your animation, switch to a voice-over to describe your product, and end with realistic sounds of chopping, slicing, and boiling to match the visual of cooks using your product in a real-life setting.

You can also tie sounds to specific *events* in Flash. For example, say you want your instructional animation to contain a button someone can press to get ordering information. You can tie the sound of a button clicking to the Down state of your button, as you'll see in Chapter 11, so that when someone clicks your button, she actually *hears* a realistic clicking sound.

Figure 8-5:
When you tell Flash to open the first in a series of sequentially numbered files (top), the program asks if you'd like to import the entire series (bottom). This trick works only if the numbers appear at the end of the file name just before the extension and if you don't skip any numbers in the series. And since Flash begins importing with the numbered file you choose, it doesn't go back and pick up files containing lower numbers.

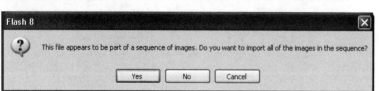

Note: Pre–Version 8, Flash shipped with a library of sound effects you could add to your animations. But Macromedia discovered that most folks weren't using them, so they pulled them in Flash 8. (Seems there isn't much call for robot noises and doorbell chimes in production-level animation circles.) Creating digitalized sounds from scratch is a big enough subject to warrant its own book, and if you're interested in the recording and editing process, you might want to check out *Producing Great Sound for Digital Video* by Jay Rose (CMP Books). But if experimenting with preproduced sound clips fits your particular project, check out the box on page 257.

Importing Sound Files

Before you can work with sound in Flash, you need to import a sound file either to the Stage, the Library, or both. Flash lets you import a variety of sound files, as you can see in Table 8-2.

Table 8-2. *Audio File Formats You Can Import into Flash*

File Type	Extension	Note
MPEG-1 Audio Layer 3	.mp3	Works on both Mac and Windows.
Windows Wave	.wav	Works on Windows only, *unless* you have QuickTime 4 (or later) installed; then you can import .wav files into Flash on the Mac, too.
Audio Interchange File format	.aiff, .aif	Works on Mac only, *unless* you have Quick-Time 4 (or later) installed; then you can import AIFF files into Flash running in Windows, too.
Sound Designer II	.sd2	Only works on Mac, and only if you have QuickTime 4 (or later) installed.
Sound-only QuickTime movies	.mov, .qtif	Works on both Windows and Mac, but only if you have QuickTime 4 (or later) installed.
Sun AU	.au	Works on both Windows and Mac, but only if you have QuickTime 4 (or later) installed.

To import a sound file:

1. Select File → Import → Import to Library.

   The Import to Library dialog box appears.

2. **In the "File name" field, type the name of the sound file you want to import (or, in the file window, click the file to have Flash fill in the name for you).**

   To see the different types of sound files you can import, you can either click the pop-up menu next to "Files of type," or check out Table 8-2.

3. Click Open.

   The Import to Library dialog box appears, and Flash places a copy of the imported sound file into the Library (Figure 8-6, top). When you click to select any of the frames in your Timeline, the sound appears in the Property Inspector.

Adding an Imported Sound to a Frame (or Series of Frames)

You can tell Flash to play an animated sound beginning with any frame of your animation. Depending on the settings you choose, Flash keeps playing the sound file either until it finishes (regardless of whether your animation is still playing or not) or until you tell it to stop.

The example below shows you how to use the *stream* option to synchronize a short sound clip of a fly buzzing to an animated sequence showing—what else?—a buzzing fly. Then you see how to start and stop a second sound (the sound of the fly becoming a frog's lunch).

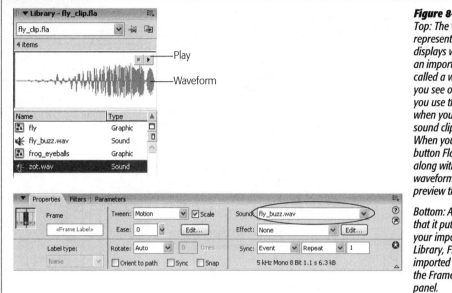

Figure 8-6:
Top: The visual representation Flash displays when you select an imported sound clip is called a waveform. (As you see on page 261, you use this waveform when you're editing a sound clip in Flash.) When you click the Play button Flash displays along with the waveform, you can preview the sound.

Bottom: At the same time that it puts a copy of your imported file in the Library, Flash makes the imported file available in the Frame Properties panel.

To add an imported sound to a series of frames:

1. **Open the file happy_frog.fla.**

   You can find this file on the "Missing CD" page. (To see a working version, check out happy_frog_sound.fla.

2. **In the Layers window, click to select the topmost layer (Guide: Layer 1).**

   Flash highlights the layer name, as well as all the frames in that layer.

3. **Select Insert → Timeline → Layer.**

   Flash creates a new layer and places it above the selected layer.

   Double-click the new layer name and type in *soundtrack*, as shown in Figure 8-7.

4. **Click the first keyframe in the soundtrack layer.**

   In the Property Inspector, Flash activates the Frame properties, including those related to sound.

5. **Click the arrow next to the Sound field and, from the drop-down list that appears, choose the imported sound file fly_buzz.wav.**

   Alternatively, you can drag the sound file symbol from the Library to the Stage. Either way, the sound properties for the file appear at the bottom of the Property Inspector, and the waveform for the buzzing fly sound appears in the soundtrack layer (Figure 8-8).

Using Sound Effectively

If you've ever watched a movie that had a breathtakingly beautiful (or laughably cheesy) musical score, you've experienced the power of sound firsthand. Effective sound can elevate a decent visual experience into the realm of art. Ineffective sound can turn that same visual experience into a nerve-shredding mess.

If you're thinking about adding sound to your animation, consider these points:

• **Why do you want to add sound?** If your answer is to add emotional punch; to cue your audience aurally to the interactive features you've added to your animation, such as buttons that *click* or draggable objects that *whoosh*; or to deliver information you can't deliver any other way (such as a voiceover explaining an animated sequence or realistic sounds to accompany the sequence); then by all means go for it. But if your answer is "Because I can," you need to rethink your decision. Sound—as much as any graphic element—needs to add to the overall message you're trying to deliver or it'll end up detracting from that message.

• **Are you sure your audience will be able to hear your sound?** Sound files are big. They take time to download. If you're planning to put your animation on a Web site, Flash gives you a couple of different options for managing download time—but keep in mind that not everyone in your audience may have a fast connection or the volume knob on her speaker turned up. (For that matter, some folks are deaf. Check out the box on page 11 for tips on providing hearing-impaired folks with an alternate way of getting your information.)

• **How important is it that your soundtrack matches your animation precisely?** Flash gives you options to help you synchronize your sound clips with your frames. But you can't match a 2-second sound clip to a 10-second animated sequence without either slowing down the sound or speeding up the animation. If you want to match a specific sound clip to a specific series of frames, you may need to edit one (or both) to get the balance right *before* you begin synchronizing them in Flash.

Note: If you don't see the waveform on the Timeline after you've added it, click on the first keyframe and then Shift-click Frame 20 to select all of the frames, from 1 to 20. Finally, choose Insert → Timeline → Insert Frame.

---

6. **In the Property Inspector, click the arrow next to the Sync field and, from the first drop-down list that appears, choose Stream.**

Your synchronization choices include:

Event. Tells Flash to give the sound its very own Timeline. In other words, Flash keeps playing the sound until the sound finishes, regardless of whether or not the animation has ended. If you repeat (or loop) the animation in the Controller, Flash begins playing a new sound clip every time the animation begins again—with the result that, after a dozen or so loops, you hear a dozen flies buzzing! Flash assumes you want your sound to behave this way unless you tell it otherwise.

DESIGN TIME

Stock Images, Sounds, and Video Clips

If you're using Flash to create stuff for work—presentations, tutorials, Web advertisements, marketing materials, or what have you—you or someone else on your team is probably going to be creating all your content from scratch. But there's a place in every Flash fan's toolkit for *stock media:* generic images, sound clips, and video clips that you purchase (or, more rarely, get for free) from companies whose job it is to produce such items.

Typically, you pay a modest fee to use stock images, sounds, and video clips. Sometimes, you also pay a royalty fee based on the number of times you use a stock element in your animation.

If you're using Flash to snazzy-up your personal Web site, you may find stock media is just what the doctor ordered: You get something cool that you can use for a relatively low price without having to invest time and money buying audio and video equipment and tracking down that twister yourself. But even professional animators have been known to rely on stock media occasionally because it lets them test out a concept quickly and cheaply.

Places to find stock images, sound clips, and video clips abound on the Web. Here are a few you might want to check out:

www.freestockfootage.com
www.bigshotmedia.com
www.wildform.com/videolibrary
www.flashkit.com/soundfx/
www.a1freesoundeffects.com/household.html
www.findsounds.com/
http://creative.gettyimages.com

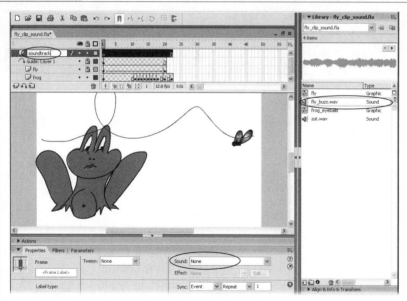

Figure 8-7:
Technically speaking, you can add a sound clip to any layer you like. But if you're smart, you create a separate layer for your sounds (some folks even create a separate layer for each sound). Creating separate layers helps keep your keyframes from becoming so cluttered that you can't see everything you've added to them. It also helps you find your sounds quickly in case you want to make a change down the road.

Tip: You add a sound to a button the same way you see demonstrated here with two exceptions: You typically add a sound file for a button to the button's third, or Down, frame (so that the sound plays when your audience clicks *down* on the button) and you leave the synchronization option set to Event. To see an example, check out the file button_sound.fla on the "Missing CD" page.

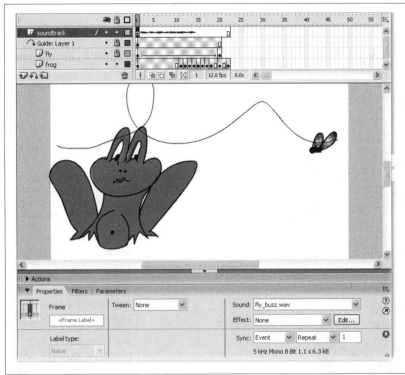

Figure 8-8:
It's rare that the length of a sound clip precisely matches the length of the animated clip to which you want to assign it. Here, the sound clip stretches only to Frame 14—but the layer showing the buzzing fly stretches all the way to Frame 20. You could cut and paste the sound to fill those last four frames so that the fly doesn't become uncharacteristically silent all of a sudden, but Flash gives you much easier ways to match a sound clip to a frame span: streaming, repeating, and looping.

Start. Similar to Event, but tells Flash *not* to begin playing a new sound if the animation repeats.

Stop. Tells Flash to stop playing the sound.

Stream. Tells Flash to match the animation to the sound clip as best it can, either by speeding up or slowing down the frames-per-second that it plays the animation. This option is the one you want for *lip-synching*, when you're trying to match a voiceover to an animated sequence featuring a talking head. Because choosing this option also tells Flash to *stream* the sound file (play it before it's fully downloaded in those cases where you've put your animation on a Web site), someone with a slow connection can get a herky-jerky animation.

Tip: To preview your newly added sound on the Stage, drag (*scrub*) the playhead along the Timeline. You can scrub forward or backward. To hear just the sound in a specific frame, Shift-click the playhead over that frame. Flash keeps playing the sound until you let up on either the Shift key or the mouse.

---

7. **From the second drop-down list next to the Sync field, choose Loop.**

   Loop tells Flash to repeat the sound clip until the animation ends. Repeat lets you tell Flash how many times you want it to play the sound clip (regardless of the length of the frame span).

---

8. **Test the soundtracked animation by choosing Control → Test Movie.**

   You hear a buzzing sound as the fly loops its way across the test movie.

9. **Add a second, short sound clip to your animation to make the scene more realistic. To do so:**

   In the soundtrack layer, click Frame 20.

   On the Stage, you see the frog's tongue appear (Figure 8-9).

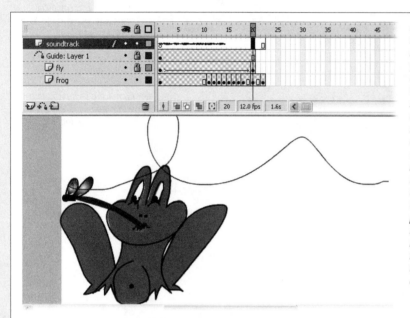

Figure 8-9:
Beginning sound clips in individual keyframes lets you change the soundtrack at the exact moment your visuals change. Here, you see the frog's tongue appear in Frame 20 of the frog layer, and it doesn't change until Frame 22 (which contains the final keyframe of the animation). So to match the zot! sound to the tongue action, you want to tell Flash to start playing the zot.wav file on Frame 20 and stop playing it on Frame 22. The following steps tell you how to match the sound and action.

10. **Select Insert → Timeline → Blank Keyframe.**

    Flash places a blank keyframe (a hollow circle) in Frame 20.

11. **In the Property Inspector, click the arrow next to Sound and then, from the drop-down list that appears, choose zot.wav.**

    Flash places the waveform for the sound file onto the Timeline, beginning with Frame 20.

12. **In the Property Inspector, click the arrow next to Sync and then, from the drop-down list that appears, choose Start.**

13. **In the soundtrack layer, click to select Frame 22.**

    On the Stage, you see a very satisfied frog (Figure 8-10).

14. **Select Insert → Timeline → Blank Keyframe.**

    Flash places a blank keyframe (a hollow circle) in Frame 22.

15. In the Property Inspector, click the arrow next to Sound and then, from the drop-down list that appears, choose zot.wav.

16. Click the arrow next to Sync and then, from the drop-down list that appears, choose Stop.

17. Test the new sound by choosing Control → Test Movie.

You hear a buzzing sound as the fly loops its way across the test movie. But as the frog's tongue appears, the buzzing stops and you hear a satisfying *zot!*

Tip: If you don't hear any sounds, select Control and see whether the checkbox next to Mute Sounds is turned on. If it is, click it to turn it off.

Figure 8-10:
Because the synchronization option for the zot! sound was set to start in Frame 20, Flash automatically stops playing the zot.wav sound file when the animation ends. Still, it's good practice to tell Flash specifically when you want it to stop playing a sound file. You'll be glad you did when you come back to the animation a week or two later because you won't have any cleanup to do before you add additional sounds to the Timeline.

Editing Sound Clips in Flash

You can change the way your imported sound clips play in Flash. You can't do anything super-fancy, like mix down multiple audio channels or add reverb—Flash isn't a sound-editing program, after all—but you *can* crop the clips, add simple fade-in/fade-out effects, and even choose which speaker (right or left) they play out of.

First, import the sound clip you want to edit, as described on page 254. To edit it, follow these steps:

1. On the Timeline, click any frame that contains a portion of the sound clip's waveform.

Flash activates the sound options you see in the Property Inspector.

---

2. **In the Property Inspector, click the drop-down box next to Edit and then choose from the following menu options:**

   Left channel. Tells Flash to play the sound through the left speaker.

   Right channel. Tells Flash to play the sound through the right speaker.

   Fade left to right. Tells Flash to begin playing the sound through the left speaker, and then switch midway through the clip to the right speaker.

   Fade right to left. Tells Flash to begin playing the sound through the right speaker, and then switch midway through the clip to the left speaker.

   Fade in. Tells Flash to start playing the sound softly and build to full volume.

   Fade out. Tells Flash to start playing the sound at full volume and taper off toward the end.

   Custom. Tells Flash to display the Edit Envelope window you see in Figure 8-11, which lets you choose the *in point* (the point where you want Flash to begin playing the sound) and the *out point* (where you want the sound clip to end). You can also choose a custom fading effect; for example, you can fade in, then out, then in again.

Note: Clicking the Property panel's Edit button displays the same Edit Envelope window you see when you choose the Custom option.

Incorporating Video

Flash animation is great for creating lot of things: cartoons, ads, presentations, tutorials, and interactive Web sites, to name a few. But sometimes, video footage is more effective. For example, video footage showing a live product demonstration, a kid blowing out the candles on his birthday cake, or an interview with a CEO can get a point across quicker than any other medium.

Note: One of the recent trends Flash is fueling is video blogging, or *vlogging:* adding video clips to plain-vanilla Web logs. You can find out more at sites like *www.vidblogs.com* and *www.wearethemedia.com*.

With Flash, you don't have to choose. You can import video files in a variety of formats (see Table 8-3) and incorporate them along with images, sounds, text, and interactive controls (such as buttons your audience can push to start and stop different sections of your video clips) to build unique multimedia animations. You can even apply effects to a video clip in Flash: for example, skewing and tinting.

Because Flash isn't set up to let you edit video files more than a few seconds long, most Flash jockeys do all their video production and editing in other specialized video editing programs (such as those listed in the box on page 266). Then they

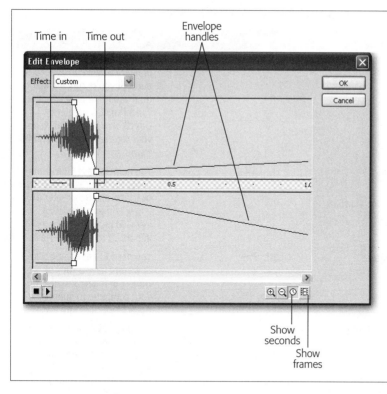

Time in   Time out   Envelope handles

Edit Envelope

Effect: Custom

OK

Cancel

0.5   1.0

Show seconds
Show frames

Figure 8-11:
The sound file you see here is a two-channel (stereo) sound, so you see two separate waveforms, one per channel. To crop the sound clip, drag the Time In and Time Out control bars left and right. Flash ignores the gray area during playback and only plays the portion of the waveform that appears with a white background; so here, Flash only plays the second half of the waveform. To create a custom fading effect, you can drag the envelope handles separately. The settings in this example tell Flash to fade out on the left channel while simultaneously fading in on the right channel. To preview your custom effect, click the Play icon.

export their video clips as separate .flv files, which they tie to their Flash anima-tions using a bit of ActionScript code. This technique works great if all you want to do is display a video in Flash along with Play/Stop buttons (the most common approach, and the one demonstrated on page 266).

Table 8-3. *Video File Formats You Can Import into Flash*

File Type	Extension	Note
QuickTime movie	.mov	You need to have QuickTime 7 or later (if you're running Mac) or QuickTime 6.5 or later (if you're running Windows) installed on your computer to import QuickTime movies into Flash.
Audio Video Interleaved	.avi	You need to have QuickTime 7 or later installed on your computer (if you're running Mac) or, if you're running Windows, you need either QuickTime 6.5 or later or DirectX 9 or later installed on your computer to import AVI movies into Flash.

Table 8-3. *Video File Formats You Can Import into Flash (continued)*

File Type	Extension	Note
Motion Picture Experts Group	.mpg, .mpeg	You need to have QuickTime 7 or later installed on your computer (if you're running Mac) or, if you're running Windows, QuickTime 6.5 or later or DirectX 9 or later installed on your computer to import MPEG movies into Flash.
Digital video	.dv, .dvi	You need to have QuickTime 7 or later (if you're running Mac) or QuickTime 6.5 or later (if you're running Windows) installed on your computer to import DV movies into Flash.
Windows Media	.asf, .wmv	You need to be running Windows *and* have a copy of DirectX 9 or later installed on your computer to import Windows Media files into Flash.
Macromedia Flash video	.flv	The easiest way to create a .flv file is by importing another type of video file into Flash, and then, by double-clicking the imported file in the Library, exporting the video again as a .flv file. (The box on page 266 shows you two more options.)

Preparing to Import Video Files

Before you can import a video clip into Flash, you first have to have a video file stored in one of the formats Table 8-3 describes. But you also need to know up front how you expect to link the video file to your finished Flash animation file at runtime: by embedding the video file directly onto your Flash Timeline, by linking to the video file at runtime, and so on.

This cart-before-the-horse requirement isn't quite as odd as it seems at first blush. Video files tend to be so huge that you can't always get away with embedding them directly into your Flash document the way you embed graphics and sound files (pages 244 and 253, respectively). So to keep the lengthy import process from being a complete waste of your valuable time, Flash doesn't let you import a video clip until it knows that *you* know how you'll be publishing, or *deploying*, the video-containing animation you intend to create.

Tip: Note: Chapter 14 tells you all you need to know about publishing Flash files, including Flash files containing video clips.

Your deployment options include:

- **Progressive download from a Web server.** In this option, you either find an .flv file or you create one (see the box on page 266) containing the video clip you want to add to your animation. Then, in your Flash document, you create ActionScript statements (page 281) that describe which .flv file to pull in at runtime and how you want your animation to interact with that file. (If all you want to do is display the video, add basic video controls, such as Play and Stop buttons. You can tell Flash to generate the necessary ActionScript code for you.) When you choose this option, you get to publish both your finished Flash animation and your .flv file to a regular, garden-variety Web server.

- **Stream from Flash Video Streaming Service.** This option is similar to Option #1, with one notable exception: Instead of publishing your finished Flash animation file and your .flv file to a regular Web server, you have to publish them to a special Web server running Flash Media Server (formerly Flash Communication Server). The Flash Video Streaming Service takes care of installing and running all the necessary server programs and hardware; all you have to do is pay for the service.

- **Stream from Flash Communication Server.** This option is similar to Option #2 above, except that you (or, more likely, your company's IT department) buy the server hardware, install the server software, and maintain the resulting system.

- **Embed video in SWF and play in Timeline.** This option represents the simplest way to embed video into your animation, but it only works for very short video clips (somewhere between 5 and 10 seconds or less). Any more than that, and the size of your animation file grows so large that you have trouble editing the file in Flash *and* your audience has trouble viewing it in their Flash Player.

- **Linked QuickTime video for publishing to QuickTime.** This option lets you import a QuickTime video file, add Flash graphics and animated effects, and then export the resulting hybrid animation as a QuickTime movie file. (QuickTime movie files run only in the QuickTime player or browser plug-in; they *don't* run in Flash Player.)

Importing Video Files

Once you have access to a video file and a handle on how you're going to deploy your video-containing animation, you're ready to begin importing the video file into Flash.

The import process varies slightly depending on which format video file you want to import (.flv, .mov, and so on), where that file is located (your computer, a Web server, a Flash Web server), and how you plan to deploy your finished video-containing animation (see "Preparing to Import Video Files" on page 264). In this section, you see step-by-step examples of the two most common scenarios: importing a Flash video file stored on a Web server and importing a QuickTime file stored on your computer.

Creating a Flash Video File

You may not be able to shoot video footage with your PC or PowerBook, but you *can* create digital video using nothing more than your copy of Flash 8 (or one of the other programs listed below). That's good news if you plan to use one of the first three animation-plus-video deployment options described on page 265, all of which require your video clip to be in Flash video file format (.flv).

To create a Flash video file, choose one of the following:

1. Import another type of video file into Flash 8. Then, in the Library, double-click the imported file to export it as a .flv file.

2. Use a third-party tool, such as Sorenson Squeeze for Macromedia Flash or Flix Pro 8 for Flash 8, that lets you import straight video capture or an existing video file and then export the clip as a Flash video file.

3. Install a QuickTime-compatible video-editing program on your computer, such as Adobe After Effects (*www.adobe.com*), Apple Final Cut Express (*www.apple.com/finalcutexpress*), Apple Final Cut Pro (*www.apple.com/finalcutstudio/finalcutpro*), or Avid Media Composer (*www.avid.com/products/composer*). Then install QuickTime and a special type of QuickTime plug-in called a Flash Video Exporter. (An exporter comes with Flash 8 Professional, but others are available from third-party companies such as On2, which you can find online at *www.on2.com*.)

With the exporter and QuickTime installed, when you edit video in one of the video editing programs, the program lets you save the video in .flv format.

Importing a Flash video file stored on a Web server (progressive download)

When you import an .flv file stored on a Web server into your Flash animation, you get a bonus: Flash lets you add prebuilt video controls (Play, Stop, Mute, and other control buttons) to let your audience decide when and how to view the video clip. The best part is, you don't have to write any of the interactive ActionScript code yourself. Flash takes care of everything. (Don't worry if you don't have a video file stored on a Web server; there's an example file you can practice with, as you'll see in the following steps.)

1. **Select File → Import → Import Video.**

   The Import Video: Select window you see in Figure 8-12 appears.

Note: Flash gives you another way to import a video file: by selecting File → Import → Import to Stage. Then, from the Import dialog box that appears, select a video file saved in one of the formats listed in Table 8-3.

---

2. **Turn on the radio box next to "Already deployed to a web server, Flash Video Streaming Service, or Flash Communication Server" (Figure 8-12). In the URL box, type** *http://examples.oreilly.com/flash8tmm/building_implode.flv* **and then click Next.**

   The Import Video: Skinning window you see in Figure 8-13 appears.

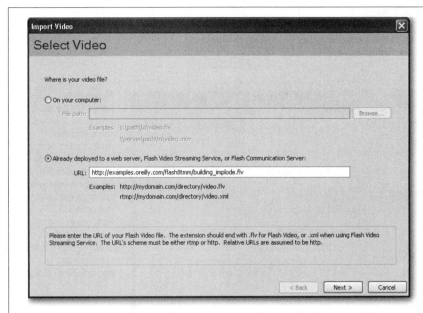

Figure 8-12:
You can import a video file stored on your computer or on a server. In this example, the Flash video file building_implode.flv is stored on a Web server. Because Flash makes assumptions based on the type of file you tell it you want to import and where that file is located (for example, .mov or .flv, your personal computer or a Web server), the Import Video dialog boxes that Flash displays after you click Next vary slightly.

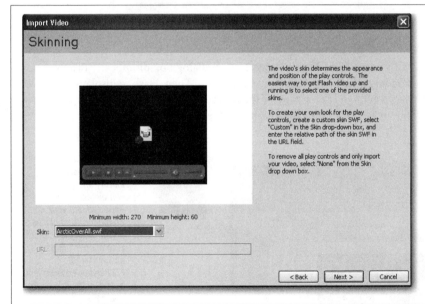

Figure 8-13:
Choosing a skin (like ArcticOverAll.swf) tells Flash which video controls you want to display and how you want those controls to look. You don't have to tell Flash to add any controls (one of the options is None), but most of the time, you should add them so your audience can control video playback. If you want more complicated playback options, you need to write your own custom ActionScript code.

3. **Click the arrow next to Skin and, from the drop-down box that appears, choose ArcticOverAll.swf.**

Flash shows you an example of the ArcticOverAll skin in the preview area.

4. **Click Next.**

Flash displays the Import Video: Finish Video Import dialog box you see in Figure 8-14.

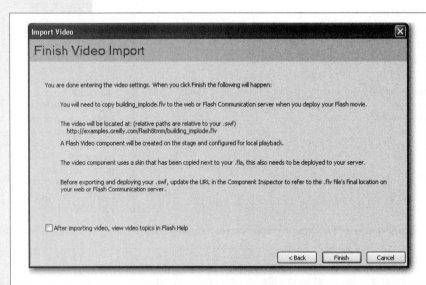

Figure 8-14:
Before Flash imports your video, it shows you a couple of confusing last-minute instructions (and the ability to open the Help panel preloaded with still more confusing instructions). Fortunately, importing video and then deploying the finished video-containing animation isn't difficult.

5. **Click Finish.**

The Import Video: Finish Video Import dialog box disappears. Briefly, you see a Loading FLV Dimensions message box. Then Flash redisplays your workspace, where you see a copy of the imported video (complete with the skin you chose in step 3) in the Library, and on the Stage (Figure 8-15).

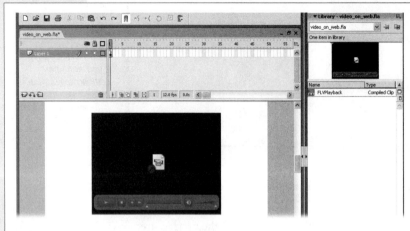

Figure 8-15:
As you can see in the Library, the video-containing skin you imported into your animation (and placed on the Stage) is actually a component. Flash customized the FLVPlayback component based on the information you gave it during the import process, so that when you test your animation, the Play, Stop, and other controls all work automatically.

6. **Choose Control → Test Movie to test your imported video.**

You see the result in Figure 8-16. (To see a finished example, download video_ on_web.fla from *www.missingmanuals.com/cds.*)

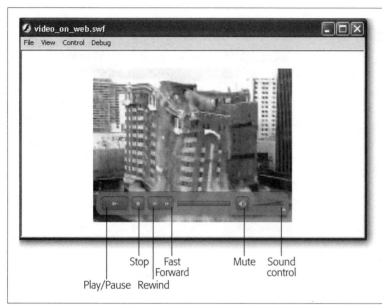

Figure 8-16:
Thanks to the behind-the-scenes ActionScript code Flash creates for you during the import process, the controller buttons let you start, pause, replay, and mute the imported (linked) video right out of the box. You can use Flash's drawing tools to add images or text to the Stage surrounding the video or even apply effects (such as skewing) to the video itself; you can also add additional sound, as described on page 253. But you can't edit or remove the sound attached to the original video: Flash treats the two as a single, uneditable entity.

Stop | Fast Forward | Mute | Sound control
Play/Pause | Rewind

Note: To deploy the video-containing animation on a Web server, all you have to do is upload the finished animation file (video_on_web.swf) and the skin you chose (ArcticOverAll.swf) to the same directory on the same Web server where you stored the Flash video file (building_implode.flv). For more on publishing, check out Chapter 14.

Importing a QuickTime file stored on your computer (embedding)

You don't have to have access to a Web server to import a video file into Flash. In fact, even if you *do* have access to a Web server, you might want to import a video file from your computer instead to save the hassle and time of uploading and downloading while you work out the kinks in your Flash animation.

This example shows you how to embed a QuickTime file directly into your animation's Timeline.

Note: Embedding a video file can make your finished animation's file size balloon to epic proportions—especially if you choose a lengthy clip or tell Flash during the import process to use a high-quality compression algorithm. And large file sizes can cause problems during playback: lengthy load time, dropped frames, audio that doesn't quite sync up, and so on. For tips on optimizing both video and your overall animation file size, check out page 397, Chapter 14.

To import a QuickTime movie stored on your computer:

1. **Select File → Import → Import Video.**

   The Import Video: Select window you see in Figure 8-17 appears.

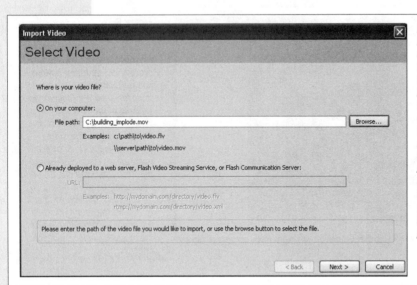

Figure 8-17:
If you know the name and location of the QuickTime file you want to import, you can type it into the "File path" box. Otherwise, click Browse to open the standard Open window, choose a file, and then have Flash type the name for you. Although it's not obvious at first glance, the text at the bottom of this window is a hint meant to help you fill out the "File path" box.

2. **Click Browse.**

   Flash displays a standard Open window similar to the one you use to open a Flash document.

3. **Click to choose the file building_implode.mov on your computer, and then click Open.**

   Flash redisplays the Import Video: Select window, this time showing the "File path" box filled in with the name of the file you chose.

4. **Click Next.**

   The Import Video: Deployment window shown in Figure 8-18 appears.

5. **Click to choose "Embed video in SWF and play in Timeline."**

   To find out more about the other options on this window, flip to page 265. You can also click the option to read the hint Flash displays in the right side of the window.

6. **Click Next.**

   The Import Video: Embedding window you see in Figure 8-19 appears.

   Next, you'll change the settings in this window to import the movie clip and its audio track separately.

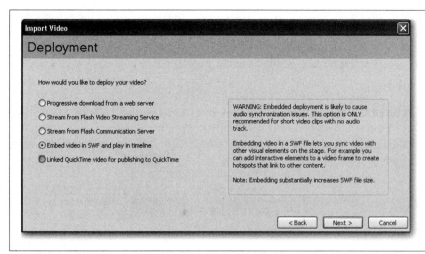

Figure 8-18:
Flash gives you several options for deploying the video-containing animation you're attempting to create. (Deploying is a combination of compiling an animation into an executable file format, and placing that file—and any other necessary files, like your video file—on a Web server where your audience can download them.)

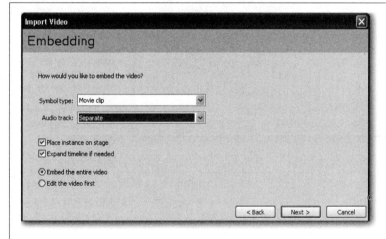

Figure 8-19:
The options in this window let you import a video file as a graphic symbol, an embedded video symbol, or a movie clip symbol. Typically, you'll choose movie clip; they're the easiest to work with in Flash and give you the most flexibility, since they're not tied frame-for-frame to your main animation. You can also keep the video's audio track separate (as shown here) or combine the two. If you're not sure whether or not you'll need to edit the audio in Flash, go ahead and choose Separate anyway— you never know.

7. **Click the arrow next to "Symbol type" and then, from the drop-down list that appears, choose "Movie clip." Then click the arrow next to "Audio track" and then choose Separate.**

The other options you can set in this window include:

Place instance on stage. Tells Flash to import a copy of the video clip to the Stage in addition to the Library.

Expand Timeline if needed. Tells Flash to create enough frames to hold the imported video clip. If you turn this checkbox off and your Timeline doesn't contain as many frames as the video clip you're trying to import, Flash truncates the video.

Embed the entire video/Edit the video first. Choosing "Embed the entire video" imports the video file as is; choosing "Edit the video first" shows you options that let you slice and dice clips of the video and then piece them together on import (see "Editing Embedded Video," page 274).

8. **Click Next.**

The Import Video: Encoding window shown in Figure 8-20 appears. You use this window to tell Flash how faithfully to reproduce the video clip—from high quality, which represents the biggest file size hit, to low quality—and also to shorten the clip.

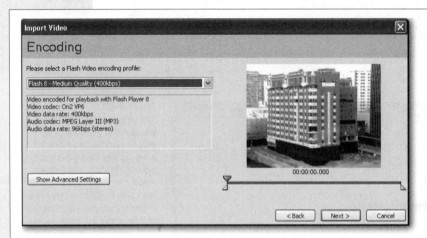

Figure 8-20:
Flash lets you choose the quality of the imported video clip. The higher the quality, the larger the file size. 400 kilobits per second is about midway between the two extremes Flash supports. Drag the triangle on top of the preview bar to view the video clip; drag the "In point" and "Out point" handles on the preview bar to crop the clip.

Note: To see a slew of additional encoding and video editing options, including options for cropping and resizing your imported video and even specifying a different compression algorithm (*codec*) for the video and audio import, click Show Advanced Settings. "Editing Embedded Video," page 274, walks you through the process.

9. **Click Next.**

The Import Video: Finish window you see in Figure 8-21 appears. Now's your chance to review your choices before you go through with the import.

10. **Click Finish.**

A Flash Video Encoding Progress window appears (Figure 8-22, top). The longer the clip you're trying to import, the longer you see this window on your screen. Finally, when Flash finishes importing your video file, the window disappears and Flash redisplays your workspace (Figure 8-22, bottom).

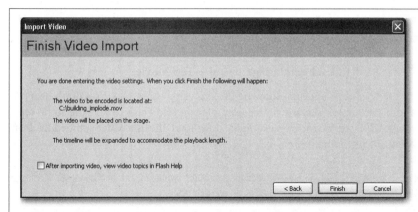

Figure 8-21:
It's a long road—but when you see this window, you're nearly finished importing your QuickTime movie. If you'd like to review or change any of the options you've set up until this point in the import process, click the Back button to step back through the Import Video widows.

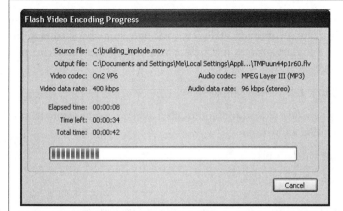

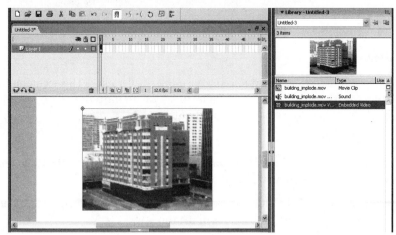

Figure 8-22:
Top: How long Flash grinds away depends on the length of the video clip, the import quality you specified, and a raft of other variables.

Bottom: Here, you see the result of a successful video import: a copy of the video on the Stage, and a copy of the embedded video symbol in the Library. If you told Flash during the import process to save a copy of the video as a movie clip symbol (or to save the soundtrack separately), you see those symbols in the Library, too.

Note: Editing the movie clip symbol (Chapter 7) lets you add effects and change the imported video frame by frame, in the movie clip symbol's Timeline.

11. **Test the animation by choosing Control → Test Movie.**

    The test window appears, showing the imported video clip. You don't hear any audio soundtrack because in this example you told Flash to save the audio separately. (To see a working example, download the file video_embed.fla from *www.missingmanuals.com/cds.*)

Note: To see how to add the building_implode.mov audio symbol to your animation, see "Adding an Imported Sound to a Frame (or Series of Frames)" on page 255.

Editing Embedded Video

If you choose to embed an imported video clip (as opposed to linking your Flash animation to a video clip at runtime), Flash lets you apply some basic edits to the video clip during the import process just before you embed the video clip into your animation. You can:

• Split a video clip into two or more smaller clips.

• Tell Flash how to encode video (and audio) clips when it comes time to save your video-containing animation.

• Crop (resize) your video display.

The following sections show you how.

Note: See how to embed a video file on page 269, "Importing a QuickTime file stored on your computer (Embedding)."

Split a video clip

Flash lets you break a video clip into one or more smaller clips. This technique is also useful for trimming clips: for example, to cut off an intro or the last few seconds of a video clip before you place it on the Stage.

To split a video clip:

1. **In the Import Video: Embedding window (Figure 8-19), turn on the radio box next to "Edit the video first", and then click Next.**

    The Import Video: Split Video window appears. As you see in Figure 8-23, your video clip appears in the preview area of the window.

2. **Click the Create New Clip icon (the + sign).**

    Flash creates a new sub-clip and places it in the list.

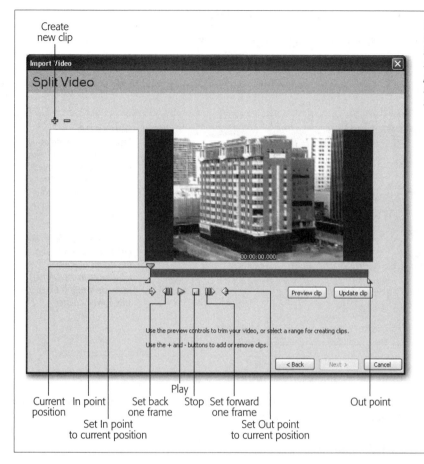

Create
new clip

Import Video

Split Video

00:00:00.000

Preview clip   Update clip

Use the preview controls to trim your video, or select a range for creating clips.

Use the + and - buttons to add or remove clips.

< Back   Next >   Cancel

Play

Current   In point   Set back   Stop   Set forward   Out point
position   one frame   one frame
        Set In point   Set Out point
    to current position   to current position

Figure 8-23:
Click the Create New Clip icon to create a named subclip; then drag in "In point" and "Out point" sliders to define the length of the new subclip.

3. **Rename the subclick by double-clicking the subclip name and typing in a new name.**

   Shoot for a short but descriptive name, such as *first_half*. The name you choose is the name Flash uses when it creates the embedded video symbol (and movie clip symbol) that it puts in the Library after it finishes the import process.

4. **Click Play to preview the video clip.**

   To back up the preview, click "Stop," and then click "Step back one frame." To slow down the preview, click "Stop," and then click "Advance by one frame."

5. **Drag the in and out points (Figure 8-23) to isolate just the part of the clip you want to keep.**

Note: If you prefer, you can drag the "In point" and "Out point" sliders directly without previewing the clip first. Or, if you're previewing the video clip and happen to stop playback at the point where you want to add an in or out point, you can click "Set in point to current position" or "Set out point to current position," respectively.

---

6. **Play the shortened version of the clip by clicking "Preview clip."**

In the preview area, Flash plays the shortened subclip you defined.

7. **Save the sub-clip by clicking "Update clip."**

Flash saves the newly created sub-clip in the list (Figure 8-24, left).

 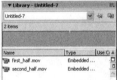

Figure 8-24:
Left: You can create as many subclips as you like. If you change your mind, you can always click to select a subclip and then click the Delete button to delete it.

Right: When you finish the import process, you see the results of your handiwork in the Library: separate symbols for each subclip you created.

8. **Continue importing the video file as usual (page 265).**

When you finish the import process, Flash places separate symbols in the Library for each subclip you defined (Figure 8-24, right).

Customize video and audio encoding

Flash lets you customize the way it encodes your video and audio clips. As Figure 8-25 (top) shows, you can tell Flash which codec (compression format) you want it to use; you can also tweak certain compression settings, such as the frame rate you want your imported video to have.

To see the options shown at left in Figure 8-25, click the Show Advanced button you see in the Import Video: Encoding window (Figure 8-20).

Here's a list of the options you can customize:

- **Encode video.** Turning on this checkbox lets you set the video encoding options listed below.

- **Video codec.** Tells Flash which video compression algorithm to use. Your options are On2 VP2 and Sorenson Spark.

Tip: Note: A *codec* is a software program that translates video into a more compact file format (and then *un*translates it for playback). Folks who frequently deal with compressed video usually have a preference for one or the other of these third-party programs that come with Flash.

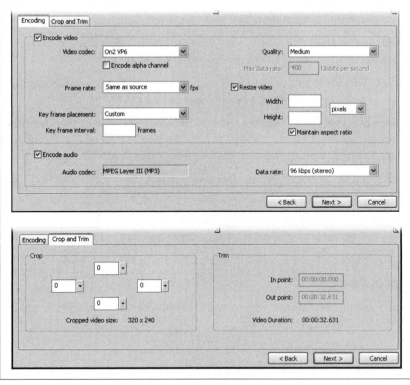

Figure 8-25:
Top: On the Encoding tab, Flash lets you customize how you want it to encode (import and then publish) both the video and the audio portions of your video file.

Bottom: The Crop and Trim tabs have options that let you crop (resize) and trim (shorten) your video clip. All you have to do is drag the crop sliders and the "In point" and "Out point" handles; Flash automatically displays the cropped dimensions and the newly edited video length. For more on editing video in Flash, see page 274.

- **Encode alpha channel.** Tells Flash to encode any transparency settings applied to the video file.

- **Frame rate.** Tells Flash how many frames per second you want your imported video to have. You can keep the frame rate of the original video clip or choose a new frame rate from 10 to 30.

- **Key frame placement.** Choosing Automatic tells Flash to import video key frames as it sees fit; choosing Custom lets you set the "Key frame interval" you want.

- **Key frame interval.** Tells Flash how many video key frames (*not* Flash key-frames) to import. The lower the number, the lower the file size (and imported video quality) you end up with.

- **Quality.** Tells Flash how closely you want it to try to recreate the original video clip in terms of visual quality and frame rate. Your choices are low, medium, high, and custom. (The higher the quality, the larger your animation file.)

- **Max data rate.** Available only if you set Quality to custom (see above), this option tells Flash how many kilobytes per second you want your imported video to run at. (The range you can specify runs from 40 to 700.)

- **Resize video.** Turning on this checkbox enables the Width, Height, and "Maintain aspect ratio" settings described next.

- **Width.** Tells Flash how wide you want to your video display to appear, expressed either as pixels or as a percent of total display size.

- **Height.** Tells Flash how tall you want to your video display to appear, expressed either as pixels or as a percent of total display size.

- **Maintain aspect ratio.** Turning on this checkbox tells Flash to automatically adjust the Width box as you type a number into the Height box (and vice versa), letting you preserve the original shape of the resized video display.

- **Encode audio.** Turning on this checkbox enables the encoding option listed below.

- **Data rate.** Tells Flash how precisely you want it to recreate the video sound track, in terms of kilobytes per second (quality) and number of channels (mono vs. stereo).

Crop video display

You can crop the display area your imported video appears in to make it smaller, either width- or height-wise (or both).

To crop your video display:

1. **Click the Crop and Trim tab you see in the Import Video: Encoding window (Figure 8-25, top).**

   The Crop and Trim options you see in Figure 8-25 (bottom) appear.

2. **In the Crop area, drag the top, bottom, left, and right sliders to tell Flash how you want it to crop the video display.**

   Flash displays the new dimensions beneath the sliders. In the preview area, Flash displays a dashed bounding box showing you the new dimensions.

Part Three:
Adding Interactivity

3

Automating Flash with ActionScript

When you've got your Flash document on your PC, you're in control. You can make it do whatever you want, whenever you want. But eventually, your creation must strike out on its own. You won't be there to tell your animation what to do when someone clicks a button or remind it to turn off the sound after the first three times through. You need to provide instructions to make your animation perform automatically—that is, *automate* it.

To automate your animation or make it interactive, you use ActionScript—Flash's built-in programming language—to act on, or *script*, the different parts of your animation. For example, you can instruct your animation to load a Web page when someone clicks a button you've added, to start playing an audio clip at the beginning of a certain scene, to play your animation in reverse, to loop certain sections of your animation, and so on.

Flash calls the chunks of ActionScript code you attach to your animation *actions*, which is a great reminder that ActionScript exists to help your audience inter*act* with your animation.

Unfortunately, mastering a scripting language like ActionScript is a bit harder than mastering a regular programming language because you have to memorize not only the language itself (including syntax and basic programming concepts such as variables, functions, parameters, and so on) but also the scripting *object model* (the internal, Flash-designated names of all the parts of your animation and all the actions you can apply to them). Fortunately, Flash offers ActionScript wizards called *behaviors* that help you construct simple actions.

This chapter acquaints you with the ActionScript language, as well as the Actions panel you use to build actions and attach them to your animation. You also learn when (and how) to use behaviors to reduce the time and effort you have to spend to create an interactive animation.

Note: You'll find additional examples of scripts in Chapters 10, 11, and 12.

How ActionScript Works

ActionScript is Flash's own scripting language, similar (but not identical) to Java-Script, the scripting language that's supported in Internet Explorer, Netscape Navigator, and most other Web browsers. Where JavaScript lets you script (act on) all the different parts of a Web page, ActionScript lets you script (act on) all the different parts of your Flash animation.

Flash calls individual snippets of ActionScript code *actions*. Here's an example of an action:

```
on (press) {
    startDrag(this);
}
```

As you can see, an action is composed of English words (well, pidgin English, perhaps). Attaching this chunk of code to an object in your animation—a button, say—tells Flash:

> *When someone presses (that is, clicks) this button, let him drag the contents of the frame around in Flash Player.*

You create and edit scripts in the Actions panel. Figure 9-1 shows what the complete script might look like.

Figure 9-1:
Flash attaches a script to an object you select on the Stage just before you display the Actions panel. Here, Flash is attaching this script to a button named rightEyeInstance. Buttons, in fact, are one of the most popular ways to bring interactivity into Flash animations, and you can see how to empower them with actions in Chapter 11.

The above action is simple and straightforward, but you can create custom actions that do pretty much anything you like—within the constraints of the ActionScript language, the Flash scripting and security models, and your own programming expertise, that is. (See the box on page 285.)

Flash gives you the following two ways to create actions:

- **By typing (or pointing and clicking) ActionScript code directly into the Actions panel (Window → Actions).** You can type ActionScript code from scratch right in the Actions panel. Or, if you're familiar with ActionScript but want to avoid typing, you can build your actions by choosing functions, statements, properties, and so on from the Action panel's drop-down menu (Figure 9-2).

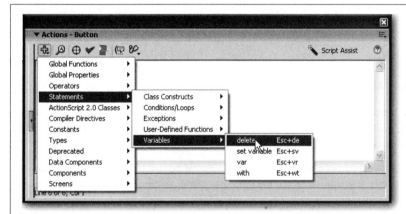

Figure 9-2:
Clicking the Add button (the + sign) lets you choose from a list of functions, statements, operators, events, and more. When you choose an item from the list, Flash types it into the script pane for you. If you know ActionScript, using this list saves you typing time and searching time. But if you don't know ActionScript, this list isn't much help.

- **By using behavior wizards.** The Flash design team came up with a brilliant idea: Build wizards to make it easy for folks to create common actions—for example, ActionScript that makes a movie clip start playing when you click a button. Flash calls these common actions *behaviors*, and you can see them (and access the wizards that help you create them) by displaying the Behaviors panel (Window → Behaviors), as shown in Figure 9-3.

The following sections show you how to create actions using the Actions panel and behaviors, respectively.

Tip: Whenever you're considering adding an action to your animation, always check the Behaviors panel first to see whether there's a behavior that fits your bill. If there is, you've just saved yourself time. If not— no harm done.

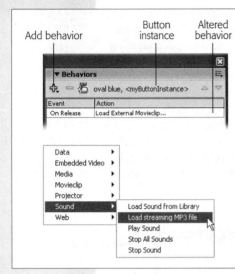

Add behavior   Button   Altered
                      instance   behavior

Figure 9-3:
Top: Flash attaches the behaviors listed in the Behaviors panel to the object shown at the top of the panel. Here, Flash is attaching a single behavior (a scrap of ActionScript code that loads a movie clip symbol when someone presses and then releases a button) to an instance of the oval blue button symbol called myButtonInstance.

Bottom: Clicking the Add Behavior icon displays all the different behaviors you can add. The behaviors you see here depend on which object you selected on the Stage just before you displayed the Behaviors panel.

Adding an Action

For an action to work, you must attach it to something in your animation. You add an action to either an object (like a component or symbol) or a frame, depending on when you want Flash to perform the action.

In this section, you see an example of adding an action to an instance of a button symbol (page 226), but the technique's the same no matter where you're putting the action. Just remember to select the object on the Stage—or a frame in the Timeline—and *then* create the action.

Note: Chapter 10 describes the differences between frame- and object-based actions and when you want to choose one over the other.

To add an action:

1. **Open the document hotspot_drag_begin.fla.**

   You can download this example file from the "Missing CD" page at *www.missingmanuals.com/cds*. It has a drawing all ready for you to practice on. (For a working copy, download hotspot_drag.fla.)

2. **Choose Window → Properties → Properties to display the Property Inspector.**

3. **On the Stage, click Smiley's left eye (see Figure 9-4).**

   Flash highlights the instance of the *leftEye* button symbol and displays instance-related properties in the Properties tab of the Property Inspector.

4. **In the Property Inspector, click the "Instance name" field type in *myLeftEye-Instance* and then hit Return.**

Help for Learning ActionScript

In addition to showing you how to add prebuilt actions called behaviors to your animations, this book gives you working examples of other useful and popular ActionScript actions (including online versions you can download and play with when you get a chance).

So for a lot of the animations you'll want to create, you're covered. But if you want to create other, more advanced actions—such as hooking up a component to a back end data source (Chapter 12) or applying a custom data-scrubbing algorithm to a text field your audience types into your Flash form—you'll need to roll up your sleeves and get jiggy with ActionScript.

Flash itself offers a *little* help in getting you up to speed on ActionScript, but it's not nearly enough. No mere mortal—except those with a very strong background in Java, C++, or JavaScript—can decipher ActionScript from the help Flash provides, which includes:

- **ActionScript documentation.** To see Flash's ActionScript documentation, select Help → Flash Help. Then, in the Help window that appears, click the arrow next to the Book Categories field and, from the drop-down menu that appears, select *ActionScript 2.0*. Two books appear: *Learning ActionScript 2.0 in Flash*, and *ActionScript 2.0 Language Reference* (Figure 10-1).

- **The Actions panel.** Theoretically, the Actions panel lets you put together actions by pointing and clicking. But while it's true that you can click the Add button to choose an ActionScript function, statement, or property to add to your action, this ability isn't much good if you don't know which functions, statements, and properties to choose (or in which order to choose them). Clicking the ScriptAssist icon tells Flash to display additional script-building hints, but these hints are as good as it gets. (Figure 9-6 has an example.)

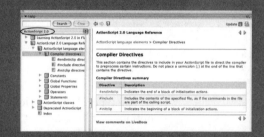

If Flash's ActionScript documentation and the Actions panel don't do it for you—and there's a good chance they won't—check out the resources listed on page 438 of the Appendix. You'll also want to consider a good a book (or three) devoted exclusively to the subject, such as *ActionScript for Flash MX 2004* and *Essential ActionScript 2.0*, both by Colin Moock (O'Reilly), and *ActionScript Cookbook,* by Joey Lott (O'Reilly).

5. **Choose Window → Actions to display the Actions panel.**

   The Actions panel displays both the type of object you selected (Button) and the instance name (myLeftEyeInstance), as shown in Figure 9-5.

6. **In the Actions panel, type the following ActionScript code:**

```
on (release) {
    stopDrag( );
}
on (press) {
    startDrag(this);
}
```

Figure 9-4:
Because many ActionScript statements require you to refer to a symbol instance by name, you want to get in the habit of always typing in a short, meaningful instance name every time you drag an instance to the Stage. You may not need it, but if you do, it's there. And even if you don't end up referencing the instance name in ActionScript, it comes in handy as a reminder of which object you're tying your action to (see Figure 9-5).

As you type, Flash occasionally "guesses" at what you want, popping up a list of options or filling in a bit of punctuation. You can either accept Flash's suggestions or just keep typing. Either way, when you finish, your Actions panel should look something like the one in Figure 9-5.

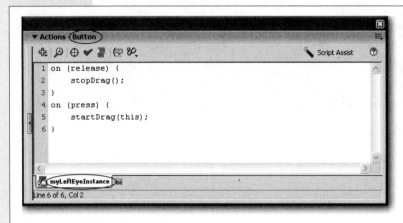

Figure 9-5:
Always double-check the Actions panel to make sure you're adding your action to the correct instance of the correct object. If you goof, your ActionScript code might be letter-perfect—but odds are, it won't work, and Flash won't be able to tell you why. (It's not a mind reader, after all.)

Tip: Clicking the Actions panel's ScriptAssist icon (it looks like a magic wand) redisplays the Actions panel with the script pane at the bottom, and ActionScript hints at the top. Each time you click a line of Action-Script code in the script pane, Flash changes the hints to match. Figure 9-6 shows you an example of the Actions panel in ScriptAssist mode. (Click the ScriptAssist icon again to toggle the Actions panel back to normal mode.)

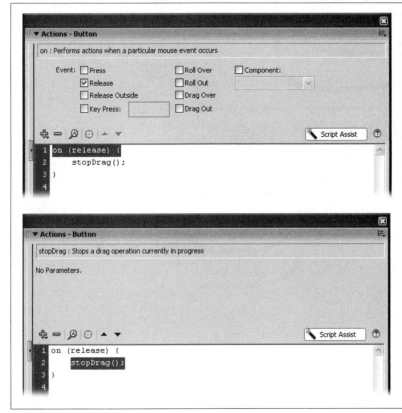

Figure 9-6:
Top: Clicking the ScriptAssist icon tells Flash to redisplay the Actions panel with hints at the top.

Bottom: Some hints are more useful than others. You can stay in ScriptAssist mode if you like and continue to type your ActionScript code in the script pane. To return to normal mode, just click the ScriptAssist icon again.

7. **Test your action by choosing Control → Test Movie.**

   The Flash Player (test window) appears. As Figure 9-7 shows, clicking on Smiley's left eye lets you drag the face around the test window. When you let up on your mouse, Flash drops Smiley right where you repositioned him.

Adding a Prebuilt Behavior

Adding a behavior in Flash is similar to adding an action: In both cases, you add ActionScript code to the Actions panel. But in the case of adding an action, *you* have to type the ActionScript code; when you add a behavior to your animation, *Flash* types the code for you.

Figure 9-7:
*Top: Smiley as he first appears,
before you move your mouse over
his left squinched-up eye.*

*Bottom: Because Smiley's left eye is
a button symbol, mousing over it
tells Flash to turn your arrow cursor
into a pointing finger. Clicking
Smiley's left eye lets you drag
Smiley around the test window. He
stays where you drop him (until
you click his left eye and drag him
again).*

Adding a behavior actually requires a few more steps and clicks than it would take
an experienced scripter to type a quick ActionScript from scratch. But behaviors let
you reap the benefits of ActionScript without learning anything about scripting.

Flash includes only a couple dozen behaviors, one of which does the same thing as
the ActionScript described in the previous section. Here's how to make a button
object draggable using a behavior:

1. **Open the document hotspot_drag_begin.fla.**

   You can download this file from the book's "Missing CD" page. For a working
   copy, download drag_behavior.fla.

2. **On the Stage, click Smiley's left eye.**

   Flash highlights the instance of the *leftEye* button symbol and displays instance-
   related properties in the Properties tab of the Property Inspector.

3. **In the Property Inspector, click the "Instance name" field, type *myLeftEye-
   Instance*, and hit Return.**

4. **Choose Window → Behaviors.**

Flash displays the empty Behaviors panel you see in Figure 9-8.

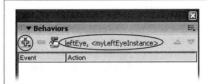

Figure 9-8:
Always select the object you want to add a behavior to before you open the Behaviors panel; not only does Flash decide which behaviors to show you based on the object you selected, but you also need to make sure Flash associates your behavior with the right object.

5. **Click the Add button (the + sign).**

   Flash displays a pop-up menu containing several different categories of behaviors.

6. **Choose Movieclip → Start Dragging Movieclip, as shown on the top of Figure 9-9. (It would be great if behaviors shielded you completely from ActionScript's scripting model, but they don't; you have to know how to drill down to the Start Dragging Movieclip behavior.)**

   The wizard Flash displays depends on the behavior you choose. In this case, Flash displays the Start Dragging Movieclip dialog box (Figure 9-9, bottom).

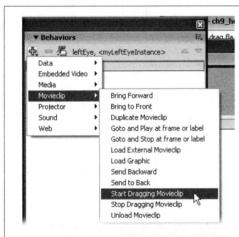

Figure 9-9:
Top: These lists are a lot shorter than the ones you see in the Actions panel—and browsing the options you see here may give you some great ideas for customizing your animation!

Bottom: Flash asks you which movie clip (animation) you want to make draggable when Smiley's left eye is clicked. The example file you work with in this section contains just one animation, so the choice is simple: _root.

7. **Click OK to accept the single option highlighted.**

The Start Dragging Movieclip dialog box disappears. The Behaviors panel shows you the results of your hard work (Figure 9-10, top).

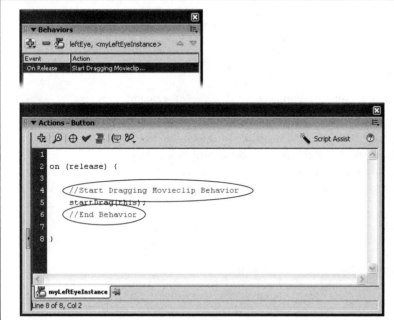

Figure 9-10:
Top: Clicking the Event or Action portion of the completed behavior pops up a list or a dialog box, respectively, that you can use to modify your behavior without typing a lick of ActionScript code.

Bottom: Opening the Actions panel shows you the code Flash generated for you. This is like the code you typed into the Actions panel yourself in the actions example, but Flash reminds you that it (and not you) wrote this code.

8. **Click the Add button again.**

Flash displays the same pop-up list of behaviors shown in Figure 9-9 (top).

9. **This time, choose Movieclip → Stop Dragging Movieclip.**

Flash displays the Stop Dragging Movieclip dialog box shown in Figure 9-11.

Figure 9-11:
Flash doesn't need any extra information from you to generate this behavior, so it displays a simple confirmation dialog box. Clicking OK tells Flash to go ahead and generate the necessary ActionScript code.

10. **Click OK.**

The Stop Dragging Movieclip dialog box disappears. In the Behaviors panel, you see the second behavior (Figure 9-12, top).

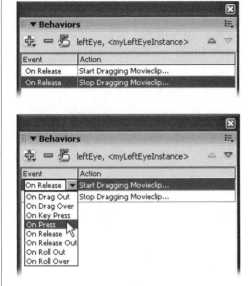

Figure 9-12:

Top: A single event (On Release) triggers both behaviors. For this example, you want On Press to trigger the Start Dragging behavior, and On Release to trigger the Stop Dragging behavior. To make that change…

Bottom: …click the On Release event next to Start Dragging Movieclip, as shown here, and then choose On Press from the drop-down list.

11. Click the On Release event next to Start Dragging Movieclip (see Figure 9-12, bottom) and then, from the drop-down list, choose On Press.

Flash redisplays the event as shown in Figure 9-13 (top).

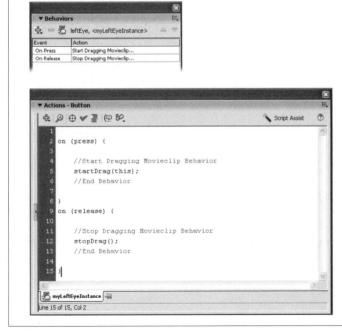

Figure 9-13:

Top: There, that's better: Now pressing Smiley's left eye should let you drag the image, and releasing it should drop the image.

Bottom: It's always a good idea to double-check the code Flash generates by opening the Actions panel. If you spot anything amiss (or just want to add some additional logic), you can tweak the code yourself.

12. **Test your newly added behaviors by selecting Control → Test Movie.**

The Flash Player (test window) appears. As expected, clicking on Smiley's left eye lets you drag the face around the test window. When you release your mouse button, Flash drops Smiley right where you repositioned him.

Controlling Animation

Ordinarily, Flash assumes you want to play your animation in sequential order from the first frame on your Timeline to the last. But sometimes start-at-the-beginning-and-quit-at-the-end isn't exactly what you want. Fortunately, by using a combination of scenes, frame labels, and ActionScript (Chapter 9), you can control your animation virtually any way you like.

For example, say you're putting together an instructional animation. You want to start with an introductory section, move on to the meat of your topic, and then wrap up with a question-and-answer section. If you organize these sections into separately named scenes, then you can play with the order of your animation quickly and easily. If you decide to reposition the question-and-answer scene directly after the introduction as a kind of pretest, for example, you can do that with a simple drag of your mouse. You can even add buttons someone can click to replay the question-and-answer scene over and over, as many times as she likes.

In this chapter, you see how to create both frame- and object-based ActionScript actions to make the most common types of nonsequential playback effects, including *looping* (replaying a section of your animation over and over again) and *reversing* (playing a section of your animation backwards). To make these effects easy to test, you'll also see how to add interactive buttons to your animations. Finally, this chapter describes how to control the overall speed at which Flash plays your animation on your audience's computers.

Slowing Down (or Speeding Up) Animation

As you saw in Chapter 1, animations are nothing more than a series of content-containing frames that Flash plays one after another so quickly that your eyes interpret the overall effect as continuous movement.

You get a pretty good idea of how your animation will appear to your audience when you test your animation on your own computer. But the speed at which Flash actually displays your frames on *someone else's* computer depends on several factors, many of which you can't control:

- **Your audience's computer hardware.** Both processor speed and memory affect animation playback, especially if the animation's very long or includes multimedia such as bitmaps, sound, or video clips (Chapter 9). You have no control over this factor unless you're developing an animation for playback on a specific set of machines: for example, if you're creating a tutorial in Flash that you know will be played only on the computers in your company's training room.

- **Your audience's Internet connection.** If you've added your animation to a Web page, the speed of your audience's Internet connection affects how quickly your animation downloads and plays on their computers. You have little or no control over this factor (beyond *preloading*, which you can learn about in Chapter 14) because even if you're targeting your animation for specific machines with, say, 56 kbps connections, Internet congestion may force download speeds of much less than that.

- **The delivery option you've chosen (if you've added video).** If you've incorporated a video clip into your animation (Chapter 9), you've had to tell Flash whether you want to:

  — **Embed the video into your Flash document.** If you've chosen this option, your animation won't begin to play until the person has downloaded the entire (enormous) Flash document, video clip and all. When the animation *does* begin to play, however, neither his Internet connection speed nor overall Internet traffic affect playback.

  — **Stream the video at runtime.** If you've chosen not to embed the video clip into your Flash document, the person's Flash Player begins playing the animation as soon as a few frames' worth of the animation file has finished downloading to their computers. When the animation *does* begin to play, however, it might run in fits and starts, depending on his computer hardware and Internet connection speed, Internet traffic, and the size of your animation and video files.

- **The size and configuration of your finished animation file.** Large animation files—files containing complex animated effects, lots of gradients and transparent images, video clips, and so on—take longer than small files to download or stream over the Internet. They can also take longer to play because large files tend to suck up all the memory on your a computer. You can control this factor by optimizing your animation to keep the file size as small as possible and by *preloading* sections of your animation. (Chapter 14 shows you how.)

- **The frame rate you've applied to your animation.** On your animation's Timeline, you can tell Flash the maximum frame rate you want it to shoot for, in frames per second (fps).

The easiest factor to control—and the only one covered in this chapter—is the last one: the frame rate. The following section shows you how to set a new frame rate for an animation.

Setting a Frame Rate

When you create a new animation, Flash assumes a maximum frame rate of 12 *fps* (frames per second). In other words, given the constraints listed in the previous section, Flash tries its best to display one frame every 1/12th of a second. Here's another way to look at frame rate: If your animation spans 240 frames, you're looking at roughly 20 seconds of screen time.

In most cases, the standard 12 fps works just fine, especially if you're planning to put your animation up on a Web site. But you can speed up or slow down your animation by setting a per-second frame rate higher (or lower) than 12, respectively.

To change your animation's frame rate:

1. **On the Timeline, double-click the Frame Rate icon (Figure 10-1).**

   The Document Properties window in Figure 10-2 appears.

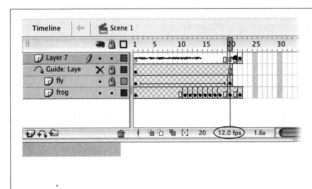

Figure 10-1:
In addition to double-clicking the Frame Rate icon (circled) on the Timeline, Flash gives you two additional ways to set your animation's frame rate. You can select Modify → Document (which pops up the window in Figure 10-2) or click the Stage and then change the frame rate directly in the Frame Properties panel that appears. Flash doesn't prevent you from changing your frame rate in the middle of building an animation, but it's such a basic characteristic that you typically want to set it once up front and only change it later if you absolutely have to.

2. **Click the "Frame rate" box and type a number from 0.01 to 120; then click OK.**

   Flash lets you type in a frame rate of anything between 0.01 and 120. But in most cases, you want to stick with a frame rate of somewhere between 12 (the standard Flash frame rate) and 24 (the standard Hollywood movie frame rate). Every animation's different, of course, and you might actually *want* to create an unusual effect. But a rate much slower than 12 tends to look herky-jerky, while a rate much higher than 24 tends to look blurry.

The Document Properties window disappears. On the Timeline, you see the new frame rate.

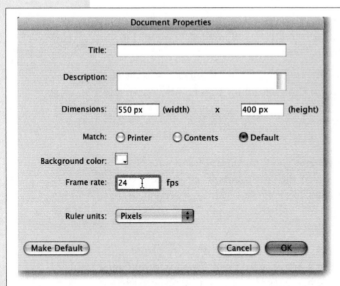

Figure 10-2:
Flash can play your movies at frame rates from 0.01 frames per second (that is, a super-slow 100 seconds per frame) to a blistering 120 frames per second. Going with a super-low or super-high frame rate, though, can cause audio synchronization problems. Keep in mind that setting the frame rate won't ensure that your animation will actually play at that frame rate: It's just a suggested maximum. Several other factors (page 294) affect playback, regardless of the frame rate you set.

3. **Test your new frame rate by choosing Control → Test Movie.**

   In the test window that appears, your animation plays faster (if you typed in a higher frame rate) or slower (if you typed in a lower frame rate).

Note: Frame rate affects the playback speed of the entire animation. If you want to speed up (or slow down) only certain sections of your animation, you change the rates by removing (or adding) frames as described on page 115.

Organizing an Animation

As you see in a lot of the examples earlier in this book, you don't have to do a thing to your standard Timeline, organization-wise. You can let Flash play your animation sequentially, from Frame 1 right through to Frame 500 (or whatever number your last frame is) with no problems.

But you can designate certain sections of your Timeline as named scenes—or even just label certain frames—and speeding up development time, as well as make your animations more flexible and interactive.

- **Organizing your animation as a series of scenes speeds up development time.** If you break an animation into scenes, then you can find what you're looking for quickly; you can also easily rearrange your animation. For example, say you create an animation containing a couple hundred frames (not an uncommon length). You might find yourself getting pretty tired of looking for that single eight-frame span that shows your cartoon character reacting to the marketing copy you're adding in as an audio voice-over. Your marketing team changes its mind on the copy, and suddenly your character has to smile. They change their minds again, and instead of smiling, your character now has to look thoughtful.

If you don't organize your animation into scenes, you have to slog through your animation frame by frame—all 200 of them—to find the specific images you want. But if you *do* organize your animation into scenes, all you have to do is zip to the scene you named ralph_reacts. And if you need to reposition the ralph_reacts scene before the product_description scene, all you have to do is open the Scene panel and drag the scene where you want it—no need to cut and paste.

• **Creating scenes and labeling frames makes your animations more flexible and interactive.** If you break an animation into named chunks with scenes and frame labels, then you give your animations the potential to be flexible and more interactive, because you can write ActionScript actions that *target* (act on) each individual chunk. For example, you can let your audience decide whether to play the ralph_reacts scene first, last, or skip it altogether.

Tip: Both scenes and labeled frames are a natural fit for creating a Web site in Flash because they let you organize your content non-sequentially. Page 305 shows you an example of linking content to navigation buttons.

Flash gives you two options when it comes to organizing your animation into named chunks: scenes and labeled frames. The following sections describe both options.

Working with Scenes

A *scene* in Flash is a series of frames that you assign a name of your choosing. For example, you can assign the first 15 frames of your animation name "intro," the next 30 frames the name "main," and the final 15 frames the name "credits."

Each time you create a new scene, Flash displays a brand new Timeline for you to fill with content. Then, when you play your animation, Flash plays each scene in top-down order, beginning with the first scene listed in the Scene panel (Figure 10-3), and ending with the last.

As the following sections show, after you create scenes, you can rename them and reorganize them with the click of a button.

Creating a scene

Flash automatically starts you out with one scene (cleverly named Scene 1) each time you create a new Flash document.

To create additional scenes:

1. **On the Timeline, create content for the frames you want in your first scene.**

   If you're using the example file scene_begin.fla, you see two layers, buttons and words, each of which extends from Frame 1 through Frame 15. (You can download this example file from the "Missing CD" page at *www.missingmanuals.com/cds.*)

2. **Choose Window → Other Panels → Scene.**

   The Scene panel appears.

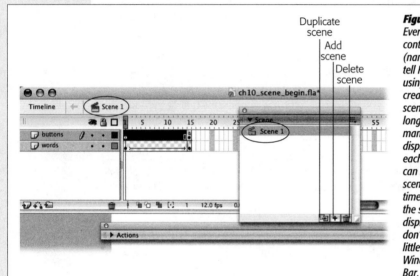

Duplicate scene
Add scene
Delete scene

Figure 10-3:
Every animation you create contains at least one scene (named Scene 1, unless you tell Flash differently). By using the Scene panel to create and name new scenes, you can organize long animations into manageable chunks. Flash displays the Timeline for each scene separately, so it can be easy to forget which scene you're in at any given time. In fact, your only cue is the scene name Flash displays in the Edit bar. If you don't see it (along with the little clapper icon), choose Window → Toolbars → Edit Bar.

3. **Click the "Add scene" icon.**

   In the Scene panel, Flash creates a new scene and then places it directly below Scene 1. Flash also displays a brand new Timeline and a clean, fresh Stage (Figure 10-4).

4. **On the Timeline, create content for the frames you want in your new scene.**

   When you're done, you may want to rename the scene (as discussed in the next section), and then test it by choosing Control → Test Scene. Or, to create additional scenes, simply repeat steps 3 and 4.

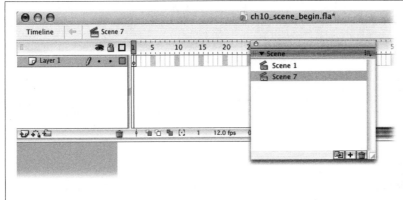

Figure 10-4:
*Each time you create a new
scene, Flash hides the
Timeline for the previous
scene and displays a
brand-new workspace. At
this point, Flash associates
everything you add to the
Stage and the Timeline to
the newly created scene—
here, Scene 7. (Flash
names scenes sequentially;
in this figure, Scenes 2
through 6 were created and
then deleted.)*

Renaming a scene

The names Flash gives each scene you create—Scene 1, Scene 2, Scene 3, and so on,
as you see in Figure 10-4—aren't particularly useful if you're using scenes as a way
to find the frames you need quickly. Fortunately, Flash makes it easy for you to
rename scenes. Here are the steps:

1. **Choose Window → Other Panels → Scene.**

   The Scene panel appears.

2. **In the Scene panel, double-click the name of the scene you want to change.**

   Flash displays the scene name in an editable text box.

3. **Type the new name.**

   You'll need to refer to this name in ActionScript code if you're planning to
   make your animation interactive, so short and meaningful is best. For example,
   you might choose *intro* for an introductory scene, *main* for the meat of your
   animation, and *credits* for the last few wrap-up frames that display your company's name and contact info.

Reorganizing scenes

Flash always plays scenes in order from the scene that appears at the top of the
Scene panel down to the scene that appears in the bottom. To change the order in
which Flash plays your scenes:

Note: Another way to change the order in which Flash plays your scenes and frames is by using Action-
Script (Chapter 9).

---

1. **Choose Window → Other Panels → Scene.**

   The Scene panel appears.

---

2. In the Scene panel, click the name of the scene you want to move, and then drag it above or below the other scenes, as shown in Figure 10-5.

The instant you let up on your mouse, Flash reorders the scenes in the Scene panel. The new order is the order in which Flash plays your animation when you choose Control → Test Movie.

Note: To play just the scene currently on the Stage, select Control → Test Scene (instead of Control → Test Movie).

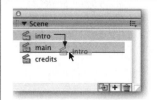

Figure 10-5:
Dragging a scene to a new location in the Scene list automatically reorganizes the sequence in which Flash plays your animation—no ActionScript necessary. The dark black line that appears as you drag a scene lets you know where Flash will put the scene when you let up on your mouse.

Scripting (targeting) a scene

In Flash parlance, *targeting* a scene means writing ActionScript code that performs some action on a scene.

The example in this section shows how to add ActionScript to buttons so that your audience can choose to play different scenes. Figure 10-6 gives you a quick overview of how the finished example looks.

Note: For more information on creating button symbols, see page 228.

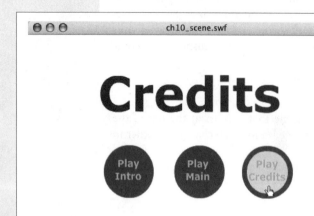

Figure 10-6:
You'll often want to break an animation into scenes so that you can give your audience the ability to play the scenes independently. Here, pressing the Play Credits button plays the credits scene, pressing the Play Main button plays the main scene, and pressing the Play Intro button plays the (you guessed it) intro scene. To put together an interactive animation, you have to first create named scenes and then tie those scenes to buttons using ActionScript code.

Note: You can download the example files for this section from the "Missing CD" page at *www. missingmanuals.com/cds*. The file scene_no_action.fla is the starting point, and scene.fla is the completed animation with ActionScripts.

1. **Open the file scene_no_action.fla.**

   In the Scene panel (Window → Other Panels → Scene), notice that the animation contains three scenes (intro, main, and credits). The Stage has three buttons labeled Play Intro, Play Main, and Play Credits, respectively.

2. **Test the animation by selecting Control → Test movie.**

   In the test window, the word "Intro" recedes; the word "Main" approaches and recedes; and the word "Credits" approaches. Clicking the Play Intro, Play Main, and Play Credits buttons—which only appear while the intro scene's playing—turns the buttons from red to yellow but has no other effect on the animation.

3. **Click the X in the upper-right (Windows) or upper-left (Mac) corner of the test window to close it and return to your workspace.**

   You're going to attach ActionScript actions to each of these buttons, starting with the Play Intro button.

4. **Click the Edit Scene icon (Figure 10-7) and then choose "intro" if it's not already chosen.**

   The Edit bar displays "intro" to let you know you're about to edit the intro scene. On the Stage, you see the three buttons shown in Figure 10-7.

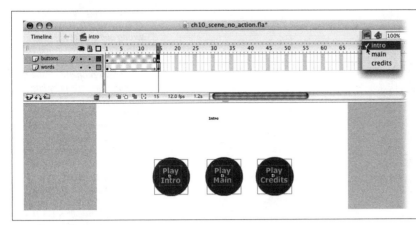

Figure 10-7:
You can switch from scene to scene in your animation using the Scene panel, but you'll probably find clicking the Edit Scene icon much handier, because the Edit Scene icon doesn't disappear while you're working.

5. **On the Stage, click to select the button marked "Play Intro."**

   In the Property Inspector, you see the button icon. If the properties you see in the Property Inspector don't appear to be button-related, make sure you haven't selected the "Play Intro" text overlaying the button by mistake.

6. **Open the Actions panel by selecting Window → Actions.**

The words "Actions—Button" appear at the top of the Actions panel.

7. **Click the Script pane, and then type the following:**

```
on (release) {
    gotoAndPlay("intro",1);
}
```

Note: In this example, you attach an action to a button release event. But Flash lets you attach actions to all kinds of events: pressing down on a button, mousing over an object, dragging or dropping an object, and so on. These actions tell Flash how to handle events, and people in programming circles call them *event handlers.*

When you finish, your Actions panel should look like the one in Figure 10-8. The ActionScript code you just typed in tells Flash to fast-forward to the first frame of the scene named *intro* and begin playing the animation as soon as your audience clicks (and then releases) the Play Intro button.

Next, you're going to add to the Play Main button an action that plays the main scene.

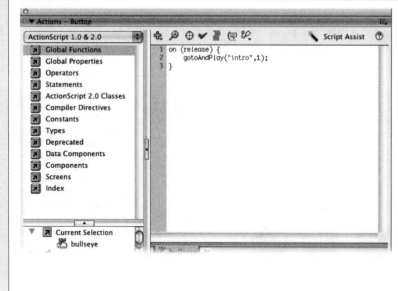

Figure 10-8:
Always double-check the Actions panel's title bar to make sure you're adding your action to the object you think you're adding it to. (If you attach your action to the wrong object—like the text overlaying a button instead of the button itself—your action won't work properly.) Instead of typing this code in by hand, you can construct it by clicking the Actions toolbox. You can double-click Global Functions → Movie Clip Control → On, choose release from the context menu, and then continue clicking and typing to build the complete ActionScript statement. But for a simple two-liner like this one, typing's usually easier.

8. **On the Stage, click to select the button marked "Play Main."**

The words Actions—Button appear at the top of the Actions panel, and the Script pane clears.

9. **Click the Script pane, and then type the following:**

```
on (release) {
    gotoAndPlay("main",1);
}
```

This ActionScript code tells Flash that as soon as your audience clicks and releases the Play Main button, you want Flash to find the first frame of the scene named *main* and begin playing the animation from there. (The only difference between this code and the code you created for the Play Intro button in step 7 is the name of the scene in quotes.)

Finally, you're going to attach to the Play Credits button an action that plays the credits scene. By now, this should feel familiar.

10. **On the Stage, click to select the button marked "Play Credits."**

The words Actions—Button appear at the top of the Actions panel, and once again the Script pane appears empty.

11. **Click the Script pane and type the code that tells Flash to begin playing the first frame of the credits scene as soon as your audience clicks and releases the Play Credits button:**

```
on (release) {
    gotoAndPlay("credits",1);
}
```

Next task: Copy the scripted buttons to the other two scenes (main and credits), so that no matter which scene your audience chooses to play, all three buttons will appear.

12. **Use the Selection tool to draw a rectangle around all three buttons.**

Flash displays selection boxes around each button, as well as each text box overlaying each button.

13. **Select Edit → Copy. Click the Edit Scene icon, and then, from the context menu that appears, select "main."**

Flash takes you to the main scene's Timeline.

14. **Click to select the first keyframe in the buttons layer of the main scene. Then, select Edit → Paste in Place.**

Flash places the scripted buttons on the Stage in the same position they appear on the Stage in the intro scene.

15. **Click the Edit Scene icon and then select "credits."**

Repeat the previous step to paste the buttons into the credits scene.

Although Flash displays the Timeline for each scene separately, as you saw in the box on page 298, in reality all scenes share the same Timeline. So when your audience clicks the Play Intro button, Flash plays the intro scene, and then continues playing the rest of the animation, including the second (main) and third (credits) scenes. Similarly, when your audience clicks the Play Main button, Flash plays the main scene (the second scene), and continues playing the rest of the animation (credits, which is the third scene). But what you *want* is for Flash to play each scene once through, and then stop until your audience clicks another button. To tell Flash to stop playing when it gets to the end of a scene, you need to add another snippet of ActionScript code to each scene, as described next:

1. **Working in the credits scene, click the layer name buttons to select the buttons layer.**

   Flash highlights the name of the layer, as well as all the frames contained in that layer.

2. **Choose Insert → Timeline → Layer.**

   Flash creates a new layer (Layer 3) and then places it above the buttons layer.

3. **Rename the new layer by double-clicking the name Layer 3 and typing in the new name *actions*.**

   When you're finished, press Return.

Tip: Get in the habit of creating a new layer (named actions) just for the actions you add to your animations. In this simple example, creating a new layer isn't a life-or-death matter; but in more complex animations, adding actions to already-filled frames can cause playback problems.

---

4. **Click to select the last frame in the scene (in this case, Frame 15).**

   Flash highlights the selected scene.

5. **Choose Insert → Timeline → Keyframe.**

   Flash places a keyframe symbol (a hollow circle) in Frame 15, as you see in Figure 10-9.

6. **Click the Script pane of the Actions panel and then type the following ActionScript statement:**

   ```
   stop( );
   ```

   This ActionScript statement tells Flash to stop playing the animation when it reaches the last frame of the credits scene.

7. **Using the Edit Scene icon to switch, add the same ActionScript to the main and intro scenes.**

8. **You can test the scripts you've just created by selecting Control → Test Movie.**

This time, clicking the Play Intro button plays the Intro scene; clicking the Play Main button plays the main scene, and clicking the Play Credits scene plays the credits scene.

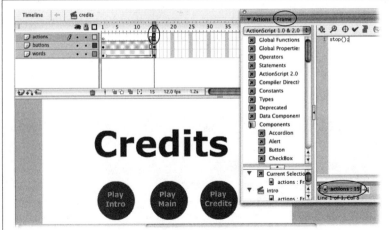

Figure 10-9:
Here's an example of adding an action to a frame. (You know it's a frame you're adding an action to by the title of the Actions panel.) After you add an action to a frame, Flash displays a tiny symbol in that frame just like the one in Frame 15 of the actions layer.

Note: With a long exercise like this, it's super-easy to miss a step. To see a working example, check out the finished file scene.fla.

Working with Labeled Frames

Like scenes, *labeled frames* make it easy for you to target a specific portion of your Timeline with an action so that you can create flexible, interactive animations.

For example, say you're using Flash to build an animated Web site. Every time someone clicks a button on your navigation bar, you want to display a different Web page. If she clicks the Contact Us button, for instance, you want to display a Web page showing your company's contact information.

Technically, you don't have to label your frames in order to accomplish this. You can hook up your button to your Contact page by attaching the *gotoAndPlay( )* function to your button and, inside the parentheses, specifying the frame number (instead of the scene name shown on page 305). The code looks like this:

```
gotoAndPlay(15);
```

The problem with this approach is that going back and adding additional frames to the beginning of your Timeline muffs up your code. If you added 10 frames to the beginning of your animation, for example, the old Frame 15 is now the new frame 25. So to make your button work again, you'd have to change the attach Action-Script code to this:

```
gotoAndPlay(25);
```

A much better approach: give Frame 15 a meaningful label, like *contact*, and write the ActionScript code this way:

```
gotoAndPlay("contact");
```

When you label a frame like this, Flash always associates the frame with the label—no matter what number that frame ends up being. So you can edit your Timeline to your heart's content without ever having to worry that you're breaking your actions.

The following sections show you how to label frames, and how to reference those labels in ActionScript code.

FREQUENTLY ASKED QUESTION

The Difference Between Scenes and Labeled Frames

It sounds like scenes and frame labels do the same thing: Both let me break up my animation into chunks and make the chunks interactive, and both let me target a frame using a name instead of just the frame number. So if they both do the same thing, when do I use one over the other?

Using labeled frames *is* very similar to using scenes. But there are three big differences between the two:

Simply dragging scenes around in the Scene panel rearranges the way Flash plays your animation. You can't drag-and-drop to rearrange labeled frames. (You *can* rearrange the way your animation plays using labeled frames, but you have to write the ActionScript code to do it.)

It's harder to break up scenes than to add labels. When you use scenes, you need to either add new content for each scene as you build your animation, or—if you've already created your animation and want to break it into scenes after the fact—you need to cut and paste frames from the original Scene 1 into your new scenes. Hardly rocket science, but it *is* extra work. Adding or changing frame labels is much quicker.

You work with scenes in separate Timelines; you work with labeled frames in one big Timeline. This difference is usually the showstopper: Some people love working with content in separate Timelines; some people hate it.

Labeling a frame

Labeling a frame is easy. All you have to do is select a frame and then, in the Property Inspector for that frame, type in the label you want.

Note: As with all content (images, sounds, actions, and so on), the label you attach to a keyframe stays in force until the next keyframe.

To label a frame:

1. **On the Timeline, click the frame you want to label to select that frame.**

   Flash highlights the selected frame, and the Property Inspector associated with that Frame appears. (If it doesn't, select Window → Properties.)

2. **In the Property Inspector, click the Frame Label box (Figure 10-10) and then type in a label.**

   On the Timeline, Flash displays a little red flag in the frame you attached the label to, followed by the label itself (Figure 10-10).

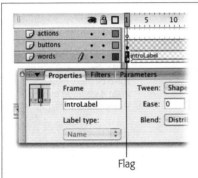

Figure 10-10:
Flash assumes a label type of Name (grayed out here), and that's exactly what you want in most circumstances. (The other label types Flash offers are Comment, which displays your label on the Timeline but doesn't allow you to access it using ActionScript, and Anchor, which lets you designate the frame as a separate HTML anchor page that your audience can "back up" to using their browser's Back button.) Here, you see the entire label name spelled out on the Timeline. But if use a really long label name or assign a label to a frame at the end of your Timeline, Flash doesn't have room to spell the whole thing out. (In that case, the red flag's your only reminder that you've labeled a frame.)

Flag

Targeting a labeled frame

After you've labeled a frame, you can reference that label in an ActionScript action. This section shows you how.

Note: The example in this section is identical to the one on page 300 except for two differences: This example shows ActionScript targeting labeled frames (using a movie clip), while the one on page 300 shows ActionScript targeting scenes (without using a movie clip).

To target a labeled frame:

1. **Open the file labeled_frames_no_action.fla, which you can download as described on page 301.**

    On the Stage, you see an instance of the movie clip symbol myMovie, which contains the word "Intro" along with three buttons labeled Play Intro, Play Main, and Play Credits. (You can also download a working example, labeled_frames.fla.)

2. **Test the animation by selecting Control → Test movie.**

    In the test window, you see the word "Intro" recede; the word "Main" approach and recede; and the word "Credits" approach. Clicking the Play Intro, Play Main, and Play Credits buttons turns the buttons from red to yellow but has no other effect on the animation.

3. **Click the X in the upper-right (Windows) or upper-left (Mac) corner of the test window to close it and return to your workspace.**

    Much as in the previous section, you're going to attach an ActionScript action to each button starting with Play Intro button.

4. **Choose Edit → Edit Symbols to edit the myMovie movie clip.**

5. **The Timeline has three labels: introLabel, mainLabel, and creditsLabel (Figure 10-11). On the Stage, you see the word "Intro" and three buttons.**

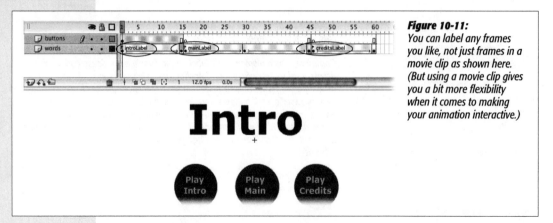

Figure 10-11:
You can label any frames you like, not just frames in a movie clip as shown here. (But using a movie clip gives you a bit more flexibility when it comes to making your animation interactive.)

6. **On the Stage, click to select the button marked "Play Intro."**

   In the Property Inspector, you see the button icon. If the properties in the Property Inspector don't appear to be button-related, make sure you haven't selected the "Play Intro" text overlaying the button by mistake.

7. **Select Window → Actions to open the Actions panel.**

   The words Actions—Button appear at the top of the Actions panel.

8. **Click the Script pane, and then type the following:**

   ```
   on (release) {
       gotoAndPlay("introLabel");
   }
   ```

   When you finish, your Actions panel should look like the one in Figure 10-12. The ActionScript code you just typed in tells Flash to fast-forward to the frame labeled *introLabel* and begin playing the animation as soon as someone clicks and releases the Play Intro button.

9. **Using the same procedure, add the following action to the Play Main button:**

   ```
   on (release) {
       gotoAndPlay("mainLabel");
   }
   ```

   This ActionScript code tells Flash that as soon as your audience clicks and releases the Play Main button, you want Flash to find the frame labeled mainLabel and begin playing the animation from there. (The only difference between this code and the code you created in step 8 is the name of the label in quotes.)

10. **Add the following action to the Play Credits button:**

    ```
    on (release) {
        gotoAndPlay("creditsLabel");
    }
    ```

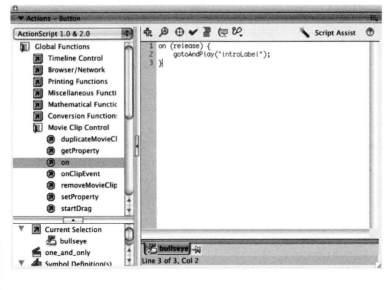

Figure 10-12:
In this example, you'd get the same result typing in gotoAndPlay(1) as you do by typing in gotoAndPlay("introLabel") because both statements tell Flash to begin playing the animation at Frame 1 as soon your audience presses (and then releases) the Play Intro button. But typing gotoAndPlay("introLabel"), as shown here, is easier to remember and get right. It also acts as a kind of insurance; if you go back and add frames to your Timeline, you don't have to worry about your additions breaking this ActionScript code.

The above ActionScript code tells Flash to zip to the frame labeled creditsLabel and then begin playing the animation (*after* someone clicks and releases the Play Credits button).

As things stand right now, Flash plays the entire animation, from the frame label right through to the last frame on the Timeline, each time someone clicks a button. Just as you did when you made buttons play scenes (page 300), you need to tell Flash when to stop. This time, you'll create three simple frame-based scripts to tell Flash where to stop when it starts playing each label—a kind of end-label, if you will:

1. **Click the layer named buttons to select the buttons layer.**

   Flash highlights the name of the layer, as well as all the frames contained in that layer.

2. **Choose Insert → Timeline → Layer.**

   Flash creates a new layer (Layer 3) and places it above the buttons layer.

3. **Rename the new layer by double-clicking the name Layer 3 and typing in the new name *actions*.**

   When you're finished, press Return.

4. **In the actions layer, click Frame 15 to select it. Then choose Insert → Timeline → Keyframe.**

   Flash places a keyframe symbol (a hollow circle) in Frame 15.

5. In the Script pane of the Actions panel, type the following ActionScript statement:

```
stop( );
```

This statement tells Flash to stop playing the animation when it reaches Frame 15.

6. In the same manner, add the *stop( );* action to Frame 45 and Frame 60 (Figure 10-13).

Make sure you're in the actions layer, and use the Timeline to select the correct frame.

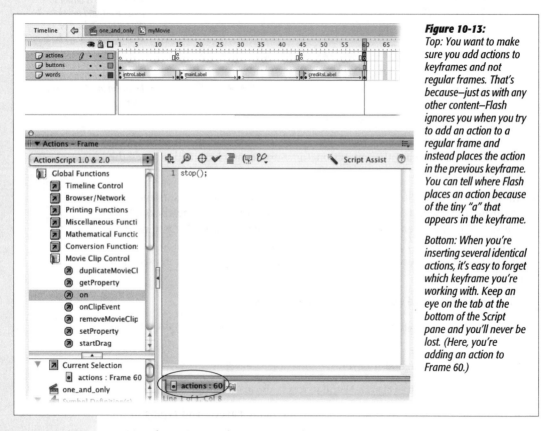

Figure 10-13:
Top: You want to make sure you add actions to keyframes and not regular frames. That's because—just as with any other content—Flash ignores you when you try to add an action to a regular frame and instead places the action in the previous keyframe. You can tell where Flash places an action because of the tiny "a" that appears in the keyframe.

Bottom: When you're inserting several identical actions, it's easy to forget which keyframe you're working with. Keep an eye on the tab at the bottom of the Script pane and you'll never be lost. (Here, you're adding an action to Frame 60.)

7. Test the scripts you've just created by selecting Control → Test Movie.

This time, you see the Intro play through once. Clicking the Play Intro button replays the Intro scene; clicking the Play Main button plays the main scene; and clicking the Play Credits Scene button plays the credits scene.

8. Click the X in the upper-left corner of the test window to close it and return to your workspace.

   Your animation's almost perfect. However, unless you tell it otherwise, Flash always plays an animation once through, from the beginning until the end—or until it reaches a *stop( )* statement—each time the animation runs. In this case, you don't want Flash to do that; you want Flash to display only the buttons and play a scene only *after* someone clicks a button. To stop the Intro from automatically playing once through, attach an action to the first frame of the main Timeline telling Flash to stop playing the movie clip as soon as it loads the movie clip into the frame.

9. Select Edit → Edit Document.

   Flash returns you to the main Timeline, whose single keyframe contains an instance of the myMovie movie clip.

10. On the Stage, click the movie clip instance to select it.

    In the Actions window, click the Script pane and then type in the following ActionScript code:

```
onClipEvent (load) {
    stop( );
}
```

11. Test the script by selecting Control → Test Movie.

    This time, the Intro doesn't play until you click the Play Intro button. (The other buttons work just as you programmed them to.)

Looping a Series of Frames

Looping—replaying a section of your animation over and over again—is an efficient way to create long-playing effects for a modest investment of effort and file size.

Say, for example, you want to create a repetitive background effect such as sunlight glinting off water, palm fronds waving in the breeze, or flickering lights. You can create the frames necessary to show the effect briefly (a couple seconds' worth or so), save the frames as a movie clip, and place an instance of that movie clip in one of the layers of your animation so that the effect spans your entire animation. Flash automatically replays the movie clip until you tell it otherwise, so you get an extended effect for a just a few frames' worth of work—and just a few frames' worth of file size, too. Such a deal. (For a more in-depth look at movie clip symbols, check out Chapter 7.)

Note: You've seen this kind of looping background effect in action if you've ever watched *The Flintstones*—or just about any other production cartoon, for that matter. Remember seeing the same two caves shoot past in the background over and over again as Fred chased Barney around Bedrock?

To loop a series of frames using a movie clip symbol:

1. **Open the file loop_no_mc.fla, which you can download from the "Missing CD" page.**

   On the Stage, you see a sprinkling of white stars on a blue background. In the Library, you see four symbols, including the *blink_lights* movie clip symbol (Figure 10-14).

   Since you've never seen this movie clip before, take a look at the preview.

Note: To loop a section of your *main* Timeline, all you have to do is attach the following action to the last frame of the section you want to loop: *gotoAndPlay(1);*. (If you want your loop to begin at a frame other than Frame 1, replace the 1 in the preceding ActionScript code with the number of the frame at which you want Flash to begin looping.)

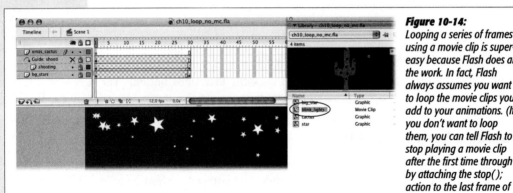

Figure 10-14:
Looping a series of frames using a movie clip is super-easy because Flash does all the work. In fact, Flash always assumes you want to loop the movie clips you add to your animations. (If you don't want to loop them, you can tell Flash to stop playing a movie clip after the first time through by attaching the stop( ); action to the last frame of your movie clip symbol.)

2. **In the Library, select the blink_lights movie clip. Then, in the Library's preview window, click the Play icon.**

   You see the lights on the cactus change from red to yellow, pink, and blue in rapid succession.

3. **Preview the main animation by selecting Control → Test Movie.**

   In the test window, you see a lone shooting star streak across the background.

4. **Click the X in the upper-left corner of the test window to return to the workspace.**

   First stop: Add an instance of the xmas_cactus movie clip to the animation.

5. **In the xmas_cactus layer, click the first keyframe (Frame 1) to select it. Then, drag the blink_lights movie clip from the Library to the Stage.**

   Choose Control → Test Movie again to see the results. In the test window that appears, you see the lights on the cactus blink repeatedly as the shooting star moves across the screen.

Note: If you *don't* want your movie clip to loop, you need to tell Flash to stop playing the movie clip after the first time through. To so instruct it, attach the *stop( );* action to the last frame of your movie clip symbol (*not* the movie clip instance).

DESIGN TIME

Power to the People

One of the beefs some people have with Flash is that the Flash Player embedded in Internet Explorer (and other Web browsers) doesn't automatically show Play, Stop, Rewind, and Pause buttons. So unlike watching an animation play in, say, Windows Media Player, your audience has no control over Flash animation playback—unless you give it to them by creating interactive (object-based) scripts, which you should get into the habit of doing.

(Theoretically, your audience can view a context menu that lets them interact with your animation by right-clicking your animation if they're running Windows, and Control-clicking your animation if they're running Mac. But because few audience members know this—and because Flash gurus who also happen to be expert ActionScript coders can modify, rearrange, add to, and delete menu options—context menus aren't particularly useful when it comes to providing consistent playback control.)

Giving your audience as much control as possible is always a good idea, but it's crucial if you're planning to put your Flash animation on the Web. You can't possibly know your Web audience's hardware configuration.

Say, for example, you create a splash page animation with a Stage size of 550 × 400 pixels, and a file size of 10 megabytes. Someone accessing your animation on a handheld, over a slow connection, or on a machine that's already maxed out running 10 other resource-hogging applications won't be able to see the animation you see on *your* machine.

But even if everyone on the planet had a high-speed connection and the latest computer hardware, giving your audience control would still be important. Why? Because no matter how kick-butt your animation is, by the 23rd time through, it's going to wear a little thin. If you don't offer at least one of the options listed below, you risk turning away repeat visitors:

- The ability to bypass your animation entirely and go straight to the site's home page

- The ability to stop and restart the animation

- The ability to choose which sections of your animation to play

- The ability to choose a low-bandwidth, reduced-length, or small-screen version of your animation

To add buttons, hotspots, text fields, and other controls that let your audience control the way they interact with your animation, you use *object-based scripts*. (Object-based scripts are so called because you attach the scripts directly to the objects, such as buttons, with which you want your audience to interact.)

To create automatic effects, such as reversing a movie clip or loading a Web page when your animation reaches Frame 12, you attach a script to a frame to create a frame-based script. Page 309 has an example of a frame-based script.

Reversing a Series of Frames

Reversing a series of frames is a useful effect. A basketball bouncing up and down, a flag waving side to side, or a boomerang advancing and receding: These things are all examples of reversing a single series of frames.

Instead of creating the two complete series of frames by hand—one showing a ball falling, for example, and another showing the same ball bouncing back up—Flash gives you two ways to generate the reverse effect using just one series of frames:

- You can copy the frame series, paste it, and use Modify → Timeline → Reverse Frames to reverse the pasted frames. This option is quick and easy, but it doubles your Timeline (and your file size, unless your pasted frames contain nothing but symbols).

- You can use ActionScript to play a series of frames in reverse. This option's a bit more difficult to create, especially if you're not familiar with programming in ActionScript. But if file size is an issue, it's the way to go, because you have to save only one series of frames in the file.

The following sections demonstrate both of these approaches.

Using Modify → Timeline → Reverse Frames

When you use Modify → Timeline → Reverse Frames in conjunction with Flash's copy-and-paste function, you can create the reverse of a series of frames quickly, right on the Timeline.

To create a reversed series of frames using Modify → Timeline → Reverse Frames:

1. **Click the first frame in the series you want to reverse. Then Shift-click the last frame in the series you want to reverse.**

   Flash highlights every frame in the series, from first to last.

2. **Select Edit → Timeline → Copy Frames. On the Timeline, click the first frame where you want to insert the reversed series of frames.**

   Flash highlights the selected frame.

3. **Select Edit → Timeline → Paste Frames.**

   Flash pastes the copied frames onto the Timeline, beginning at the selected frame.

4. **If the pasted frame series isn't highlighted, select it (Figure 10-15, top).**

5. **Choose Modify → Timeline → Reverse Frames (Figure 10-15, bottom).**

   Flash reverses the frames on the Timeline.

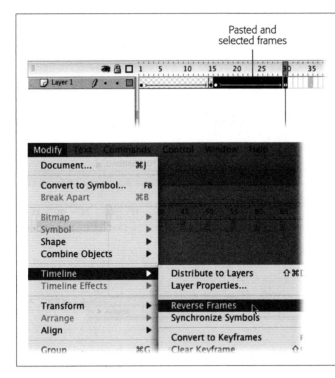

Pasted and
selected frames

Using ActionScript

Since there's no function called *playBackwards( )*, the most efficient way to reverse
a series of frames is to use ActionScript to tell Flash to step backwards through the
series one frame at a time. Using this approach, you have only to create (and save
to disk) one series of frames, which helps keep the size of your finished animation
file as small as possible.

Note: Actions that play animations backward are like potato salad recipes: Everyone seems to have one,
and everyone seems to think hers is the only good one. The example in this section represents *one* way to
play a series of frames backwards—not *the* way. (The Appendix lists sites that offer additional approaches.)

To reverse a series of frames using ActionScript:

1. **Open the file reverse_no_action.fla, which you can download from the "Missing CD" page.**

   (If you like, you can check your work against the already-finished, ActionScript-containing example file, reverse.fla, which you can download from the same place.)

   On the Stage, you see an instance of the movie clip symbol *rollerball*, which
   contains the word "Flash!" along with a blue-gray ball.

2. **Test the animation by selecting Control → Test movie.**

   In the test window, the word "Flash!" approaches. At the same time, the ball rolls from left to right.

3. **Click the X in the upper-left corner of the test window to close it and return to your workspace.**

   In the next few steps, you'll attach some ActionScript designed to reverse playback of the movie clip.

4. **On the Stage, click the movie clip instance to select it. Then choose Window → Actions.**

   The Actions panel appears. In the title bar, you see Actions—Movie Clip.

5. **In the Actions panel, click the Script pane and then type the following Action-Script code:**

   ```
   onClipEvent (load) {
       gotoAndStop(20);
   }


   onClipEvent(enterFrame) {
       if (_currentframe > 1) {
           prevFrame( );
       }
   }
   ```

   The above ActionScript code gives Flash two separate instructions:

   As soon as you (meaning Flash) load the movie clip into the frame, go to the last frame in the movie clip (Frame 20) and stop.
   As soon as you (Flash) start to play a frame, play the previous frame. Repeat until you run out of frames (in other words, until all frames have been played, from 20 backwards through to 1).

6. **Test the action by choosing Control → Test movie.**

   In the test window, you see the animation run backwards: The word "Flash!" recedes as the ball rolls from right to left.

Tip: In the ActionScript code above, you can replace *20* with *_totalframes* and let Flash figure out the last frame of the movie clip. To see the other movie clip properties you can access (besides _currentframe and _totalframes): In the Actions panel, click "Add a new item to the script" and then click ActionScript 2.0 Classes → Movie → Movie Clip → Properties.

Interacting with Your Audience

Chapter 9 introduced you to actions and behaviors, both of which let your audience interact with your animation by pushing buttons, dragging images, typing in text, and so on. In this chapter, you see examples of common actions and behaviors that you can adapt to fit your own project. Think of them as recipes. You'll find out how to insert dynamic text into an animation at runtime, how to capture the information your audience types into a text field, how to create rollovers, how to add actions to buttons and Flash components, and more.

Note: For more examples of actions, check out Chapter 10.

Dynamic Text

Dynamic text is text that you insert into your animation at *runtime*, when the animation plays on your audience's computer (as opposed to when you create the animation).

Dynamic text's great for adding late-breaking updates to your animation: Think sports scores, weather reports, and news headlines. Dynamic text is also a good way to incorporate customized text into your animation without having to go to all the trouble of reworking the animation itself. For example, using dynamic text, you can create a single, basic animation and switch out the header text at runtime so that three different clients can play the same animation and see three different messages (Figure 11-1).

Loading dynamic text into your animation requires a dynamic text box (you can think of it as a placeholder), some data (in this case, it's a text file, but you could

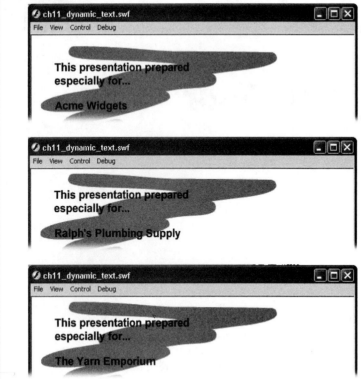

Figure 11-1:
One animation with three different messages, all thanks to one dynamic text element and three separate .txt files. In addition to text, you can also load images and even whole animations at runtime (see pages 327 and 333, respectively, for details).

also use data you've calculated using ActionScript), and a simple action that ties the two together. The following example walks you through the process.

To create dynamic text:

1. **Open the Flash file dynamic_text_example.fla.**

   You can download this example file from the "Missing CD" page at *www. missingmanuals.com/cds*.

   If you don't see the Property Inspector, choose Window → Properties → Properties to display it.

2. **Using the Text tool, add a text element to the Stage as shown in Figure 11-2. Then, with the text element still selected, choose "Dynamic Text" from the Text type drop-down box in the Property Inspector.**

   Flash redisplays the Property Inspector to include dynamic text–related properties.

3. **Click the "Instance name" field and type a short, unique name (such as *myDynamicTextInstance*) for this instance of dynamic text (Figure 11-3).**

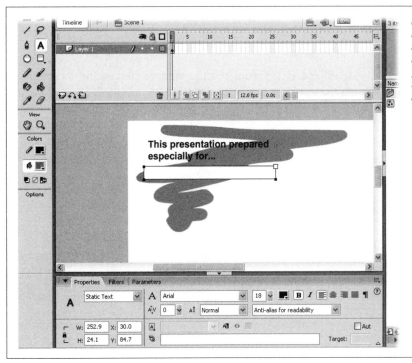

Then, in the Variable field, type *theActualText*, which is the name for the text you're going to associate with this dynamic element.

The variable name refers to just the dynamic text you'll be creating (as opposed to the whole text element complete with its associated font, color, and other characteristics, which is what the instance name refers to).

In the next few steps, you'll create the text file you want Flash to pull in at runtime.

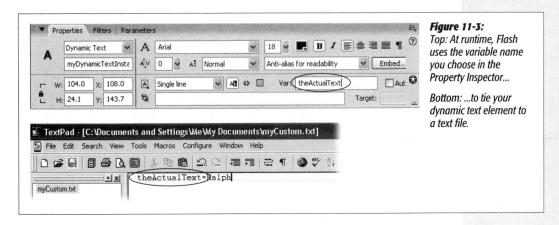

Figure 11-3:
Top: At runtime, Flash uses the variable name you choose in the Property Inspector...

Bottom: ...to tie your dynamic text element to a text file.

4. **Using a text editor program, create a text file named myCustom.txt containing the following single line of text:**

```
theActualText=Ralph
```

As you can see in Figure 11-3, your text file needs to contain the variable name you typed into the Property Inspector, followed by the equal sign, followed by the text you want Flash to load into your animation at runtime. (In computer-ese, the term for this standard *something=something* format is *name-value pair*.) Your text can include spaces and punctuation.

Tip: If you like, you can include HTML tags in your text file. (For example, you can surround a bit of text with the HTML tags *<FONT COLOR="red">your text here</FONT>* to pull in red text at runtime.) If you do include HTML tags in your text file, though, make sure you click the "Render text as HTML file" icon in the Property Inspector. If you don't, Flash displays your HTML tags instead of interpreting them.

---

5. **Save your myCustom.txt file in the same folder that you save your Flash file for this example.**

Next, you'll create an action that ties the contents of your dynamic text element to this .txt file.

Note: Flash lets you name your text file anything you like. But for the purposes of this example, stick to myCustom.txt.

---

6. **Click Frame 1 to select it.**

You're creating a frame-based action (as opposed to a text element–based action) because you want Flash to load your dynamic text as soon as it loads your frame.

7. **Choose Window → Actions *or*, if the collapsed Actions panel is visible, click Actions.**

Flash displays (or expands) the Actions panel. Make sure the title of the panel reads "Actions—Frame;" if it doesn't, repeat the previous step.

8. **In the Actions panel, type the following ActionScript code:**

```
loadVariables("myCustom.txt", this);
```

The above line of ActionScript code tells Flash to load the contents of the myCustom.txt file into this animation. When Flash loads the text file, the contents of the file tell Flash what variable you want to plug text into (the variable *theActualText*), and what the text is (*Ralph*).

9. **Test your dynamic text element by choosing Control → Test Movie.**

The Flash Player you see in Figure 11-4 appears.

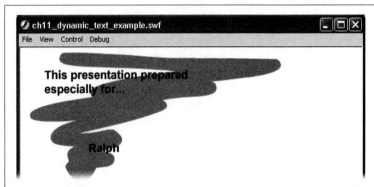

Figure 11-4:
If you can't get your dynamic text to work (or just want to save yourself a bit of typing), no sweat; you can find working files for this dynamic text example (dynamic_text_working.fla and myCustom.txt) online at www.missingmanuals.com/cds.

Note: Flash doesn't require you to create the text file yourself. If you're a programmer type, you can generate it at runtime using a server-side program, or even have someone else create it using a text editor. You can also change where Flash expects to find the text file. (Out of the box, Flash expects to find the text file in the same directory as the .fla file that references it.) For details, search Flash Help for "loadVariables."

Input Text

You're familiar with *input text* if you've ever bought anything online: Chances are you had to type your name, address, and credit card information into input text fields created in either HTML or Flash. The input text fields you create in Flash let you gather information from your audience and then process it, either inside Flash (using ActionScript) or by sending it to a server-side program for processing.

Note: The steps you need to take to exchange, or *integrate*, data with other programs is so program- and computer-dependent that they can't be covered here. Instead, this section shows you how to create input text elements and access the data your audience types in. For more on how to get that data to your server, check out Flash Help and the other resources discussed in the Appendix.

You create an input text field in Flash using the Text tool, similar to the way you create static and dynamic text. Then, by setting a few options in the Property Inspector, you can let your audience type their own text. You access that text using ActionScript. The following steps show how.

Note: The InputText and InputTextArea components that Flash offers are similar in some ways to the input text element, or field, you create using the Text tool, but the components are a bit more powerful and a bit more difficult to use. Check out Chapter 12 for details on these (and other) components.

1. **Open the file input_text.fla.**

   You can find all the files you need for this example—unfinished (input_text.fla) and finished (input_text_working.fla)—on the "Missing CD" page.

Controlling Dynamic and Input Text Appearance

Normally, when you add static text to your animation, the text looks to your audience the same way it looks to you, no matter what Flash Player or operating system they're running. (That's because Flash automatically embeds all the font information it needs for static text right in the .fla file.)

But there are two exceptions to this rule:

- **Static text with a device font.** If you choose a *device font* such as _sans, _serif, or _typewriter in the Property Inspector (scroll all the way up to the top of the list to see them), Flash doesn't embed font information. Instead, it picks the closest font it can on the person's computer and uses that font to display the static text. You can find out more about static text on page 163.

- **Dynamic and input text elements.** When you load text from an external file or let your audience type text, Flash can only guess at how you want that dynamic (or input) text to appear, *even if you specified in the Property Inspector how you want it to look*. In other words, if your audience happens to have the font you selected in the Property Inspector installed on their computer, that's the font Flash uses to display your dynamic or input text. If your audience *doesn't* happen to have that font installed, however, Flash uses the closest device font it can find installed on that computer (which may or may not be close to what you intended).

This lack of display control may be fine with you. (Every Flash form doesn't have to be a masterpiece of detail, after all.) But if it's *not* OK with you, you can take a couple of extra steps to make sure Flash shows your audience dynamic and input text exactly the way you want it to.

To control the appearance of dynamic and input text, you need to add *font outlines* to your animation. Here's how:

1. On the Stage, select the dynamic or input text element whose display you want to control.

2. In the Property Inspector, click the Font rendering method and choose either the Bitmap (as-is) option or one of the Anti-Alias (smoothing) options.

3. Click the Embed button.

4. In the Character Embedding dialog box that appears, select the character sets you expect your audience to type (or that you expect Flash to pull in). If you're creating a numeric input field, for example, select Numerals. If you're creating an input field you know you'll be constraining to the letters S, M, L, and XL, click in the "Include these characters field", and then type *SMLX* to tell Flash to display only the uppercase letters S, M, L, and X.

5. When you finish, click OK.

Adding font outlines kicks up your animation file size, so if you don't much care how Flash displays input and dynamic text, you may want to skip this process. (You'll find more on the topic of optimization in Chapter 14.)

If you don't see the Property Inspector, choose Window → Properties → Properties to display it.

2. Using the Text tool, add a text element to the Stage as shown in Figure 11-5. Then, with the text element still selected, choose Input Text from the Text type drop-down box in the Property Inspector.

Flash redisplays the Property Inspector to include input text–related properties (Figure 11-5).

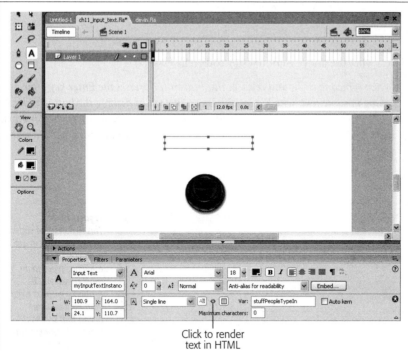

Figure 11-5:
These input text–related properties let you tell Flash how you want to accept and deal with the text your audience types in. (If you like the button in this example, you'll want to check out Window → Common Libraries → Buttons. There you'll find this and more realistic-looking button symbols, all courtesy of Flash.)

Click to render
text in HTML

3. Click in the "Instance name" field and then type *myInputTextInstance*. In the Variable field, type *stuffPeopleTypeIn*.

You'll be referencing this variable name in the action you create next.

Note: As you're clicking around the Property Inspector, make sure you don't accidentally click the "Render as HTML" button (Figure 11-5). This button must be turned off for the input text element to work properly. If you turn it on, your audience won't be able to click in the text box—much less type anything.

---

4. Click the Selection tool and then, on the Stage, click the button (that big one in the middle) to select it. Then choose Window → Actions.

In the Actions panel that appears, you see the title Actions—Button.

5. Click the Actions panel and type the following ActionScript code as shown in Figure 11-6:

```
on (release, keyPress "<Enter>" ) {
    if (stuffPeopleTypeIn != undefined && stuffPeopleTypeIn != "") {
        trace("You typed :" + stuffPeopleTypeIn + ":");
    }
    else {
```

```
        trace("No text was typed in.");
    }
}
```

Here's what the above ActionScript code tells Flash:

When someone clicks and releases this button (or presses the Enter key after typing in some text, which a lot of folks do instead of clicking the button), check to see what— if anything—he typed into the input text element. If you find text, log it in the Output panel. If you don't find any text, log the message "No text was typed in" instead.

Next, you'll test your input text field.

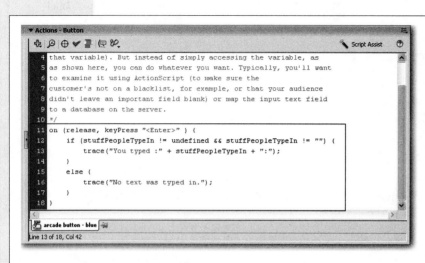

Figure 11-6:
This ActionScript code shows you how to get to the text your audience types in. In most cases, you'll probably want to write your own custom action that scrubs the input data (makes sure someone didn't type numbers instead of a last name, for example) or an action that transfers the data to a server-side database or program for scrubbing and storage.

6. **Select Control → Test Movie.**

   In the Flash Player that appears, you see your button and input text field.

7. **Click the button.**

   Flash displays the Output panel and logs the "No text was typed in" message, as shown in Figure 11-7 (top).

8. **Type text into the input text field and either click the button again or press Enter.**

   This time, Flash logs your typed-in text in the Output panel (see Figure 11-7, bottom).

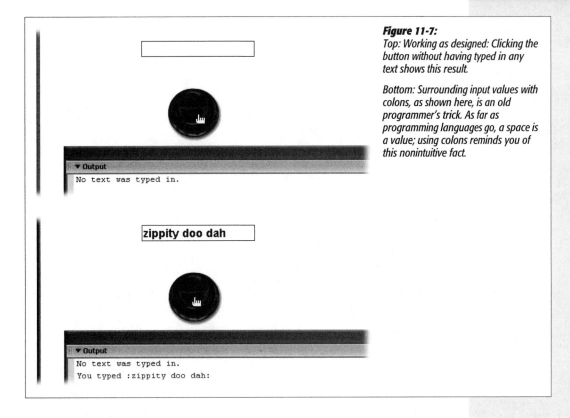

Figure 11-7:
Top: Working as designed: Clicking the button without having typed in any text shows this result.

Bottom: Surrounding input values with colons, as shown here, is an old programmer's trick. As far as programming languages go, a space is a value; using colons reminds you of this nonintuitive fact.

Tying Actions to Events

Flash keeps track of every event that occurs while your animation plays, beginning with the instant Flash Player loads your animation and continuing through every frame Flash plays, every button your audience clicks, every key they press—basically, just about everything that happens in (or to) your animation.

You can tie an action to any event. The following sections show you how to tie actions to the most common events: when your animation loads, and when your audience clicks a button, mouses over a hotspot, or chooses an option from a list.

Triggering an Event When Your Audience Clicks a Button

In Chapter 7, you saw how to create groovy-looking button symbols (and where to find the button symbols that come with Flash), as well as how to change the appearance of a button when someone mouses over it.

This section shows you how to tie a button to an action so that when your audience clicks the button, Flash does something.

The example below uses a quick and easy behavior to tell Flash to load an additional animation when your audience clicks a button. But you can substitute a different behavior (or your own custom ActionScript code) to tell Flash to go to a

Handling Events

An *event* in Flash is something that happens. Flash recognizes two different types of events: *user events* (things your audience does to your animation, such as clicking a button, dragging a mouse, or typing in some text) and *system events* (things Flash does automatically, like loading an animation and moving from frame to frame).

If you want to tie an action to an event—in other words, tell Flash to do something when a particular event, such as a button click, occurs—you need to use an *event handler*. An event handler is simply an ActionScript function (OK, technically, a special kind of function called a *method*) that recognizes all the events that can affect a certain type of object.

For example, the built-in event handler shown in this chapter is the mighty *on( )* event handler, which lets you handle all the events that can happen to a button: *press, release, releaseOutside, rollOver, rollOut, dragOver, keyPress ("<Enter>"), keyPress("<Space>"), keyPress("<Up>"), keyPress("<Down>")*, and so on. (Flash made the button's *on( )* event handler handle *keyPress* events because a lot of folks use the keypad to click an active button or to move from button to button.)

After you select an event handler, you have to add in your own custom ActionScript code to tell Flash how, specifically, you want it to handle the event. This chapter gives several examples.

Flash also supports something called a *listener event model*, which is a set of ActionScript classes that let you tell any object in your animation to "listen" for an event that happens to any other object. For example, you can tell a button to "listen" to an input text field and become active when the text in the field changes. Page 337 has an example of the listener event model.

Handling events is a huge, relatively complex topic—not just in Flash, but in every programming language. To find out more, search for *Handling Events* in Flash Help (see the Appendix for tips on using Flash Help).

The two separate
events you want
to handle

Flash's built-in
event handler

The ActionScript
code you write to
handle the events
(this code tells
Flash what to do
when the events
occur)

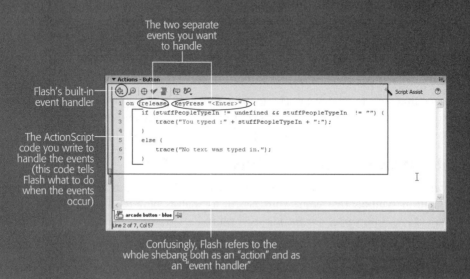

Confusingly, Flash refers to the
whole shebang both as an "action" and as
an "event handler"

different frame in the current animation, load a Web page, play a sound—just about anything you like.

To tie an action to a button:

1. **Open the file button_event.fla.**

   You can download this file from the "Missing CD" page. Make sure the Property Inspector is visible (select Window → Properties → Properties).

2. **On the Stage, click the button to select it.**

   Button-related properties appear in the Property Inspector.

3. **Click the "Instance name" field (see Figure 11-8), and then type *myButton-Instance*.**

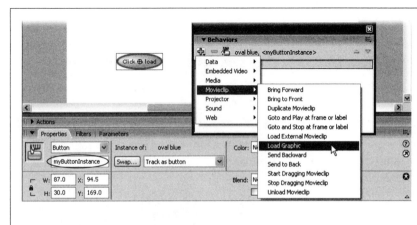

Figure 11-8:
The quickest and easiest way to make your button do something when someone clicks it is to add a behavior to your button. If Flash doesn't offer a behavior that does what you want, you can always roll up your sleeves, write some ActionScript code, and add the code to your button the old-fashioned way using the Actions panel (see page 283).

4. **Select Window → Behaviors.**

   The Behaviors panel in Figure 11-8 appears.

5. **Click on Add Behavior (the plus sign) and, from the pop-up menu, choose Movieclip → Load Graphic.**

   Flash displays the Load Graphic dialog box you see in Figure 11-9.

6. **Click the URL field and then type *http://examples.oreilly.com/flash8tmm/ elevator.jpg***

   This action tells Flash to load the image file named elevator.jpg.

7. **Choose Control → Test Movie to test your button.**

   The Flash Player you see in Figure 11-10 (left) appears.

8. **In Flash Player, click the "Click to load" button.**

   Flash replaces the contents of the first animation (the button) with the contents of the elevator.jpg file, as shown in Figure 11-10 (right).

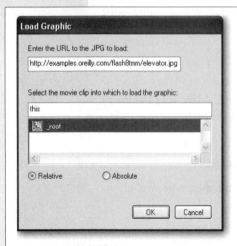

Figure 11-9:
Here, you're telling Flash to load an image file located on a server. You could tell Flash to load the image in a Loader component, a Window component, or a nested movie clip, if this animation happened to contain any. Instead, leaving _root selected tells Flash to replace the current animation with the loaded image.

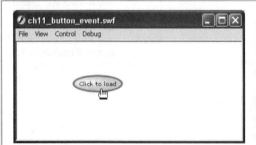

Figure 11-10:
Left: Thanks to the ActionScript code that Flash generated when you created your behavior, clicking this button loads the image on the right. (You can expand the borders of the window Flash chooses for you by dragging them.)

Right: Adding conditional statements to the ActionScript code (such as the ActionScript if...else and switch statements) lets you load a different image based on a certain condition: for example, the text an audience typed in.

Creating Hotspots and Rollovers

If you've surfed the Web much, you've probably encountered hotspots and rollovers. A *hotspot* is a clickable portion of an image. The most popular way to use hotspots is to create a big, fancy splash page image, and then display different images or Web pages as someone mouses over or clicks different areas of the image. See Figure 11-11 for an example.

A *rollover* is a special type of hotspot. When your audience mouses over a rollover, the area changes visually ("rolls over")—turns a different color, displays a different bit of text, or something to that effect). Rollovers—which many folks use in navigation bars—are useful when you want to give your audience a big, fat, unmistakable visual cue that they've moused over something they can click.

In this section, you'll create both a hotspot and a rollover. Clicking the hotspot embeds a second animation in the main animation using an instance of the Loader component; clicking the rollover embeds a third animation.

Note: Components, like the Loader in this example, are canned animation features that you can add to any Flash document. Chapter 12 covers components in detail.

Figure 11-11:
Hotspots and rollovers let you turn any image into a fancy navigation "bar." Here, mousing over the image on the left side of the splash page (or over the crossword-style text on the right) pops up descriptive text; clicking any part of the image whisks you off to the appropriate section of the Web site. Underneath their sophisticated covers, hotspots and rollovers are really just buttons.

Note: You can download a working version of this example file (hotspot_working.fla), plus the files you need for the following tutorial (hotspot.fla, apple.swf, and hoppy.swf), from the "Missing CD" page. This tutorial assumes you have these files on your hard drive.

---

1. **Open the file hotspot.fla.**

   The child's face is an imported bitmap that was turned into an editable image using Modify → Break Apart (page 250). First, you'll turn the child's face into a hotspot.

2. **Use the Lasso tool to draw a circle around the child's face (Figure 11-12).**

   Flash highlights (selects) the portion of the image inside the lasso.

3. **Select Modify → Convert to Symbol.**

   Flash displays the Convert to Symbol dialog box.

4. **In the Convert to Symbol dialog box, click the Name field and then type** *childFace.* **Select the Button symbol type, and then click OK.**

   Flash places your button symbol in the Library. The button instance you'll be working with remains on the Stage.

Figure 11-12:
Top: The Lasso tool lets you describe irregular shapes. When you try this on your own bitmap image, choose Modify → Break Apart after you import your image and before you draw your hotspot on it. If you forget, Flash won't let you select just a portion of your image.

Bottom: You can create as many hotspots on an image as you like, but make sure you don't overlap them.

5. **On the Stage, click to select the button instance.**

   Flash redisplays the Property Inspector to show button instance–related properties. (If you don't see the Property Inspector, choose Window → Properties → Properties.)

6. **In the Property Inspector, click the "Instance name" field and type** *faceInstance.*

   Your hotpot is complete. Next, you'll turn the child's hat into a rollover.

7. **Use the Lasso tool to draw a circle around the child's hat (Figure 11-12, bottom).**

   Once again, Flash highlights the portion of the image inside the lasso.

8. **Select Modify → Convert to Symbol.**

   Flash displays the Convert to Symbol dialog box.

9. **In the Convert to Symbol dialog box, click the Name field and then type** *childHat.* **Then select the Button symbol type. When you're finished, click OK.**

   Flash places your childHat button symbol in the Library. The button instance you'll be working with remains on the Stage.

10. **On the Stage, click the Selection tool and then double-click the childHat instance.**

    Flash pops you into symbol editing mode (see Figure 11-13).

11. **In the symbol Timeline, click the Over frame.**

    Because this is the frame Flash displays when your audience mouses *over* your button, any changes you make to your symbol here appear as a rollover effect.

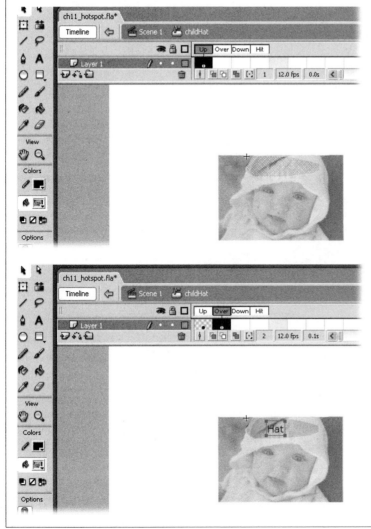

Figure 11-13:
Top: As sophisticated and time-intensive as hotspots and rollovers appear, they're really nothing more than glorified buttons, as the standard button Up, Over, Down, and Hit frames here show.

Bottom: The Over frame (often referred to in programming circles as the Over state) is what distinguishes a rollover from both a regular button and a hotspot. Any changes you make to the Over frame appear when your audience mouses over the button to create the so-called rollover effect.

12. Choose Insert → Timeline → Keyframe.

Flash displays a round dot in the Over frame to let you know it's a keyframe now and that you can make changes on the Stage.

13. Using the Text tool, add the static text *Hat* to the symbol Stage.

Be sure to position it directly over the hat symbol as shown in Figure 11-13 (bottom).

14. Choose Edit → Edit Document to return to the main document Timeline. Then, with the instance still selected on the Stage, head to the Property Inspector, click the "Instance name" field, and then type *hatInstance*.

In the next few steps, you'll add an instance of the Loader component to the stage and use it to play (that is, *load*) a new animation when your audience clicks the child's face hotspot.

15. **Choose Window → Components.**

Flash displays the Components panel (Figure 11-14).

Figure 11-14:
The Loader component, which page 350 describes in more detail, lets you embed an image or another animation directly into the main animation.

16. **From the Components panel, drag an instance of the Loader component (you'll find it in the User Interface folder) to the Stage.**

Where you place the component doesn't matter for this example. Just make sure it's on the Stage but not touching your image. (Flash doesn't actually place your new animation inside the Loader component; the Loader component just tells Flash to pull in the new animation and play it.)

Note: You can't refer to an instance until you've given it a name, so *always* name your instances immediately after you drag them to the Stage (even if you're not planning to involve them in an action right away).

---

17. **In the Property Inspector, with the Loader component still selected, click the "Instance name" field and then type *myLoader*.**

Now that the loader's on the Stage and properly named, you can tell Flash what animation to load. And to do *that*, you add a behavior to the *childFace* button instance.

18. **On the Stage, click the childFace instance to select it. Then choose Window → Behavior.**

The Behaviors panel appears.

19. Click the Add Behavior icon. From the drop-down list, choose Movieclip → Load External Movieclip.

Flash displays the Load External Movieclip dialog box shown in Figure 11-15.

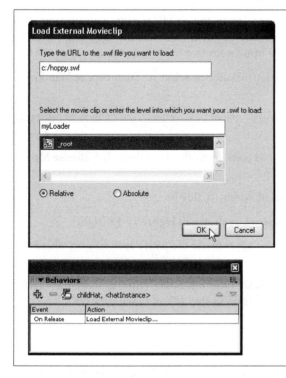

Figure 11-15:
Top: Tell Flash which animation to load when someone clicks the childFace hotspot (and where to load it). myLoader is the instance name you typed in for the Loader component.

Bottom: This behavior tells Flash to display a different animation in the same Loader component when someone clicks the childHat rollover.

Note: Out of the box, Flash's security model prevents you from loading an animation on a Web site into an animation on your computer. So, to demonstrate adding an action to a button, this example shows you how to load an animation located on your own computer. For the nitty-gritty technical details of Flash's security model, choose Flash Help and search for "understanding security."

20. In the URL field, type *c:/hoppy.swf* as shown in Figure 11-15 (left).

This example assumes you saved the hoppy.swf file on a Windows computer's C: drive. If you saved it in a folder, type the path to that folder. (If you have a Mac, the path might look like *Macintosh HD/Users/<Your Account Name>/ Desktop/hoppy.swf.*)

Tip: If you saved the file in the same place you saved hotspot.fla, you can simply type the file name (*hoppy.swf*) in the URL field.

21. In the "movie clip or level" field, type *myLoader* (the name of the Loader instance you added to your animation in step 17) and then click OK.

    In the Behaviors panel, Flash displays a new behavior showing the event *On Release* and the action *Load External Movieclip*.

    Finally, you'll add another behavior to the childHat button instance so that when your audience clicks the rollover positioned over the child's hat, a different animation loads. Just a few more steps to go:

22. On the Stage, click the childHat instance to select it. Then choose Window → Behavior.

    Flash redisplays the Behaviors panel to reflect the childHat instance (Figure 11-15, right).

23. Click the Add Behavior icon and then, from the drop-down list, choose Movieclip → Load External Movieclip.

    Flash displays a Load External Movieclip dialog box.

24. In the URL field, type *c:/hoppy.swf,* as shown in Figure 11-15 (right).

    As explained in step 20, type the appropriate file path depending on where you saved this file.

25. In the "movie clip or level" field, type *myLoader* (the name of the Loader instance you added to your animation in step 17) and then click OK.

    Time to test your handiwork:

26. Select Control → Test Movie.

    The Flash Player window appears. To make sure you're seeing everything, maximize the Flash Player window by clicking the Maximize button in the window's upper-right corner.

27. Move your mouse over the child's hat.

    As your cursor changes to a pointing finger to let you know you're over a clickable region, the word "Hat" appears (Figure 11-16, top).

28. Click the child's hat.

    The apple.swf animation begins playing at the bottom of the Flash Player (Figure 11-16, middle).

29. Click the child's face.

    The apple.swf animation disappears, and the hoppy.swf animation appears in its place (Figure 11-16, bottom).

Figure 11-16:

Top: Mousing over the child's hat changes your pointer, letting you know you're over a clickable region. The rollover effect (the word Hat) also appears. In place of adding text as shown here, you might choose to change the color, transparency, or size of the button, or add special effects—anything you think will fit the look of your animation and get your audience's attention.

Middle: Clicking the hat embeds the apple.swf animation by loading it into the Loader component you added in step 16 on page 332.

Bottom: Clicking the child's face replaces the apple.swf animation with the hoppy.swf animation.

Tying an Event to a Component

Just as you can tell Flash what to do when your audience clicks a button, you can tell it what to do when your audience interacts with a component. (Chapter 12 describes the components Flash includes and shows you how to add them to your animations.) When it comes to interactivity, though, you can add actions to a component instance exactly as you would to a button or movie clip instance, a hotspot, and so on.

The example below shows how to add an action to a ComboBox component (a drop-down list) so that when someone chooses a Web page from the list, Flash launches his Web browser preloaded with that Web page.

To tie an event to a component:

1. **Open the file component_action.fla.**

   You can download this file from the "Missing CD" page.

   The Stage shows an instance of the ComboBox component (Figure 11-17).

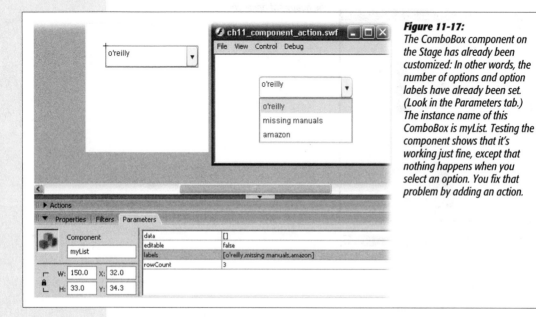

Figure 11-17:
The ComboBox component on the Stage has already been customized: In other words, the number of options and option labels have already been set. (Look in the Parameters tab.) The instance name of this ComboBox is myList. Testing the component shows that it's working just fine, except that nothing happens when you select an option. You fix that problem by adding an action.

2. **Test the component by selecting Control → Test Movie.**

   The Flash Player in Figure 11-17 appears.

3. **Click the drop-down box, and then select from the list of Web sites.**

   Flash highlights the option you select. When you release your mouse, Flash displays your option in the field—but nothing else happens.

   Next, you'll tell Flash what you want to happen. In the next few steps, you'll add a frame-based action that tells Flash to wait until your audience has selected an option and then display the selected Web site.

4. **Click Frame 1 to select it. Then select Window → Actions.**

   The Actions frame titled Actions—Frame appears.

5. Click in the script pane, and then type the following ActionScript code:

```
1    var comboListener:Object = new Object();
2
3    comboListener.dropdown = function(eventInfo) {
4        var comboValue:String = eventInfo.target.value;
5        switch (comboValue) {
6            case "o'reilly" :
7                getURL("http://www.oreilly.com");
8                break;
9            case "missing manuals" :
10               getURL("http://www.missingmanuals.com");
11               break;
12           case "amazon" :
13               getURL("http://www.amazon.com");
14               break;
15           default :
16               trace("error in component or action");
17       }
18   };
19   myList.addEventListener("change",comboListener.dropdown);
```

Note: You can download a working version of this example, complete with ActionScript code (component_action_working.fla) from the "Missing CD" page—good news if you're not much for typing.

Here's what the above ActionScript does: First, in lines 1 through 18, it creates a variable called comboListener that describes what you want Flash to inspect (the option your audience selects from a drop-down list).

Then, on line 19, the code associates the comboListener both with the Combo-Box instance named *myList*—so Flash knows which specific ComboBox you're talking about—and with the *change* event, so Flash knows when you want it to check which option your audience has selected. (There's no sense in telling Flash to check every 2 seconds; it only makes sense to tell it to wait until the option has changed.)

Time to test your action:

6. Select Control → Test Movie.

The Flash Player appears, showing contents similar to what's in Figure 11-18 (top).

7. From the drop-down box, choose Missing Manuals.

Flash launches your Web browser, and then loads the Missing Manuals home page. Selecting another option tells Flash to open an additional browser window.

Figure 11-18:
Top: Thanks to the built-in ActionScript function getURL( ), choosing an option from the drop-down list...

Bottom: ...displays the Web site you associated with the option.

Communicating with Your Audience's Web Browser and Mail Client

You can do more with Flash's built-in *getURL( )* function than simply load a Web page (although that *is* pretty cool). You can also:

- **Communicate with the Web page in which you've embedded your animation.** For example, you can pass a JavaScript statement to the Web browser. (To test this out, attach the following ActionScript code to the first frame of your animation, make sure you've selected HTML in the Format tab of the Publish Settings window, and then choose Publish Preview.)

```
getURL("javascript:alert('Hi from
inside a Flash animation!')");
```

- **Trigger your audience's mail client.** The following ActionScript code launches your audience's email program with the "To:" field prefilled with *santa@northpole.org:*

```
getURL("mailto:santa@northpole.org");
```

For more on exchanging data between Flash and other programs, including sending data via the HTML GET and POST methods, head to Flash Help and search for "working with external data."

Components for Interactivity

Creating common Flash elements like playback controls (Play and Pause buttons), text fields, checkboxes, and menus can add up to a lot of grunt work. Since they pretty much look the same in every animation, some kind Flash developers did the grunt work for you and put ready-made versions of these Flash bits and pieces—called *components*—right in the program.

A component is a compiled, prebuilt movie clip that you can drag onto the Stage and customize (Figure 12-1). Flash Professional 8 comes with some three dozen components, and Flash Basic 8 has about half that number.

If you do a lot of work in Flash, you'll appreciate the time that components can save you. But another great thing about components is the consistency they offer. For example, say you're creating three Web sites in Flash for a single corporate client: one site for their employees, one for their customers, and one for their business partners. Your client wants the sites to have a slightly different look and feel based on their intended audiences, but also wants the sites to be similar when it comes to navigation and usability.

If you're ActionScript-savvy, you can create the menus you'll need from scratch. But if you use the prebuilt MenuBar component that comes with Flash, you not only save time, you also ensure that the strip of menu buttons you display at the top of each page of each site looks and behaves predictably. From a design perspective, this consistency can mean the difference between someone being able to get around your site and someone surfing away in frustration.

This chapter shows you how to add Flash's built-in components to your animation and how to customize them. You also see where to find additional components on the Web.

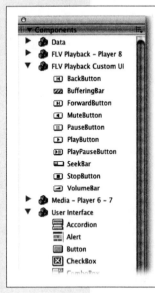

Figure 12-1:
Flash Professional 8 comes with over 40 components in three different categories: Data components to transfer data from your Flash animation to a server; Playback components to add playback controls to your animation; and User Interface controls to create interactive buttons, boxes, and lists (similar to HTML form controls). The examples in this chapter focus on the components available in both Flash Basic and Flash Professional, but the techniques apply to all components.

Note: *Using* components requires a good deal of ActionScript knowledge. But *creating* your own components is an even more ActionScript-intensive proposition. If you'd like to explore creating your own components, check out both the Components Language Reference you find in Flash Help (see the Appendix), and a good book that covers both ActionScript and object-oriented design. Colin Moock's *Essential ActionScript 2.0* (O'Reilly) is one of the best on the market.

The Built-in Components

The components that ship with Flash are generic, customizable elements that fall into three main categories:

- **Data components.** These components let you transfer data from your Flash animation to a server (such as a Web server). You'll want to use data components if you're creating a Flash data-entry form, an ecommerce Web site, a tutorial—any situation in which you need to capture information from your audience (in Flash) and then examine or process that information (on the back end, using a program on your server).

- **Playback components.** These components let you add as many or as few playback controls to your animation as you like. Examples of playback controls include the Mute, Pause, and Play buttons.

- **User Interface components.** Similar to HTML components, Flash User Interface components include buttons, checkboxes, lists, text fields and windows—everything you need to create a Flash form and collect data from your audience.

Note: This chapter focuses on the User Interface components for two reasons: They're by far the most popular Flash components, and they're the only components that come standard with both Flash Basic and Flash Professional. For detailed descriptions and examples of the Data and Playback components, check out Flash Help in the Appendix.

To see the components described in the following sections, select Window → Components to display the Components panel.

Data Components

If all you want to do is create a simple, noninteractive Flash animation, you don't need to bother with data components (Window → Components, then choose Data). *Data components* come into play only when you want to capture information in Flash and then send it to another program (such as a database) running on a server. Data components bridge the gap, so to speak, between your Flash animation and your back end.

For example, imagine you're using Flash to create a Web site for a retail store. The store wants to be able to accept credit card orders online and then send the collected order information to its order entry system for processing and shipping.

The actual steps you need to take to transfer Flash data to an order entry system depend on the specifics of the computer hardware and programs that make up the retail store's back end. The two major steps, however, are always the same:

- Use Flash's interface components (page 347) to create a Flash form that accepts order information.

- Use one or more of the data components you find in Table 12-1—along with ActionScript in your Flash program as well as various server-side technologies —to transfer Flash data to your server-side program in a form that program can use. Server-side technologies include Java servlets, ColdFusion components, SQL databases, and XML data files.

Note: Because creating data components is both programming-intensive and completely dependent on the server-side program to which you want to transfer data, it's beyond the scope of this book. For more information on data components and the related data binding and Web service ActionScript classes that work with them, check out Flash Help in the Appendix.

Table 12-1. Flash Data Components (Flash Professional Only)

Component	Description
DataHolder	Lets you tell Flash to watch certain data values and let you know when they change.
DataSet	Lets you work with other component data (sort component data, search it, filter it, and so on) as well as data pulled in from a server-side program.
RDBMSResolver	You use this component in conjunction with the DataSet component to save the data you collect (or generate) in Flash to a relational database running on a server. (You're responsible for parsing the XML code that this component generates into the server-side SQL statements necessary to populate your database.)
WebService Connector	Lets you access remote (server-side) APIs that conform to the industry-standard Simple Object Access Protocol from inside a running Flash animation.
XMLConnector	Lets you hook up Flash components with external XML data sources by letting you read and write XML documents.
XUpdateResolver	Works with the DataSet component to let you save the data you collect (or generate) in Flash to an external XUpdate-supporting data source, such as an XML database.

Playback Components

Flash's playback components (Window → Components) let you give your audience control over how and when they play the audio and video clips you've added to your animation. Giving your audience the ability to pause, mute, restart, and otherwise control media playback makes good sense. Say, for example, that your animation contains a long video clip, so it takes a while to download. The person using your Web site runs out to grab a cup of coffee. Now imagine she's waylaid at the water cooler. By the time she makes it back to her seat, your animation and video have finished downloading and playing. If you didn't include playback controls, your audience has no choice but to go through the whole process again (or, more likely, surf to a more user-friendly Web site). You get playback components only as part of Flash Professional 8; Flash Basic 8 doesn't come with them. Table 12-2 describes the playback components; Figure 12-2 shows you an example of one of the components (the streaming video player FLVPlayback) in action.

Note: To find out more about embedding audio, video, and other non-Flash media files into your animation, see Chapter 8.

Table 12-2. *Flash Playback Components (Flash Professional Only)*

Component Group	Components	Notes
FLVPlayback–Player 8	FLVPlayback	New in Flash 8, this component lets you add progressive streaming video to your animation through a video player (Figure 12-2) that contains a full set of playback controls. You can choose a *skin* for this component to customize its look and feel. (For more on skinning, check out the box on page 344.)
FLVPlayback Custom UI	BackButton, BufferingBar, ForwardButton, MuteButton, PauseButton, PlayButton, PlayPauseButton, SeekBar, StopButton, VolumeBar	Let you add video playback controls individually (useful if you're planning to create your own skin).
Media–Player 6-7	MediaController, MediaDisplay, MediaPlayback	Use these older playback components if you're targeting an earlier version of the Flash Player (Version 6 or 7; earlier versions don't support playback components). The MediaDisplay component lets your audience play video and audio, but not control the playback. The MediaController component (when you use it in conjunction with either the MediaDisplay or MediaPlayback component) lets your audience control media playback. The MediaPlayback component is a combination of the MediaController and MediaDisplay components.

Note: Each component comes with different parameters you can set to customize the component. For example, you can set the Button component's label parameter to tell Flash what text to display on the button, and the Window component's contentPath parameter to tell Flash which image (or animation) file you want to load into the window. Find out more in the section "Customizing Components" later in this chapter. For a complete rundown of each and every parameter for each and every component, search Flash → Flash Help for "types of components."

Figure 12-2:
Top: It's a good idea to give your audience the ability to pause, mute, restart, and otherwise control media playback.

Middle: Flash gives you a variety of ways to skin your playback component (change the appearance of your playback controls), as described in the box below.

Bottom: You don't have to show all the playback controls all the time; sometimes, a stripped-down skin (component set) fits the bill.

More Than One Way to Skin a Component

In computer parlance, a *skin* is a set of visual characteristics you can apply to a feature (such as the FLVPlayback component shown in Figure 12-2 with three different skins applied). Skins don't affect how the feature works, just how it looks.

Flash includes a few dozen skins you can apply to the FLV-Playback component. You can change its color and transparency as well as how many playback controls appear.

To apply a skin:

1. On the Stage, select the instance of FLVPlayback you want to skin.

2. Open the Component Inspector (Window → Component Inspector).

3. Click the Parameters tab.

4. Click in the Value column next to skin; then click the magnifying glass icon that appears to display the Select Skin dialog box.

5. In the Select Skin dialog box, choose a skin (such as ClearOverAll.swf) from the drop-down list. Flash automatically previews the skin for you right there in the dialog box.

6. When you're happy with the way your component looks, click OK.

Because Flash skins are nothing more or less than published animation (.swf) files that you add to your main animation, you can create your own skins if you don't find one you like in the Select Skin dialog box. For help in creating a skin, search for "creating a new skin" in Flash Help (page 437). To specify a custom skin, in the Select Skin dialog box, choose Custom Skin URL; then type the file name of your custom skin.

User Interface Components

Similar to HTML form components, Flash's popular *user interface components* (Figure 12-3) let you interact with your audience and gather information. Examples of user interface components include buttons, checkboxes, text fields, and drop-down lists.

Note: Some user interface components are available only in Flash Professional 8, not in Flash Basic 8. The following sections tell you which are which.

Figure 12-3:
To see the User Interface components that come with Flash, display the Components panel (Window → Components) and then click User Interface. If you're running Flash Basic 8, you don't see as many components as this section describes.

Accordion

(Flash Professional 8 only.) The *Accordion* component (Figure 12-4) is a clickable menu to display different Flash content (such as multiple movie clips) in the same space-saving frame.

An example of when you might want to use the accordion component: You're creating a Flash Web site and you want to display three different customer forms—say, for billing address, ship-to address, and credit card info—depending on which menu option someone clicks.

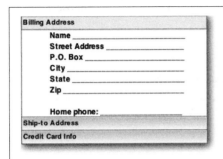

Figure 12-4:
Clicking a frame title (such as Billing Address, shown here) tells Flash to display the content for that frame. Similar to HTML frames, the Accordion component lets your audience see lots of different content without having to surf to lots of different Web pages. Because people always sees the same background page when you use the Accordion component, they're less likely to become confused.

Alert

(Flash Professional 8 only.) Similar to the JavaScript *alert( )* dialog boxes that seem to spring out of nowhere while you're innocently clicking around the Web, the *Alert* component is a pop-up message to communicate with your audience. For example, if you're creating a Flash form, you can use the Alert component to let people know when they've typed in an invalid email address.

Button

You see an example of the clickable Button component in Figure 12-5.

Typically, you want to use a Button component when you're creating a Flash form. If you need a fancier button, you can either create your own button symbol, or check out Flash's button symbols (page 226).

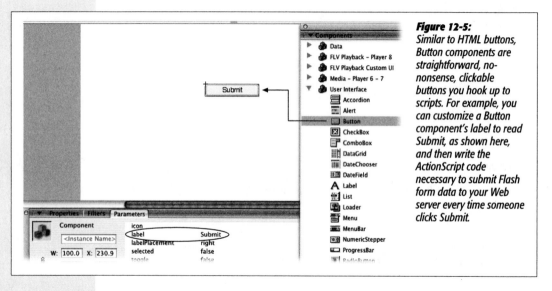

Figure 12-5:
Similar to HTML buttons, Button components are straightforward, no-nonsense, clickable buttons you hook up to scripts. For example, you can customize a Button component's label to read Submit, as shown here, and then write the ActionScript code necessary to submit Flash form data to your Web server every time someone clicks Submit.

Checkbox

The CheckBox component lets you offer folks an easy way to choose multiple options, as shown in Figure 12-6.

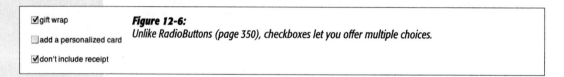

Figure 12-6:
Unlike RadioButtons (page 350), checkboxes let you offer multiple choices.

ComboBox

As Figure 12-7 shows, the ComboBox component lets you display a drop-down list of options.

You use this component when you want to offer people an easy way to choose a single option (such as which animation they want to play, or which Web page they want to hop to) from a predefined list.

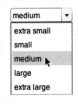

Figure 12-7:
Flash automatically adds a scrollbar to your ComboBox component if you create a long list (over six options). Short list or long, the ComboBox lets your audience choose only one option. If you want to offer people a list from which they can Shift-click or Control-click multiple options, use the List component (page 348).

DataGrid

(Flash Professional 8 only.) The DataGrid component lets you display a table containing multiple rows and columns of data.

Typically, you use this component when you want to transfer data from your server (for example, product names, descriptions, and prices) and display it in Flash in table form. But you can also use it to display the data you collect (or create) in your Flash animation.

DateChooser

(Flash Professional 8 only.) Presenting your audience with the clickable calendar Flash calls a DateChooser component (Figure 12-8) makes it easy for people to select a date—much easier than making them guess what format you want, and then type a date from scratch.

This component comes in handy when, for example, you're putting together an online event scheduler and you want people to be able to click different dates to see a list of the events your company's scheduled for each date.

Figure 12-8:
When your audience clicks the left and right arrows, the DateChooser component automatically scrolls to the previous and next months, respectively. You can customize the way the calendar looks (see "Customizing Components", page 353). For example, you can specify blackout days or display Monday as the first day of the week instead of Sunday.

DateField

(Flash Professional 8 only.) A combination of the DateChooser component (see above) and a text field, the DateField component visually reinforces a person's choice by filling a text field with the date he selects (Figure 12-9).

Figure 12-9:
Left: Clicking the calendar icon next to the text field...

Middle: ...displays a calendar someone can scroll through to pick a date. Once she clicks a date to select it...

Right: ...Flash hides the calendar and types the selected date into the text field.

Label

A Label component lets you add a single line of noneditable, nonclickable text to your Flash creation. As shown in Figure 12-10, many folks find this component useful for adding short descriptions of other user interface components.

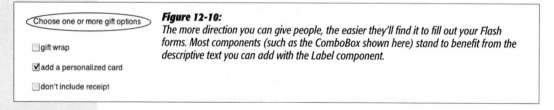

Figure 12-10:
The more direction you can give people, the easier they'll find it to fill out your Flash forms. Most components (such as the ComboBox shown here) stand to benefit from the descriptive text you can add with the Label component.

List

You use the List component (Figure 12-11) to create a clickable, scrollable list from which someone can Shift-click to select multiple options.

Figure 12-11:
The List component is similar to multiple checkboxes (see above) in that both let your audience select multiple options (once you customize the List component by setting multipleSelection to true in the Property Inspector). But because list components are scrollable, they tend to take up less screen real estate than checkboxes, and so they're helpful when your Stage is already packed with graphics and other components.

Loader

A *Loader component* is a nonscrollable window that lets you display an animation or bitmap image along with your main animation. By customizing the Loader component (page 353), you can show the animation or bitmap full-size or modify it to match the Loader dimensions you set.

Figure 12-12 shows you an example of using the Loader component to display a small, thumbnail version of an animation in the corner of your main animation.

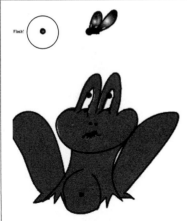

Figure 12-12:
You can create all kinds of nifty effects with the Loader component, such as this thumbnail animation inset in the upper-left corner of the main animation. You can even create recursive animations (loading the same animation into itself). Because Flash keeps track of when it loads each animation or bitmap image, you can use ActionScript to tie an action (such as stopping all sounds) to a successfully loaded file.

Menu

(Flash Professional 8 only.) The Menu component is useful if you're creating a full-fledged program in Flash and want to let your audience navigate your program by choosing from familiar drop-down menus. The menus you create using the Menu component are similar in style and function to the File and Edit menus in Flash (and many other software programs), although you *do* have to have quite a bit of ActionScript knowledge under your belt to customize and use them.

MenuBar

(Flash Professional 8 only.) The MenuBar component is a horizontal bar of clickable button-like menu options. This component's handy if, for example, you're creating a complex Web site in Flash and you want to display an identical, space-saving menu bar at the top of each Web page (see Figure 12-13).

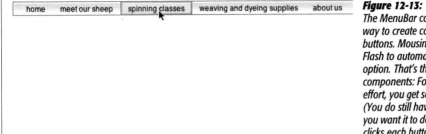

Figure 12-13:
The MenuBar component is an easy way to create compact rows of buttons. Mousing over a button tells Flash to automatically highlight the option. That's the beauty of components: For drag-and-drop effort, you get sophisticated behavior. (You do still have to tell Flash what you want it to do when your audience clicks each button, as described on page 335.)

NumericStepper

You use the NumericStepper component to create the clickable list of numbers shown in Figure 12-14. Simpler for people to use than a type-in-your-own-number text field, this component makes it easy for you to limit your audience's choices to a predefined set of valid numbers.

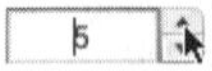

Figure 12-14:
When you use the NumericStepper component, your audience gets an easy way to specify a number, and you don't have to use ActionScript to examine the number and see whether it's valid (the way you would if you let them type any number they want).

ProgressBar

The horizontal ProgressBar component, shown in Figure 12-15, is a visual indicator of how long Flash expects to take to complete a process (such as loading a file).

LOADING 0%

Figure 12-15:
This component is useful when you want to give people a visual indication of how long they have left to wait for an animation (or a Web page) to load.

RadioButton

When you want to make sure your audience chooses just one of several mutually exclusive options, use a group of RadioButton components (Figure 12-16).

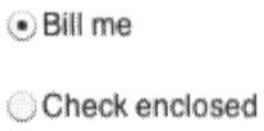

Figure 12-16:
RadioButton components let you offer your audience mutually exclusive options, so you never use just one; you always use RadioButton components in groups of two or more. (If you think you want a single RadioButton, you probably want a checkbox.) Turning on one radio button tells Flash to turn off all the other radio buttons.

ScrollPane

Similar to the Loader component (page 348), the ScrollPane component lets you include an additional animation or bitmap imagine in your main animation. But unlike the Loader component, the ScrollPane component includes scrollbars your audience can use to control the content they see.

Figure 12-17 shows you the ScrollPane component in action.

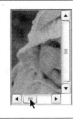

Figure 12-17:
When you display an animation or image using the ScrollPane component, Flash automatically tacks on scrollbars people can use to choose which part of the animation they want to see through the window.

TextArea

The TextArea component (Figure 12-18, top) is a multiline, scrollable text field that's useful when you want your audience to be able to type a long comment, or any other information longer than a few words.

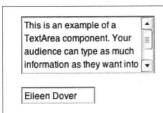

Figure 12-18:
Top: The TextArea and TextInput components both let your audience type text, but the TextArea component (shown here) lets them type a lot of text. Flash automatically adds scrollbars if someone types in more text than the TextArea component's dimensions can display.

Bottom: People can type as much text as they like into a TextInput component, but only a single line of text (based on the dimensions you set) appears. This component is most useful when you want to limit people to a few words or less.

TextInput

The TextInput component (Figure 12-18, bottom) lets you create a single-line text field. Using this component lets you give your audience a freeform text field just long enough to type what you want them to type (for example, a name, phone number, or email address).

Tree

(Flash Professional 8 only.) Similar to the List component (page 348), the Tree component displays information (such as the contents of a folder) in a hierarchical fashion.

This component's useful if, for example, you're creating a complex Web site and you want to add a site map option that shows your audience the hierarchical view of your site, from the home page down.

UIScrollBar

The UIScrollBar component is a fancy, color-customizable scrollbar you can add to a TextInput or TextArea field to make your text fields match your overall color scheme.

Window

The Window component (Figure 12-19) is a movable, titled window to display an animation or a bitmap file.

You might want to use this when you're creating a tutorial in Flash and you want to display each how-to animation in a separate window so that your audience can reposition each window and close it easily when they're ready to move on to the next topic.

Window Title Goes Here

Flash!

Figure 12-19:
The Window component shown here is similar to the Loader and ScrollPane components. The main differences are control (your audience can reposition and close a Window component) and familiarity (Window components look and act like standard display windows, so there's a good chance people will know how to interact with them).

Adding Components

Adding a component to your animation is the first step in using that component. As you see in the following sections, adding an instance of a component to the Stage is similar to adding an instance of a symbol: all you have to do is drag and drop. But instead of dragging a component from the Library panel, you drag components from the Component panel.

Note: After you add the component, you still need to customize it and—depending on the component you choose—add the ActionScript code necessary to tie the component to your back end. (See "Customizing Components" on page 353.)

To add a component to your animation:

1. Select Window → Components.

    The Components panel appears.

2. In the Components panel, click to a select the component you want and then drag it to the Stage.

    As Figure 12-20 shows, Flash displays an instance of the component on the Stage. It also places a copy of the component in the Library (Window → Library).

Tip: Flash gives you another way to add a component: In the Components panel, double-click the component. When you do, Flash immediately places an instance of the component on the center of your Stage.

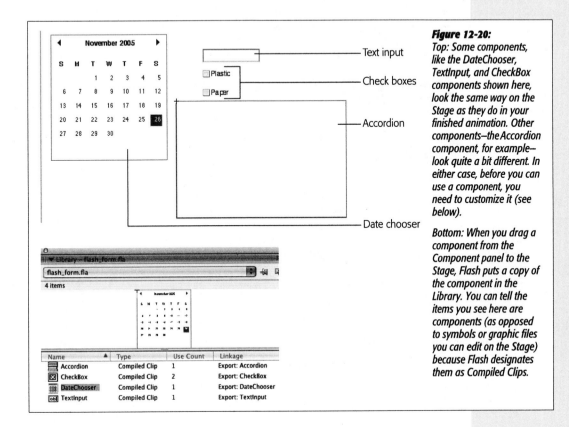

Figure 12-20:
Top: Some components, like the DateChooser, TextInput, and CheckBox components shown here, look the same way on the Stage as they do in your finished animation. Other components—the Accordion component, for example—look quite a bit different. In either case, before you can use a component, you need to customize it (see below).

Bottom: When you drag a component from the Component panel to the Stage, Flash puts a copy of the component in the Library. You can tell the items you see here are components (as opposed to symbols or graphic files you can edit on the Stage) because Flash designates them as Compiled Clips.

Customizing Components

After you've dragged a component to the Stage, you can begin customizing it. For example, if you add a CheckBox component to the Stage, you want to change the standard CheckBox label to a specific label that fits your needs. If you add a Button component to the Stage, in addition to changing the button's label (from Button to Submit Form, say), you want to tell Flash what to do when someone clicks the button.

You can't customize a component using Flash's editing tools the way you modify a symbol or an image. Instead, Flash gives you three separate panels to customize a component: the Properties and Parameters panels, the Component Inspector, and the Actions panel. How many (and which) panels you need to use depends both on the component you're customizing and on which characteristics of the component you want to change. For example, you can customize the labels of the

MenuBar component using the Parameters panel, but to customize the labels of the Menu component, you need to create ActionScript actions, which you do in the Actions panel.

Note: Components are sometimes referred to as *black boxes* because you can't inspect their inner workings. The only things you can look at or change are the characteristics that the developer *exposes* (lets you access) through the Property Inspector, the Component Inspector, or ActionScript classes.

Customizing Components Using the Properties and Parameters Panels

After you drag a component to the Stage, Flash displays the component's customizable characteristics in the Property Inspector and its customizable parameters in the Parameters panel.

As you can see in Figure 12-21, *properties* (including width, height, and instance name) affect the entire component; *parameters* let you customize the way individual component features work.

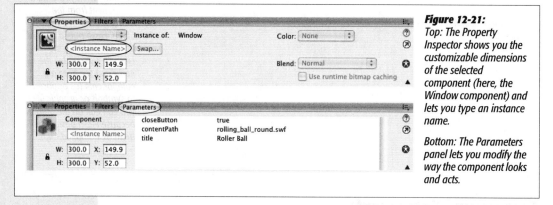

Figure 12-21:
Top: The Property Inspector shows you the customizable dimensions of the selected component (here, the Window component) and lets you type an instance name.

Bottom: The Parameters panel lets you modify the way the component looks and acts.

To customize a component using the Property Inspector:

1. **On the Stage, select the component you want to customize. Then select Window → Properties → Properties.**

   The Property Inspector appears with the Properties tab selected, as shown in Figure 12-21 (top).

2. **Click the "Instance name" field and then type an instance name for this component.**

   The instance name refers to this instance in any ActionScript code you write, so make sure you type a short, meaningful, easy-to-remember name.

3. **If you like, use the "Selection width" and "Selection height" fields to change the size of the component.**

Simply type the new dimensions in pixels. When you click Enter, Flash redisplays the component based on the new dimensions you just set.

4. **If you like, use the "Selection X position" and "Selection Y position" fields to change the component's position.**

The X position is the number of pixels you want between the left edge of the Stage and the left edge of your component; Y is the number of pixels you want between the top of the Stage and the top of your component.

Note: You can also reposition your component by dragging it around on the Stage. When you do, Flash automatically fills in the Selection X and Selection Y positions.

To customize a component using the Parameters panel:

1. **On the Stage, select the component you want to customize. Then select Window → Properties → Parameters.**

The Property Inspector appears with the Parameters tab selected.

2. **Click the parameter you want to change.**

Flash highlights the value of the parameter (Figure 12-22, top).

3. **Either type a new value, click the drop-down box to select a new value as shown in Figure 12-22 (bottom), or click the magnifying glass icon (Figure 12-23, top) to enter a list of values (Figure 12-23, bottom).**

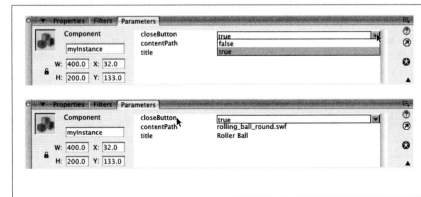

Figure 12-22:
Top: Clicking anywhere on the name of the parameter or on the current value tells Flash to select the value so you can change it.

Bottom: Flash offers you lists of options for some parameters. To set other options (such as title), you need to type your own value.

4. Repeat steps 2–3 for each parameter you want to change. When you finish, test the component by choosing Control → Test Movie.

Customizing Components Using the Component Inspector

Using the Component Inspector (Figure 12-24), you can set additional parameters (page 354), bindings, and schema for a selected component.

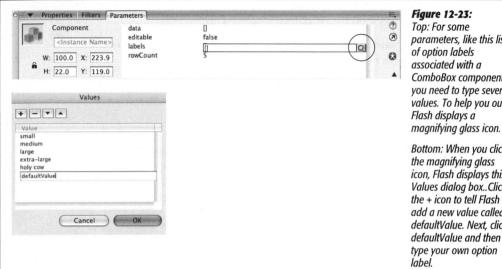

Figure 12-23:
Top: For some parameters, like this list of option labels associated with a ComboBox component, you need to type several values. To help you out, Flash displays a magnifying glass icon.

Bottom: When you click the magnifying glass icon, Flash displays this Values dialog box..Click the + icon to tell Flash to add a new value called defaultValue. Next, click defaultValue and then type your own option label.

Note: Only Flash Professional 8 lets you specify bindings and schema; these features aren't included in Flash Basic 8.

Bindings let you tell Flash how to connect your component's data to a back end data source, such as a database or other program running on a Web server.

The *schema* let you add bindable properties to a component; they also let you tell Flash how you'd like it to constrain properties. For example, one of the constraints you can set for the value of a TextInput component is data type. You can tell Flash to set the data type to Date (so that your audience can only type data in date format). Other data types include PhoneNumber, SocialSecurity, Integer, and ZipCode.

Note: Schema let you describe each of the parameters associated with your component. But to put those descriptions to use—for example, to examine the data someone types into your TextInput field, recognize that the data's not in date format, and then display an error message—you need to add Action-Script to your component (page 361).

Parameters tab

The parameters that Flash lets you customize using the Component Inspector's Parameters tab include the same parameters you set using the Parameters tab of the Property Inspector—plus a whole lot more.

1. On the Stage, select the component you want to customize. Then select Window → Component Inspector.

FREQUENTLY ASKED QUESTION

Knowing What to Type for a Parameter

I understand the concept of parameters and values. But if I don't know what a parameter does—and frankly, the Parameters panel doesn't give me much in the way of clues. How do I know what to type for the parameter's value?

The parameters Flash lets you set in the Parameters and Component Inspector panels vary from, component to component. In some cases, you can figure out the value you're supposed to type by looking at the name of the parameter. For example, it doesn't take a rocket scientist to guess what you're supposed to type for the Window component's title parameter: the text you want Flash to display in the title bar of your Window.

But you can't always so easily decipher the values Flash expects for other parameters (or the values for the component bindings and schema you're introduced to on page 356—not by a long shot).

In the upper-right corner of the Component Inspector, there's a wizard icon.(It looks like a little magic wand.) The hope is that Adobe will eventually make wizards available for each component that comes with Flash. As this book goes to press, however, clicking the wizard icon has no effect (unless you count the pop-up message "No wizards for this component"). That's because only one wizard—the

Data Connection wizard—is available, and Macromedia designed it to help you specify only certain data bindings. (If you're interested, you can download this wizard: just go to *www.macromedia.com/devnet/flash/articles/datawizards.html*.)

Until that wonderful day when Flash comes with a full set of component wizards, you need to select Help → Flash Help and search on the name of the component you're customizing to get the skinny on parameters. When you do, you see a parameter list for the component you searched on, as well as descriptions of the kinds of values you need to type for each parameter.

Note: Unfortunately, if you're working with a third-party component you've found on the Internet and installed using the Macromedia Extension Manager (see the box on page 364), Flash Help doesn't help: You need to contact the component author and ask for documentation.

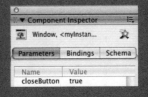

The Component Inspector appears. The panel has a Parameters tab, shown in Figure 12-24, where you can view and, if you want, change the component's parameters.

The parameters you see depend on the selected component. In the example of the Window component in Figure 12-24, the parameters you can set include *closeButton* (whether you want Flash to display a little X in the title bar that your audience can click to close the window), *contentPath* (the name of the image or animation file you want to load into the Window component), and *title* (the text you want to appear in the title of the window).

2. **If the Parameters tab isn't already selected, click to select it.**

   Flash displays all of the parameters you can change.

3. **Click anywhere on the name or value of the parameter you want to change.**

   Flash highlights the selected value.

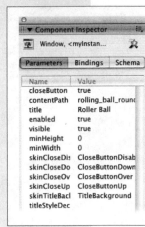

Figure 12-24:
The Component Inspector's Parameters tab (shown here) lets you inspect and modify all the parameters associated with a component (not just the most-often modified parameters shown in the Parameters tab of the Property Inspector, as Figure 12-22 shows). Clicking the Bindings and Schema tabs lets you change how your component transmits data to other programs and how Flash constrains your component's properties and parameters, respectively.

4. **Either type a new value for the parameter, or choose a value from the drop-down list Flash displays.**

   For example, if you click the value *true* next to the *closeButton* (see Figure 12-24), Flash displays a drop-down box from which you can choose either true or false.

   When you're done, or if you don't need to change any parameters, read on to work on the bindings.

Note: Because data bindings link specific component fields (such as the value of a TextInput component) to specific external-to-Flash programs (such as a ColdFusion script or Active Server Page running on a server), this book can't provide you with working examples. Instead, you see how to add and delete bindings in general using the Component Inspector. For help in binding your specific components to your specific server-side programs, start by searching Flash Help for data binding classes (see the Appendix for tips on accessing Flash Help). Then check out Macromedia's cache of data integration articles, which you can find online at the Flash Developer Center (*www.macromedia.com/devnet/flash/data_integration.html*).

Bindings tab

The Bindings tab of the Component Inspector *binds*, or maps, individual data fields of your component to individual data fields in a server-side program, such as a ColdFusion script or relational database.

Note: Before you can add a binding to your component, you need to know the inner workings of your server-side program. For example, you need to know which server-side data field you want to map your component data to and how you want to format your component data. (Typically, you know this information either because you've written the server-side program yourself, or because you've asked the IT folks who have.)

---

1. **In the Component Inspector, click the Bindings tab.**

   Flash displays the data bindings associated with the selected component.

2. **Click the Add button.**

   Flash displays the Add Binding dialog box (Figure 12-25, top).

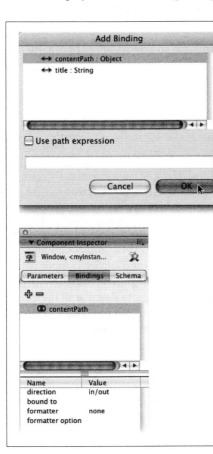

Figure 12-25:
In the Add Binding dialog box (top), you can add a data binding to more than one parameter, or data field, although you do need to add bindings one at a time. Selecting a data field and clicking OK displays your new binding in the Component Inspector window (bottom). Now you can build your binding with the newly activated binding parameters (direction, bound to, and so on).

3. **Click to select the field you want to bind.**

   Typically, you want to bind a component field to a field in a database or some other program running on a server.

4. **Click OK.**

   Flash redisplays the Component Inspector, showing your newly created binding (Figure 12-25, bottom).

5. **With your newly created binding still selected, click the name of the binding parameter you want to change.**

   Flash highlights the parameter's value.

6. **Either type a new value, or choose a value from the drop-down menu.**

For example, clicking the in/out value you find next to the *direction* parameter (Figure 12-25, bottom) displays a drop-down menu containing three choices: in, out, and in/out.

When you're done, you can click the Schema tab to add additional properties to your component, as discussed next.

Schema tab

The Schema tab lets you add additional properties (data fields) to a component, which you can then bind to a server-side program. Typically, you use this tab for one of two reasons:

- **You want to make an existing property bindable.** Adding the name of a component property that already exists to the Schema tab tells Flash to let you bind that property (see the "Bindings tab" section, above) to a server-side program.

- **You want to add a brand-new bindable property to a DataSet component.** Flash gives you several ways to transfer data between your animation and your server-side program, most of which involve using the DataSet component in conjunction with one or more of the other data integration components (see Table 12-1). Typically, you use the DataSet component to describe all the different fields you want to transfer. (For more information on the DataSet component, search Flash → Flash Help for "using the DataSet component.")

To add a bindable property to a component:

1. **In the Component Inspector, click the Schema tab.**

Flash displays the schema (the detailed description of each bindable property, including the name of the property, which type of data it can hold, and so on) for the selected component, as shown in Figure 12-26.

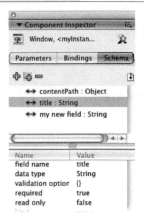

Figure 12-26:
You use the Schema tab both to add new bindable properties (fields) to a component and to describe or constrain existing bindable properties. Here are all the parameters for this instance of the Window component's title property, including the name of the property (title), the internal data type of the property (String), and so on. You can tell Flash to calculate the contents of the title property (kind), format the contents for display (formatter), or format the contents for transfer to an external-to-Flash program (encoder).

2. **If you like, you can add one or more bindable properties to the component. To add a property, click the Add button.**

   Flash displays a new property (field) called new field.

   You can customize the property you just added, or any of the existing ones, as described next.

Note: To delete a property, first select it; then click the Delete button (the one that looks like a – sign, as shown in Figure 12-26).

---

3. **Click to select the property you want to change.**

   In the bottom half of the Component Inspector, Flash displays the schema settings associated with that property.

4. **Click the name of the schema setting you want to change.**

   Flash highlights the schema setting's value.

   Either type a new value for the schema setting, or choose a value from the drop-down menu Flash displays. For example, clicking the {} value next to validation option (Figure 12-26) lets you type the minimum and maximum length of the string you want this field to contain.

Customizing Components Using the Actions Panel

To make a component do something useful—to make a Button component send Flash form data to a database running on a server after someone clicks it, for example, or to display a different Web page depending on the option someone chooses from a list—you have to write your own ActionScript code.

You also have to write your own ActionScript code if you want to make a change to the way a component looks, that you can't make using the Property Inspector or the Component Inspector, such as adding a skin to a component (see the box on page 344).

Note: In some cases, you need to use ActionScript to customize the way a component looks as well as how it behaves. For example, you can't change the appearance of the Menu component using the Property or Component Inspector; you need to use the Actions panel and ActionScript.

You use the Actions panel (Window → Actions) to write ActionScript code. But while the Actions panel offers assistance in the form of a clickable object model and code hints, the fact is that you need to know a good deal about ActionScript if you want to make a component do something useful.

Figure 12-27 shows you an example. Not only do you need to understand Action-Script language constructs (such as the *switch* and *function* statements and how to declare a variable); you also need to be familiar with the *eventInfo* object and understand the *listener event model* (the messages Flash sends out every time some-one clicks a button, chooses from a drop-down list, drags a window, or otherwise interacts with a component).

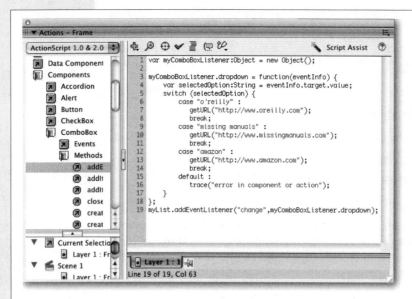

Figure 12-27:
Here's an example of a short action that connects a ComboBox component (page 346) to an ActionScript statement—getURL( )—whose purpose in life is to load a Web page. Choose O'reilly from the drop-down list, and Flash launches a Web browser preloaded with O'Reilly's home page; choose missing manuals, and the Missing Manual home page loads; and so on. There's no getting around it: If you want to use components, you need to know ActionScript.

If you're serious about learning ActionScript, the first thing to do is explore the examples and language reference in Flash Help. Then check out Help → Flash Developer Center and invest in a good book on the topic, such as Joey Lott's *ActionScript Cookbook* (O'Reilly).

Note: You'll find ActionScript examples in Chapters 10 and 11. Chapter 11 also has examples of using the ActionScript wizards Flash calls *behaviors*.

Finding Additional Components

In addition to the components that ship with Flash Professional 8 and Flash Basic 8, you can also find components on the Web (try searching the Web for "Flash components" using *www.google.com* or your favorite search engine).

Below are a few of the most popular sources for Flash components as this book goes to press:

- **Flash Exchange.** Adobe hosts a Web site called Flash Exchange (see Figure 12-28). Adobe itself doesn't create the components on the Flash Exchange; instead, regular folks and third-party software companies submit the components and the site categorizes and rates them. To visit the Flash Exchange, select Help → Flash Exchange.

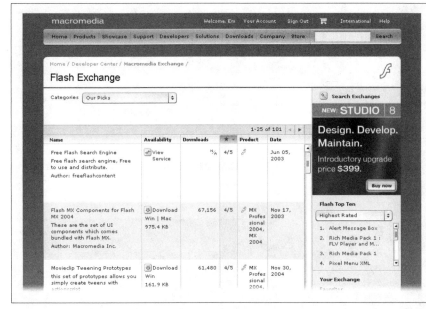

Figure 12-28:
The Flash Exchange Web site (which you can surf to by selecting Help → Flash Exchange) lists hundreds of components in nearly a dozen different categories, from Navigation to Commerce and Accessibility. Some you pay for; others you can download for free. Use the component specifications, number of downloads, and rating associated with each component to help you decide which ones to try.

- **The Flash components network** (*www.flashcomponents.net*). Similar to Macromedia's Flash Exchange, this site lists and rates Flash components submitted by a variety of Flash enthusiasts and software companies.

- **ActionScript.org** (*www.actionscript.org/components*). This everything-Flash site lists dozens of freely downloadable components.

Note: Because anyone with time, inclination, and ActionScript experience can create a Flash component, Flash enthusiasts (as opposed to established software companies) create most of the Flash components on the Web. Many of the components are free, too. But there's a downside: Components don't always come with the documentation you need to customize them, and they virtually never come with a guarantee—either that they'll work as promised, or that they don't harbor viruses that can damage your machine. Don't be afraid to try out useful components, but do exercise the same care and caution you use when you download and install any other software program.

UP TO SPEED

Installing Third-Party Components

After you find and download a component (page 362 lists several online component resources), you need to install the component so that you can use it in Flash. You do this installing with the Macromedia Extension Manager:

1. Select Help → Manage Extensions. The Macromedia Extension Manager window appears.

2. Click the Install icon.

3. In the Install Extension window that appears, type (or surf to) the name of the component file you want to install, and then click Install (Windows) or Open (Mac). Component file names all have .mxp extensions. Flash installs the component and updates the Macromedia Extension Manager window.

Close Flash (File → Exit), and then launch it again. The newly installed component appears in the Components panel.

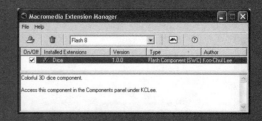

Part Four: Delivering Your Animation to Its Audience

4

Testing and Debugging

Testing your animation is a lot like filing your income taxes. Both can be tedious, time-consuming, and frustrating—but they've got to be done. Even if your animation is short, straightforward, and you've whipped out 700 exactly like it over the past 2 years, you still need to test it before you release it into the world. Why? Murphy's Law: Anything that *can* go wrong *will* go wrong. Choosing a motion tween when you meant to choose a shape tween, adding content to a frame instead of a keyframe, tying actions to the wrong frame or object, and mistyping an Action-Script keyword are just a few of the ways a slip of your fingers can translate into a broken animation. And it's far better that you find out about these problems *before* your audience sees your handiwork rather than after.

Throughout this book, you've seen examples of testing an animation using the Control → Test Movie option (for example, Figure 3-5). This chapter expands on that simple test option, plus it shows you how to test animation playback at a variety of connection speeds. And if you've added ActionScript actions or behaviors to your animation, this chapter shows you how to unsnarl uncooperative Action-Script code using Flash's debugging tools.

Testing Strategies

All your audience ever sees is the finished product, not your intentions. So no matter how sophisticated your animation or how cleverly constructed your Action-Script code, if you don't test your animation and make sure it works the way you want it to, all your hard work will have been in vain.

The following section shows you how to prepare for testing from the very beginning by following good Flash development policies. Also, you find out the differences between testing on the Stage and testing in Flash Player, along with tips for testing your animation in a Web browser.

Planning Ahead

The more complex your animation, the more you need a thorough plan for testing it. Few of the guidelines in the next two sections are specific to testing in Flash. Instead, they're tried-and-true suggestions culled from all walks of programming life. Following them pays off in higher-quality animations and reduced time spent chasing bugs.

Ideally, you should begin thinking about testing before you've created a single frame of your animation. Here are some preanimation strategies that pay off big:

Separate potentially troublesome elements

ActionScript actions are very powerful, but they can also cause a lot of grief. Get into the habit of putting them into a separate layer named actions, either at the top of your list of layers or at the bottom, so that you'll always know where to find it. Putting all your sounds into a separate layer (named sounds) is a good idea, too.

Reuse as much as possible

Instead of cutting and pasting an image or a series of frames, create a graphic symbol and reuse it. That way, if a bug raises its ugly head, you'll have fewer places to go hunting. You can cut down on bugs by reusing ActionScript code, too. Instead of attaching four similar ActionScript actions to four different frames or buttons, create a single ActionScript function and call it four times.

Be generous with comments

Before you know it, you'll forget which layers contain which images, why you added certain actions to certain objects, or even why you ordered your Action-Script statements the way you did. In addition to adding descriptive comments to all of the actions you create (there's an example at the end of this chapter, in Figure 13-19), get in the habit of adding an overall comment to the first frame of your animation. Make it as long as you want and be sure to mention your name, the date, and anything else pertinent you can think of. You create a comment in ActionScript two different ways, as shown below.

```
// This is an example of a single-line ActionScript comment.

/* This type of ActionScript comment can span more than one line. All you
have to remember is to begin your multi-line comment with a slash-asterisk
and end it with an asterisk-slash, as you see here. */
```

Stick with consistent names

Referring to a background image in one animation as "bg," in another animation as "back_ground," and in still another as "Background" is just asking for trouble. Even if you don't have trouble remembering which is which, odds are your office teammates will—and referring to an incorrectly spelled variable in ActionScript causes your animation to misbehave quietly. In other words, type *Backgruond* instead of *Background*, and Flash doesn't pop up an error message; your animation just looks or acts odd for no apparent reason. Devise a naming convention you're comfortable with and stick with it. For example, you might decide always to use uppercase, lowercase, or mixed case. You might decide always to spell words out, or always to abbreviate them the same way. The particulars don't matter so much as your consistency in applying them.

Note: Capitalization counts. Because Flash is case-sensitive, it treats background, Background, and BACK-GROUND as three different names.

Techniques for Better Testing

The following strategies are crucial if you're creating complex animations as part of a development team. But they're also helpful if it's just you creating a short, simple animation by your lonesome.

- **Test early, test often.** Don't wait until you've attached actions to 16 different objects to begin testing. Test the first action, and then test each additional action as you go along. This iterative approach helps you identify problems while they're still small and manageable.

- **Test everything.** Instead of assuming the best-case scenario, see what happens when you access your animation over a slow connection or using an older version of Flash Player. What happens when you type the wrong kind of data into an input text field or click buttons in the wrong order? (Believe this: Your audience will do all of these things, and more.)

- **Test blind.** In other words, let someone who's unfamiliar with how your animation's supposed to work test it. In programming circles, this type of testing is known as *usability testing*, and it can flush out problems you never dreamed existed.

- **Test in "real world" mode.** Begin your testing in the Flash authoring environment, as you see on page 370, but don't end there. Always test your animation in a production environment before you go live. For example, if you're planning to publish your animation to a Web site, upload your files (including your .swf file and any external files your animation depends on) to a Web server and test it there, using a computer running the operating system, connection speed, browser, and Flash Player plug-in version you expect your audience to be running. (Sure, transferring a few files isn't *supposed* to make a difference—but it often does.) Chapter 14 covers publishing to the Web, as well as other publishing options.

Testing on the Stage vs. Testing in Flash Player

Flash gives you two options for testing your animation: on the Stage and in the built-in Flash Player. Testing on the Stage is faster, and it's good for checking your work as you go along, but in order to try out your animation exactly as your audience will see it, you must eventually fire it up in Flash Player. Here's some more advice on when to choose each:

- **Testing on Stage** is the quick and easy option, using the Controller toolbar and the associated menu options (Control → Play, Control → Stop, Control → Rewind, Control → Step Forward One Frame, Control → Step Backward One Frame, and Control → Go to End). Testing on the Stage is quicker than testing in Flash Player, because you don't have to wait for Flash to compile (*export*) your Flash document and then load it into the Player. Instead, when you test on the Stage, Flash immediately resets the playhead and moves it along the Timeline frame by frame. For simple animations, testing on the Stage can be easier as well as quicker than testing in Flash Player because you can position the Controller toolbar on your workspace where it's handy—no need to wait for Flash Player's menu options to appear.

The downside to testing on the Stage is that it doesn't always test what you think it's testing. For example, if you test a frame containing a movie clip instance, you don't see the movie clip playing; you have to switch to symbol editing mode and test the symbol there to see the movie clip in action. And if your animation contains a button instance and you forget to turn on the checkbox next to Control → Enable Simple Buttons, the button doesn't work on the Stage—even though it may work perfectly well when you test it in Flash Player.

- **Testing in the built-in Flash Player (Control → Test Movie and Control → Test Scene)** is the more accurate option. When you test an animation by selecting Control → Test Movie or Control → Test Scene, Flash generates a .swf file. For example, if you're testing a Flash document named myDocument.fla, Flash generates a file called myDocument.swf (or myDocument_myScene.swf, if you're testing a scene) and automatically loads that .swf file into Flash Player (test window) that's part and parcel of the Flash development environment. This testing option shows you exactly what your audience will see, not counting computer hardware and connection differences (page 294).

Testing on the Stage

If all you want to do is check out a few simple frames' worth of action, this is the option to use. It's also the best choice if you want to see your motion path or *not* see the layers you've marked as hidden. (For the skinny on hiding and showing layers, check out page 120.)

To test your animation on the Stage:

1. **Select Window → Toolbars → Controller.**

   The Controller toolbar you see in Figure 13-1 appears.

2. **Turn on the checkbox next to one or more of the following options:**

   Control → Loop Playback. Tells Flash to loop playback over and over again after you click Play on the Controller. Flash keeps looping your animation until

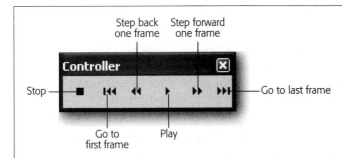

Step back one frame Step forward one frame

Controller ☒

Stop

Go to last frame

Go to first frame Play

Figure 13-1:
You can reposition the Controller by dragging it to wherever it's most convenient for you. Or, if you prefer, you can skip the Controller altogether and use the button-equivalent menu options: Control → Stop, Control → Rewind, Control → Step Forward One Frame, Control → Play, Control → Step Backward One Frame, and Control → Go to End.

you click Stop. If you don't turn on this option, Flash just plays the animation once.

Control → Play All Scenes. Tells Flash to play all the scenes in your animation, not just the scene currently visible on the Stage.

Control → Enable Simple Frame Actions. Tells Flash to play the actions you've added to frames on the Timeline. If you don't turn on this option, Flash ignores all frame actions.

Control → Enable Simple Buttons. Tells Flash to make your buttons work on the Stage. (If you don't turn on the checkbox next to this option, neither mousing over a button nor clicking it on the Stage has any effect.)

Control → Enable Live Preview. Tells Flash to display any components you've added to the Stage the way they'll appear in Flash Player. (The components don't work on the Stage, but you see how they're supposed to look.) If you have components on the Stage and you don't choose this option, only the outlines of your components appear.

Control → Mute Sounds. Tells Flash not to play any of the sound clips you've added to your animation.

3. **Make sure that what you want to test is at least partially visible on the Timeline.**

    If you want to test a particular scene, for example, click the Edit Symbols icon in the Edit bar and then choose a scene to display the Timeline for that scene. If you want to test a movie clip symbol, select Edit → Symbols to display the Timeline for that movie clip.

4. **In the Controller toolbar, click Play to begin testing. Your other options include:**

    Stop. Clicking this square icon stops playback.

    Go to first frame. Clicking this icon rewinds your animation. That is, it moves the playhead back to Frame 1.

Step back one frame. Clicking this double-left-arrow icon moves the playhead back one frame. If the playhead is already at Frame 1, this button has no effect.

Play. Clicking this right-arrow toggle button alternately runs your animation on the Stage, and stops it. Playback begins at the playhead. In other words, playback begins with the frame you selected in the Timeline and runs either until the end of your animation, or until you press the Stop button.

Step forward one frame. Clicking this double-right-arrow icon moves the playhead forward one frame (unless the playhead is already at the last frame, in which case clicking this icon has no effect).

Go to last frame. Clicking this icon fast-forwards your animation to the very end. That is, it sets the playhead to the last frame in your animation.

Note: You can also drag the playhead back and forth along the Timeline to test your animation on the Stage (a technique called *scrubbing*).

Flash plays your animation on the Stage based on the options you chose in step 2.

Testing in Flash Player

Flash 8's Test mode shows you a closer approximation of how your animation will actually appear to your audience than testing on the Stage. When you fire up the Test Movie command, your animation plays in the Flash Player that comes with Flash 8. Test mode is your best bet if your animation contains movie clips, buttons, scenes, hidden layers, or actions, since it shows you *all* the parts of your animation—not just the parts currently visible on the Stage.

Note: Motion paths don't appear when you test your animation in Flash Player, for good reason: Flash designed them to be invisible at runtime. If you want to see your motion paths in action, you need to test your animation on the Stage.

To test your animation in Flash Player:

1. **Select Control → Test Movie.**

   The export dialog box in Figure 13-2 appears, followed by your animation running in Flash Player (test window) similar to the one in Figure 13-3.

Figure 13-2:
When you see this dialog box, you know Flash is exporting your animation and creating an .swf file. If you've tested this particular animation before, Flash erases the .swf file it previously created and replaces it with the new one. Finishing an export can be fast or slow depending on the size and complexity of your animation and your computer's processing speed and memory.

2. **To control playback—to stop the animation and then rewind it, for example—
choose options from the Control menu.**

In you're running Windows, the Control menu appears in Flash Player; on a
Mac, you get the Control menu in Flash 8 itself. (In Windows you can also see
the Control menu in Flash itself if you turn on tabbed viewing in Preferences.
See the box on page 374 for details.)

3. **To close Flash Player, select File → Close or click the X in the upper-right
(Windows) or upper-left (Mac) corner of the window.**

Note: The Flash Player's View options are described in the box on page 382; Figure 13-13 acquaints you
with Flash Player's Debug menu options.

Figure 13-3:
*Normally, when you select Control → Test Movie or
Control → Test Scene, Flash opens up Flash Player in
its own window. To control playback, you have a
couple of choices: You can choose options from the
File, View, Control, and Debug menus, or you can right-
click in the window if you're running Windows
(Control-click if you're running Mac) and choose
options from the context menus that appear.*

Note: Testing your animation in Flash Player gives you a great sense of what your audience will see. But
factors such as connection speed and hardware differences come into play when you actually publish your
animation, so you'll want to test your animation in a real-life production setting (using the same kind of
computer, same connection speed, and same version browser as you expect your audience to use) before
you go live (see page 369).

Testing Inside a Web Page

In addition to letting you test your animation in Flash Player, Flash lets you test
your animation embedded in a Web page. This option lets you see how your animation looks in a Web browser based on the animation alignment, scale, and size
options Flash lets you set.

Testing Multiple Animations

Some folks find a tabbed page—like the tabs in some Web browsers—easier to pop back to, especially if they're trying to test several different animations at once. If you'd rather Flash Player appear in a tabbed page, select Edit → Preferences (Windows) or Flash → Preferences (Mac).

In the Preferences window that appears, click the General category. Turn on the checkbox next to "Open test movie in tabs." Then, exit and relaunch Flash, reopen your document, and then choose Control → Test Movie. This time, Flash Player appears as a tab. When you click the tab, the Flash developer menu options change to the Flash Player options.

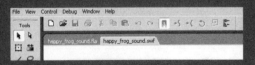

Here's how it works. You tell Flash in the Formats tab of the Publish Settings window (Figure 13-4, left) that you want to embed your animation in a Web page. Then, in the HTML tab, you tell Flash how you want your animation to appear in the Web page (Figure 13-4, right). When you choose File → Publish Preview, Flash constructs an HTML file containing your animation, and then loads it automatically into the Web browser on your computer.

Note: Tucking your animation into a Web page is the most popular publishing option, but it's not the only one Flash offers. You get acquainted with the other publishing options, including publishing your animation as a QuickTime movie and a standalone Flash projector file, in Chapter 14.

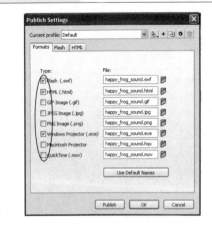
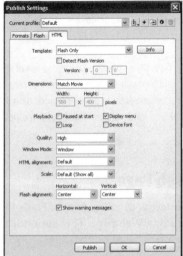

Figure 13-4:
Left: Flash offers several publishing options, one of which is embedding your animation into an HTML file.

Right: Flash constructs an animation-containing HTML file based on the options you choose in this tab. The name Flash uses for your HTML file is the name of your Flash document, but with an .html extension.

To test your animation inside a Web page:

1. **Choose File → Publish Settings.**

   The Publish Settings dialog box in Figure 13-4 (left) appears.

2. **Make sure the "HTML (.html)" checkbox is turned on, then click the HTML
   tab.**

   Flash displays the contents of the HTML tab shown in Figure 13-4 (right).

3. **Click the arrow next to Template, and then, from the drop-down box that
   appears, choose "Flash only."**

4. **Click OK.**

5. **Flash accepts your changes and closes the Publish Settings dialog box.**

Note: For a description of each of the settings on this tab, see page 405.

---

6. **Choose File → Publish Preview.**

7. **The Publishing dialog box in Figure 13-5 (left) appears briefly to let you know
   Flash is creating an HTML file. When the dialog box disappears, Flash loads
   the completed HTML, including your embedded animation, into the Web
   browser on your computer (Figure 13-5, right).**

   Right-clicking (Windows) or Control-clicking (Mac) the running animation
   shows you standard menu options you can use to control playback inside the
   browser, although how many options you see depends on whether you turned
   off the checkbox next to "Display menu" in the Publish Settings dialog box.

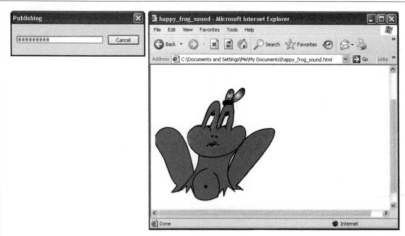

Figure 13-5:
*Left: When you see this
dialog box, you know
Flash is busy creating an
HTML file based on the
options you set in the
Publish Settings dialog
box.*

*Right: In addition to
creating an HTML file,
choosing File Publish
Preview launches your
Web browser preloaded
with that file.*

Testing Download Time

If you're planning to publish your animation on the Web, you need to know about how long it takes your animation to download from a Web server to somebody's computer. Chapter 14 gives you several optimization techniques, including tips for preloading content and reducing your animation's file size; but before you begin to optimize your animation, you need to know just how bad the situation is and where the bottlenecks are. The following sections show you how.

Simulating Downloads

You *could* set up a bank of test machines, each connected to the Internet at a different transfer speed, to determine the average download time your audience will eventually have to sit through. But Flash gives you an easier option: simulating downloads at a variety of transfer speeds with the click of a button. The simulation takes into consideration any additional, non-Flash media files that you've included in your animation, such as sound and video clips.

To simulate different download speeds:

1. **Choose Control → Test Movie.**

   The Flash Player (test window) appears.

2. **In the test window, select View → Download Settings (Figure 13-6) and then, from the submenu, select the connection speed you expect your audience to be running.**

   Your choices range from 14.4 (1.2 kbps) to T1 speed (131.2 kbps). If you need to simulate a faster speed, check out Figure 13-7.

Note: Unless you're planning to allow only certain folks to view your animation (for example, students in your company's training classes), you can't possibly know for sure what connection rates your audience will be using. The best approach is to test a likely range. If the animation plays excruciatingly slowly at the lowest connection speed in your test range, consider either optimizing or offering a low-bandwidth version. Chapter 14 (page 395), tells you how.

---

3. **Choose View → Simulate Download.**

   The test window clears, and Flash plays your animation at the rate it would play it if it had to download your file from a Web server at the connection speed you chose in step 3.

4. **Repeat steps 3 and 4 for each connection speed you want to test.**

If you're like most folks, you'll find that your animation takes too long to play at one—or even all—of the simulated connection speeds you test. Fortunately, Flash gives you additional tools to help you pinpoint which frames take longest to download (so that you know which frames to optimize). Read on for details.

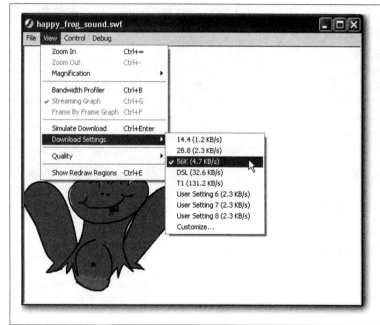

Figure 13-6:
If you're used to testing your animation inside the Flash development environment, you'll be shocked when you see how long it takes to download and play your animation over the Web. Flash automatically adjusts for standard line congestion to give you a more realistic picture. So, for example, when you choose the 14.4 kbps setting, Flash actually simulates the transfer at the slightly lower rate of 12.0 kbps.

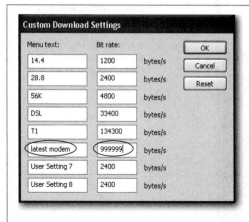

Figure 13-7:
To keep up with the latest advances in transfer technology, you can select a faster transfer rate than any of the options Flash offers. To do so, select View → Download Settings → Customize and type a label and the new transfer speed you want to test (from 1 byte per second to 100,000,00).

Pinpointing bottlenecks with a bandwidth profiler report

Simulating downloads at different connection speeds gives you a general, overall feel for whether or not you'll need to optimize your animation or offer your audience a low-bandwidth alternative (or both). But to get more precise information, such as which frames represent the greatest bottlenecks, you need to run a *bandwidth profiler report* (Figure 13-8).

The report gives you information you can use to figure out which frames of your animation are hogging all the bandwidth. There are a Timeline and a playhead at

Size Reports

Flash offers a second statistical report called a *size report*. This report is much less useful than the bandwidth profiler report in terms of testing, because all it describes is how much of your .fla file is devoted to each frame, scene, and so forth—and typically, it's the .swf file you're interested in, because that's the file that your audience downloads. But you *may* find the size report useful if you want to print out a record of all the ActionScript actions, scenes, symbols and fonts you've included in your animation.

To create a size report, choose File → Publish Settings → Flash, and then turn on the checkbox next to "Generate size report." Make sure you can see the Output window (Window → Output). Then, when you choose File → Publish, Flash displays the size report in the Output window. It also automatically generates a text file named yourFlashFile Report.txt that you can pull into a text editor or word processor.

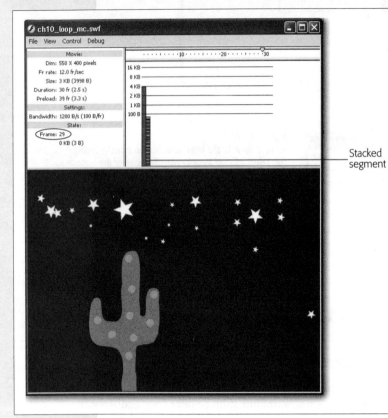

Figure 13-8:
Flash assumes you want it to display your bandwidth reports in Streaming Graph format, as shown here, unless you tell it otherwise. Unfortunately, analyzing the graph on this kind of report can be tricky; to match a stacked segment to a particular frame, you have to click the stacked segment. When you do, Flash displays the associated frame in the Frame field on the left side of the report.

Stacked segment

the top of the report. As your animation plays, the playhead moves along the Timeline to help you see at a glance which frames are causing Flash to display those tall bandwidth-hogging frame bars. *Preload*, the most useful number, tells you how long your audience will have to sit and wait before your animation begins playing. Additional download details in the bandwidth profiler report include:

- **Dimensions.** The width and height of the Stage in pixels (page 37).

- **Frame rate.** The frame rate you set for this animation (page 295).

- **Size.** The size of the .swf file Flash created when you exported (began testing) the movie.

- **Duration.** The number of frames in this animation, followed by the number of seconds the frames take to play based on the frame rate you set.

- **Preload.** The total number of seconds it takes Flash to begin playing the animation at the bandwidth setting you chose (see page 403).

- **Bandwidth.** The connection simulation speed you chose by selecting View → Download Settings.

- **Frame.** The frame Flash is currently loading.

- **KB.** The percentage of the total file (and number of frames) Flash has currently loaded.

- **Loaded.** The number of kilobytes Flash has currently loaded.

To generate a bandwidth profiler report:

1. **Choose Control → Test Movie.**

   The Flash Player (test window) appears containing your running animation.

2. **In the test window, select View → Bandwidth Profiler.**

   In the top half of the window, Flash displays a report similar to the one in Figure 13-8.

3. **Select View → Frame By Frame Graph.**

   The graph Flash displays when you choose the Frame By Frame option makes detecting rogue frames much easier than if you stick with Flash's suggested View → Streaming Graph option shown in Figure 13-8. Figure 13-9 has an example of a Frame By Frame graph.

4. **Select View → Simulate Download.**

   The progress bar at the top of the bandwidth profiler report moves as Flash simulates a download.

If your animation played just fine, try testing it using a slower simulated connection. (Your goal is to make sure as much of your potential audience can enjoy your animation as possible—even folks running over slow connections and congested networks.) To do this test, redisplay the bandwidth profiler report, this time using a different connection simulation speed, as described next.

1. **Choose View → Download Settings.**

   A submenu menu appears, showing a list of possible connection simulation speeds, such as 28.8, 56K, and T1.

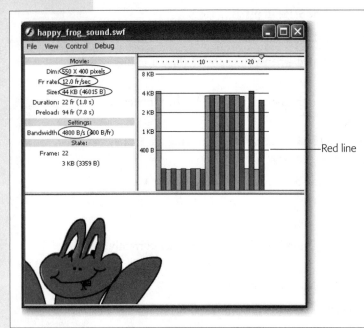

Figure 13-9:
On the left side of this Frame By Frame bandwidth profiler report, you see animation properties pertinent to playback, including the .swf file size and the Stage dimensions and frame rate you set in Flash. The right side of the report shows you a frame-by-frame picture of the download process. Frame bars that appear above the red line (here, Flash has drawn the red line at 400B) mean a wait for data. So Frame 1, along with most of the frames between Frame 10 and Frame 22, are the culprits in this slow-playing animation; at a connection speed of 56 kbps, they make Flash pause the animation while they're being downloaded.

2. **Choose the new simulation speed you want to test. Then choose View → Simulate Download again.**

   A new bandwidth profiler report appears, based on the new connection speed (Figure 13-10).

The Art of Debugging

Imagine, for an instant, that your animation isn't behaving the way you think it should. Testing it on the Stage or in Flash Player and then eyeballing the results, as described in the previous section, is a good place to start tracking down the problem.

But if you've added ActionScript to your animation, chances are you need more firepower. You need to be able to step through your animation frame by frame and examine the inner workings of your ActionScript code—the variables, instance names, function calls, and so on—to help you figure out what's wrong.

You need the Flash debugger, shown in Figure 13-11. Unfortunately, unless you're familiar with ActionScript, much of the information the debugger displays isn't helpful. But even if you're new to ActionScript, the debugging tools you see in this section will give your bug-fixing skills a boost.

Because the Flash debugger shows you a combination of ActionScript code and the Flash object model, its usefulness in debugging your animations is directly proportional to your knowledge of these two things.

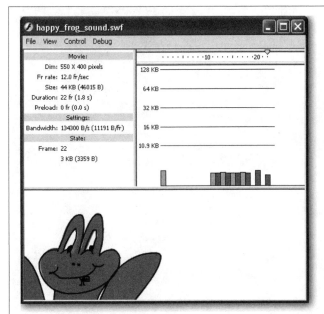

Figure 13-10:
Oh, what a difference a faster connection speed makes! Here, every last one of the frames in the animation appears below the red line that Flash has drawn at 10.9 KB, meaning that audiences running T1 connections don't have to wait one split second for the animation to download and begin playing.

For example, if you have no idea how function calls work or what parameters a specific ActionScript function call requires, seeing the function call displayed in the debugger isn't going to help you figure out what—if anything—is wrong with the call. It's the same with the objects you add to your animations (Figure 13-12, middle) and the object properties and methods that Flash creates for you each time you add an object (Figure 13-12, bottom).

Luckily, some of Flash's debugging tools are more accessible than others. The next three sections cover different debugging strategies, all of which are both simple to use and most helpful in tracking down problems.

Note: Flash lets you debug your animations remotely after you've uploaded them to a Web server. This book doesn't cover remote debugging, but you can find out more about it in Flash's help files.

Using the trace() Statement

The ActionScript *trace( )* statement isn't the only way to debug your ActionScript code, but it's by far the easiest—and it delivers the biggest bang for your debugging buck, too. The *trace( )* statement is the hammer in your Flash debugging toolkit: straightforward, dependable, and useful in so many different types of situations that even ActionScript pros routinely use it to figure out why their code isn't working properly.

Here's how it works. You add a *trace( )* statement to the action you suspect may be causing a problem. Then, when you test your animation, Flash prints out the contents of that statement in the Output window so you can examine them. This section explains the process step by step.

The Flash Player View Menu Options

Flash Player offers several menu options you can use to change the way your animation appears as it's playing. If you turned on the checkbox next to *Display menu* in the Publish Settings dialog box (Figure 14-1), your audience can see some of these same options, by right-clicking (Windows) or Control-clicking (Mac).

Note: If you're running a Mac, the following menu options don't appear directly in Flash Player; instead, they appear in the Flash menu.

- **View → Zoom In.** Tells Flash to enlarge your animation. This option's useful if you want to examine your artwork close-up.

- **View → Zoom Out.** Tells Flash to shrink your animation.

- **View → Magnification.** Displays a menu of percentage options you can choose from to tell Flash to enlarge or shrink your animation.

- **View → Bandwidth Profiler.** Creates a bandwidth profiler report (page 377).

- **View → Streaming Graph.** Tells Flash to display download data in stacked bars when it creates a bandwidth profiler report (Figure 13-8).

- **View → Frame By Frame Graph.** Tells Flash to display the download time for each frame separately when it creates a bandwidth profiler report (Figure 13-9).

- **View → Simulate Download.** Tells Flash to pretend to download your animation from a Web server based on the download settings you select using View → Download Settings.

- **View → Download Settings.** Displays a list of connection speeds, from 14.4 to T1, to test the download speed of your animation on a variety of different computers.

- **View → Quality.** Tells Flash to display your animation's artwork in one of three different quality modes: low, medium, or high. Flash assumes you want high quality unless you tell it differently. (Choosing low or medium quality doesn't reduce simulation download time, but reducing image quality in the Flash authoring environment *does* reduce your animation's file size, which in turn speeds up download time.)

- **View → Show Redraw Regions.** Displays borders around the moving images in your animation.

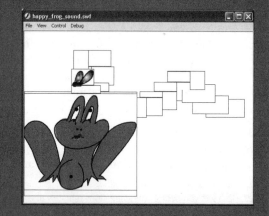

To add a *trace( )* statement to an action:

1. **Open the file reverse_debug.fla.**

   If you're playing along at home, you can download this animation from the "Missing CD" page at *www.missingmanuals.com/cds.*

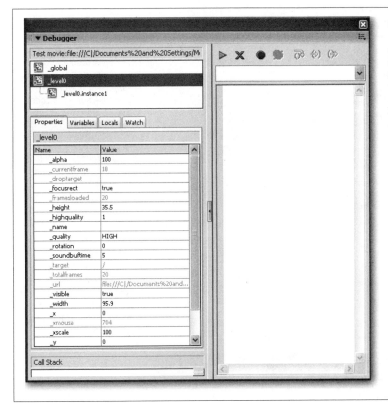

Figure 13-11:
The Debugger shows you what Flash is thinking behind the scenes. This panel shows the instance names, property values, variable names and values, and other ActionScript keywords and statements that either you (or Flash) added to your animation.

When you open the file, you see a one-frame Timeline and an instance of a movie clip (Figure 13-13).

2. **On the Stage, click the instance to select it.**

3. **Select Window → Actions.**

   The Actions window appears, containing the two separate actions in Figure 13-13.

4. **Select Window → Library.**

   The Library panel appears, containing a single movie clip symbol named *rollerball.*

   Time to test the clip, so you can start tracking down the problem, as described next.

5. **In the Library panel, click rollerball. Then, in the same panel's preview pane, click the Play button.**

   In the preview pane, the ball rolls from left to right, and the word "Flash!" grows from small to large.

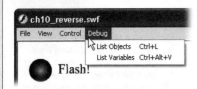

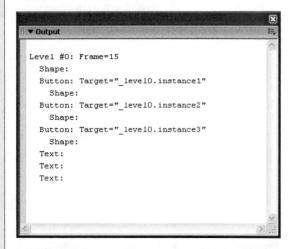

Figure 13-12:
Top: Even the basic debug menu options that appear in Flash Player produce output that's pretty much incomprehensible unless you're an ActionScript code jockey.

Middle: For example, here's what choosing Debug → List Objects dumps to the Output window for one animation. You can tell Frame 15 contains three instances of a button symbol and three chunks of text, but not much else.

Bottom: For the same animation, selecting Debug → List Variables creates this report. Page 381 shows you how to create a friendlier report using the ActionScript trace( ) statement.

```
Level #0:
Variable _level0.$version = "WIN 8,0,22,0"
Button: Target="_level0.instance1"
Variable _level0.instance1.scale9Grid = [getter/setter] undefined
Variable _level0.instance1.filters = [getter/setter] [object #1, class
 'Array'] []
Variable _level0.instance1.cacheAsBitmap = [getter/setter] false
Variable _level0.instance1.blendMode = [getter/setter] "normal"
Variable _level0.instance1.tabIndex = [getter/setter] undefined
Button: Target="_level0.instance2"
Variable _level0.instance2.scale9Grid = [getter/setter] undefined
Variable _level0.instance2.filters = [getter/setter] [object #2, class
 'Array'] []
Variable _level0.instance2.cacheAsBitmap = [getter/setter] false
Variable _level0.instance2.blendMode = [getter/setter] "normal"
Variable _level0.instance2.tabIndex = [getter/setter] undefined
Button: Target="_level0.instance3"
Variable _level0.instance3.scale9Grid = [getter/setter] undefined
Variable _level0.instance3.filters = [getter/setter] [object #3, class
 'Array'] []
Variable _level0.instance3.cacheAsBitmap = [getter/setter] false
Variable _level0.instance3.blendMode = [getter/setter] "normal"
Variable _level0.instance3.tabIndex = [getter/setter] undefined
```

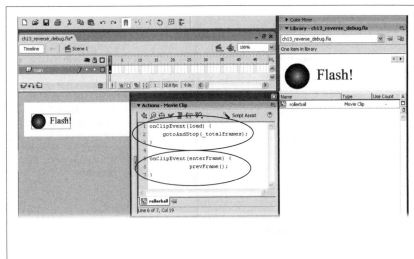

Figure 13-13:
Here are two actions attached to an instance of the rollerball movie clip. The first action tells Flash to go immediately to the last frame of the move clip. The second action tells Flash to back up one frame the instant it enters a frame. So when the playhead enters the last frame, as instructed, Flash immediately plays the previous frame, then the frame before that, then the frame before that, and so on.

6. **Test the animation by choosing Control → Test Movie.**

In the Flash Player that appears, the movie clip appears to run backwards: The ball rolls from right to left, and the word "Flash!" shrinks. The animation doesn't repeat: one time through, and it stops. This is exactly the result the ActionScript code was designed to produce, so at first blush, everything seems A-OK. But if you leave the Flash Player up and continue working in Flash for any length of time, Flash begins to respond sluggishly. (*Very* sluggishly after a couple minutes.)

7. **In the Flash Player, choose File → Close.**

The Flash Player disappears. Since you can't yet be sure which script action's causing the problem, add the *trace( )* statement to both of them:

8. **In the Actions panel, click in the Script pane and type the following Action-Script addition to the first action:**

   ```
   trace("last frame of clip is " + _totalframes);
   ```

9. **Using the same procedure, add the following addition to the second action:**

   ```
   trace("currFrame is " + _currentframe);
   ```

The text phrases "frames total in this clip" and "currFrame is " aren't strictly necessary, but they do add a welcome human touch: These snippets of text make the trace output much more readable. Figure 13-14 shows what your Actions panel should look like.

10. **Test the animation again by selecting Control → Test Movie.**

Flash Player appears, once again showing the movie clip running backwards. But another window—the Output window—also appears. As Figure 13-15

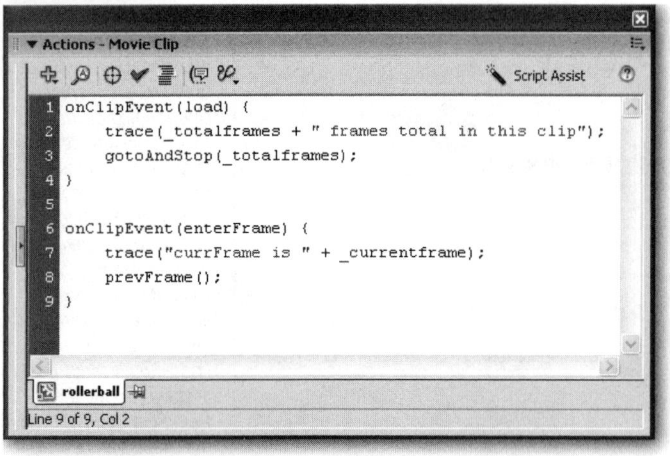

Figure 13-14:
The trace( ) statement displays the contents of a single parameter. (A parameter can include both text and variable names, as long as you remember to include a + sign to string them all together as shown here.) In this example, the ActionScript code references both the _totalframes and _currentframe variables, so it's important to see what Flash thinks the contents of these variables are as the animation runs its course.

shows, the Output window displays the contents of the *trace( )* statements you added to your actions. Your job as debugger-in-chief is to watch for the results of the trace statements in this window and see what they reveal about how the animation is working (or not working).

Tip: If you don't see your trace statement in the Output window, select File → Publish Settings → Flash, and make sure the checkbox next to "Omit trace actions" is turned off.

As Figure 13-15 explains, Flash appears to be trying to back up one frame even after it's reached the first frame of the movie clip. So, one possible bug fix is to check whether or not Flash has reached the first frame, and if it has, to tell it to stop trying to back up.

Note: In programming circles, this kind of never-ending behavior is called an *endless loop*. Endless loops are pretty serious bugs, because they chew up computer resources in the background without contributing anything useful.

Flash guru that you are, you'll make a slight adjustment to the second action based on the results shown in the Output window (and in Figure 13-15). Now that you have a plan in mind, close Flash Player (File → Close), and go on to the next step.

11. **To try out the possible fix, click the Action panel's Script pane and type the following (bolded) ActionScript code, adding it to the existing second action:**

```
if (_currentframe > 1) {
    trace("currFrame is " + _currentframe);
        prevFrame();
}
```

The contents of your Actions panel should look similar to the one in Figure 13-16.

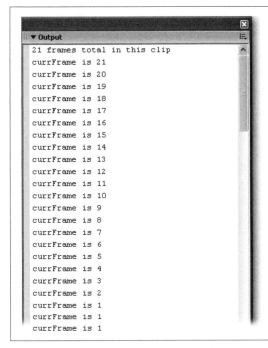

Figure 13-15:
As the animation runs, Flash obediently displays the contents of the trace( ) statements it encounters. Flash detected 21 frames in the movie clip (in other words, the value of the _totalframes property is 21). Then, as expected, Flash immediately printed out the contents of the second trace( ) statement, at which point the value of _currentframe was 21. Then Flash backed up one frame. As it entered the previous frame, it encountered the second trace( ) statement once again, so once again it printed the value of the _currentframe variable (this time, the value was 20). Flash backed up again. This time, the value of _currentframe was 19. And so on. So far, so good—until the value of _currentframe hit 1. As you can see by the Output window's scrollbar, after Flash had backed up all the way to the first frame it got stuck, encountering that second trace( ) statement over and over and over again.

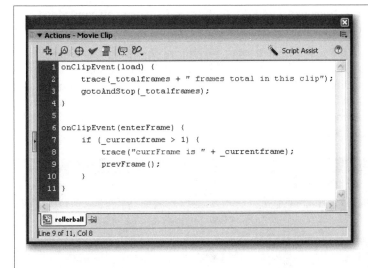

Figure 13-16:
The great thing about using trace( ) statements is that they offer instant gratification. You can add as many as you like to your actions, and you can dump out the contents of as many variables as you like. In this example, the fact that there are only two (fairly short) actions makes debugging relatively easy. But even in larger, complex actions, trace( ) statements can help you identify buggy code in short order. Of course, a requirement for using trace( ) statements—or any other debugging strategy, for that matter—is that you know what the contents of any given variable should be during the course of the animation (so that you'll know when Flash prints out variable contents that are incorrect).

12. **Retest the animation by selecting Control → Test Movie.**

Once again, Flash Player appears, showing the movie clip running backwards. But this time the content in the Output window has changed, as Figure 13-17 shows. Success!

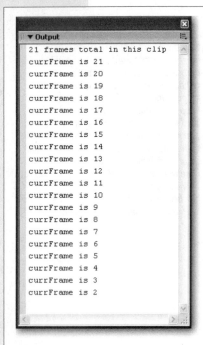

Figure 13-17:
Problem solved! As you can see here, Flash steps backward frame by frame from the last frame (21) to the second frame, backs up one more time, and then stops; it doesn't keep trying to back up to a nonexistent Frame 0 the way it did before.

13. **Return to the Actions panel and delete the *trace( )* statements you added earlier. Close the Actions panel when you're done.**

After you've fixed a bug, you'll want to remove the *trace( )* statements you added to your ActionScript code. The Output panel doesn't appear when you publish your animation (in other words, your audience won't see your *trace( )* statements), but it's still a good idea to remove any unnecessary statements. Cleaning up keeps your ActionScript as short and uncluttered as possible. (Or, you can conceal them in comments as described in the box below.)

TRICK OF THE TRADE

Comment Me Out

If you're planning to keep working on your ActionScript action and think you'll need to reuse these *trace( )* statements at some point down the road, you don't have to delete them and then type them in again later. Instead, you can "comment them out" by placing two slashes in front of each line, like this:

When you stick two slashes at the beginning of a line of ActionScript code, Flash ignores everything it finds on the line after those slashes. In other words, it treats the code as if it were a plain old comment (page 368). Later, when you want to use that *trace( )* statement again, all you have to do is remove the slashes and you're back in business.

```
// trace("currFrame is " + _currentframe);
```

Deciphering the Actions Panel's Color Code

One quick way to spot problems in your ActionScript code is to examine the colors Flash uses to display your code in the Actions panel.

Right out of the box, Flash displays ActionScript keywords in blue, comments in light gray, text strings (text surrounded by quotes) in green, and stuff it doesn't recognize in black. So if you notice a function call or a property that appears black, you know there's a problem. Properly spelled function calls and properties should appear blue, so if they're black, chances are your finger slipped. In the example you see below, for example, the function *gotoAndStop( )* is misspelled *gotoAnddStop( )*, and the property *_currentframe* is misspelled as *_currentframes*.

If Flash's ActionScript coloring scheme is too subtle for your tastes, you can change the colors it uses. To change colors:

1. Select Edit → Preferences (Windows) or Flash → Preferences (Mac).

2. In the Preferences panel that appears, select the ActionScript category. Make sure the checkbox next to "Code coloring" is turned on.

3. Click the color pickers next to Foreground, Keywords, Identifiers, Background, Comments, and Strings to choose different colors for each of these ActionScript code elements.

For example, if you have trouble making out the text strings in your scripts due to red-green color-blindness, you can change Strings to a different hue.

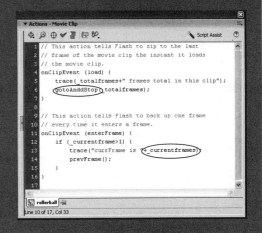

Displaying Property Names and Values

The *trace( )* statement lets you examine the contents of individual properties while your animation is running. But if you want to examine the contents of *all* the properties in your animation in one fell swoop, there's an easier way, using the Debug Movie command.

The Debug Movie command lets you choose any movie clip in your animation (even one you've nested in another movie clip), view all the properties for that movie clip, and even change editable properties on the fly.

1. **Select Control → Debug Movie.**

   Flash pops up the debugger panel shown in Figure 13-18.

2. **In the display list, click the name of the Timeline you want to examine.**

   In the Properties tab, Flash lists all the properties the Timeline contains, including values for properties that have them.

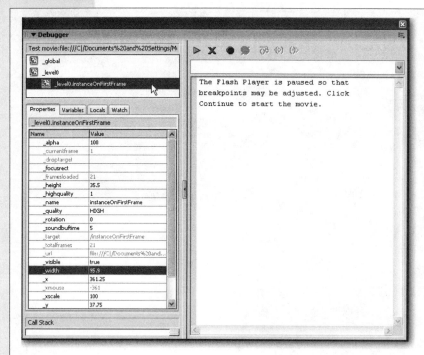

▼ Debugger

Test movie:file:///C|/Documents%20and%20Settings/M|

_global

_level0

_level0.instanceOnFirstFrame

Properties | Variables | Locals | Watch

_level0.instanceOnFirstFrame

Name	Value
_alpha	100
_currentframe	1
_droptarget	
_focusrect	
_framesloaded	21
_height	35.5
_highquality	1
_name	instanceOnFirstFrame
_quality	HIGH
_rotation	0
_soundbuftime	5
_target	/instanceOnFirstFrame
_totalframes	21
_url	file:///C|/Documents%20and...
_visible	true
_width	95.9
_x	361.25
_xmouse	-361
_xscale	100
_y	37.75

Call Stack

The Flash Player is paused so that
breakpoints may be adjusted. Click
Continue to start the movie.

Figure 13-18:
In the display list, Flash lists your main animation (_level0) and any nested Timelines (movie clips) you've added to your main animation. Here, the movie clip instance named instanceOnFirstFrame is selected, so all the property names and corresponding values in the Properties tab belong to that movie clip instance. Selecting _level0 shows property names and values associated with the main animation.

Figure 13-18, for example, shows that there are 21 total number frames in the movie clip instance (*_totalframes*), Flash has succeeded in loading all 21 (*_frames-loaded*), and the playhead's currently on Frame 1 (*_currentframe*).

Note: Technically, you can let Flash name your symbol instances (instance1, instance2, and so on). But for debugging purposes, naming your instances yourself makes identifying them much easier. To name a symbol instance, select the instance on the Stage and then, in the Property Inspector, type the name you want into the "Instance name" field.

Setting and Using Breakpoints

One of the most important debugging tools in any well-stocked ActionScript programmer's arsenal is the *breakpoint*. A breakpoint is an artificial stopping point— sort of a roadblock—that you can insert into your ActionScript code to stop Flash Player in its tracks. Setting breakpoints lets you examine your animation at different points during playback so that you can pinpoint where a bug first occurs.

Flash lets you set breakpoints at specific lines in your ActionScript code. Setting a breakpoint lets you play the animation only up until Flash encounters that breakpoint. The instant Flash encounters a line with a breakpoint, it immediately stops the animation so that you can either examine object property values (as described in the previous section) or step through the remaining code in your action slowly, line by line, watching what happens as you go.

Setting breakpoints is a great way to track down logic errors in your ActionScript code. For example, say you've created a chunk of code containing a lot of *if...else* and *do...while* statements. Stopping playback just before you enter that long stretch of code lets you follow Flash as it works through the statements one at a time. By stepping through statements in the order Flash actually executes them (as opposed to the order you thought Flash was supposed to execute them), you may find the cause of your problem is that Flash never reaches the *else* section of your *if...else* statement, for example, or never performs any of the statements inside your *do...while* block because the *while* condition is never met.

Note: For more information on using *if...else, do...while,* and other logical statements in ActionScript, check out Colin Moock's *ActionScript: The Definitive Guide* (O'Reilly). It has detailed coverage of more advanced ActionScript topics that are beyond the scope of this book.

To set a breakpoint:

1. **Open the file reverse_debug.fla. (It's the same one used earlier in this chapter; see page 382 for download instructions.)**

   A one-frame movie containing an instance of the rollerball movie clip symbol appears in your workspace.

2. **On the Stage, click the instance of the movie clip to select it.**

   Flash displays a blue selection box around the movie clip.

3. **Select Window → Actions.**

   The Actions panel in Figure 13-19 (top) appears.

4. **In the Action panel's Script pane, click anywhere on line 12.**

5. **Click the down arrow next to the Debug options icon, and then choose Set Breakpoint (Figure 13-19, bottom).**

   In the Script pane, Flash displays a red dot next to line 12 to let you know you've successfully set a breakpoint.

Tip: Another way to set a breakpoint is to click in the Script pane just to the left of the Line number at which you want to set a breakpoint. When you do, Flash displays the breakpoint icon (the red dot). To remove the breakpoint, simply click the red dot.

---

6. **Select Control → Debug Movie.**

   The Debugger panel appears.

7. **In the Debugger panel, click the Continue icon.**

   Flash begins playing the animation, and then stops. In the Script pane of the Debugger panel, there's a small red arrow pointing at the line where Flash stopped (in this case, in Figure 13-20, that line is Line 12).

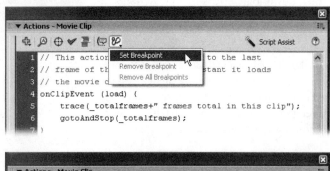

Figure 13-19:
Top: You have to click on a line of ActionScript code before Flash lets you set a breakpoint.

Bottom: After you select Set Breakpoint, Flash shows a little red dot next to the breakpoint line. You can add as many breakpoints to your code as you like, with one caveat: You can add a breakpoint only to a "live," or executable, line of code. For example, you can't add a breakpoint to a line containing nothing but a closing brace, such as Line 15 or 16.

Now you can step through the remaining ActionScript code line by line.

8. **Click the Step Over icon at the top of the Debugger panel (labeled in Figure 13-20).**

   Flash executes Line 12 and moves to Line 13, as in Figure 13-21.

9. **Click Step Over again.**

   Flash executes Line 13 and moves to Line 14. In the Output panel, you see the results of Flash having executed Line 13: the message "currFrame is 21."

10. **Continue clicking Step Over until either the animation finishes playing or you spot a problem.**

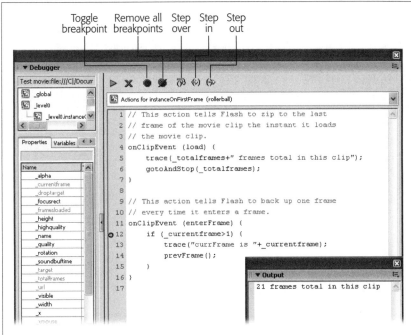

Toggle Remove all Step Step Step
breakpoint breakpoints over in out

Figure 13-20:
*Flash displays the
contents of the trace( )
statement in the Output
window because the
trace( ) statement is on
Line 5, and Flash doesn't
stop playing the
application until it
encounters the
breakpoint on Line 12. At
this point, you can
examine your
animation's object
properties and values
(see page 145), or you
can step into the
ActionScript code as
shown below.*

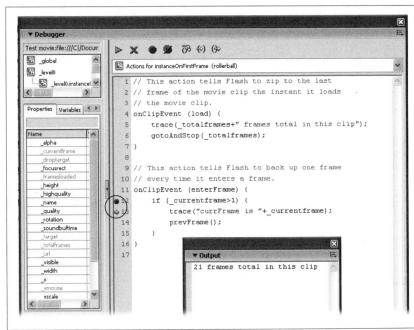

Figure 13-21:
*Flash always displays the
breakpoint icon (the red
dot) next to the line
where you set the
breakpoint. But as you
step through your code,
Flash moves the yellow
arrow so that you always
know which line Flash
will execute the next time
you click Continue.*

Note: Stepping *over* a line of code, as shown in this example, tells Flash to execute the line of code—even if the line happens to contain a function call. But if you want to explore the inner workings of a function call, you can set a breakpoint at a line containing a function call, and then click Step Into. This action tells Flash to step *into* the called function and begin working through each line of the called function. To pop back out of the called function and return to the calling code, click Step Out.

Publishing and Exporting

When you've finished creating an animation in Flash, you'll want to do one of two things with it: You'll want to either *publish* it, which means packaging it in a form your audience can play using the Flash Player they've installed on their computers; or you'll want to *export* it, which means packaging it in a form you can edit using another graphics or animation program (such as Adobe Illustrator or Macromedia/Adobe Fireworks).

Note: *Publishing* means something different in Flash (where it means "creating an executable Flash file") from what it means in the larger world of Web development (where it means "transferring files to a Web server").

In this chapter, you'll learn how to do both.

Using Flash's publishing settings (Figure 14-1), you'll see how to tell Flash to publish your animation as part of a Web page, and as a standalone *projector*. You'll also see how to export the artwork in your animation as editable image files. But before you publish or export, you need to learn how to *optimize* your animation (reduce your animation's file size) so that it runs as quickly and efficiently as possible—a real concern if you're planning to publish your animation on the Web (see the box on page 397).

Optimizing Flash Documents

The larger your published Flash animation file size, the longer it takes for your audience to download it off the Web, and the more stress it puts on their computers when it does begin to play. (Find out more about the difference between an

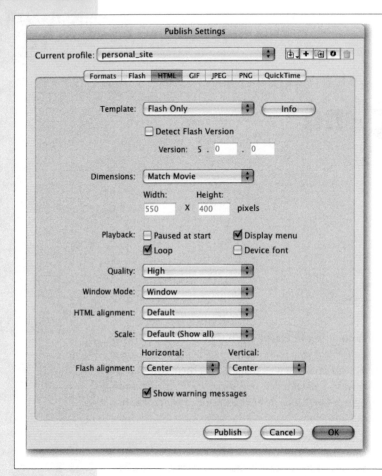

Figure 14-1:
Flash lets you choose how to deliver your compiled animation: as a standalone projector file (a self-contained executable file you double-click to run, with no need for a Web browser or a separate Flash Player), a QuickTime movie, an image file, or embedded in a Web page (shown here).

editable .fla Flash document and a published, ready-to-roll .swf document on page 403.) A large file size can cause someone to stare at a blank screen for seconds or even minutes at a time, while she waits for your animation to download and begin playing. A large file size can also cause your animation (including any sound files it contains) to play in fits and starts once it *does* begin.

Optimizing your animation means paring down file size by making various changes to your images, text, and other elements—all while making sure your animation continues to play the way you want it to. You can think of optimization as low-fat cooking for the animation set: The goal is to get rid of the fat without getting rid of the flavor. And, like low-fat cooking, Flash doesn't offer a single approach to optimization; instead—because every animation and target audience is different—you need to experiment, tweak, and retest using the strategies outlined below.

The Importance of Being Optimized

In an era where lightning-fast connections, high-speed processors, and multimegabyte memory cards abound, why should I bother optimizing my Flash documents?

Here's why: Not everyone has access to the latest, greatest equipment and Internet service. In many parts of the world, people don't have access to affordable T1 connections, for example. Also, folks relying on the computers at their schools or jobs don't have control over their equipment. And, of course, not everyone has the time, money, or patience necessary to upgrade every time a new "revolution" in hardware or software technology hits the market.

There's a tendency among some animators (especially those who don't have a background in building non-Flash software programs) to resist the extra effort that optimizing their animations (as you see on page 400) requires. But here's the fact: If people can't see your animation, nothing else matters. Not the beauty or cleverness of your artwork, nor the sophistication of your animated sequences, nor the appropriateness of your perfectly synchronized background music.

Here's a short list of the most common excuses some animators give for not optimizing their animations (and the reasons why these excuses don't fly):

- **It looks great on my machine. If my audience doesn't have a fast enough connection, they need to upgrade.** Animators and others using Flash tend to be running high-end equipment—much faster and more powerful than the equipment their audiences are running. That's why testing your animation at a variety of connection speeds (as discussed on page 378) and even on a variety of machines, if possible, is so important. As noted above, not everyone *can* upgrade, and not everyone *wants* to. But even if they do, chances are they're not going to do it just to see your animation.

- **So what if it takes 5 minutes to download my animation file? My animation is so fantastic it's worth waiting for.** It doesn't matter if your animation is in line for the next Webby Award: If your audience can't run it (or surfs away impatiently instead of waiting for it to download and stutter across their screens), you haven't communicated effectively—and communicating effectively is, or should be, the goal of every animation you create in Flash.

- **The big boys (Hollywood trailer-makers, high-end advertisers, and super-sophisticated, high-traffic sites) don't worry about optimization. Why should I?** It's true that some folks would still check out the latest Hollywood teaser even if it took all day to download. But they don't have to because the big boys pay an army of professional testers and software designers to optimize their animations using the techniques in this chapter.

The bottom line, as you've read over and over in this book, is to determine the needs of your target audience *first* and then construct your animation to meet those needs. If you're delivering your animation as a standalone file on DVD, you're absolutely sure that your audience will be running high-end equipment, and you know for a fact they're highly motivated to run your animation (for example, they have to work through the Flash training tutorial you created in order to keep their jobs), then by all means take optimization with a grain of salt. But if your audience fits any other profile, ignore optimization at your own risk.

Tip: As you check out the optimization strategies in this section, keep in mind that effective optimization is always a balancing act. You may decide some effects are worth the bloated file size they require, and some aren't. In still other cases, you'll want to compromise. For example, you might choose to remove half of the gradient effects you've applied to your images so that you reduce file size, but keep the other half. In Flash, you're the director, so you get to decide how much is enough.

Ten Optimization Strategies

Below you'll find 10 different strategies for keeping file size down by tweaking the images you draw, the bitmaps you import, the graphic effects you apply, and more. Apply as many of the strategies as you can. You can use any of these techniques to trim down a completed animation. Better yet, keep them in mind as you create your next animation. That way, you'll end up with a streamlined animation without a lot of extra, after-the-fact work.

Choose tweens over frame-by-frame animations

Every time you add a keyframe to your Timeline, the size of your file goes up dramatically. In contrast, when you use a motion or shape tween (Chapter 3), Flash only has to keep track of the beginning and ending keyframes; for the in-between frames it generates, it has to save only a few calculations. (Obviously, there are times you need to use frame-by-frame animation to create the effect you're after; but for those times when tweening will do the job, use it.)

Choose the Pencil tool over the Brush tool

Brush tool fills are more complex than the lines you create with the Pencil tool, so brush strokes take up more file space. When you feel both strokes are equally acceptable, choose the Pencil.

Choose solid over dashed or dotted lines

Through the Property Inspector, Flash lets you apply a handful of dash-and-dot effects to the lines you draw on Stage using the Pencil, Pen, Line, and Shape tools (page 58). But do so sparingly, because these line effects increase file size.

Simplify curves

The less points that make up your lined curves and fill outlines, the less information Flash has to keep track of—and the smaller your file size. Flash even gives you a special Optimize command to remove superfluous points from your shapes. Here's how to use it:

1. Select the curved line or fill outline you want to optimize and then choose Modify → Shape → Optimize.

    The Optimize Curves dialog box you see in Figure 14-2 (top) appears.

2. **Drag the smoothing slider to tell Flash how much optimization to apply, from none to maximum, and then click OK.**

   Flash displays a message (Figure 14-2, bottom) letting you know what percentage of the selected line or outline it was able to dispense with.

3. **Click OK.**

   On the Stage, you see the (subtle) results of the optimization.

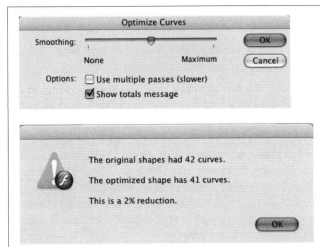

Figure 14-2:
Top: Optimizing a line doesn't straighten it out or even smooth it the way that Modify → Shape → Straighten and Modify → Shape → Smooth do; instead, it ever-so-subtly shifts the points that make up the line. If you want to see how successful the optimization is, make sure you leave the Show totals message checkbox turned on.

Bottom: Because optimization is a final tweak meant for you to do after your image already looks the way you want it to look, you don't see a huge reduction in size here. Still, depending on the number of curved lines and fill outlines your animation contains, the saved bytes can add up fast.

Use symbols

Creating a reusable symbol (Chapter 7) allows you to add multiple instances of a shape or drawing to your animation without dramatically increasing file size. Even shrinking, rotating, or recoloring your instances costs less in file size than creating separate images.

Avoid bitmaps (or optimize them)

Bitmaps are expensive in terms of file size. If you can do without them, do so; if not, crop them (so that you use as little of them as possible) or optimize them by choosing a higher-than-standard compression option, as described below.

Note: You can also optimize bitmaps in the Publish settings (page 405).

To optimize a bitmap:

1. **Import the bitmap into your document's Library panel.**

   The steps, if you need a refresher, are in Chapter 8 (page 246).

In the Library, double-click the icon next to the imported bitmap's file name. (Or select the bitmap, and then, from the Options menu in the upper-right corner of the Library, choose Properties.)

Either way, the Bitmap Properties window you see in Figure 14-3 appears.

2. **From the Compression drop-down list, choose either "Photo (JPEG)" or "Lossless (PNG/GIF)."**

   Choose the first option if your image contains a lot of different colors or transparent effects; choose the second if it contains a few solid lumps of color. Find out more about JPEGs, PNGs, and GIFs beginning on page 403.

   Flash calculates a percent compression rate and displays it near the bottom of the Bitmap Properties window.

   If you chose "Photo (JPEG)", you can compress the image further. Turn off the "Use imported JPEG data" checkbox and then type a number into the Quality box that appears (Figure 14-3).

Tip: Flash starts you out with a quality rate of 50. You need to experiment to find out the lowest number that gives you an acceptable tradeoff between file size and quality, but one way to begin is to jot down the current file size (Flash displays it just below the Quality field), type *25,* and then click OK. When you open the Bitmap Properties window again, Flash displays the new file size for the bitmap based on a file quality of 25. If the image looks OK, type a lower number; if not, type a higher number. The higher the number, the larger the file size; the lower the number, the lower the file size.

3. **Take a look at your newly optimized image by clicking the Test button.**

   The preview area shows the way the image looks using the optimization settings you chose. Near the bottom of the Bitmap Properties window, you see the percent compression rate Flash has calculated based on the Quality setting you typed in. If the image quality looks horrible, repeat step 2 with a higher quality setting; if the quality looks okay but the compression rate doesn't seem low enough, try again with a lower quality setting. (Sometimes, depending on your image, a lower quality setting will look practically identical to a slightly higher quality setting.)

4. **When you're satisfied with the quality-vs.-file size tradeoff, click OK.**

   Flash hides the Bitmap Properties window and returns you to your workspace.

Note: The image doesn't appear optimized in the Library preview area, and when you drag an instance of the bitmap symbol to the Stage, the image doesn't appear optimized there, either. To see the effects of your optimization settings on the Stage, select Control → Test Movie.

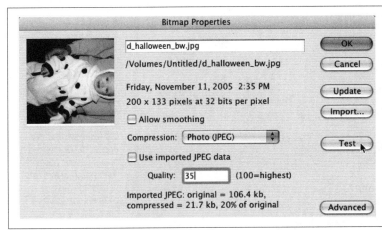

Figure 14-3:
Everything in life's a tradeoff, and bitmap optimization in Flash is no exception. If you find you can't balance image quality with compression—for example, by the time you reach an acceptably high compression rate, your image appears nearly unrecognizable—consider cropping the bitmap (page 250) or turning it into a vector drawing (page 250).

Keep sound clips to a minimum; when you do use them, optimize them.

Sound clips can quickly swell your animation size. Always use the shortest clips you can get by with (page 261 shows you how to shorten sound clips) and optimize them by compressing them as much as possible without sacrificing too much sound quality.

To optimize a sound file:

1. **Import the sound file into your document's Library panel.**

   Page 254 has the full detail on importing audio files.

2. **In the Library, double-click the icon next to the imported sound file's name.**

   Alternatively, select the sound file, and then, from the Options menu in the upper-right corner of the Library, choose Properties.

   Either way, the Sound Properties window you see in Figure 14-4 appears.

3. **From the Compression drop-down list, choose a compression scheme.**

   Page 409 describes the different schemes.

4. **When you're satisfied with the quality-vs.-file size tradeoff, click OK.**

   Flash hides the Sound Properties window and returns you to your workspace.

Note: To make sure Flash uses the compression option you set in the Sound Properties window, turn off the "Override sound settings" checkbox in the Publish Settings dialog box. Page 409 has details.

Group elements

Grouping shapes, lines, and other portions of your drawings (by selecting them and then choosing Modify → Group) cuts down on file size because Flash can streamline in the information it needs to store. Chapter 5 (page 133) has full instructions.

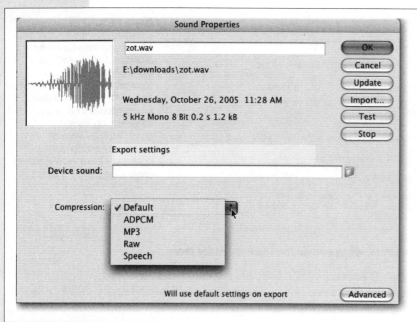

Figure 14-4:
If you leave Compression set to Default, Flash uses the compression option you set in the Publish Settings window (page 396) to figure out how to compress this sound clip. Otherwise, Flash applies the Compression option you set here (unless you've told Flash to override this compression setting; see page 409 for details).

Avoid the extraneous

The more you add to your animation, the larger your file size. If you absolutely, positively need to pare down your file, consider removing or simplifying some (or all) of your drawings, multimedia files, and graphic effects, paying particular attention to these space hogs:

- Sound files, embedded video clips, and bitmaps

- Gradient effects

- Alpha (transparency) effects

- Custom colors

Tip: If you can't bring yourself to do without media files altogether, go ahead and use them—but abbreviate them. For example, instead of using a long sound clip, loop a short one. Or use a single sound clip a bunch of different ways (soft, loud, the first half, the second half) to create multiple sound effects for minimal overhead. Instead of embedding a video clip as is, try adjusting the in and out points to clip off any nonessential intro or outro frames when you import it into Flash (page 262). And if you're using a mask layer (page 197), make sure you clip off every scrap of the background image not revealed by the mask.

Tell Flash to keep your file size down

One of the options you want to make sure you set when you're ready to publish your animation is the "Compress movie" option in the Publish Settings dialog box (page 396). (Out of the box, Flash turns on this option, but do double-check that you haven't inadvertently turned it off.) Choosing this option tells Flash to squeeze your animation file as much as it can without sacrificing content. How much Flash compresses your file depends on the specific elements and effects you've included in your animation; the more text and ActionScript code your animation contains, for example, the more "bloat" Flash can squeeze out of your file.

POWER USERS' CLINIC

Preloading

If you drop in on Flash user groups, you may hear talk of *preloading*, which is a strategy related to optimization. Preloading means that you use a frame-based script (Chapter 10) to download as much of your animation as you can before you actually need it. For example, to keep your audience entertained–in other words, to keep them from getting so bored waiting for your animation to download that they surf away in frustration–you might want to display a quick-to-download scene and loop it a few times while your real, byte-intensive animation quietly downloads in the background.

The ActionScript required to create your own preloader script is beyond the scope of this book, but Flash Help has details. Simply choose Help → Flash Help and search for "about loading and working with external media." (See the Appendix for more tips on using Flash Help.)

Publishing Your Animations

Publishing your animation is Flash shorthand for "using the editable .fla file you work with in Flash to generate a noneditable file your audience can play."

The kind of noneditable file Flash produces depends on how you decide to publish your animation. Your choices include:

- **A compiled Flash file (.swf).** Flash Players, including the Flash Player plug-in that comes with most browsers, play .swf files. If you plan to include your Flash animation in a hand-coded HTML file (or to import it into a Web site creation program such as Microsoft's FrontPage), you want this option.

- **A Web page (.html, .swf).** Choose this option if you want Flash to put together a simple Web page for you that includes your animation. (You can always tweak the HTML file later, either by hand or using another Web site creation program.)

- **An image file (.jpg, .gif, or .png).** This option lets you display one of the frames of your animation as an image file or as an animated GIF file—useful for those times when your audience doesn't have a Flash Player installed because at least they can see *part* of your animation. (For more advice on using ActionScript to detect your audience's Flash Player at runtime and offer alternatives, see the box on page 413.)

Note: Flash gives you another way to turn your artwork into an image file: by *exporting* it (page 425).

- **A standalone projector file (.exe, .hqx).** A *projector* file is a self-contained Flash-player-plus-your-animation file. Your audience can run a projector file to play your animation even if they don't have a copy of Flash Player installed. Typically, you choose this option if you plan to deliver your animation to your audience on CD or DVD (as opposed to over the Web). Projector files for Windows carry the .exe extension. On Mac, the projector file doesn't have an extension, but if you create a Mac projector file in Windows, the projector extension that Flash creates is .hqx.

- **A QuickTime movie (.mov).** Flash lets you publish your animation as a QuickTime movie so that folks with the QuickTime player can see it. This option has become a bit less popular now that most Web browsers can play Flash files on their own. To view a QuickTime movie, audiences have to go to the trouble of downloading and installing the free QuickTime player (But if you insist, see the box on page 425 for help in publishing your animation as a QuickTime movie.)

You can choose more than one publishing option at a time, simply by turning on as many checkboxes as you like in the Publish Settings dialog box. For example, you can publish your animation as a compiled Flash file, a Web page, and a standalone projector file all at once when you click Publish.

The following sections show you each of these five publishing options in detail.

Publishing as a Compiled Flash (.swf) File

When you publish your animation as an .swf file, your audience can run it using a Flash Player—either a standalone version of Flash Player, or a Web browser plug-in version. Publishing as an .swf file gives you the flexibility of including your animation in a from-scratch Web page.

Note: If you've worked through any of the examples in this book, you're already familiar with .swf files. Each time you test your animation using Control → Test Movie, Flash automatically generates an .swf file and plays it in the Flash Player that comes with Flash.

To publish your animation as a compiled Flash (.swf) file:

1. **Choose File → Publish Settings.**

   A Publish Settings dialog box, similar to the one in Figure 14-5 appears. Here's where you tell Flash what kind of files to publish, and you can choose as few or as many as you like. When you turn on a checkbox, Flash shows you a panel where you can choose settings specific to that file type.

2. **Turn on the checkbox next to "Flash (.swf)" and then turn off all the other checkboxes.**

   The Flash tab appears next to the Formats tab.

3. **Click the Flash tab.**

   The Flash settings in Figure 14-6 appear.

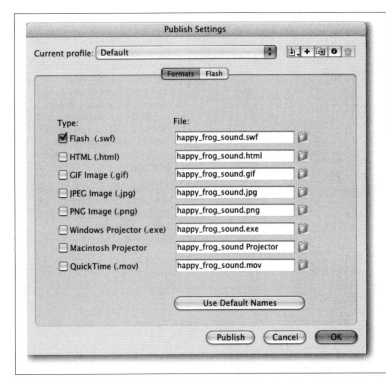

Figure 14-5:
*Each time you turn on a Type
checkbox, Flash adds a
corresponding tab to the Publish
Settings dialog box; each time you
turn off a checkbox, Flash removes
the corresponding tab. Here, the
tab matches the one type chosen:
Flash.*

4. **Change one or more of the following settings:**

Version. Lets you select the version of Flash Player you want to be able to run your animation. Choose the latest version (Flash Player 8) if you've included any of the new-in-Flash-8 features (page 5) or if you're not sure whether or not you've included any new features. If you know your audience is running an earlier version of Flash Player (for example, Flash Player 7) and you know you won't be using any new-in-Flash-8 features, you can choose the earlier version.

Flash activates the relatively unhelpful *Info* button only when you choose one of the Flash Lite versions. Flash Lite is a special Flash Player designed for handhelds, such as Pocket PCs. (This book doesn't cover Flash Lite, but you can find out more about it by visiting the online sources listed in the Appendix.)

Note: If you choose Flash Player 8 and it turns out your audience is running an earlier version of the player, such as Flash Player 7, they may need to download and install Flash Player 8 in order to play your animation (depending on the features you included in your animation). Macromedia (now Adobe) makes a free downloadable copy of the latest Flash Player available at *www.macromedia.com/software/flashplayer*, but it's your responsibility to let your audience know when (or if) they need to surf there and download a new player. For more information, see the box on page 414.

Load order. Tells Flash to either load your layers from the bottom of the stack up (Flash does this automatically), or from the top down. This option affects

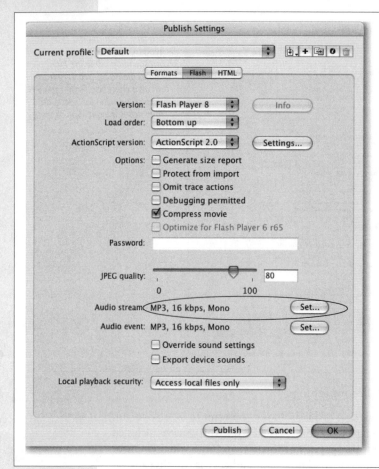

Figure 14-6:
The settings here let you fine-tune the .swf file that Flash generates when you click Publish. Normally, you don't have to make any changes to these settings. But in some cases—for example, when you know your target audience is running a back-level version of Flash Player—you do want to change them. These pages explain each setting.

If you don't like the audio format Flash picks for you (circled), click the Set button to display the Sound Settings dialog box shown in Figure 14-8.

only the first frame of your animation, so unless someone is running a very slow Internet connection, chances are your file will load and begin playing so quickly that load order isn't an issue.

ActionScript version. Tells Flash which version of ActionScript to use. In most cases, you want to leave ActionScript 2.0 selected.

Note: If you're an ActionScript programmer and know for sure that your audience is running Flash Player 6 or earlier (or the Flash Lite player) and that you haven't included any ActionScript 2.0 statements in your actions, go ahead and choose ActionScript 1.0.

Generate size report. Tells Flash to list the bytes in your .fla file by frame, scene, action, and so on. While this report isn't as useful for testing as the bandwidth profiler report (page 377), you may find it useful for keeping track of which content you've added to your animation.

Protect from import. Theoretically, this option tells Flash to encode your .swf file so that other folks can't import it into Flash and edit (steal!) your animation. Unfortunately, human nature being what it is, you can find programs floating around the Web that let folks bypass this encoding. So if you need to reference sensitive information in your Flash animation (such as passwords or confidential company info) don't store that information in Flash; instead, store it safely on a protected server and get it at runtime.

Omit trace actions. Tells Flash to ignore any *trace( )* statements you've added to your ActionScript actions (page 381).

Note: Flash Player won't display the Output window or any *trace( )* actions even if you *don't* turn on this checkbox. The only time you need to turn on this checkbox is if you plan to debug your animation remotely, using the special Flash Debug Player, but for some reason don't want to see your *trace( )* statements.

Debugging permitted. Tells Flash to let you debug your animation remotely (over the Web) using the special Flash Debug Player browser plug-in. This book doesn't cover remote debugging, but you can find out more about it using Flash Help (see the Appendix).

Compress movie. Tells Flash to reduce .swf file size as much as possible without sacrificing your animation's quality. Make sure this option's turned on. (Flash can't compress animations targeting pre-6 versions of Flash Player, but odds are you aren't doing that anyway.)

Optimize for Flash Player 6 r65. This option targets your animation especially for playback on an interim version of the Flash 6 Player, so you almost never want to check it.

Password. If you've chosen "Protect from import" or "Debugging permitted," type a password in this box. Typing a password lets anyone with the password import the compiled .swf file into Flash at a later date and edit it—a potential security risk if your ActionScript code contains confidential company information. Typing a password also lets anyone with the password debug the .swf file remotely. (This book doesn't cover remote debugging.)

JPEG quality. This option lets you set the quality (and therefore the size) of the bitmaps you've added to your animation—but only for those bitmaps for which you've turned on the "Use document default quality" checkbox in the Bitmap Properties dialog box (Figure 14-7, top). To set JPEG quality, either drag the slider or, in the box, type a number from 1 to 100 (Figure 14-7, bottom).

Audio stream. Tells Flash which compression scheme you want it to use for streaming audio clips for which you haven't already specified a compression scheme (page 401). Flash displays the compression scheme it assumes you want. To specify another one, click the Set button and then, in the Sound Settings dialog box that appears (Figure 14-8), choose the compression scheme you want.

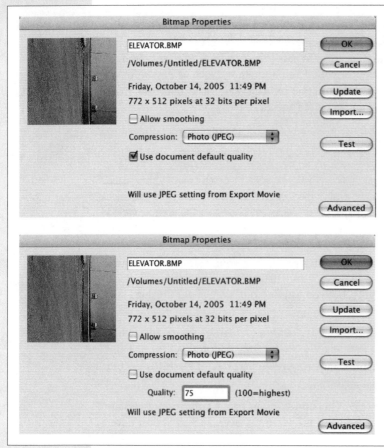

Figure 14-7:
*Top: If you turn on the checkbox
next to Use document default
quality, as shown here, Flash lets
you set bitmap quality using the
JPEG quality checkbox in the
Publish Settings window's Flash
tab.*

*Bottom: If you set the quality of
your bitmap using the Bitmap
Properties dialog box, however,
Flash ignores the JPEG quality
checkbox in the Publish Settings
window. In other words, you
can't tell Flash to compress the
same image twice.*

Note: Flash gives you two ways to specify a compression scheme for your sound clips. You can specify a compression scheme for individual sound clips using the Sound Properties dialog box (page 402) or you can specify one for all of the sound clips in your animation using the Audio Stream and Audio Event options you find in the Publish Settings window. (See below for more detail on the difference between audio streams and audio events.)

Audio event. Tells Flash which compression scheme you want it to use for audio events for which you haven't already specified a compression scheme, using the Sound Properties dialog box. Flash displays the compression scheme it assumes you want. To specify another one, click the Set button next to "Audio event," and then, in the Sound Settings dialog box that appears, choose another compression scheme. Your options are identical to the options Flash gives you for setting "Audio stream" (see Figure 14-8), and they don't override individual sound properties unless you turn on "Override sound settings."

Note: Specifying a high-quality compression scheme doesn't improve a low-quality sound clip; Flash can only work with what you give it.

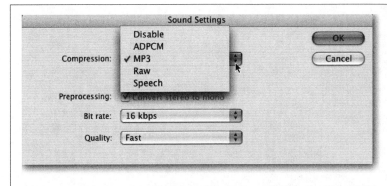

Figure 14-8:
Clicking the Set button (circled in Figure 14-6) opens the Sound Settings dialog box. Here, you can choose from high-quality compression schemes (such as MP3, suitable for long, continuous clips like soundtracks) and lower-quality, byte-saving schemes (such as Speech or ADPCM. Choosing Raw tells Flash not to compress your sounds at all.

Override sound settings. Tells Flash to ignore the compression schemes you set for your sound clips using the Sound Properties dialog box (page 402) and use the compression schemes (both streaming and event) you set in the Publish Settings window instead. If you *don't* turn on this checkbox, Flash uses the compression settings you set in the Publish Settings window only for those sound clips assigned a Default setting in Sound Properties dialog box.

Export device sounds. Tells Flash to include MIDI and other device sound files with the .swf file. Turn on this option only if you're targeting mobile devices.

Local playback security. New in Flash 8, this option lets you tell Flash if you want your .swf to be able to exchange information with *local files* (files located on your audience's computers) or *network files* (files located elsewhere on the Web). If you don't choose either of these options, Flash lets your .swf file read information from both local and network files, but not write information to either.

5. **Click Publish.**

The Publish Settings window disappears, and Flash generates a Flash file based on the name you set in the Formats tab. If you didn't type a name of your own choosing, Flash names the file similar to your .fla file. For example, if the name of your Flash document is myAnimation.fla, Flash generates a file named myAnimation.swf.

Tip: You don't have to go through the Publish Settings window every time you want to publish your animation. Once you've got the settings the way you want them, all you have to do is select File → Publish.

Publishing as a Web Page

If you want to put your animation on a Web page, an .swf file by itself isn't sufficient: You also have to create an HTML file (a Web page) that embeds that .swf file. You can create the HTML file either by using your favorite HTML editor or by telling Flash to generate a simple HTML file for you.

Creating a Publish Profile

Customizing all the different publishing settings Flash offers can be time-consuming. If you suspect you'll want to reuse a batch of options—because, for example, your boss wants you to publish each animation both as a QuickTime movie and a Flash file and wants to see both versions embedded in different-looking Web pages—you can save each batch of settings as a named profile: say, myQuickTimeProfile and myFlashProfile.

That way, when you want to publish an HTML embedding the QuickTime version of your animation (for example), all you have to do is specify your QuickTime profile. When you want to change gears and publish an HTML that embeds an .swf file, you can switch to your Flash profile (instead of having to hunt through all the options, figure out which ones to change, and change them…again…and again… and again).

To create a publish profile:

1. In the Publish Settings dialog box, click the "Create new profile icon." (It looks like a + sign.)

2. In the Create New Profile dialog box that appears, type a name for your profile, and then click OK.

3. Flash saves all your current settings to that profile. As you continue to make changes in the Publish Settings window, Flash continues to save those changes to your profile.

You can create as many profiles as you like. To change profiles, click Current Profile and then select a profile from the drop-down list.

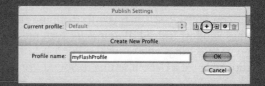

At a minimum, the HTML file needs to tells the Web browser how to display the .swf file: at the top of the page or in the middle, whether you want the animation to begin playing immediately or wait until the audience clicks a button, and so on.

Because most people who use Flash want to put their animations on the Web, Flash simplifies the process by letting you create an .swf in addition to a simple Web page (.html) in one fell swoop, using the Publish Settings dialog box.

To publish your animation as a Web page (.html and .swf):

1. Choose File → Publish Settings.

   The Publish Settings dialog box appears.

2. **Make sure the checkboxes next to "Flash (.swf)" and "HTML (.html)" are turned on; if they're not, turn them both on now.**

   The Flash and HTML tabs appear next to the Formats tab, as shown in Figure 14-9.

3. **Click the Flash tab and then set up your .swf file.**

   For the details, see step 4 on page 405.

4. **Click the HTML tab.**

   The HTML publish settings you see in Figure 14-10 appear.

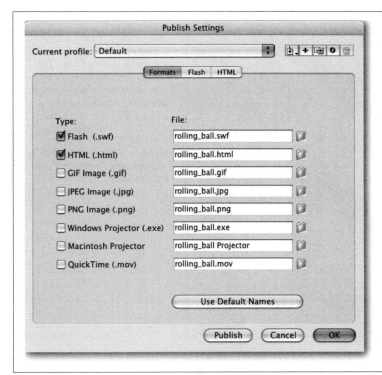

Figure 14-9:
Flash assumes you want to publish your animation on the Web—for which you need both an .swf file and a .html file—unless you tell it otherwise. You can change the suggested file names, all of which begin with the name of your Flash document (here, rolling_ball).

5. **If you like, change the template setting.**

Most of the time, you want to stick with the "Flash only" template that Flash assumes you want. But if you've added certain elements to your animation, or if you want to target a specific Web browser, Flash needs to insert special HTML tags into the template it uses. In that case, you may need one of the following options:

Flash for Pocket PC 2003. Creates an HTML file that runs on Pocket PC 2003.

Flash HTTPS. Choose this option if you plan to upload your HTML and .swf file to a secure Web server (https://).

Flash only. Creates a basic HTML file that runs in any Web browser.

Flash with AICC Tracking. Choose this option if you've added Learning Interaction components (Window → Common Libraries → Learning Interactions) to your animation and plan to have these components interact with an AICC learning management system. (AICC stands for Aviation Industry CBT Committee.)

Flash with FSCommand. Choose this option if you've included the Action-Script *fscommand( )* statement in your animation. (*fscommand( )* lets your Flash animation call a JavaScript statement. JavaScript is the scripting language supported by most Web browsers.)

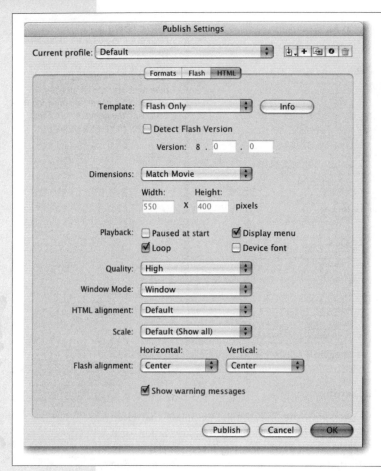

Figure 14-10:
*These settings let you tell Flash
how you want your animation
included in your Web page. This
option's great for testing the way
your animation looks on the Web,
as well as for creating simple
pages. But if you want a really
sophisticated Web page, you need
to edit the HTML file that Flash
produces—in either a text editor, or
in a Web page creation tool such
as Dreamweaver.*

Flash with Named Anchors. Choose this option if you've organized your animation into named scenes (Chapter 10). Flash generates the tags necessary to let people surf directly from scene to scene using their browsers' Back buttons.

Flash with SCORM 1.2 Tracking and **Flash with SCORM 2004 Tracking.** Choose one of these options if you've added Learning Interaction components (Window → Common Libraries → Learning Interactions) to your animation, and plan to have these components interact with a SCORM learning management system. (SCORM stands for Shareable Content Object Reference Model.)

Image Map. Choosing this option tells Flash to create an HTML image map (which an HTML-savvy person can turn into hotspots). For this option to work, you need to have added the frame label *#map* to the frame you want Flash to turn into an image map, and you have to have chosen GIF Image (.gif), JPEG Image (.jpg) or PNG Image (.png) in addition to HTML (.html) in the Formats tab of the Publish Settings window. (Chapter 10 explains how to add frame labels.)

QuickTime. Choose this option if you chose QuickTime in the Formats tab of the Publish Settings window. Flash embeds your animation as a QuickTime .mov file (instead of a Flash .swf file).

6. **If you chose "Flash only" or "Flash HTTPS" in the previous step, you can now turn on Detect Flash Version/Version to help make sure your audience has the correct version of Flash Player to view your animation.**

   When you turn on the checkbox for this option, your audience sees a Web page telling them where to download the latest Flash Player (but only if the version of Flash Player they have installed doesn't match the version of Flash Player you specify in the Version box). For example, if you type a Version of 8.0.0, someone trying to run your animation with version 7.0 Flash Player sees a Web page similar to the one shown in Figure 14-11. When you turn on Detect Flash Version, anyone who doesn't have the version of Flash Player you specify sees this Web page (instead of the Web page containing your animation). Clicking the Get Flash link whisks your audience to Macromedia (now Adobe), where they can download a free copy of the correct Flash browser. You can edit this HTML file if you'd like to reword the message, and of course you have to upload it to your Web server along with the .swf file in order for your audience to see its contents. (See the box on page 414 for further advice.)

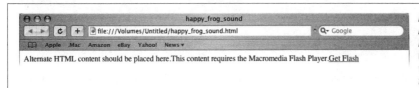

Figure 14-11:
If you turn on Detect Flash Version, anyone who doesn't have the version of Flash Player that you specify sees this Web page.

7. **Turn on any of the following settings if you'd like you tweak how your animation appears in the Web page—which may be different from how it appears in Flash on the Stage:**

   Dimensions. Lets you tell Flash how large you want your animation to appear in the Web page. Your options are Match Movie, which tells Flash to use the dimensions of the Stage you specified in the Document Properties window (page 48); Pixels, which tells Flash you want to specify new height and width dimensions in pixels (see below); and Percent, which tells Flash you want to specify new height and width dimensions as a percentage of the Web page display (see below).

   Width/Height. Lets you specify your animation's width and height in the Web page in pixels or in a percentage of the Web page.

   Paused at start. Tells Flash *not* to begin playing your animation as soon as your audience loads your Web page into their browser. If you choose this option, make sure you either turn on Display menu (see below) or—a better solution—

The Problem with Detecting Your Audience's Flash Version

If you create an animation that uses Flash 8-only features, your audience won't be able to play it in an earlier version of Flash Player. But how do you know which version of Flash Player your audience has installed? And if it turns out they *are* running an earlier version, how can they see your animation?

The easiest approach to this dilemma is the one most Flash-ianados opt for: using the Detect Flash Version publishing option described on page 413.

But making people jump through hoops before they can see your animation isn't always the best design choice. For one thing, not everyone wants to stop what they're doing and download yet another plug-in. For another, folks in many corporate settings aren't allowed to download and install software of any kind, even a free Flash Player.

Fortunately, hoop-jumping isn't necessary: Computers excel at this kind of automatic detect-this-and-do-that process. With a little bit of elbow grease, you can devise a more seamless, professional approach, such as:

- Detecting your audience's installed Flash Player and automatically displaying a version of your animation that runs in that player

- Having your HTML file substitute a static image or animated GIF file if it doesn't find the correct Flash Player

- Having your animation download and install the correct version of Flash Player for your audience so they don't have to

Macromedia (now Adobe) maintains a Web site devoted to this oh-so-common design problem, and with any luck Adobe will continue to maintain it. As this book goes to press, you'll find descriptions, examples. and sample code at *www.macromedia.com/software/flashplayer/download/detection_kit*.

make sure you've included an obvious visible Play button in your animation. Otherwise, your audience won't be able to play your masterpiece.

Display menu. Tells Flash to include a shortcut menu for your animation so that when your audience right-clicks (Windows) or Control-clicks (Mac), they see animation controller options such as Zoom In, Zoom Out, Play, Loop, Rewind, Forward, and Back.

Loop. Tells Flash to automatically play your animation over and over again.

Device font. Tells Flash to check your audience's Windows computer for fonts that match the fonts in your animation. If Flash doesn't find any matching fonts, it substitutes the closest system fonts it can find on your audience's computer. (This option only applies to Windows computers.)

Quality. Tells Flash how precisely (and how processor-intensively) you want it to *render*, or draw, your animation on your audience's computer. Your options range from Low to Best.

8. **Choose one of the following Window Mode settings to tell Flash how you want your animation to appear with respect to HTML/DHTML content that you add to your .html file:**

Window. This standard mode tells Flash to place your animation in a rectangular area on the Web page. HTML content can appear around the animation.

Opaque Windowless. Tells Flash to place your animation on top of HTML content.

Transparent Windowless. Tells Flash to erase the background of your animation (the blank parts of the stage) so that HTML and DHTML content can show through.

HTML alignment. Tells Flash how you want it to align your animation with respect to the rest of your Web page—the text, images, and so on you plan to add to your HTML file. Your options include Default (center), Left, Right, Top, or Bottom.

9. **Choose one of the following Scale options to tell Flash whether to stretch or crop your animation in those cases where your Stage size doesn't match the height/width dimensions you set in the Publish Settings window (page 396).**

Default (Show All). Fits as much of the animation into the height/width dimensions you set as possible without stretching or distorting the animation. If there's extra room left over, Flash fills in the empty spaces with black bands, letterbox style.

No border. Fits as much of the animation into the height/width dimensions you set as possible without stretching or distorting the animation. If there's extra room left over, Flash crops it.

Exact fit. Stretches (or squishes) the animation to fit the height/weight dimensions you set.

No scale. Tells Flash to preserve the Stage height/width dimensions you set in the Document Properties dialog box.

Flash alignment: Horizontal. Tells Flash how you want to align your animation with respect to the dimensions you set in the Publish Settings dialog box—in other words, how you want to position your animation horizontally inside the width-and-height box you're adding to your Web page. Your options include Left, Center, and Right.

Note: See "HTML Alignment" in the previous step if you want to align the width-and-height box with respect to your Web page (as opposed to aligning your animation with respect to the width-and-height box, which you do using "Flash alignment").

Flash alignment: Vertical. Tells Flash how you want to align your animation with respect to the dimensions you set in the Publish Settings dialog box; in other words, how you want to position your animation vertically inside the width-and-height box you're adding to your Web page. Your options include Top, Center, and Bottom.

Note: You need to know when Flash encounters problems so that you can fix them, so make sure the "Show warning messages" option is always turned on. Turning on this option tells Flash to pop up any errors that occur during the publishing process.

10. **Click Publish.**

The Publish Settings window disappears, and Flash generates both an HTML file and a Flash file based on the names you set in the Formats tab. If you didn't type names of your own choosing, Flash names both files similar to your .fla file. For example, if the name of your Flash document is myAnimation.fla, Flash generates a file named myAnimation.html and myAnimation.swf. To make your HTML file and Flash animation available on the Web, you'll need to upload both of these files to your Web server.

Publishing a Frame as a Static Image File

It may seem odd that Flash lets you publish a frame of your animation as a single, static image—after all, the point of using Flash is creating animations, not images. But publishing your animation as an image file (in addition to publishing it as a Flash file) can be a savvy design choice: If some people don't have a Flash Player installed on their machines and so can't see your animation, at least they can see your opening frame.

Note: When you *do* choose to publish an image file, you're the one who needs to create the HTML to display that image file; Flash doesn't do it for you when you select the "HTML (.html)" option in the Formats tab of the Publish Settings window.

Publishing a Static GIF

GIF (Graphic Interchange Format) files are super-small, thanks in part to the fact that they limit your image to 256 colors. GIF files are the best choice for vector images containing just a few areas of solid color.

Note: Another way to create static images is to export them by choosing File → Export Image (page 425).

To publish a frame of your animation as a static GIF file:

1. **On the Timeline, click to select the frame whose content you want to publish.**

Flash highlights the selected frame. On the Stage, you see the image you're about to publish.

Note: Another way to tell Flash which frame you want to publish is to add the frame label *#Static* to the frame you want to publish. Chapter 10 (page 306) shows you how to label a frame.

2. **Choose File → Publish Settings.**

A Publish Settings dialog box appears.

3. **Turn on the checkbox next to "GIF Image (.gif)."**

   The GIF tab appears next to the Formats tab.

4. **Click the GIF tab.**

   The GIF publishing options shown in Figure 14-12 appear.

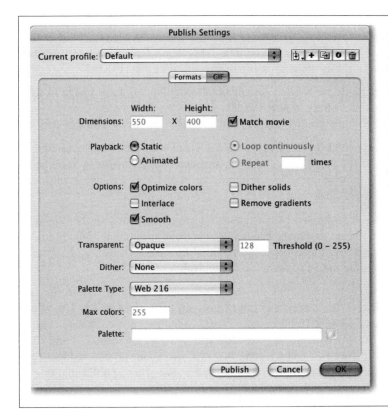

Figure 14-12:
GIFs are generally the most compact of the three static image file formats, but they're also the most restrictive: They can display only 256 colors. (If the image you're exporting contains a bunch of custom colors, your GIF may look slightly off.) Two different types of GIFs exist: static and animated. In this section, you see how to publish frame content to a static GIF.

5. **Choose one or more of the following publishing options:**

   Dimensions (Width/Height). Tells Flash how large you want the GIF file to be, in pixels. These options are available only if you haven't checked Match movie (see below).

   Match movie. Tells Flash to create a GIF image the same size as the Stage.

   Static/Animated. Tells Flash whether to create a static GIF file or an animated GIF file. Make sure you turn on Static. (Page 423 shows you how to create an animated GIF file.)

   Optimize colors. Lowers file size as much as possible without sacrificing image quality. Always make sure you turn this option on.

Interlace. Tells Flash to create a GIF that downloads in several passes, so that a fuzzy version appears first, then a clearer version, then a still clearer version, and so on. Turning on this option doesn't reduce download time, but it does give your audience quick successive "tastes" of the image while they're waiting—useful for very large images.

Smooth. Tells Flash to smooth (anti-alias) your image. Turning on this option may improve the look of any text your image contains; it can also save a few bytes.

Dither solids. Tells Flash to attempt to match any solid custom colors you've used as closely as it can by combining two colors. If you don't turn on this option, Flash chooses the nearest-in-shade solid color in its palette.

Remove gradients. Tells Flash to convert the gradients in your image to solid colors. (Gradient effects don't translate well to the GIF format anyway, so if your image contains gradient effects, you probably want to turn on this option.)

Transparent. Lets you specify the transparency of your image background (the blank area of the Stage). Your options include *Opaque* (a regular, solid background), *Transparent* (no background), or *Alpha* and *Threshold* (lets you choose how transparent you want the background to appear).

Dither. Tells Flash to *dither* (mix two colors) to try to match all the non-solid areas of your image as closely as possible. Your options include *None* (no dithering), *Ordered* (minimal dithering, minimal file size increase), and *Diffusion* (maximum dithering, maximum file size increase).

Palette Type. Lets you tell Flash which 256 colors to use to create the GIF image. (GIFs are limited to 256 colors, but you get to pick which 256.) Your options include Web 216 (Web-safe colors), Adaptive (non-Web-safe colors), Web Snap Adaptive (a mix of Web-safe and non-Web-safe colors), and Custom (lets you specify a color palette you've saved as an .act file, using a program such as Fireworks). Depending on the image you're publishing, one of these options may yield better-looking results—although in most cases, you want to leave this option set to Web 216.

Max colors. Available only if you've selected a Palette Type of Adaptive or Web Snap Adaptive (see above), this option lets you specify a maximum number of colors lower than 256 to save on file size.

Palette. Available only if you've selected a Palette Type of Custom (see above), this option lets you type the file name of your own custom color palette. You must have created the palette using another program, such as Fireworks, and saved it with the .act file extension. If you prefer, you can click the file icon to browse your computer for the palette file name.

6. Click Publish.

The Publish Settings window disappears, and Flash generates a GIF file based on the name you set in the Formats tab. If you didn't type a name, Flash names the GIF file similar to your .fla file. For example, if the name of your Flash document is myAnimation.fla, Flash generates a file named myAnimation.gif.

Publishing a JPEG

JPEG (Joint Photographic Experts Group) files typically don't end up being as small as GIF files, but they can contain many more colors. Sometimes referred to as the "photo format," JPEG is the best choice if your image, like a scanned-in photograph, contains lots of colors, subtle shading, or gradient effects.

To publish a frame of your animation as a JPEG file:

1. **On the Timeline, click to select the frame whose content you want to publish.**

    Flash highlights the selected frame. On the Stage, you see the image you're about to publish.

2. **Choose File → Publish Settings.**

    A Publish Settings dialog box appears.

3. **Turn on the checkbox next to "JPEG Image (.jpg)."**

    The JPEG tab appears next to the Formats tab.

4. **Click the JPEG tab.**

    The JPEG publishing options shown in Figure 14-13 appear.

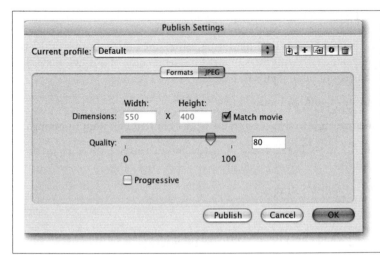

Figure 14-13:
Publishing a frame of your animation as a JPEG file is a pretty cut-and-dried process. As you can see here, the only options Flash gives you are to specify your image's JPEG version's size and quality.

5. **Choose one or more of the following publishing options:**

    Dimensions (Width/Height). Tells Flash how large you want the JPEG file to be, in pixels. These options are available only if you haven't turned on "Match movie," described next.

    Match movie. Tells Flash to create a JPEG image the same size as the Stage.

    Quality. Tells Flash how much detail you want it to include. The larger the number you type (or specify by dragging the slider), the better your JPEG image will look, and the larger your JPEG file size will be. (Depending on your particular image, the image quality may appear similar enough at different quality levels that you can get away with a lower number, thereby whittling away at your animation's finished file size. See page 398 for more on optimization.)

    Progressive. Similar to the GIF's Interlace option (page 418), turning on this option tells Flash to create a JPEG that downloads in several passes, so that a fuzzy version appears first, then a clearer version, then a still clearer version, and so on. Turning on this option doesn't reduce download time, but it does give your audience quick successive "tastes" of the image while they're waiting, which some audiences appreciate.

6. **Click Publish.**

    The Publish Settings window disappears, and Flash generates a JPEG file based on the name you set in the Formats tab. If you didn't type a name, Flash names the JPEG file similar to your .fla file. For example, if the name of your Flash document is myAnimation.fla, Flash generates a file named myAnimation.jpg.

Publishing a PNG

Developed to replace and improve on the GIF file format (back when it looked like Web developers would have to pay royalties for every GIF they produced), the PNG (Portable Network Graphics) file format offers the best of both worlds: the tiny file size of a static GIF with the support for 24-bit color of a JPEG. PNG files can include transparent (alpha) effects, too.

To publish a frame of your animation as a PNG file:

1. **On the Timeline, click to select the frame whose content you want to publish.**

    Flash highlights the selected frame. On the Stage, you see the image you're about to publish.

2. **Choose File → Publish Settings.**

    A Publish Settings dialog box appears.

3. **Turn on the checkbox next to "PNG Image (.png)."**

    The PNG tab appears next to the Formats tab.

4. **Click the PNG tab.**

The PNG publishing options shown in Figure 14-14 appear.

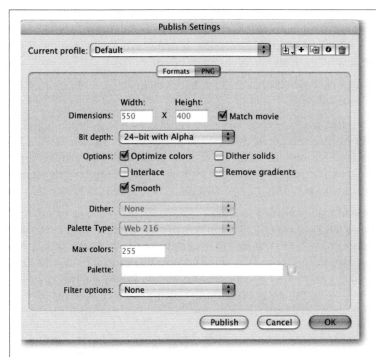

Figure 14-14:
Some older Web browsers—for example, Internet Explorer versions 6 and earlier—don't offer complete support for PNG files. If you want to publish a static image but you're not sure which browser your audience has installed, you may want to opt for GIF or JPEG instead.

5. **Choose one or more of the following publishing options:**

Dimensions (Width/Height). Tells Flash how large you want the PNG file to be, in pixels. These options are available only if you haven't turned on "Match movie," described next.

Match movie. Tells Flash to create a PNG image the same size as the Stage.

Bit depth. Tells Flash how many colors you want the PNG to be able to render. Your options include 8-bit (256 colors, the same as GIF), 24-bit (16.7 million colors), and 24-bit with Alpha (16.7 million colors plus the ability to render your image background as transparent). The more colors, the larger the file size.

Optimize colors. Reduces file size without sacrificing the quality of your image. You always want to turn this option on.

Interlace. Tells Flash to create a PNG that downloads in several passes, so that a fuzzy version appears first, then a clearer version, then a still clearer version, and so on. Turning on this option doesn't reduce download time, but it does give your audience quick successive "tastes" of the image while they're waiting—useful for very large images.

Smooth. Tells Flash to smooth (anti-alias) your image. Turning on this option may improve the look of any text your image contains; it can also save a few bytes of file size.

Dither solids. Tells Flash to attempt to match any solid custom colors you've used as closely as it can by combining two colors (only necessary if you choose a Bit depth of 8-bit as described above). If you don't turn on this option, Flash chooses the nearest-in-shade solid color in its palette.

Remove gradients. Tells Flash to convert the gradients in your image to solid colors to save on file size.

Dither. Tells Flash to *dither* (mix two colors) to try to match all the nonsolid areas of your image as closely as possible (only necessary if you've chosen a Bit depth of 8-bit). Your options include None (no dithering), Ordered (minimal dithering, minimal file size increase), and Diffusion (maximum dithering, maximum file size increase).

Palette Type. Available only if you choose a bit depth of 8-bit (see above), this option lets you tell Flash which 256 colors to use to create the PNG image. Your options include Web 216 (Web-safe colors), Adaptive (non-Web-safe colors), Web Snap Adaptive (a mix of Web-safe and non-Web-safe colors), and Custom (lets you specify a color palette you've saved as an .act file, using a program such as Fireworks). Depending on the image you're publishing, one of these options may yield better-looking results—although in most cases, you want to leave this option set to Web 216.

Max colors. Available only if you've selected a Palette Type of Adaptive or Web Snap Adaptive (see above), this option lets you specify a maximum number of colors lower than 256.

Palette. Available only if you've selected a Palette Type of Custom (see above), this option lets you type the file name of your own custom color palette. You must have created the palette using another program, such as Fireworks, and saved it with the .act file extension. If you prefer, you can click the file icon to browse your computer for the palette file name.

Filter options. This option lets you tell Flash to apply an additional compression algorithm when it's creating your PNG file. Normally, you don't use this option unless you're trying to pare down your PNG file by a few bytes. Your options include None, Sub, Up, Average, Path, and Adaptive.

6. **Click Publish.**

The Publish Settings window disappears, and Flash generates a PNG file based on the name you set in the Formats tab. If you didn't type a name, Flash names the PNG file similar to your .fla file. For example, if the name of your Flash document is myAnimation.fla, Flash generates a file named myAnimation.png.

Publishing as an Animated GIF

In addition to static images, the GIF file format lets you create animated images. Animated GIFs are mini-animations that play right in the Web browser, with no need for a Flash browser. The quality isn't always stellar and your audience can't interact with them (which is why Flash was invented). But depending on how long your animation is and what quality of playback you're shooting for, they can be an impressive alternative.

To publish your animation as an animated GIF file:

1. **Choose File → Publish Settings.**

   A Publish Settings dialog box appears.

2. **Turn on the checkbox next to GIF Image (.gif).**

   The GIF tab appears next to the Formats tab.

3. **Click the GIF tab.**

   The GIF publishing options shown in Figure 14-15 appear.

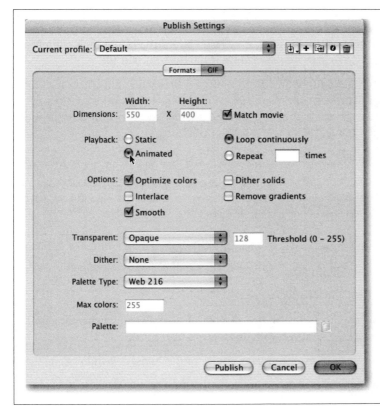

Figure 14-15:
Animated GIFs are amazing creatures: small, decent quality (especially if you're only talking about a few frames), and as easy to include in an HTML file as a static GIF file (the basic line of HTML code you need is <IMG SRC="yourGIF.gif">). The only extra settings you have to specify for an animated GIF, as opposed to a static GIF, are whether you want the animated GIF to loop continuously, loop a few times, or not loop at all.

4. Set the publishing options you see in Figure 14-15 just as you would for a static GIF file (page 416) *except* for the following:

   Static/Animated. This option tells Flash whether to create a static or animated GIF file. Make sure you turn on Animated.

   Loop continuously. Turn on this option to tell Flash to replay the animated GIF over and over again. (If you include the GIF in an HTML file, your audience can stop the animated GIF by clicking their Web browser's Stop button.)

   Repeat. Tells Flash to create an animated GIF that automatically plays the number of times you type into the times box.

5. Click Publish.

   The Publish Settings window disappears, and Flash generates a GIF file based on the name you set in the Formats tab. If you didn't type a name, Flash names the GIF file similar to your .fla file. For example, if the name of your Flash document is myAnimation.fla, Flash generates a file named myAnimation.gif.

Publishing as a Standalone Projector

A *projector* is the equivalent of an .swf file and a copy of Flash Player all rolled up into a single executable file. When you create a projector, your audience doesn't need to have either a Web browser or a Flash Player installed on their computers: All they need to do to play your animation is run the projector file.

You'll want to choose this option if you want to deliver your animation on a CD or DVD (as opposed to over the Web). Tutorials, product demonstrations, and program mock-ups (as well as the programs themselves) are all examples of the kinds of animations you might want to publish as projectors.

Note: If you plan to distribute a Flash projector to folks outside your company, take a look at the Macromedia Flash Run-Time Distribution License, a legal-ese description of what you can and can't do with your projector files. Adobe may change the location of this document, but the time of this writing, you can find a copy online at *www.macromedia.com/software/eula/tools/flashplayer_usage.html*.

To publish your animation as a standalone projector:

1. Choose File → Publish Settings.

   A Publish Settings dialog box appears.

2. Turn on the checkbox next to one or both of the following, depending on the operating system you expect your audience to be running:

   Windows Projector (.exe) to create a projector that runs on Windows.

   Macintosh Projector to create a projector that runs on the Mac.

3. Click Publish.

If you chose "Windows Projector (.exe)", Flash generates an .exe file. If you chose Macintosh Projector, Flash generates an .hqx file (if you're running Windows) or a self-running animation file with no extension (if you're running Mac). (Running the zipped .hqx file on a Mac automatically unzips the projector file and runs it.) Flash names the files based on the names displayed in the Formats tab. For example, if the name of your Flash document is myAnimation.fla, Flash generates files named myAnimation.exe or myAnimation.hqx.

FREQUENTLY ASKED QUESTION

Publishing Flash as QuickTime

Every time I try to publish my animation as a QuickTime movie, I get an error. What's up?

Technically, Flash lets you publish your animation as a QuickTime movie, so that folks who've installed the QuickTime player on their machines can play your animation without having a Flash Player installed.

The thing is, QuickTime support for Flash stopped at Version 5. If you create an animation using Flash 8, you have to target it for a Flash 5 player to be able to publish it as a QuickTime movie. Put another way, you can't use any of the features Macromedia introduced in Flash Versions 6, 7, or 8 in your published QuickTime movie.

If you still want to publish your Flash animation as a QuickTime movie—because your audience is running machines with only the QuickTime player installed, for example—follow these steps:

1. Choose File → Publish Settings.

2. In the Format tab of the Publish Settings window, turn on the checkbox next to both "Flash (.swf)" and "QuickTime (.mov)."

3. In the Flash tab, specify a "Version of Flash Player 5."

4. In the QuickTime tab, find the Controller drop-down box, and then select Standard.

Click Publish. When you do, Flash generates a .mov file you can play in the QuickTime player.

The installed version of QuickTime does not support this type of Macromedia Flash movie. QuickTime requires Macromedia Flash version 5 or before.

Please select "Version: Flash Player 5" in the Flash tab of the Publish Settings dialog.

OK

Exporting Flash to Other Formats

Exporting your entire animation—or one or more of the individual frames that make up your animation—is very similar to publishing. In both cases, you get to specify which file format you'd like Flash to convert your .fla file into, and in both cases, you get to tweak file settings based on the file format you choose. The only real difference, in fact, is that Flash designated the most common file formats (.html, .swf, .gif, .jpg, .png, .mov, and projector files) as publishing destinations and all other file formats as export destinations. Most of the time, you'll export (rather than publish) an image, sound, or your entire animation because you want to work with it in another graphics or animation program.

Flash lets you export to all the file formats you see in Table 14-1.

Table 14-1. File Formats to Which You Can Export Your Flash Animation

Format	Extension	Platform	Note
Flash movie	.swf	Windows, Mac	Image (single frame) and animation
PICT file	.pct	Mac	Image and animation (as a sequence of images)
Enhanced metafile	.emf	Windows	Image and animation (as a sequence of images)
Windows metafile	.wmf	Windows	Image and animation (as a sequence of images)
EPS 3.0	.eps	Windows, Mac	Image and animation (as a sequence of images)
Adobe Illustrator	.ai	Windows, Mac	Image and animation (as a sequence of images)
AutoCAD DXF	.dxf	Windows, Mac	Image and animation (as a sequence of images)
JPEG Image	.jpg	Windows, Mac	Image and animation (as a sequence of images)
GIF Image	.gif	Windows, Mac	Image and animation (as a sequence of images)
PNG Image	.png	Windows, Mac	Image and animation (as a sequence of images)
Bitmap Image	.bmp	Windows	Image and animation (as a sequence of images)
Flash Movie	.swf	Windows, Mac	Animation
QuickTime	.mov	Windows, Mac	Animation
Animated GIF	.gif	Windows, Mac	Animation
Wave form audio format	.wav	Windows	Animation (sound)
Audio Video Interleave	.avi	Windows	Animation

Exporting the Contents of a Single Frame

Exporting the contents of a single frame of your animation lets you create a one-frame animation or (much more commonly) an image file you can edit with another image-editing program.

Note: Exporting an image from one animation and then importing the image into another animation is one way to share images between Flash documents. You can also share by saving the image as a graphic symbol in one animation and then using the Library panel's drop-down list to add the symbol to another animation, as described in Chapter 7.

---

1. **On the Stage, click to select the frame you want to export.**

   Flash highlights the selected frame.

2. **Choose File → Export → Export Image.**

   The Export Image dialog box you see in Figure 14-16 appears.

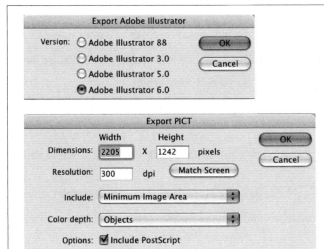

Figure 14-16:
The Export Image dialog box lets you export a frame to any of the following image formats: Flash movie, PICT, EPS 3.0, Adobe Illustrator, AutoCAD DXF, MPEG, GIF, or PNG file.

3. **From the pop-up menu, choose the file format to which you want to export.**

   In Windows, this menu's called "Save as type;" on the Mac, it's called Format.

4. **In the Save As box, type a name for your exported file.**

   Leave the file extension Flash suggests.

5. **Click Save.**

   Flash displays an Export window containing format-specific settings, as shown in Figure 14-17.

Figure 14-17:
Top: The settings window you see after you click Save (and even whether you see one or not) depends on the format you're exporting to. Here, you see the settings window for the Adobe Illustrator format.

Bottom: The PICT file format lets you specify different file settings. For explanations of the image settings for GIF, JPEG, and PNG formats (which are either identical, or very similar, to the settings here and in the other export windows) see page 416.

6. In the Export window, set one or more export options and then click OK.

Flash exports the contents of your frame to the file format you chose in step 3.

Exporting an Entire Animation

Exporting your animation to another file format lets you edit the animation using another animation program, such as Apple's QuickTime. You might want to do this if, for example, you want to combine frames from both Flash and QuickTime animations into a single animation.

1. Choose File → Export → Export Movie.

The Export Image dialog box you see in Figure 14-18 appears.

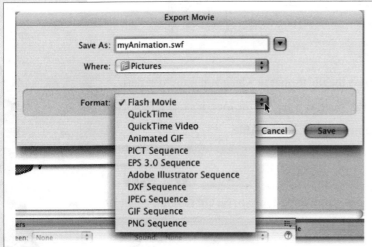

Figure 14-18:
The Export Movie dialog box lets you export your animation to a variety of formats, several of which will be familiar to you if you've had a chance to check out the section on publishing (page 403).

2. From the pop-up menu, choose the file format to which you want to export.

In Windows, this menu is called "Save as type;" on the Mac, it's called Format.

3. In the Save As box, type a name for your exported file.

Leave the file extension Flash suggests.

4. Click Save.

Flash displays an Export window containing format-specific settings, as shown in Figure 14-19.

5. In the Export window, set one or more export options, and then click OK.

Flash exports the contents of your frame to the file format you chose in step 2.

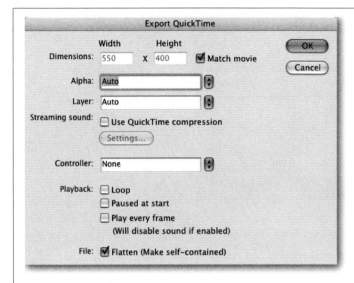

Figure 14-19:
When you export your animation, Flash displays the same settings you see when you publish your animation. From Flash's perspective, the two processes are the same, but you may appreciate the convenience of publishing over exporting. For example, when you publish your animation, Flash lets you save your settings in an easy-to-reuse publish profile (see the box on page 410). Not so when you export your animation.

Part Five: Appendix

5

Installation and Help

It's 2:00 a.m., you're *this close* to finishing your animation, and you run into a snag. If you can't find the answer to your question in the pages of this book, you have plenty of other possibilities. First of all, Flash has its own built-in help system, which may give you the answer you need on the spot. For more complex problems, you can seek technical support from the developer (now Adobe, as mentioned on page 436) or from fellow Flash fans via the Web. This appendix outlines all these options.

First, in case you need help getting Flash installed on your computer, some basic instructions follow.

Tip: While the Flash box lists minimum requirements, *minimum's* the operative word. You'll want at least 20 gigabytes free on your hard disk—not just for the program installation, but to give you room to create and store your Flash masterpieces and import additional files (such as previously created images, sound files, and movies) from elsewhere.

Installing and Activating Flash 8

As with most programs, before you can use Flash, you need to install it on your computer and activate it. Fortunately, this one-time process is fairly painless. To get started, grab your Flash installation CD and the jacket that it comes in. (You need the jacket because it contains the serial number you need to activate Flash.)

Then follow these steps:

1. **Close any other programs you have open.**

Flash demands all your computer's attention during the installation and configuration process, so you don't want any other files or programs open when it installs. Close your Internet connection, too.

2. **Insert the Flash installation disc into your CD/DVD drive.**

   If you're in Windows, the installation screen appears automatically.

   If you're on a Mac, you have an extra step: On the desktop, double-click the CD/DVD icon; then double-click the name of installation program (for example, FL_Client_Installer). Then the installation screen appears.

Note: If the installation screen doesn't appear when you insert your Flash installation disk (and you're running Windows), click Start → My Computer and then double-click the drive letter for your CD or DVD drive. The installation disc's contents—including something called a Setup file—appear in your My Computer window. Double-click the Setup file to start the installation.

---

3. **Follow the onscreen installation instructions on the next few screens, telling Flash that you want to accept its license agreement (you can't install the program unless you do) and confirming that you want to install the free Flash Player plug-in.**

   When you finish, a message appears to let you know you've successfully installed Flash.

   The first time you launch the program, it asks you for your serial number.

4. **Launch your newly installed copy of Flash.**

   You can use any of the methods described on page 16, like the Start menu (Windows) or the Dock (Mac).

5. **Type your serial number, and then click Next to activate your copy of Flash.**

   An optional registration screen appears.

6. **If you wish to register, type your name, your email address, and the country where you're located.**

   Registering your copy of Flash gives Adobe a record of your purchase in case you run into any snags down the line.

7. **Click Finish.**

   You're good to go.

Getting Help from Flash

Flash's documentation isn't especially thorough or well-written, but it offers you a good place to start. You can search for a specific topic or read through multipage documents devoted to everything from Flash basics to ActionScript syntax and class definitions.

Flash Documentation: The Help Window

The Help window lets you search the Flash and ActionScript documentation you automatically installed on your computer when you installed Flash.

To use the Help window:

1. **Select Help → Flash Help.**

   The Help window in Figure A-1 appears.

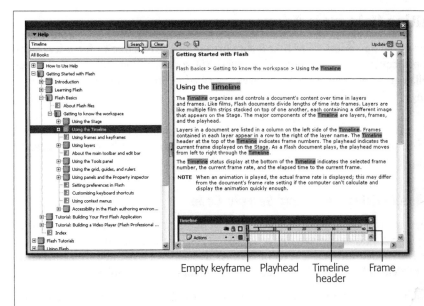

Figure A-1:
To use Flash's Help window, type the word or phrase you're looking for in the search box and then click Search. To narrow your search, you can tell Flash to look only in a specific set of documentation books (such as Features, Components, or Tutorials & Samples). But in most cases, you'll want to search All Books, as shown here. (If you knew enough about the term to know what book it belongs in, chances are you wouldn't have to search for help with it in the first place!)

Empty keyframe   Playhead   Timeline header   Frame

2. **In the search box (Figure A-1), type the word or phrase with which you need help.**

   Flash displays a list of topics in the left-hand side of the Help window.

3. **Click the topic that looks like the closest match to what you're searching for.**

   Flash displays the text for that topic in the Help window's right-hand side. You may have to repeat this step several times to zero in on the information you want.

Note: To view Flash documentation online, choose either Help → Flash LiveDocs or Help → Flash Documentation Resource Center.

Flash Overview and Tutorials

Flash includes a quick overview of the product (what it is and what you can do with it) along with a handful of tutorials that cover different Flash features, such as using layers and creating motion tweens.

To view the Flash overview and tutorials, select Help → Getting Started with Flash. When you do, the Help window in Figure A-1 appears, preloaded with links to the overview and tutorials.

Getting Help from Adobe

Adobe offers a variety of technical support options, from free to for-a-fee. Since Adobe acquired Flash's original developer, Macromedia, you still see the Macromedia name on many of the Web pages described in this section, but expect that to change in the future.

Note: As of this writing, all "macromedia.com" URLs listed in this appendix still work, or at least take you to the relevant page on Adobe's Web site. To make sure you get to the most up-to-date support page, use the Help menu, described next, instead of typing in a URL.

Online Articles, FAQs, and Sample Code

Adobe maintains two different Web sites containing articles on Flash, as well as sample code and answers to frequently asked Flash-related questions. One of these sites is designed for a basic level of Flash skill (Help → Flash Support Center); the other (Help → Flash Developer Center) focuses on advanced topics.

If you're interested in creating animations that folks can play on mobile devices such as mobile phones and PDAs, check out the Mobile and Devices Developer Center at *www.macromedia.com/devnet/devices/flashlite.html*.

Forums

As of this writing, Adobe is continuing Macromedia's *user-to-user forums*, where anyone can ask a question about Flash and anyone can answer. User-to-user means that Adobe employees don't officially monitor the forums or answer any questions, so the feedback you get has no official sanction or guarantee of accuracy. Still, the best and fastest answers and advice often come from other folks in the trenches, so if you've worked your way through Macromedia Knowledge Base (online articles), FAQs, and documentation, these forums (Help → Macromedia Online Forums) are definitely worth a look.

Direct Person-to-Person Help

Sometimes, nothing will do but asking a real, live technical support person for help. If you've purchased a supported copy of Flash (as opposed to a 30-day trial version), you get two freebie questions; after that, you have to pay Adobe's technical support staff $100 per question. (No, that's not a typo.)

To find out more or to sign up for for-fee technical support, select Help → Flash Support Center, and then, from the Macromedia Flash Support Center Web site, click Contact Product Support.

Finding Flash Gurus

Flash is one of those programs that people tend to get passionate about, so it's not surprising that there are hundreds of great resources on the Web offering everything from example code to free components, articles, tutorials, and more. Here are a few that are definitely worth checking out:

- **FlashGuru** (*www.flashguru.co.uk*): With its professional-quality articles and tutorials, this wondrous Flash blog would be useful enough by itself; but it also lists dozens of other Flash blogs maintained by heavy-hitters in the Flash world.

- **Flash Insider** (*www.flashinsider.com*): This "Unofficial Flash Weblog" tracks Flash-related news and events. It also offers online forums, articles on everything from ActionScript to ad design and free downloadable Flash components.

- **Flash Kit** (*www.flashkit.com*): Surprisingly badly designed for a site that focuses on a design program, Flash Kit nevertheless offers a wealth of sound effects, fonts, components, and movie clips. It also hosts a well-attended online forum.

- **Best Flash Animation Site** (*www.bestflashanimationsite.com*) and **Webby Awards** (*www.webbyawards.com*): There's nothing like watching a beautifully constructed Flash animation to get you thinking about good design. On these two sites you can nominate the coolest Flash animation you've ever seen (including your own) or simply visit the sites others have nominated.

- **Macromedia Mobile User Group of Boston** (*www.flashmobilegroup.org*): If you're interested in creating Flash content for mobile devices (such as mobile phones), you'll want to check out this site, which offers Flash Lite–specific articles, seminars, links, and live chats.

- **FlashPro Mailing list** (*http://www.muinar.org*): FlashPro is an open and non-moderated email list "for professional Flash designers and ActionScript coders." This is where the big dogs run, so you may want to exhaust some of the resources listed above (and comb through FlashPro's archived posts) before posting a question.

Index

File Extensions

as, 42
.asc, 42
.exe, 42, 404, 425
.fla, 42
.flp, 42
.gif, 405
.hqx, 42, 404, 425
.html, 405
.jpg, 405
.jsfl, 42
.mov, 404
.png, 403
.swf, 42, 403–404

A

accessibility, 26
Accessibility panel, 25
Accordion component, 345
actions, 281
    adding, 284
    tying to events, 325
Actions panel, 25, 282
ActionScript, 1, 281
    comments and testing, 368
    creating communication file, 17
    debugger panel, 25
    language constructs, 361
    specifying a version, 406
    to control embedded video, 269
    where to find documentation, 285
activating, 433
Active Server Page, 358
Adobe Illustrator, 248
    exporting to, 427
Alert component, 346
Align panel, 26
aligning objects, 67
    using snapping and guide layers, 158
alpha, 167
Alpha (transparency), 170
anchor points, 61
animation, 293–316
    anatomy of, 5
    controlling, 293
    file saving, 40
    other terms for, 7
    playing, 39
    slowing and speeding, 294
anti-aliasing, 5
audio, 253–262
    customizing encoding, 276
    file formats (Flash-friendly), 254–255

B

background (Stage) color setting, 49
bandwidth profiler report, 377
    creating, 379

FLASH 8: THE MISSING MANUAL

Colophon

Reba Libby was the production editor and the proofreader for *Flash 8: The Missing Manual*. Matt Hutchinson and Marlowe Shaeffer provided quality control. E. A. Vander Veer wrote the index.

The cover of this book is based on a series design by David Freedman. Karen Montgomery produced the cover layout with Adobe InDesign CS using Adobe's Minion and Gill Sans fonts.

David Futato designed the interior layout, based on a series design by Phil Simpson. This book was converted by Keith Fahlgren to FrameMaker 5.5.6. The text font is Adobe Minion; the heading font is Adobe Formata Condensed; and the code font is LucasFont's TheSans Mono Condensed. The illustrations that appear in the book were produced by Robert Romano, Jessamyn Read, and Lesley Borash using Macromedia FreeHand MX and Adobe Photoshop CS.

Better than e-books

Buy *Flash 8: The Missing Manual* and access
the digital edition FREE on Safari for 45 days.

Go to www.oreilly.com/go/safarienabled
and type in coupon code T8R4-TQYQ-8CGX-ZXQS-H1MB

Search
thousands of
top tech books

Download
whole chapters

Cut and Paste
code examples

Find
answers fast

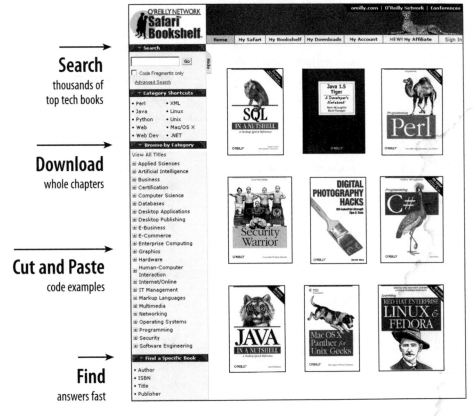

Search Safari! The premier electronic reference
library for programmers and IT professionals.

Related Titles from O'Reilly

Web Programming

ActionScript Cookbook

ActionScript for Flash MX: The Definitive Guide, *2nd Edition*

Ajax Hacks

Dynamic HTML: The Definitive Reference, *2nd Edition*

Flash Hacks

Essential PHP Security

Google Advertising Tools

Google Hacks, *2nd Edition*

Google Map Hacks

Google Pocket Guide

Google: The Missing Manual, *2nd Edition*

HTTP: The Definitive Guide

JavaScript & DHTML Cookbook

JavaScript Pocket Reference, *2nd Edition*

JavaScript: The Definitive Guide, *4th Edition*

Learning PHP 5

PHP Cookbook

PHP Hacks

PHP in a Nutshell

PHP Pocket Reference, *2nd Edition*

PHPUnit Pocket Guide

Programming ColdFusion MX, *2nd Edition*

Programming PHP

Upgrading to PHP 5

Web Database Applications with PHP and MySQL, *2nd Edition*

Web Site Cookbook

Webmaster in a Nutshell, *3rd Edition*

Web Administration

Apache Cookbook

Apache Pocket Reference

Apache: The Definitive Guide, *3rd Edition*

Perl for Web Site Management

Squid: The Definitive Guide

Web Performance Tuning, *2nd Edition*